Dynamic Oneness

Dynamic Oneness

The Significance and Flexibility of Paul's One-God Language

SUZANNE NICHOLSON

PICKWICK *Publications* • Eugene, Oregon

DYNAMIC ONENESS
The Significance and Flexibility of Paul's One-God Language

Pickwick Publications
An imprint of Wipf and Stock Publishers
199 W. 8th Ave., Suite 3
Eugene, OR 97401

www.wipfandstock.com

ISBN 13: 978-1-60608-326-0

Cataloguing-in-Publication data:

Nicholson, Suzanne

Dynamic oneness : the significance and flexibility of Paul's one-God language / Suzanne Nicholson

xviii + 294 p. ; 23 cm. Includes bibliographical references and indices.

ISBN 13: 978-1-60608-326-0

1. Bible. N.T. Epistles of Paul—Criticism, interpretation, etc. 2. Bible. N.T. Epistles of Paul—Language, style. 3. Monotheism. I. Title.

BS2650.2 N55 2010

Manufactured in the U.S.A.

For Lee, Connor, and Alex

Contents

Acknowledgments

THIS BOOK IS A reworking of my 2007 doctoral dissertation, and so I would be remiss if I did not express my deep gratitude to those who helped me throughout the process. I would like to thank A Foundation for Theological Education for supporting my studies through the award of a John Wesley Fellowship, and Durham University's Department of Religion and Theology for its award of the Evans Scholarship in 2001/2 and 2002/3. My thanks also go out to St. Mary's College for their support and encouragement during the time I served as chaplain there, and to St. John's College for the use of their Postgraduate Study Centre, in which I spent many a long hour studying and learning to drink tea the British way. I am very grateful for my dear friends Nigel and Anne Oakley, who without a second thought graciously offered their support in so many practical ways.

I also wish to express my gratitude to Malone University for their support of my studies, including the award of a summer research grant in 2009 to put the finishing touches on this project. I would also like to thank the library staff for putting up with my many requests for interlibrary loans.

I wish to thank N. T. Wright for offering helpful comments on an early draft of portions of this thesis, and also for providing a prepublication manuscript of his recent book on Paul. I also appreciate the comments offered by Stephen Barton while my supervisor was on sabbatical . . . which leads to the great thanks I owe to my supervisor, Professor Loren Stuckenbruck. His understanding and support of my complicated personal circumstances, as well as his insightful comments, made the dissertation far better.

I would like to offer special thanks to my family: to my parents, for all their support (and for putting up with the fact that their grandchildren lived on another continent for four years), to my children, Connor and Alex, and especially to my husband, Lee, without whose support and sacrifice this book would not have been possible.

Finally, I thank God for giving me the strength and encouragement to complete this process.

Abbreviations

BIBLE CITATIONS

1/2 Chr	1/2 Chronicles
1/2 Cor	1/2 Corinthians
1/2 Kgs	1/2 Kings
1/2 Sam	1/2 Samuel
1/2 Thess	1/2 Thessalonians
1/2 Tim	1/2 Timothy
Col	Colossians
Dan	Daniel
Deut	Deuteronomy
Eph	Ephesians
Exod	Exodus
Ezek	Ezekiel
Gal	Galatians
Gen	Genesis
Hab	Habakkuk
Hag	Haggai
Heb	Hebrews
Hos	Hosea
Isa	Isaiah
Jer	Jeremiah
Lev	Leviticus
Mal	Malachi
Matt	Matthew
Mic	Micah
Neh	Nehemiah
Num	Numbers
Phil	Philippians
Phlm	Philemon

Prov	Proverbs
Ps	Psalms
Rom	Romans
Song	Song of Songs
Zech	Zechariah
Zeph	Zephaniah

MT	Masoretic Text
LXX	Septuagint

Apocrypha

2/4 Macc	2/4 Maccabees
Sir	Sirach
Tob	Tobit
Wis	Wisdom of Solomon

Old Testament Pseudepigrapha

2 Bar.	*2 Baruch*
1/3 En.	*1/3 Enoch*
Apoc. Ab.	*Apocalypse of Abraham*
Apoc. Zeph.	*Apocalypse of Zephaniah*
As. Mos.	*Assumption of Moses*
Ezek. Trag.	Ezekiel the Tragedian
Jos. Asen.	*Joseph and Aseneth*
Jub.	*Jubilees*
L.A.B.	*Liber antiquitatum bilicarum* (Pseudo-Philo)
L.A.E.	*Life of Adam and Eve*
Let. Aris.	*Letter of Aristeas*
P. Jos.	*Prayer of Joseph*
Ps.-Phoc.	Pseudo-Phocylides
Pss. Sol.	*Psalms of Solomon*
Sib. Or.	*Sibylline Oracles*
T. 12 Patr.	*Testaments of the Twelve Patriarchs*
T. Ab.	*Testament of Abraham*
T. Benj.	*Testament of Benjamin*
T. Dan	*Testament of Dan*
T. Iss.	*Testament of Issachar*

T. Levi	*Testament of Levi*
T. Mos.	*Testament of Moses*
T. Naph.	*Testament of Naphtali*

Dead Sea Scrolls

1QH	*Thanksgiving Hymns*
1QM	*War Scroll*
1QpHab	*Pesher Habakkuk*
1QS	*Rule of the Community*
4Q174	*Florilegium*
4Q504	*Words of the Luminaries*
11QMelch	*Melchizedek*
CD	*Damascus Document*

Josephus

Ant.	*Jewish Antiquities*
Ag. Ap.	*Against Apion*

Philo

Abr.	*De Abrahamo*
Cher.	*De cherubim*
Conf.	*De confusione linguarum*
Congr.	*De congressu eruditionis gratia*
Decal.	*De decalogo*
Det.	*Quod deterius potiori insidari soleat*
Deus.	*Quod Deus sit immutabilis*
Fug.	*De fuga et inventione*
Her.	*Quis rerum divinarum heres sit*
Leg.	*Legum allegoriae*
Legat.	*Legatio ad Gaium*
Migr.	*De migratione Abrahami*
Mos.	*De vita Mosis*
Mut.	*De mutatione nominum*
Opif.	*Dc opificio mundi*
Plant.	*De plantatione*
Post.	*De posteritate Caini*
Praem.	*De praemiis et poenis*

QE	*Quaestiones et solutions in Exodum*
QG	*Quaestiones et solutions in Genesin*
Sacr.	*De sacrificiis Abelis et Caini*
Somn.	*De somniis*
Spec.	*De specialibus legibus*
Virt.	*De virtutibus*

OTHER ANCIENT LITERATURE

Aristotle

[*Mund.*]	*De mundo*

Tertullian

Marc.	*Adversus Marcionem*

Seneca

Ep.	*Epistulae morales*

Marcus Aurelius

Medit.	*Meditations*

Rabbinic Works

'Abot R. Nat.	*Avot of Rabbi Nathan*
Hor.	*Horayot*
m. Ber.	*Mishnah Berakhot*
Mek.	*Mekilta*
Midr.	*Midrash*
Pesiq. Rab.	*Pesiqta Rabbati*
Pesiq. Rab. Kah.	*Pesiqta of Rab Kahana*
Rab.	*Rabbah*
S. Eli. Rab.	*Seder Eliyahu Rabbah*
Šabb.	*Shabbat*
Sanh.	*Sanhedrin*
Sipre	*Sifre*
Tanḥ.	*Tanhuma*
y. Sanh.	*Jerusalem Sanhedrin*
Yal.	*Yalqut*

MODERN ABBREVIATIONS

AB	Anchor Bible
ABD	*Anchor Bible Dictionary*, edited by D. N. Freedman, 6 vols. (New York, 1992)
ANTC	Abingdon New Testament Commentaries
BDAG	F. W. Danker, W. Bauer, W. F. Arndt, F. W. Gingrich, *Greek-English Lexicon of the New Testament and Other Early Christian Literature*, 3rd ed. (Chicago, 2000)
Bib	*Biblica*
BJS	Brown Judaic Studies
BNTC	Black's New Testament Commentaries
CBQ	*Catholic Biblical Quarterly*
CTJ	*Calvin Theological Journal*
DPL	*Dictionary of Paul and His Letters*, edited by G. F. Hawthorne and R. P. Martin (Downers Grove, 1993)
DSD	*Dead Sea Discoveries*
EDNT	*Exegetical Dictionary of the New Testament*, edited by H. Balz and G. Schneider (Grand Rapids, 1990–93)
EKKNT	Evangelisch-katholischer Kommentar zum Neuen Testament
EncJud	*Encyclopedia Judaica*, 16 vols. (Jerusalem, 1972)
EvT	*Evangelische Theologie*
ExAud	*Ex auditu*
ExpTim	*Expository Times*
HBT	*Horizons in Biblical Theology*
HNT	Handbuch zum Neuen Testament
HTKNT	Herders theologischer Kommentar zum Neuen Testament
HTR	*Harvard Theological Review*
HUCA	*Hebrew Union College Annual*
IBC	Interpretation: A Bible Commentary for Teaching and Preaching
ICC	International Critical Commentary
Int	*Interpretation*
JBL	*Journal of Biblical Literature*

JETS	*Journal of the Evangelical Theological Society*
JJS	*Journal of Jewish Studies*
JQR	*Jewish Quarterly Review*
JSNT	*Journal for the Study of the New Testament*
JSNTSup	Journal for the Study of the New Testament: Supplement Series
JSOTSup	Journal for the Study of the Old Testament: Supplement Series
JTS	*Journal of Theological Studies*
KEK	Kritisch-exegetischer Kommentar über das Neue Testament
LCL	Loeb Classical Library
MNTC	Moffatt New Testament Commentary
NAC	New American Commentary
NCB	New Century Bible
NIBCNT	New International Biblical Commentary on the New Testament
NIBCOT	New International Biblical Commentary on the Old Testament
NICNT	New International Commentary on the New Testament
NIDNTT	*New International Dictionary of New Testament Theology*, edited by C. Brown, 4 vols. (Grand Rapids, 1975–85)
NIGTC	New International Greek Testament Commentary
NovT	*Novum Testamentum*
NovTSup	Supplements to Novum Testamentum
NTS	*New Testament Studies*
OiC	*One in Christ*
OTL	Old Testament Library
PRSt	*Perspectives in Religious Studies*
PSB	*Princeton Seminary Bulletin*
RB	*Revue biblique*
SBLDS	Society of Biblical Literature Dissertation Series
SBLSP	*Society of Biblical Literature Seminar Papers*
SHR	Studies in the History of Religions (supplement to *Numen*)
SJLA	Studies in Judaism in Late Antiquity
SJT	*Scottish Journal of Theology*

SNTSMS	Society for New Testament Studies Monograph Series
SP	Sacra pagina
SR	*Studies in Religion*
TDNT	*Theological Dictionary of the New Testament*, edited by G. Kittel and G. Friedrich, translated by G. W. Bromiley, 10 vols. (Grand Rapids, 1964–76)
TJ	*Trinity Journal*
TynBul	*Tyndale Bulletin*
VT	*Vetus Testamentum*
VTSup	Supplements to Vetus Testamentum
WBC	Word Biblical Commentary
WTJ	*Westminster Theological Journal*
WUNT	Wissenschaftliche Untersuchungen zum Neuen Testament
ZNW	*Zeitschrift für die neutestamentliche Wissenschaft und die Kunde der älteren Kirche*

1

Introduction

The Need for Further Study

THE PROBLEM

DESPITE THE VAST AMOUNTS of energy expended by biblical scholars toward an understanding of the theology of Paul the apostle, most of the effort has been devoted to Paul's soteriology, Christology, eschatology, ecclesiology, and ethics. Few scholars start at the beginning: Paul's understanding of God. James D. G. Dunn highlights the dilemma when he comments, "The problem for us, however, is that Paul's convictions about God are all too axiomatic. Because they were axioms, Paul never made much effort to expound them. They belong to the foundations of his theology and so are largely hidden from view."[1] As a result, scholars all too often skip over Paul's convictions about God in favor of the more obvious statements he makes about justification, grace, and works of the law. Indeed, one proposition on which most scholars would agree is that Paul was consumed with a passion for spreading the gospel of Christ. As scholars focus on exploring this christological emphasis, they frequently become myopic, narrowly focusing on Christ's identity without exploring the interrelationship of Christ and God.[2] Thus, this present study will attempt to address this gap in schol-

1. Dunn, *Theology of Paul*, 28.

2. Dahl argues that the problem occurs throughout all of New Testament scholarship, not just in Pauline studies: "When considering treatments of New Testament Christology, we note that most pay astonishingly little attention to the relationship between faith in Christ and faith in God, to the transfer of divine names, attributes, and predicates to Jesus, or to the emergence of 'trinitarian' formulations" (*Jesus the Christ*, 155).

arship by investigating the meaning and significance of Paul's strongest monotheistic statements.

A few examples serve to illustrate the necessity for such a study. Calvin J. Roetzel, while offering an investigation into Paul, spends very little time considering the question of the place of God in Paul's belief system.[3] Paul's strongest monotheistic statements receive scant attention in Roetzel's work. In particular, he does not mention Paul's monotheistic reference in Gal 3:20; his comments on 1 Cor 8:4–6 and Rom 3:30 are very brief and serve only as a way of referring to the factions in Corinth in the former and to Paul's universalizing tendency in the latter. When Roetzel does broach an in-depth discussion of God in his book, he does so within a discussion of how Paul's ethics are connected to the holiness of God.[4] In a section that summarizes Paul's theological views, he offers a single paragraph on God as creator, redeemer, and judge.[5] Similar to Dunn, Roetzel notes that Paul's theological presuppositions were not explicit: "Like the grammar and syntax of the language he spoke they were simply taken for granted."[6] Unfortunately, however, Roetzel misinterprets this lack of explicit God language as an indication that Paul's theology is only peripheral to his Christology. The study presented here will suggest that the opposite is true: Paul's understanding of God was never merely an assumption, but rather provided a conscious foundation that intentionally shaped the rest of his arguments.

Other scholars have adopted an approach similar to that of Roetzel. C. K. Barrett has organized his discussion of Paul's theology into the following categories: the reign of evil, law and covenant, grace and righteousness, Christ crucified, the church, and the Holy Spirit and ethics.[7] Although Barrett does discuss Paul's understanding of God peripherally and sporadically within these various subsections, he does not directly address Paul's fundamental understanding of the one God. Once again it is taken for granted and thus, perhaps unintentionally, depreciated.

Jürgen Becker takes a more direct approach to downplaying the role of God in Paul's theology when he argues that it is a mistake for scholars

3. Roetzel, *Paul.*

4. Ibid., 31–38.

5. Ibid., 94–95.

6. Ibid., 94.

7. Barrett, *Paul.*

to describe Paul as first trying to extend Old Testament Judaism into the new Christian religion; rather, everything is grounded in Paul's experience of the gospel of Christ.[8] Having declared this, he nonetheless discusses (albeit briefly) Paul's understanding of God the creator, humans as creatures of God, and the imminent judgment of God. Becker quickly dismisses Paul's statements about Christ's involvement in creation, concluding that "Paul understands the final determination of human beings and the God of salvation christologically but otherwise deals separately with God as creator and with God's relationship to creation."[9] This compartmentalization of Paul's thought about God and Christ, and of Old Testament Judaism and the new Christian perspective, is simply not born out in Paul's letters, as this study will show.[10]

In contrast to many scholars, then, this study explores what it may mean to take Paul's understanding of God as a point of departure for his understanding of Christ. More specifically, this study asks how a Jew like Paul—who had been "zealous for the traditions of [his] ancestors"[11]—could simultaneously proclaim loyalty to the one God of the Jews and affirm Jesus Christ as Lord. Thus, this study investigates the question of how Paul's monotheistic convictions affect his overall christological argument.

THE METHODOLOGY OF THE STUDY

Rather than approach the conundrum just described from a perspective of christological monotheism, i.e., investigating all of the texts regarding Christ and his exalted status in relation to God,[12] this study will approach

8. J. Becker, *Paul*, 374.

9. Ibid., 380. Other scholars who similarly offer little consideration of the role of monotheistic belief in Paul's theology include Schoeps, *Paul*; Ridderbos, *Paul*; Furnish, *Theology and Ethics*, but see also *Theology of First Corinthians*, 67–75, where Furnish considers the one-God language but argues that monotheistic belief is subordinated to the existential reality of belonging to God; and Segal, "Paul's Jewish Presuppositions."

10. A notable exception to this paucity of theological focus can be found in the writings of N. T. Wright. He has consistently argued that monotheism and election provide the fundamental structure of Jewish thinking, and as a result provide the fundamental structure for Paul's thinking as well. Wright correctly analyzes the importance of Paul's monotheistic statements, although in this study I will disagree with some of his conclusions regarding interpretations of specific passages.

11. Gal 1:14.

12. This approach has been explored previously by scholars such as Wright and Hurtado.

the question from the opposite direction. We will examine the contexts and themes of the most explicit one-God statements in Paul's undisputed letters—1 Cor 8:4–6, Gal 3:20, and Rom 3:30—and inquire into how these monotheistic passages contribute toward an understanding of Paul's further argument. What role does this one-God language play? What does this tell us about Paul's conception of God and the rest of his argument? Furthermore, we will explore whether this strong one-God language affects Paul's language about Christ elsewhere in the letter. How does Paul conceive of the relationship between God and Jesus within the text? In those contexts where his monotheistic language is the strongest, does Paul's language about Christ diminish Jesus's lordship, or does it nevertheless remain unaffected? What does this tell us about Paul's understanding of the identity of Christ?

Such an in-depth study of these three passages has not been undertaken previously; often, the texts are referred to in scholarly works, but rarely have they undergone intense scrutiny that focuses specifically on Paul's understanding of the relationship between God and Christ contained therein.[13] Many commentaries provide only a cursory description of the one-God formula, treating the language as mere background material.[14] As a result, these commentators miss the significance that Paul's monotheistic theology has within his larger argument.

The title of this book reflects my desire to correct this oversight. The main thrust of the term "dynamic" emphasizes that Paul's one-God theology is *not* an unreflected concept that occasionally appears in Paul's writing by rote; rather, Paul intentionally utilizes his understanding of the one God in order to underscore his overall argument. It is crucial for Paul's logic. Thus, my primary use of this term concerns Paul's argumentation; nonetheless, a secondary nuance of the term alludes to Paul's specific understanding of the oneness of God, which focuses on uniqueness more so than numerical oneness. Indeed, in chapter 2 I will argue that Paul's understanding of God involves a complex oneness.

13. Giblin focuses on these three passages, but only in the brief article "Three Monotheistic Texts in Paul."

14. See, e.g., Tobin, *Paul's Rhetoric*, 142–43. Tobin acknowledges that Rom 3:30 is a reference to Deut 6:4 and says that Paul uses it as part of a *reductio ad absurdum* argument (God cannot be god only of the Jews, since he is one). But Tobin does not further discuss any further significance of this aspect of Paul's theology.

My use of the term "flexibility" also reflects Paul's argumentation. Paul applies his one-God language in very different contexts and with different goals in each case. Whereas the term "dynamic" suggests the intentional shaping of Paul's arguments with one-God concepts, the term "flexibility" emphasizes that such shaping occurs within a variety of contexts. Paul is not constrained to use his monotheistic ideas in only one setting.

PROLEGOMENA

As we explore Paul's one-God language, a number of related issues must be investigated. Because these issues touch upon more than a single text, it is best to begin the discussion here.

One of the key presuppositions of this study is that Paul was firmly grounded in, and drew upon, his Jewish heritage. Although during much of the last two centuries scholars found profound Hellenistic influences in Paul's thought, Pauline scholarship has recently come to understand that Paul's fundamental paradigm was Jewish.[15] The apocalyptic elements in Paul's thought[16] and his extensive use of the Jewish Scriptures in support of his arguments[17] argue strongly in favor of a profound Jewish influence on Paul. This background makes the question of Paul's understanding of God and Christ even more difficult, because at the heart of Judaism lay the conviction that God is one and at the heart of the new belief in the risen Christ lay the conviction that Jesus is Lord. We will explore the intersection of these various concepts throughout the thesis.

We will begin examining Paul's Jewish background by investigating the meaning of the difficult term "monotheism." It is not clear from the term itself how monotheism relates externally to other ideas about divine beings. Specifically, does "monotheism" describe the worship of one god to the exclusion of all other existing gods, or does it describe the belief in one god alone along with the conviction that no other gods exist? In response to this question, a number of more specific terms have emerged in the last two centuries of biblical scholarship, including "henotheism," "monolatry," "inclusive monotheism," and "exclusive monotheism."

15. See Ridderbos, *Paul*, 13–43, for a discussion of the historical development of Pauline theology in this regard.

16. See Beker, *Paul the Apostle*, and *Triumph of God.*

17. See Rosner, *Paul, Scripture and Ethics.*

It is important to note that the term "monotheism" first arose in the seventeenth century when it was coined by Henry More. More's usage, however, reflects his interest in attempting to classify religions according to their philosophical beliefs.[18] This stands in contrast to the concerns of the early Christian churches, which construed the issue (albeit not under the designation "monotheism") in relation to the idolatrous practices in pagan culture and not as merely an intellectual assent to various propositions.[19]

Scholars have tried to refine More's definition in order to illustrate a development within Judaism. H. H. Rowley, for example, has traced the seeds of monotheism back to Moses while, however, describing Moses as a henotheist; Moses did not deny that other gods exist. This view then develops fully in the time of Deutero-Isaiah into a belief that there is only one deity, namely, the God of Israel.[20] John Sawyer has also argued for such a development, noting that the Israelite notion of "one God" began with an understanding of Yahweh's uniqueness, and later developed into a belief in the sole existence of the God of Israel.[21] Other scholars, however, deny that "monotheism" is at all an appropriate term to use. Peter Hayman, for instance, argues that Judaism never fully emerged from its polytheistic roots.[22]

Clearly, the question of "monotheism" is not as straightforward as a "one god" lexical analysis of the word might suggest. Our understanding is further clouded by the rise of interest in intermediary figures during the Second Temple period. Angels, archangels, exalted patriarchs, divine "hypostases," and angelomorphic figures—which of these may be included in the "identity of God,"[23] and what criteria are used for their inclusion? This is an issue to which we will return below.

All of these developments cause one to question whether the term "monotheism" provides an appropriate designation, since the phrase can encompass so much—and may not even reflect a biblical understanding of belief in the one God. Unfortunately, the alternative terms betray

18. MacDonald, "Origin of 'Monotheism.'"

19. See Moberly, "How Appropriate Is 'Monotheism'?"

20. Rowley, "Living Issues."

21. Sawyer, "Biblical Alternatives to Monotheism."

22. Hayman, "Monotheism—A Misused Word?"

23. This is the term used by Richard Bauckham. See the discussion in the following note and on pages 8–9.

similar assumptions. As a result, in this study I will most often refer to the more generic "one-God language" in Paul. In this way I hope to avoid some of the presuppositions that accompany the other terms. By using the expression "one-God language," I intend to connote the specifically Jewish understanding of the one God, Yahweh, who is the unique creator, sustainer, and ruler of all that exists and who has determined to have a special relationship with Israel, which includes Israel's exclusive devotion to Yahweh.[24] The question of whether Paul believed other gods existed will be discussed in chapter 2. At times, however, it may be necessary to use the adjective "monotheistic" as a description of Paul's thought. In those cases, I do not wish to imply More's philosophical understanding, but instead simply intend an adjectival understanding of the Jewish perspective outlined above.

Strongly related to the issue above is the question of further defining the internal parameters of Jewish concepts of the one God. Does the Jewish understanding of Yahweh limit God's person to one, or does Jewish monotheistic belief allow more than one person within God's identity? Does this question unduly place an emphasis on the ontological status of God in contrast to Jewish methods of conceptualizing the divine? Is monotheistic belief, rather, to be defined along other lines, such as unique activity?

One possible interpretation of Jewish one-God concepts is that Jews considered God's oneness in a strictly numerical sense.[25] The rabbis, for example, were clearly concerned with a numerical oneness of God. The rabbinic literature discusses the "two powers" heresy which arose in the second century. The rabbis reacted very strongly to any suggestion that there might be two powers in heaven.[26] We should keep in mind, however, that the rabbinic texts were written after the first century, and therefore

24. Similarly, Bauckham ("Throne of God," 45) argues that Yahweh's identity is understood as unique because God alone is both creator and sovereign over all things. See also his discussion in "Biblical Theology," in which Bauckham defines Jewish monotheism as the belief in "YHWH's transcendant uniqueness . . . a form of uniqueness that puts YHWH in a class of his own" (211).

25. See, e.g., the views of Cohon ("Unity of God"), de Jonge ("Monotheism and Christology"), and Harvey ("Son of God"). De Jonge and Harvey both argue that Jesus could not have been worshipped in the early church because such an act would have defied monotheistic belief.

26. For a good survey of these disputes, see Segal, *Two Powers in Heaven*.

the recorded focus on numerical oneness is likely a reaction, at least in part, to the spread of Christianity.[27]

It is also possible that Jewish monotheistic concepts may have had more to do with an understanding of God's uniqueness. Charles Giblin, for example, argues that Paul viewed God as a unique society of persons whose goal is to communicate with humanity through divine self-disclosure; it is because of this that he thinks Paul emphasizes the relational character of God.[28] N. T. Wright would also agree that the emphasis on numerical oneness is misplaced. For Wright, monotheistic beliefs have less to do with numerical analysis and more to do with providing a polemic against paganism—a polemic that comes through an understanding of the uniqueness of Yahweh. He notes that the passages that are the most fiercely monotheistic (e.g., 1 Cor 8:6) occur within the context of refuting paganism.[29]

An important work for consideration in this area is Richard Bauckham's *God Crucified: Monotheism and Christology in the New Testament*. Bauckham argues that Jewish monotheistic belief during the Second Temple period was strictly monotheistic; that is, divinity involved creation and rule and did not include intermediary or other exalted figures. Descriptions of Jesus's involvement in creation and rule, however, meant that he was included within the unique identity of the one God.[30] Bauckham argues that the Jews did not use a Greek metaphysical framework for defining nature; rather, they were concerned with God's identity as he revealed himself through his mighty acts.[31] Thus, the traditional distinction in New Testament scholarship between functional Christology and ontological Christology (in which Jesus may appear to function as divine even though ontologically he is not divine) presents a false dichotomy. For Judaism, function and ontology were inseparable; as a result, the actions and identity of Jesus were one. The New Testament writers

27. Segal suggests that Christianity was identified by the rabbis as a "two powers heresy," but he argues that the charge of "two powers" may not necessarily have originated with Christianity or been used exclusively against the new sect ("'Two Powers in Heaven,'" 80.

28. Giblin, "Three Monotheistic Texts."

29. Wright, "One God, One Lord."

30. Bauckham, *God Crucified*.

31. Schnelle similarly comments on Paul's theology that "Gott kommt jedoch nicht in seinem Sosein, sondern immer als Handelnder in den Blick" (*Paulus*, 441).

(including Paul), Bauckham argues, intended to include Jesus within the divine identity because they deliberately described him as creator and ruler and thus considered him worthy of worship.

Bauckham's approach has merit in that it brings into focus a more accurate picture of the holistic nature of Jewish thought. Nonetheless, his argument raises several questions. If the identity of the one God may include anyone who participates in the mighty acts, then what is to prevent others beside Jesus and the Holy Spirit from being described as part of Yahweh's deity? As Tertullian argued, "For I must first ask why, if there are two, there should not be more: because if divinity were capable of number we should need to believe it the more richly endowed (the more there were of it)."[32] What is to prevent Wisdom (as some have argued in recent years[33]) or the Glory or other aspects of God's identity from being described as separate persons? It seems such a move could easily lead in the direction of the Greek pantheon.

Furthermore, occasional passages in Jewish literature suggest that angels or other beings participate in creation or rule.[34] While these passages may not appear frequently, they nonetheless pose a problem for Bauckham's definition and must be addressed. Is there a way to distinguish between angelic figures whom God allows to participate in rule or creation and a more strict sense of "divinity"? Would this muddy the waters as far as which category might include Jesus?

Paul's lack of explicit delineation of the nuances of his own understanding of the oneness of God, combined with the variety of possible interpretations of Jewish one-God language, make it necessary to carefully analyze Paul's use of such phrases. If he interpreted monotheistic belief as entailing numerical oneness, then why did he make such strong statements about Jesus in juxtaposition with God within a context that attempts to be explicitly monotheistic (e.g., 1 Cor 8:6)? If numerical oneness was not his concern, then how did Paul conceive of his Jewish monotheistic

32. "Primo enim exigam, cur non plura, si duo, quando locupletiorem oporteret credi substantiam divinitatis, si competeret ei numerus" (Tertullian *Marc.* I.5.1).

33. See, for example, Penchansky, *Twilight of the Gods*. He argues that "Proverbs 8 presents Hokmah as an Israelite goddess, the daughter of Yahweh" (65).

34. The Son of Man in *1 Enoch* sits on a throne and participates in rule and judgment (46:4–5, 49:4, 51:3, 61:8–9, 69:27), and Melchizedek in 11QMelch judges "the holy ones of God." In a much later text, *3 Enoch*, Metatron/ Enoch is called a prince and ruler (4:1, 5, 8; 10:3) and judges the heavenly beings (16:1; 48c:8).

roots? What latitude did his conviction that there is one God grant him in shaping his understanding of Jesus's identity? Where were the boundary markers for his definition of the divine identity? Too often scholars have briefly acknowledged that Paul embraced Jewish belief in the one God and have not critically explored exactly what these beliefs about the one God involved. This foundational question, however, has ramifications for the rest of Paul's theology and needs to be more fully investigated.

In order to comprehend better the potential boundaries for Paul's monotheistic understanding and his resulting view of the relationship between God and Christ, it is important to analyze the concepts of intermediary figures and angelology in Second Temple Judaism. This discussion will help us understand the degree of flexibility that Jews would allow regarding the inclusion of various figures within the definition of the one God.

The rise of intermediary figures and angelology in Second Temple Judaism is well documented.[35] Nearly a century ago, Wilhelm Bousset suggested that this increased interest in angelology resulted from an emphasis on God's transcendence; these intermediary beings then became the means through which this faraway God related to his creation. Jews then began to worship these authoritative angelic beings. Bousset argued that pagan influences caused these changes from a previously "pure" form of monotheism; the worship of Christ as a deity was thus a further development of this angel worship.[36]

More recently, a number of scholars have taken issue with Bousset's conclusions. Larry Hurtado and Loren Stuckenbruck, for example, have responded that Second Temple Judaism did not evolve in the manner that Bousset contends; rather, even within great variety and despite foreign influences, monotheistic belief remained a pillar of Judaism. There was no compromise of monotheism from a pure to a weakened form.[37] In addition, angelological ideas had not developed to such an extent so as to engender an organized "angel cult."[38] In fact, there is little evidence of

35. See Hurtado, *One God, One Lord*; Stuckenbruck, *Angel Veneration and Christology*; Gieschen, *Angelomorphic Christology*.

36. See Bousset, *Die Religion des Judentums*.

37. Stuckenbruck, *Angel Veneration*, 8–9.

38. Hurtado, *One God*, 24–35.

outright angel worship. Earliest Christianity evolved, instead, out of a "mutation" (Hurtado's term) of Jewish ideas.[39]

This debate highlights the difficulty in explaining the development of Christian theology. The first Christ worshippers were Jews, yet Jews worshipped only one God, Yahweh. Thus it behooves us to explore the range of first-century beliefs regarding God and the specific intermediary figures who in some way serve God. Several categories of comparison arise for our consideration. First, some prophets, patriarchs, and priests were exalted to a high status in heaven. Moses and Enoch are two key figures in this discussion. For example, Ezekiel the Tragedian recorded a dream of Moses wherein Moses saw himself enthroned in heaven.[40] In addition, Philo considered Moses to be the ultimate example of godliness.[41] Enoch could also be held in very high esteem. According to the Similitudes, Enoch sits on a throne in heaven (*1 En.* 45:3); he is described as the Son of Man who is involved in judgment (49:4, 61:8–9). According to a later tradition preserved in *3 Enoch*, he is transformed into the exalted angel Metatron. Some scholars, such as Margaret Barker, argue that the priests themselves became God when they ministered in the holy of holies; these priests were exalted higher than any angel.[42] Similarly, Crispin Fletcher-Louis notes that Sirach 50 records a hymn in praise of the high priest Simon ben Onias; in the priestly office, Simon is the embodiment of the glory of God and is the incarnation of Wisdom.[43] Within this category of exalted humans, other figures have been named as having glorified status (e.g., they are venerated or transformed into angels), including Adam, Elijah, Abel, Noah, Jacob, Levi and Melchizedek.[44]

39. Ibid., 124.

40. Lines 68–89 in Jacobson, Exagoge *of Ezekiel*, 55.

41. Philo's texts concerning Moses's exalted status include *Det.* 162; *Leg.* 1.40–41; *Migr.* 84; *Mos.* 1.58; *QE* 2.29, 40; *Somn.* 1.189; *Mut.* 128–29; *Sacr.* 8–10; *QG* 4.8; and *Post.* 27–28.

42. Barker, "High Priest," 99. See also her monograph, *Great Angel.*

43. Fletcher-Louis, "Worship of Divine Humanity," 115–18.

44. For arguments on this perspective, see Fletcher-Louis (ibid.) who cites worship of Adam in *L.A.E.* 12–16. In addition, Gieschen cites numerous Jewish traditions, including: the belief that Elijah (having been assumed into heaven by a chariot of fire) was one of only three men who entered the company of angels without facing death and who supposedly returned to earth as an angel; the belief that Abel is the one like a Son of Man in Dan 7; the detail in *The Book of Noah* where Noah has an appearance like an angel; the reference in the *Prayer of Joseph* to the angel Israel who manifests himself as Jacob; and

The question we must ask when considering the influence of the exaltation of patriarchs, prophets, and priests on the development of Christology is whether these figures were exalted to such an extent that they were thought either to threaten or to redefine monotheistic beliefs. In this case, however, it seems clear that these figures were not given equal standing with God, so that these beliefs did not significantly influence monotheistic understanding. The interpretation of the Tragedian's dream of Moses, for example, should be guided by the manner in which the Tragedian understands the dream—and he interprets it figuratively.[45] The Enoch tradition provides probably the most extensive record of a highly exalted patriarch, and in fact, the tradition eventually led to a rabbinic aberration known as the "two powers" heresy, which arose when Rabbi Elisha ben Avuyah (Acher) saw Metatron sitting on a throne and declared that there were "two powers in heaven."[46] Yet it is important to note that Enoch/Metatron was chastised in heaven for not standing before God (*3 En.* 16:5); he was treated similarly to the other angels and thus does not appear in the text itself to have had equality with God.[47] The question of whether the rabbinic texts are reacting to a hypothetical or real problem is one to which we will return below. As for arguments that the priests became God when operating in their official capacity, Barker and Fletcher-Louis make bold claims on the basis of data taken out of context and disregard the nature of the language used in the texts. The hymn to Simon ben Onias, for example, is sung in response to the call "to sing the praises of famous men," not in response to a call to sing the praises of Yahweh! Although the priests are said to wear the Glory, this appears to be figurative and not literal language about becoming the Glory. The approaches of Barker and Fletcher-Louis do not take into account the nature and function of language, i.e., whether the language has a metaphorical sense that portrays a particular social function (in this case, the performance of the

---

the tradition that Levi put on the garments of the high priest and served before God in heaven. Also, Hurtado (*One God*) and Gieschen (*Angelomorphic Christology*) both refer to Melchizedek and such texts as Gen 14; Ps 110; and 11QMelch.

45. Bauckham, "Throne of God," 55–57. He gives additional examples of dreams which clearly were intended to be interpreted figuratively, such as Joseph's dream of the sun, moon and stars bowing down to him, which represented his brothers bowing down to him.

46. See Segal's *Two Powers in Heaven* for an extensive analysis of the rabbinic texts addressing the heresy.

47. Hengel, *Studies in Early Christology*, 192–93.

cultic rituals). Barker and Fletcher-Louis need to further define the criteria they use in determining how the language should be understood in each instance. Furthermore, the texts from which they draw their conclusions are many and diverse. If a tradition has survived that describes the high priest as becoming God, one would expect a stronger unity among the writings.

But perhaps the strongest criterion to use in evaluating these ideas is that of cultic worship.[48] As Hurtado argues, there is no evidence that the exaltation of figures such as Enoch modified devotion to the one God in any substantial way.[49] These figures simply were not exalted to the point of being worshipped in an organized sense.[50] While it is true that *1 Enoch* can depict Enoch as an object of worship, this only occurs at the last judgment and not prior to that time.[51] In addition, Enoch's role is limited in a way that Christ's is not.[52] Thus it appears that the worship of Jesus did not have a comprehensive parallel so that it could be explained by the exaltation of patriarchs, prophets, or priests.

The second category of intermediary figures to consider is that of the angels themselves. Several "principal" angels are named throughout Jewish literature, but Michael is the name that appears most frequently.[53]

48. In evaluating Christian cultic worship, Hurtado (*One God*, 93–124) finds six features that signify cultic devotion: hymnic practices, prayer, the use of the name of Christ, the Lord's Supper, confessions of faith, and prophetic announcements of the risen Christ. It is precisely the absence of such *organized* veneration that leads Hurtado to dismiss angel worship as a precursor of the exaltation of Christ. While cultic devotion provides a strong criterion which scholars such as Hurtado, Stuckenbruck, and Knight would endorse, it is not without its difficulties. Fletcher-Louis, for example, uses this criterion and achieves dramatically different results. Thus, the criterion perhaps needs to be defined more distinctly in order to provide a clearer direction.

49. Hurtado, *One God*, 67.

50. Stuckenbruck (*Angel Veneration*, 264) argues that such "worship" is actually possible, but that even this does not infringe upon the uniqueness of God. He notes, for example, several passages where angels appear to be worshipped in the same breath as God, yet the usage itself makes every attempt to preserve a monotheistic perspective. In Tob 11:14–15, the Rheneia (Delos) inscription, and the Kalecik inscription, for example, angels are included in the praise language, but the singular usage of various terms indicates that this all-encompassing praise is nonetheless directed to God.

51. *1 En.* 46:5; 48:5; 62:6, 9.

52. Bauckham (*God Crucified*, 19–20) notes that Enoch is clearly a creature who does not himself participate in the act of creation, unlike Christ, who participates with God in creating the world.

53. Texts referring to Michael include Dan 10:13, 21; 12:1; *1 En.* 20:5; *T. Ab.*; 2 Macc 11:6–8; 1QM 17:6–8.

Michael's primary role is as guardian, commander, or warrior for Israel.[54] Gabriel's name is also frequently mentioned, as are Raphael, Uriel, Israel, Yahoel, Eremiel, and Metatron.[55] Gieschen notes that the angels in Second Temple Judaism become increasingly distinct from God.[56] One of the keys to their authority, however, is listed in Exod 23:20–21, where the Divine Name is said to be in the angel. Thus, the angels are distinct from God and do his bidding, yet they carry his authority.[57]

Much of the discussion concerning angelology revolves around whether these intermediary beings were actually worshipped in Judaism. Certainly the rabbinic literature proscribes the veneration of angels through sacrifices, images, prayers or outright worship.[58] The question arises as to whether this proscription addressed actual practices within Judaism, or if it served simply as a preventive, rather than corrective, measure. Stuckenbruck argues that it is plausible that some Jews held beliefs that the rabbis considered threatening,[59] whereas Hurtado believes the evidence for this is not sufficient.[60] Despite the lack of evidence, it is reasonable to conclude that if the rabbis took the time to debate and chronicle their response to angel worship, the cultural milieu must have presented a significant possibility of such behavior. The rabbis were adamant that any worship belonged solely to the one God of Israel. This deep-rooted conviction is also supported by a "refusal tradition": at times, in the context of angelophanic visions, the seer would assume a reverent posture before a prominent angel, but the angel would explicitly reject any kind of veneration and try to steer the worship back toward God.[61]

Veneration of angels is found in the form of invocations, reverence, and thanksgiving, yet this does not amount to "cultic devotion" to angels as such, as Stuckenbruck argues. Furthermore, angel veneration, where it occurs, does not function as a substitute for the worship of the one God;

54. Gieschen, *Angelomorphic Christology*, 126. See also Hannah, *Michael and Christ*.

55. *3 En.*, the text which mentions Metatron, is a late document, dating probably to the fifth century.

56. Gieschen, *Angelomorphic Christology*, 151. See also Fossum, *Name of God*; and Rowland, *Open Heaven*.

57. See below for a discussion of this authority.

58. Stuckenbruck, *Angel Veneration*, 52.

59. Ibid., 52–75.

60. Hurtado, *One God*, 30–31.

61. Stuckenbruck, *Angel Veneration*, 80–101.

angel veneration is thus not a weakened form of monotheism.[62] Certainly the idea of principal angels may have offered Christians a basic scheme for exalting Jesus without departing from monotheistic belief, but as Hurtado argues, the concept does not account for the unique "binitarian" shape of early Christianity.[63] Most scholars agree that early Christians did not understand Jesus, in the strict sense, to be an angel.[64] The category of principal angels, then, does not seem adequate to alter our conception of monotheistic belief and what that means for the identity of Jesus.

The question becomes somewhat more murky, however, when one considers the category of angelomorphic beings. Charles Gieschen has discussed this issue in depth in his *Angelomorphic Christology: Antecedents and Early Evidence*. He argues that the distinction between Christ and angels does not rule out the possibility of an angelomorphic figure, which he defines as one who has some forms and functions of an angel without necessarily being, in the strict sense, an angel.[65] In fact, God's primary form of self-revelation in Jewish literature is as an angelomorphic figure; angelomorphic Christology, in turn, is evident in several early Christian documents.[66]

The problem of God's self-revelation to Israel is a thorny one. How does the Almighty, whom tradition holds to be invisible, make himself known to his people—especially when no one may look upon the Lord and live (Exod 33:20)? Yahweh certainly used a variety of forms to make himself known, from a burning bush (Exod 3) to a pillar of clouds (Exod 13:21). In several Jewish texts, the form in which God appears is מַלְאָךְ, or a messenger. The Angel of the Lord sometimes is not clearly distinguished from God, such as in Exod 3:2, while at other times the Angel of the Lord is portrayed as distinct. There is no uniformity in the tradition. Exod 23:20–21, however, may provide important insights for understanding the angelomorphic tradition. In these verses, God identifies an angel and says "my Name is in him" (v. 21). Gieschen thus proposes that a separate

62. Ibid., 200–201.

63. Hurtado, *One God*, 82.

64. Ibid., 73. See also, e.g., Dunn, *Christology in the Making*, 161–62.

65. Gieschen, *Angelomorphic Christology*, 3 n. 2.

66. Ibid., 6.

being can operate with God's authority through the possession of this Divine Name.[67]

We must make a clear distinction, however, between God himself appearing in the form of an angel and angels who appear with God's authority.[68] When God appears as an angel and is worshipped, there is obviously no threat to monotheism, because the figure is operating representationally; whether God appears as a burning bush, a pillar of cloud or as an angel, he is still YHWH the Lord of Israel. For angels, however, who carry the Divine Name, the question must be raised: What is the true ontological identity of the angelic being? Does carrying the Divine Name involve a transformation of the identity of the messenger itself, or does it simply transfer God's authority (and not his divinity) to the angelic being? Gieschen argues that the Divine Name is a hypostasis of presence. But again, this raises the issue of what precisely is the nature of the Name—the presence—"in" the angel. Given the evidence noted above that angelic figures refused worship and encouraged others to worship the true God, it seems unlikely that a tradition developed within Second Temple Judaism whereby principal angels came to be worshipped as God. While some diversity may have existed within Jewish thinking, angel veneration does not seem to have made a significant impact on religious practice during Second Temple Judaism. Thus, it appears that these highly exalted angels who had the Divine Name in them were not themselves included within God's identity, but rather served as God's vice-regents, and therefore did not alter the substance of monotheistic belief.

The final category to consider under the concept of intermediary figures is divine attributes and hypostases. A hypostasis is "an aspect of the deity that is depicted with independent personhood of varying degrees."[69] The Wisdom and Logos of God are included in this final category, and are frequently mentioned throughout Jewish literature. Proverbs, Wisdom of Solomon, and Sirach, for example, describe Wisdom in vividly personal

67. See also Fossum, who argues that the Angel of the Lord in Exod 23:20 is "an extension of YHWH's personality, because the proper Name of God signifies the divine nature. Thus, the Angel of the Lord has full divine authority by virtue of possessing God's Name . . ." (*Name of God*, 86).

68. Gieschen does make this distinction between divine hypostases (see below) and angelic beings who have the divine NAME in them.

69. Gieschen, *Angelomorphic Christology*, 45.

terms.[70] In addition, Philo frequently personified the Wisdom and Logos of God, and at times even referred to Logos as the "second god."[71] Scholars disagree on how to interpret these descriptions of God and the degree of independence from God that these personifications achieve.[72] But it is precisely this degree of independence which could have a significant effect on monotheistic faith and Christology. On the one hand, simple personifications do not appear to affect Jewish monotheistic belief in any way, since these are simply portraying highlights of God's identity.[73] On the other hand, the notion of a hypostasis poses intriguing implications for Christology, perhaps providing a framework for the earliest Christians to embrace as they considered Christ's identity.

Nonetheless, the argument that Jews understood these personifications to have semi-independent status remains unconvincing for two reasons. First, the interpretive shift from personification to hypostasis does not adequately take into account the genre of Hebrew poetry and its often metaphorical language. Poetry is not intended to convey literal, factual descriptions (e.g., that Wisdom is an independent being); rather, it intends to evoke an emotional response (e.g., that God's wisdom is powerful and should be sought after diligently).[74] Sirach 24, for example, is clearly a poem that borrows heavily from Proverbs not only in content, but also in poetical structure.[75] The vivid imagery of this poetry is intended not

70. See, for example, Prov 1:20–33; 4:6–9; 8:1—9:12; Wis 1:6; 7:22—8:1; 9:9–11; 10:1—11:1; Sir 24. See also *1 En.* 42.

71. Philo *QG* 2.62.

72. Moore, e.g., states, "The Jews identified the divine wisdom with the Torah, which is also sometimes personified. Wisdom and Torah, like the word, were for them realities, not mere names or concepts; but they never gave them personal existence" (*Judaism in the First Centuries*, 1:415–16). Similarly, Hurtado (*One God*, 46) does not regard these personifications as establishing the Wisdom or Logos as separate entities alongside God. Gieschen (*Angelomorphic Christology*, 70–123), on the other hand, believes that the Wisdom and Logos, among others (Name, Glory, Power, and Spirit) are hypostases that have a degree of distinct personhood. These figures take part in creation and rule.

73. Bauckham (*God Crucified*, 17, 21–22) also includes the Word, Spirit and Wisdom in God's identity as personifications. He notes that both the Word and Wisdom take part in creation and are intrinsic to the unique divine identity.

74. Stein states, "The use of poetry in ancient times, as in our own, indicates that the writer is less concerned with precise description or scientific accuracy than with evoking emotions and creating certain impressions. Poetry is clearly 'commissive' rather than 'referential' in nature . . ." (*Playing by the Rules*, 102).

75. For an analysis, see Skehan and Di Lella, *Wisdom of Ben Sira*, 331–38.

to promote worship of a hypostatic being but to describe in a picturesque manner an aspect of God's being. Indeed, the language itself is ambiguous and flexible. On the one hand, Wisdom is described as covering the earth like a mist (24:3), calling to mind the image of God's creative Spirit in Gen 1:2; on the other hand, the author characterizes Wisdom as a created being (24:8–9). Ultimately, Ben Sira identifies Wisdom with the Torah in 24:23, thus further emphasizing the metaphorical, fluid nature of the language.

Second, the understanding of what a hypostasis might have meant in first-century Judaism is nebulous at best. How does an attribute bear *partial* personhood? Rather, personhood, by its very nature, must be distinct.[76] The difficulty in determining whether any given text describes merely a personification of a divine attribute or an actual semi-independent hypostasis suggests that we seek external criteria in order to resolve the dispute. Hurtado's focus on cultic devotion thus becomes instructive. There is no evidence that the Logos and Wisdom were worshipped as separate deities apart from YHWH, especially given the monotheistic context.[77] If these descriptions truly had attained an independent identity that nonetheless involved ontological divinity, then why were these beings never worshipped as such? Where are the cultic rituals, the offerings, the prayers dedicated to these beings?

Ultimately, then, the category collapses back to one of simple personifications. Furthermore, it would not have been simple for early Jewish Christians to use this category to aid in their interpretation of the significance of Christ, since the human Jesus clearly was an independent person. That is not to say that Christians could not equate Christ with Wisdom and Logos (for clearly they did), but in order to do so, the early Christians would be making a particularly bold and radical claim about Jesus's identity, since the Wisdom and Logos were considered to be part of God's very identity.

As this preliminary overview shows, no ready-made, easy category of Jewish intermediary figures existed for Christians to use in explaining

76. Gunton, e.g., emphasizes the importance of this distinctiveness ("particularity") as constitutive of personhood within the Trinity: "Father, Son and Spirit through the shape—the *taxis*—of their inseparable relatedness confer particularity and freedom on each other. That is their personal being" ("Trinity, Ontology and Anthropology," 56).

77. As noted by both Hurtado (*One God*, 48) and Dunn (*Christology in the Making*, 170). Ringgren, although he identifies hypostases within Israelite religion, nonetheless states that "the strict monotheistic belief did not allow the hypostases to become real deities" (*Word and Wisdom*, 192).

the identity of the exalted Christ. Although many intermediary figures of high status existed in Jewish traditions, no distinct entities reached a clear status of divinity alongside God. Thus, we are left in somewhat of a quandary. Three options present themselves: either 1) Christ did not achieve divine status in the eyes of the first Christians because of Jewish monotheistic beliefs;[78] 2) the first Christians ascribed divinity to Jesus through an intentional departure from a traditional Jewish understanding of the One God;[79] or 3) early Christians believed Jesus was divine, and in affirming this belief, they came to understand the parameters of Jewish monotheism in a new way while simultaneously believing they remained faithful to the tenets of Judaism. A thorough investigation of the strongest one-God texts in Paul's undisputed letters will help to resolve this dilemma.

If it is accurate that Paul understands Jesus to be in some way divine, then we must also consider how Paul specifically envisions the relationship between God and Christ. Throughout his letters, Paul clearly attributes to Jesus a high status.[80] But to what level, exactly, is Christ exalted? If Paul raises Jesus to the level of divinity, does he simultaneously limit Jesus's divinity through some sort of hierarchy? Does Paul subordinate Christ to God, and if so, how far does this subordination go? 1 Cor 3:23 and 15:24–28 both seem to indicate such a hierarchy. The question must be asked, then, what is the nature of this subordination? This relates to the question of deity itself—is it possible to be considered part of the Jewish understanding of Yahweh and yet not be "over all," since Christ is not over God? Or is this a false distinction between two equal members of the divine identity? Is Paul even consistent in his presentation of the relationship between God and Christ?

In addressing these questions, it is helpful to begin by noting that Paul considers Christ's lordship to include everything except God himself (1 Cor 11:3, 15:27). This seems to be a consistent theme—in the hymn in Phil 2, every knee bows to Christ "to the glory of God the Father" (v. 11). Thus, by emphasizing these texts, one could conclude that (for Paul) Jesus never attains the same status as Yahweh. Indeed, this is the position taken by Dunn, who argues that Paul's use of the term κύριος was not so much

78. Dunn reaches this conclusion. See below.

79. Bousset, e.g., takes this position.

80. See, e.g., Phil 2:5–11; Gal 1:1; Rom 1:3–4, 9:5; 1 Cor 1:24, 8:6.

a way to identify Jesus with God as it was a way to distinguish Christ from God. He also maintains that Paul was reluctant to use the term "God" for Jesus and never prayed directly to Jesus.[81] In Dunn's view, the full-fledged deification of Christ occurred only later in the Christian church.

By emphasizing other texts, however, one may also find it possible to argue that Paul elevated Jesus to the level of deity, making him fully equal with God. Phil 2:6, 1 Cor 8:6, and Rom 9:5, for example, appear to place Jesus on par with Yahweh. Jesus also shares the functions of Yahweh, such as sitting on the judgment seat (2 Cor 5:10). In addition, it is important to consider that God's functions are intimately tied to the life, death, and resurrection of Christ. Yahweh is the God who sent his Son, the God who raised Jesus from the dead. It is just such a dynamic relationship that leads Francis Watson to argue that divine identity and divine action are inseparable, and thus God's own identity is determined by his relationship to Jesus, just as Jesus's identity is determined by his relationship to God.[82] "God is indeed still one and sovereign, but the oneness and the sovereignty are not extraneous to the mutually constitutive relation of 'Father' and 'Son.'"[83]

A third interpretation is also possible. Clearly Paul wrote both kinds of texts: those that appear to exalt Christ to the level of deity, and those that appear to subordinate Christ to God the Father. What if he is not being inconsistent, but rather holds both to be true; that is, Christ is divine but does not achieve the same status as Yahweh? Donald Hagner, for example, argues that Paul considered Jesus to be divine, yet at the same time created a "subordination of economy" to preserve Jewish monotheism.[84] Jesus the Son is the agent of God and himself directly represents deity to the people, Hagner argues. He does not, however, go into detail regarding the nature and extent of the subordination of Christ. He merely states

81. Dunn, *Unity and Diversity*, 53.

82. Watson, "Triune Divine Identity," 105. While Watson's work offers an important corrective to Dunn, problems may arise for Watson when the early Jewish literature is consulted. Does the attribution of a divine function to an intermediary being, such as an angel or prophet, therefore mean that the intermediary being is divine? If Watson does not intend such an implication, then he needs to define his parameters more closely.

83. Ibid., 117–18.

84. Hagner, "Paul's Christology," 29.

that, given 1 Cor 8:6, "the deity of Christ is an unavoidable conclusion," and also asserts that the same time Christ was subordinate to God.[85]

In order to characterize further Paul's understanding of the relationship between God and Christ, we will look closely not only at the strongest one-God texts in Paul's letters, but also at the surrounding context. Does the use of strongly monotheistic language cause Paul to limit his descriptions of Christ elsewhere in the letter, or does Christ's exalted status remain unaffected? Which is more prevalent—passages that appear to exalt Christ or passages that appear to subordinate him to God? Did Paul regard Jesus as divine in all contexts? Or did Paul's monotheistic framework prevent him from stating that Jesus would ever be equal with God? Just what did Paul mean in those verses where he speaks of Jesus's relationship to God the Father? Resolution of these questions is central to understanding Paul's overall theology.

One aspect of Paul's writing that will help us get to the center of these difficult issues is an exploration of his use of Jewish Scriptures as they apply to God and to Jesus. Paul frequently refers to the Old Testament and uses a variety of texts to support his positions. Of interest for this study is the observation that Paul takes a number of Old Testament texts that originally referred to God and transforms them into texts that refer to Jesus. David Capes has analyzed these Yahweh texts—the Old Testament texts that include the Divine Name, YHWH—in order to determine when Paul uses "Lord" to keep the original referent (God) and when he uses the term to substitute Jesus in the reference normally attributed to God.[86] In fourteen specific citations of Yahweh texts, Paul refers to God seven times, while seven times he refers to Jesus. Furthermore, Capes finds that in all allusions to Yahweh texts Jesus is the referent.[87] He concludes: "The evidence from Paul's letters and particularly his use of Yahweh texts suggests that he identifies Jesus as Yahweh manifest and thus his Christology is already 'high.'"[88]

Capes's analysis is convincing, but it results in the difficult question of how to explain Paul's shift in referents. How could a Jew (presumably) committed to the one God of Scripture suddenly apply these texts to

85. Ibid.

86. Capes, *Old Testament Yahweh Texts.*

87. Ibid., 160.

88. Ibid., 183.

a human who very recently had died a shameful death? What justifies Paul's radical reconceptualizing of Scripture? A recent study by Francis Watson may help to solve this dilemma. In *Paul and the Hermeneutics of Faith*, Watson provides an illuminating analysis of Paul's interpretive approach to the Jewish Scriptures.[89] Through comparisons with Jewish exegetes roughly contemporary with Paul, Watson demonstrates that many of the apparent contradictions in Paul's thinking originate within the Torah itself. Thus, Paul's pessimistic view of humanity's ability to fulfill the requirements of the Law is not a Pauline invention, but originates in Deut 30 and Israel's own history of rebellion. Paul's hermeneutic is "fundamentally antithetical" in the way that it exploits the tensions inherent in the story of Israel.[90] Watson argues that Paul does not simply start with christological convictions that he then reads back into the Old Testament; rather, Scripture provides the matrix within which Paul's Christology takes shape. The one informs the other, and vice versa: "The Christ who sheds light on scripture is also and above all the Christ on whom scripture simultaneously sheds its own light."[91]

Watson's study primarily focuses on Paul's view of the Law, but his analysis can be used to inform our understanding of Paul's view of the one God. Are there tensions inherent in the Jewish Scriptures regarding the oneness of God? Does Paul exploit these tensions when he uses exalted language to describe Christ? The tentative answer is yes. Psalm 110:1 provides a good example. The interpretive significance of this psalm for the early church has been long recognized.[92] Indeed, Hengel finds three main Old Testament texts connected to the use of Ps 110:1—Isa 52:13, Isa 14:13, and Dan 7:9–14. The last of these contains the most significance for this study. Hengel argues that in Dan 7 the one like a man almost takes the place of God; divine authority and judgment are transferred to this figure, who then participates directly in God's reign.[93] Paul uses this suggestion

89. Watson, *Paul and the Hermeneutics of Faith*.

90. Ibid., 24.

91. Ibid., 17.

92. Hengel, for example, argues that the Psalm already significantly influenced the Church by the early 50s CE, because Paul in his writings assumes that his congregations understand the concepts associated with the reference (*Studies in Early Christology*, 172).

93. Ibid., 185.

of heavenly authority in Rom 8:34 and 1 Cor 15:25.[94] Thus, the significance he places on Christ's identity is grounded in the Jewish Scriptures.

The question of whether the first Christians deified Christ is not without controversy, however, and the texts investigated are open to a number of interpretive possibilities. Dunn, for one, agrees that Ps 110:1 significantly influenced the early church, but he would not go so far as to state that the first generation of Christians deified Christ. This is a development that came only later (see discussion above). For Dunn, the exaltation of Christ in Paul's writings can be explained in other ways. For example, the Christ hymn in Phil 2, which references Isa 45:23, is an expression of Adam Christology and not an expression of Christ's deification.[95] Foundational to Dunn's argument is the conviction that Jewish monotheistic beliefs would not permit such an understanding. But Watson's analysis of Paul's hermeneutic suggests that Paul is willing and able to identify tensions within the Jewish Scriptures and exploit these in developing his Christology. What I propose here is that Paul, aware of scriptures such as Dan 7 and Ps 110:1 that describe another exalted figure alongside God, is able to use one-God language while simultaneously exalting Christ. Paul's antithetical hermeneutic suggests that we should avoid ruling out a priori the possibility of Christ's deification within a Jewish (Christian) context.

Understanding Paul's interpretive matrix thus helps to clarify how he is able to use Yahweh texts interchangeably for Jesus and God. Certainly a former Pharisee, a zealous Jew, like Paul would understand the theological implications of such statements. If Paul had wanted to avoid any misunderstandings, if he had wanted to preserve a strictly numerical understanding of the one God, he would have taken great care to avoid any confusion between God and Christ when making these formulations. Yet what we see in Paul's writings is an affinity for blurring the lines between God and Christ. Although Paul's Jewish contemporaries appear to have avoided the possibility of interpreting Ps 110:1 or Dan 7 in such a manner as to alter their understanding of the one God, it appears that Paul may not have had any such reservations. His hermeneutic elsewhere, as

94. See also Eph 1:20 and Col 3:1.

95. Dunn, *Christology in the Making*, 118.

Watson shows, allows him to interpret the Jewish Scriptures in atypical yet thoroughly Jewish ways.[96]

Closely related to the question of Paul's use of the Jewish Scriptures is the question of the titles that Paul uses for Jesus and the ramifications of those names. The titles Paul uses most frequently are "Christ," "Lord," and "Son of God." Of these, the latter two have generated the most discussion. "Christ" (Χριστός) started as a messianic title but quickly developed into a proper name for Jesus. This may have occurred because "Christ" did not have a personal meaning in Greek (i.e., "to be rubbed in"), whereas its equivalent in Hebrew meant "anointed" and thus referred to the Messiah. The confession "Jesus is Messiah," therefore, quickly turned into "Christ Jesus."[97] The Hebrew understanding of the Messiah, it appears, did not include a view that the Messiah was divine, and thus the term "Christ" *in and of itself* does not make a statement about Jesus's divinity. Nonetheless, the statements that the early church made about this Christ, such as his exaltation to the right hand of God, did involve audacious new claims about the Christ. As Hengel states, "That Jesus of Nazareth, the Messiah/ Son of Man, who was hanged on the tree of shame and was resurrected by God, was exalted to the right hand of his heavenly father and is participant in his divine power, was a claim of fanatic boldness; it was intellectual dynamite which could sound like blasphemy in the ears of Jewish listeners."[98] Thus, while the term *originally* did not have connotations of divinity, it may have come to be understood that way as the result of its specific attachment to the exalted Jesus.

The term "Lord" (κύριος), however, contains within the title itself the capacity for exalting Christ to the level of God. It is commonly known that κύριος was used in the LXX for the divine Tetragrammaton. It must be noted, however, that in pre-Christian Jewish Greek documents, the Tetragrammaton was either left in untranslated Hebrew or was written as ΠΙΠΙ; the term "Lord" was not inserted into these manuscripts until

96. This is not to say that Paul would not have been regarded as a heretic by many of his Jewish contemporaries. Rather, it is to say that Paul did not simply import ideas from Hellenistic philosophies or religions in order to achieve his understanding of Christ. His foundation was the Jewish Scriptures themselves, even if he interpreted them in a radically new way.

97. Hengel, *Studies in Early Christology*, 384–85.

98. Ibid., 174.

a post-Christian date.[99] Such information, however, does not change the fact that regardless of the written form, when the text was read, κύριος was spoken in place of the Divine Name.[100] Despite the manuscript evidence, then, it is appropriate to conclude that synagogue-attending Jews would have been aware of the divine implications of the term. Given this evidence, it is significant that Paul uses the term some 230 times to refer to Jesus.[101] It is equally important to note, however, that κύριος was not a term that was used exclusively for God; it could also be used of humans to mean teacher, master, or king.[102]

The question arises, then, whether Paul's continual references to Jesus as "Lord" meant more than simply a revered human. That "Lord" can designate a god, combined with Paul's affinity for ascribing Old Testament Yahweh texts to Jesus, certainly suggests that deification was his intended connotation. In addition, the formula "to call on the name of the Lord" (1 Cor 1:2) is a regular Old Testament formula for worship and prayer to God.[103] As will become evident throughout this investigation, Paul continually ascribed functions to Christ that normally resided with God. Unless Paul was extremely careless to the point of being absentminded, it is difficult to believe that he was unaware of the implications of his word choice.

Nonetheless, we should consider whether a difference exists between the evidence of worship of God and the evidence of worship of Christ in the Pauline Epistles. According to P. M. Casey, texts where Paul refers to calling on the name of the Lord or uses Yahweh texts to refer to Jesus are not as clear-cut as some scholars would have us believe: "The transference of items from God to an intermediary figure . . . does not imply their deification. At one level, the mere transference of a passage alters its meaning, and we may never assume that there is no other change in meaning."[104] Furthermore, Casey notes the variety of meanings for the term κύριος

99. Kahle, *Cairo Geniza*, 222.

100. De Lacey, "'One Lord' in Pauline Christology," 193. De Lacey supports his argument with testimony from Origen, including statements about the "Hellenes" reading the Tetragrammaton as *kyrios* while the Hebrews pronounce it *adonai*.

101. Dunn, *Christology in the Making*, 17.

102. Foerster, "κύριος."

103. France, "Worship of Jesus," 30.

104. Casey, "Monotheism, Worship," 225. See also Casey's monograph, *Jewish Prophet to Gentile God*.

and states that this diversity is precisely the reason that the term was so useful during a period of rapid christological development. As a result, one should not be too specific about the term's meaning. Certainly it indicated Christ that was a superior being with authority, but "it does not equate him with God, and its exact force could be differently perceived by different people."[105]

Although Casey provides an important caution that the process of transferring a text inherently alters the meaning, this does not change the fact that Paul *intentionally* transferred these texts, which originally referred to God, to the risen Christ. Such a transfer happened in multiple instances, not just on one or two occasions as one might expect if Paul had absentmindedly transferred these texts to Jesus. In addition, despite the diversity of possible meanings for the term, κύριος in the Old Testament Yahweh texts contained no ambiguity. Furthermore, Paul's strong Jewish background as a Pharisee suggests that he was fully aware both of the fundamental importance of monotheistic beliefs and of the meaning of the texts in their original context. He certainly could have used another term for Jesus (such as "rabbi") and avoided transferring Yahweh texts to Christ, had he intended to maintain a conventional understanding of the one God. We must not confuse the diversity of *possible* meanings of κύριος with an ambiguity in *intended* meaning. Although Paul's readers could certainly interpret the term κύριος in a variety of ways, it does not follow that Paul lacked a *specific* meaning when he used it.

The final title we will consider is "Son of God." The concept occurs only fifteen times in Paul's writing; compared to Paul's usage of the term "Lord," "Son of God" may appear to be of relative insignificance for Paul. Nonetheless, Hengel asserts that the places where Paul does use the term are climactic in Paul's argument.[106] We will study some of these occurrences more fully in the investigation that follows. For now, however, I will note in general that this concept, like "Lord," has a wide range of meanings, including righteous individuals, angels, kings, and the people of Israel.[107] Thus, the term does not necessarily connote divinity. Within Judaism, however, the use of "Son of God" is connected to such traditions as Enoch and divine Wisdom. As such, the term can involve ideas of preexistence,

105. Casey, "Monotheism, Worship," 225–26.

106. Hengel, *Son of God*, 14.

107. Schneemelcher, "υἱός."

mediation at creation, and sending into the world.[108] Hengel argues that because Christianity provided its own original stamp for these ideas, this caused friction with Judaism: "We cannot therefore over-exaggerate the scandal of Pauline Christology and soteriology, precisely *because* it was fed from Jewish sources."[109]

But Paul's use of "Son of God" is decidedly more ambiguous than his use of "Lord."[110] A. E. Harvey, for instance, argues that human, and not divine, categories were used to express Jesus's unique authority.[111] Harvey finds three aspects of the title "Son of God" to be significant: it connoted Jesus's obedience to his father, his position as apprentice and conveyor of the teachings of the Father, and his service as the agent and representative who held the authority of the Father.[112] "To this extent, the phrase 'Son of God' as applied to Jesus acquired new precision and a new range of meaning; but there was nothing new in the conceptions it made use of."[113] Furthermore, Jewish monotheistic beliefs were effective in restraining a broader application of this term.[114]

Certainly Harvey is correct that Jesus's obedience (some would say "faithfulness"), teachings, and authority are integral to his designation as son. But if Paul elsewhere ascribes terms and functions to Jesus that are reserved for God, then it is certainly *possible* (especially given the connection with Wisdom) that Paul does the same with the phrase "Son of God." We cannot simply rule out this possibility a priori on the grounds that Judaism would not allow it.

As we progress through our study of texts, therefore, it is necessary to keep Paul's usage of these terms in mind. Paul at times does appear to ascribe divine titles and functions to Christ; nonetheless, some of these terms have multiple possible meanings and we must not assume that Paul's use of a phrase in one context indicates that he always intends the term to be used in such a manner. We should take care, however, not to rule out from the beginning the full range of possible meanings, both di-

108. Hengel, *Son of God*, 57.

109. Ibid., 74.

110. Obviously there are no Yahweh texts in this instance which transfer a description of Yahweh as "son of God" to Jesus.

111. Harvey, "Son of God," 158.

112. Ibid., 159–62.

113. Ibid., 164.

114. Ibid., 157.

vine and human, simply on the assumption that "Judaism" does not allow such an interpretation. As noted in the discussion of Paul's hermeneutics, the Torah itself contains inherent tensions which Paul may well have exploited to the advantage of his christological theology.

Another tension present in Judaism's concept of the one God is the belief that God is God over all (universalism) and yet simultaneously that God has chosen the people of Israel to receive his special protection and favor (particularism). While first-century Jews tended to emphasize particularism, in Paul's explication of God's plan for salvation history he focused on universalism. Yahweh justifies Jews and Gentiles alike by faith, and thus he is God of the Gentiles too, Paul argued. Paul thus expanded the Jewish understanding of God's blessings, stating that the Gentiles would also share in God's promises.

One of the major avenues of investigation necessary for understanding the correlation between Paul's theology and that of Jews in general, then, is the attitude of first-century Jews toward Gentiles. Were the Jews content to let Gentiles be Gentiles? Or did they aggressively try to convert Gentiles to Judaism? Were Jews antagonistic toward Gentiles, leaving them to God's wrath, or did they perceive a future for Gentiles within the kingdom of God? We will explore this contextual background more fully in chapter 4.

For now I will simply make the observation that Paul actively sought out Gentiles and invited them into the kingdom, into the place reserved for Jews. Not only that, but Paul preached that circumcision was not necessary; certainly this would have made the new faith more attractive to the Gentiles than Judaism. In response, the Gentiles came in droves. As a result, the Jews found themselves asking several unsettling questions about this new movement. If Gentiles were now being allowed to enter the circle of God's blessings, and were allowed to do so without observing Jewish law, then what did this mean for Jews? Were they no longer God's specially chosen people? What, then, was the meaning of Israel's election? How could the Jew receive any special promise, if both Jew and Gentile were treated alike in God's plan? Did God lie about Israel's status?

All of this uneasiness arises from the implications of the nature and scope of the one God's impartiality, justice, and authority. The point I want to emphasize here is that the question of the inclusion of the Gentiles—a major issue in the early church, as evidenced by the regular debates in Paul's letters—cannot be divorced from the theological understanding of the one God. Paul appears to be stating, especially in Rom 3:30, that the inclusion of the Gentiles is not simply coincidental to God's identity as the one God over all. Rather, Paul maintains that God's identity from the beginning was and is tied to his salvific acts in Christ, and thus the inclusion of the Gentiles is not an added "extra" to salvation history, but was part of God's original plan. Such a thesis was extremely jarring to those Jews who took pride in their special election. Paul's monotheistic beliefs, then, made a great impact on the question of salvation history and thus need to be more fully investigated.

Another issue arising from Paul's monotheistic beliefs, and one that is closely connected to the preceding subject, concerns the horizontal social dimension of God's oneness. Paul's monotheistic assertions frequently appear within the context of a call for Christian unity: 1 Cor 8:6 appears in the midst of calls for the (theologically) stronger in the church to put aside their freedom for the sake of the weaker; Gal 3:20 discusses faith as the basis of salvation, and a few verses later Paul summarizes that all believers—regardless of race, social status or gender—are one in Christ Jesus; and Rom 3:30 concerns the inclusion of the Gentiles into the blessings of God. Thus the question arises as to the extent that Paul's monotheistic framework affected his ethics.

In some respects, it may appear that Paul's ethics are rather haphazard and are not based in the Jewish Scriptures. Certainly Paul does not lay out a systematic list of "thou shall" and "thou shall not." He does not offer a new Pentateuch or present new stone tablets detailing appropriate behavior. Rather, he responds to the current circumstances in his individual churches and exhorts the communities to respectful, loving behavior. Joseph Fitzmyer describes Paul's ethical statements as examples of the Christian principle of "love reacting to communal situations."[115] Unfortunately, this situational aspect of Paul's exhortations has led some scholars to overlook the strength of the connection of Paul's ethics to his one-God theology. Richard Hays, for example, wishes to show the theological underpinnings of Paul's ethics, yet he does little to explicitly address the three strongest monotheistic statements in Paul's writings.[116]

115. Fitzmyer, *To Advance the Gospel*, 198.

116. Hays, *Moral Vision*. Hays fails to mention Gal 3:20 or Rom 3:30. In his discussion of the ethics of eating idol meat in Corinth, he mentions 1 Cor 8:4 only to describe the position of the strong and does not address 8:6 (42–43). He offers a brief comment on 1 Cor 8:6 in his discussion of the ethics of abortion (450).

Despite the circumstantial nature of Paul's ethical exhortations, we should keep in mind the Jewish foundations of Paul's belief system. This is borne out by his use of the Jewish Scriptures throughout his letters. Although direct citations may be infrequent in Paul's ethical exhortations, it is clear nonetheless that he relies heavily on his Jewish heritage. Brian Rosner, for example, has demonstrated that the Jewish Scriptures "are a crucial and formative source" for Paul's ethics.[117] In what he considers a representative sample of Paul's ethics, Rosner has investigated 1 Cor 5–7 and determined that not only does Paul directly depend on Scripture, but Paul depends on Jewish moral teaching, which is itself dependent on Scripture.

Any such argument, however, must deal with those texts whereby Paul appears to set aside the Law (e.g., Rom 10:4). In Rosner's interpretation, Paul does not set aside all aspects of the Law; rather, Paul retains the idea of the Law as revealing God's will and the Law as Scripture. In other places, where Paul appears to set aside Scripture, it is important to note that Paul only sets aside those parts that make a distinction between Jew and Gentile and thus restrict God's people to the Jews. In addition, Rosner argues that the reason Paul quotes Scripture so rarely in ethical sections is that these are places where he departs the least from Jewish tradition; he quotes Scripture more frequently when he is defending his radical doctrine.[118]

Furthermore, and especially important for this study, Paul relies quite heavily on Deuteronomy when formulating his ethics.[119] This supports the argument that Paul is aware of and influenced by the Shema.[120] It is not coincidental that the Shema appears in ethical contexts. Indeed, this connection between the unity of the people of God and the unity of the one God is not unique to Paul, and in fact, it has very Jewish roots. Stephen Barton describes the unity of the people as bound up integrally with the oneness of God. Anything that threatens God's oneness, e.g., the worship of idols, threatens the community's unity. Conversely, "anything which divides the people—the activity of false teachers, prophets or mes-

117. Rosner, *Paul, Scripture and Ethics*, 177.

118. Ibid., 182–94.

119. Ibid., 178.

120. Indeed, Rosner notes that Deut 6 was "a prominent text in both the Scriptures and early Jewish literature" and he concludes that it was "on Paul's mind" when he wrote 1 Cor 8:6 (ibid., 164).

siahs, for example—undermines the common witness of the people to the oneness of God."[121]

It is thus easy to see how the unique identity of Jesus caused such uproar within the Jewish community. The definition of God was being uniquely connected to the identity of Jesus, and this in turn raised the question of who comprised the people of God and how to reconstitute that definition without invalidating God's promises to Israel. Furthermore, the everyday behaviors of some members of this new group of people involved a variety of practices that appeared at odds with Jewish tradition. What was at stake in the proclamation of Christ was the very unity of the people of God. It is therefore important to ask how Paul's understanding of God's oneness defined for him the boundaries of God's people. How much diversity was allowed, and of what kind, within a unified body? Who was included among the people of God? What were the expectations of those within the community for community life? To what extent were these decisions derived from an understanding of the identity of the one God? These questions will be addressed throughout the following chapters.

SUMMARY AND TRAJECTORIES

In summary, we have briefly explored several major issues that arise from an inquiry into Paul's use of one-God language; for some of these issues I have offered tentative conclusions, while others remain to be more fully investigated in the following chapters. Although the term "monotheism" has been frequently employed to describe Jewish belief in the one God, this investigation has shown that the term lacks precision and derives from later philosophical approaches. Accordingly, I will attempt to refer to Paul's "one-God language," although at times I may be forced to use the adjective "monotheistic." In those cases, the term is specifically intended to connote the Jewish understanding of the one God, Yahweh, who uniquely is the creator, sustainer, and ruler of the world and who has chosen to maintain a special relationship with the people of Israel. At times this belief in the one God seems to have emphasized a numerical oneness, while at other times it has emphasized God's unique activity. Thus, the following study will need to explore the ways in which Paul navigates this course.

121. Barton, "Christian Community," 290.

In considering the Jewish understanding of the one God, we have surveyed various intermediary figures in Judaism—exalted patriarchs, angels, angelomorphic beings, and divine hypostases. Ultimately, none of these categories has proved satisfactory in providing a ready-made category for explaining the exaltation of the risen Christ. In considering how the first Christians, many of whom were Jews, were able to describe Christ in highly exalted terms and yet believe themselves to be remaining faithful to Judaism, I noted that some passages in the Pauline corpus appear to subordinate Christ to God. Thus, the precise extent of Jesus's exaltation needs to be further scrutinized. Nonetheless, Paul's hermeneutical practices provide optimism for resolving some of these difficulties. Paul was clearly immersed in the Jewish Scriptures and was aware of various tensions contained therein. He exploited these tensions in order to make sense out of his experience of the risen Christ. Thus, Paul was able to take Old Testament texts that originally referred to Yahweh and apply them to Jesus. This usage was intentional, and Paul the former Pharisee certainly understood the significant implications of such reinterpretation of Scripture. In concert with this, Paul's language for Jesus—while at times ambiguous—often intended to convey lordship in the divine sense of the term. Other titles, such as Son of God, are not so clear in their connotations and must be investigated further.

Paul exploited further tensions within the Torah when he argued that the Gentiles should be included in the people of God. This discussion of salvation history cannot be separated from a discussion of the oneness of God, for it is precisely from God's oneness, and thus his universal impartiality, justice and authority, that Paul derives the warrant for the inclusion of the Gentiles. The full rationale for this argument will be explored more completely within the discussion of Rom 3:30.

Finally, I have discussed the connection between Paul's ethical exhortations and his understanding of the one God. Despite the varying contexts of his one-God citations, they all deal with proper relationships between people. Since the rightness of behavior is connected directly to the rightness of one's relationship with God (a link which I will establish more firmly in the next chapter), we must further explore this dynamic. It is important to bring this connection between the oneness of God and ethics into focus, since this underpinning appears to have been deemphasized in recent scholarship.

These issues form the background and context within which to investigate Paul's monotheistic beliefs and their implications. I will thus perform an exegetical examination of those passages that are the most explicitly monotheistic in Paul's writings: 1 Cor 8:4–6, Gal 3:20 and Rom 3:30.[122] In investigating these three texts, I will begin with a brief discussion of previous scholarly approaches, and then proceed to analyze the specific verses within their historical, cultural, and grammatical contexts. I will also explore Paul's understanding of the relationship between Jesus and God throughout each letter in order to determine whether Paul's one-God language affects his theology elsewhere.

In chapter 2 I will explore the extent to which Paul's one-God language in 1 Cor 8:4–6 supports his argument regarding the ethics of the church community. I will also consider the relationship between God and Christ, as described in 8:4–6, and ask how this one-God language affects Paul's portrayal of Christ elsewhere in the letter. In places Christ appears to be exalted to the level of deity, while elsewhere the language seems quite hierarchical. Ultimately I will demonstrate that Paul's one-God language is crucial to understanding his ethics. Furthermore, this study will reveal an underlying coherence in the interplay between Paul's theology and Christology, despite appearances to the contrary.

In chapter 3 I will attempt to unravel the cryptic verse in Gal 3:19–20 regarding the identity of the mediator, and wherein the emphasis lies in Paul's argument. In order to do so, I will explore Paul's angelology and Jewish views of mediation, as well as the role of the oneness language itself. This study will conclude that traditional interpretations, which take issue either with angelic origins of the Law or with the nature of mediation, fail to fully consider a number of issues. In addition, the context of Paul's argument, in which he contrasts the Law and the promise, will help to pinpoint the way in which this passage contrasts two different mediators.

In chapter 4 I will investigate how Paul uses one-God language in Rom 3:29–30 to support his argument for the inclusion of the Gentiles

122. Here I must focus on the undisputed Pauline literature. It is important to examine the core of Paul's monotheistic beliefs in order to provide a baseline against which to judge other, disputed texts, such as Eph 4:4–6 and 1 Tim 2:5. At times, however, this study will cite passages from the disputed literature; the purpose of such citations is to show any potential continuity with the Pauline passages explored here and the beliefs of the early church, especially within the Pauline school.

within the people of God. The importance of the *character* of God for Paul's conclusions will become apparent. In addition, despite Paul's emphasis on God throughout the letter, I will argue that Paul's exaltation of Christ does not diminish. Rather, Paul continually refers to God through Christ and Christ through God, so that the two define one another.

Finally, in chapter 5 I will offer the conclusion that Paul's conception of the one God is not perfunctory, static, or deemphasized. Rather it is vital, dynamic and integral to Paul's argumentation. Paul's concept of the one God lies at the core of, and profoundly influences the rest of, his arguments. If the new Christians he addresses do not behave appropriately, it is because they do not have a proper understanding of what it means to be in relationship with the one God. If the Jews are improperly focused on the old way of doing things, it is because they do not adequately comprehend the fullness of the Christ-event as the defining moment of the one God's plan for Israel and the world. If the Jews do not wish to include the Gentiles in the people of God, it is because they have not fully considered the implications of the impartiality and faithfulness of the one God. Whatever the context, Paul's dynamic understanding of the one God lays the foundation from which the rest of his beliefs emerge.

2

The Function and Coherence of Paul's Monotheistic Concepts

1 Corinthians 8:4–6

INTRODUCTION

THE PASSAGE THAT PERHAPS presents the most puzzlement regarding Paul's monotheistic belief is 1 Cor 8:4–6, since it is here that Paul appears to place Jesus alongside God. In this chapter, we will examine the text itself and then turn to the rest of 1 Corinthians for further enlightenment regarding the function of Paul's monotheistic language in his exhortation to the Corinthian church. While 8:4–6 itself seems to exalt Jesus to an almost inconceivable status (at least from a Jewish perspective), other passages in the letter do not appear unanimous in this positioning. Thus, after looking at 8:4–6, we will turn to those texts that also imply a functional correlation between Jesus and God, and then we will examine those texts that ostensibly place Jesus in a subordinate role. In the conclusion of this section, we will consider whether Paul maintains a coherent monotheistic framework within 1 Corinthians.

This exploration will show that, despite appearances to the contrary, Paul does in fact maintain a coherent understanding of the one God. The contextual considerations of his argument significantly influence the emphasis he places on the roles of Christ and God. Nonetheless, Paul consistently exalts Christ to the level of divinity and intentionally emphasizes unity between Christ and God. The two define one another so that God is not "all in all" apart from the actions of Christ. Nonetheless, Paul emphasizes that the salvific work accomplished through Christ does not establish a new plan or set up Christ as a new, better God. This is where the seemingly hierarchical language arises. Rather, Paul wishes to communicate that the Christ-event is the culmination of God's plan. For Paul, it is only in the unified work of God and Christ that the purposes and ultimate goals of the one God can truly be understood.

Although many scholars have taken an interest in 8:4–6 and the larger context of chapters 8–10, few seem to acknowledge the theological underpinnings of Paul's argument. Many, in fact, ignore the monotheistic statements within Paul's instructions. Much of this oversight is due to the nature of the book itself: the conflict in Corinth demands, at least in part, a consideration of sociological factors such as class and gender, as well as an investigation into Paul's rhetoric. It will be helpful, then, to review some of the approaches to this section of Paul's letter and consider how these factors have influenced Paul's theological understanding, while keeping in mind that they do not entirely account for Paul's descriptions of Christ.

We will begin by considering Gerd Theissen's work, which involves a sociological approach to interpreting 1 Corinthians. Theissen offers important insight into the first-century class system and the parallels between Paul's thought and the ability of individuals to advance within society.[1] Theissen's approach, however, is perhaps too heavily weighted in the direction of sociological processes. His arguments seem to indicate that Paul's theology is a result of societal forces, and Theissen does not give enough weight to the theological motivations for Paul's viewpoints. His emphasis leads one to surmise that religion is mostly a construction of sociological pressures, rather than a reflection of a truth that, at least partially, stands outside of society itself.

Because of Theissen's focus on sociological factors, he does not fully address the specifically theological question of Paul's motivation in 1 Cor 8. He does mention the symbolism of reconciliation as God's surrender of love, as well as the connection of love and the death of Christ (the "dying" formula) in 1 Cor 8:1, 11.[2] Yet he fails to address the deeper motivations for Paul's command to love in 1 Corinthians and elsewhere.

1. See Theissen, *Social Reality*, 187–201. Among the examples of social mobility Theissen cites are the status of slaves within a prestigious household, the manumission of slaves, the client/ patron relationship, and the acquisition of Roman citizenship after service in the army. It is this possibility of social mobility which helps the Corinthians to understand Christ's exaltation after an ignoble death, Theissen argues (190).

2. Ibid., 172.

Theissen does not mention the monotheistic underpinnings of the Jewish faith and the impact this understanding had on the sociological and ethical outworking of Paul's beliefs.

Other scholars do not adequately address the question either. David Horrell also takes a sociological approach, but he looks more closely at 1 Cor 8 and moves somewhat closer to addressing Paul's viewpoints. Horrell offers a structuralist perspective, in which Paul's Christianity provides the structure of the Christian community and simultaneously is an outcome of that community.[3] In 1 Cor 8 specifically, Horrell finds that Paul accepts the γνῶσις of verse 4, but he stresses love and the building up of the community. In general, Paul agrees with the basic theological opinions of the strong, but he emphasizes a different value for guiding one's actions—the self-limitation of one's rights for the benefit of others.[4] Horrell goes so far as to say that "Christian conduct has quite a *different* foundation and motivation" than the theology espoused in verses 4–6.[5] While Horrell agrees, in general, that theology and ethics are not to be separated in Paul's thought, he maintains that theological principles—here, specifically, the monotheistic confession—are not used as a basis for ethical action: "In essence, Paul argues here that Christian ethics are founded not upon theological principles but upon a christological praxis. The basis for action is not (theological, monotheistic) knowledge, but (christomorphic) love (8:1–3)."[6]

Horrell's argument, however, presents a false dichotomy. Theology and Christology are so thoroughly tied together in Paul's thought that one cannot speak of Christology apart from theology (see below). Who Christ is cannot be separated from who God is. It is the one God who, through Christ, creates and redeems, and the one God who, through Christ's example, calls every believer to an ethic of self-sacrificial love for one another. The theological principles set forth in verses 4–6, when properly understood, call the believer to this kind of ethic. The problem in Corinth is that those who "have knowledge" do not fully understand what it means to be one people under one God. While on the surface they and Paul agree that there is one God and one Lord, Paul tries to explain to those "in the know" that they don't really know (v. 2), because true knowledge involves

3. Horrell, *Social Ethos*, 55.

4. Ibid., 149.

5. Horrell, "Theological Principle?" 90.

6. Ibid., 105–6.

love. The rest of chapters 8–10 provides Paul's explanation of this love ethic—an ethic that is based in, and cannot be separated from, an understanding of the oneness of God.

The difficulty for Horrell's argument is evidenced by the fact that he does not provide an explanation for *why* Paul comes to a different conclusion than the "strong" regarding appropriate action toward the weak. If their theological premises are basically the same, then what brings Paul to an opposite conclusion from the strong in chapter 8? Why is he willing to set aside his rights (ch. 9), but the strong are not? If he is simply choosing a love ethic over theological knowledge, what criteria does he use to value the christological ethic over against the theological principles? The monotheistic affirmation is one of the basic tenets of Judaism, going to the heart of Jewish (and Christian) faith—what would give Paul the right to override the implications of these principles? If one acknowledges, however, that it is precisely the proper understanding of these theological principles that is at issue, then an adequate explanation exists for why Paul can be critical of the actions of the strong.

Margaret Mitchell takes a different approach when she offers a rhetorical analysis of 1 Corinthians and provides convincing arguments for the unity of the letter. Mitchell concludes that Paul sees all the topics of consideration in 1 Corinthians "to be related to the problem of party strife."[7] She views Paul's overriding concern in chapter 8 as ecclesiological and argues that Paul agrees theologically with both sides of the idol-meat dispute. Paul adds "the common baptismal acclamation" of 8:6 as a reminder of the Corinthians's theological unity.[8] Paul concludes that there is no personal advantage in either point of view; rather, one must consult the community advantage in deciding whether to eat meat sacrificed to idols. The argument is linked to freedom, and Paul sets the standard that if one's freedom causes offense and divides the community, then it is wrong.[9]

7. Mitchell, *Paul and Rhetoric of Reconciliation*, 301. She bases her understanding of unity on several factors, including terms and *topoi* promoting unity throughout the book, the affinity of this language with Greco-Roman calls for social and political unity, and the rhetorical structure of deliberative rhetoric. Furthermore, she argues that 1 Corinthians is a uniquely Pauline creation, not simply a matter of Paul following the structure of the Corinthians's letter to him (190). For a contrasting, but less convincing, viewpoint, see Yeo, *Rhetorical Interaction*.

8. Mitchell, *Paul and Rhetoric of Reconciliation*, 241.

9. Ibid., 242.

Mitchell's structural analysis of 1 Corinthians is helpful in understanding Paul's coherence and overall frame of mind in writing the letter. Rhetorical analysis, in general, is very informative in this way, as far as it goes. But rhetorical analysis only shows us the structure of an argument, the "how" of Paul's argument—not necessarily the "why." As such, Mitchell's treatment of chapter 8 does not get to the heart of the issue. Her statement that Paul agrees theologically with both sides is a bit confusing. Since the implications of their theologies are different, and thus their ethics are different, then how can Paul ultimately agree with both? While Paul agrees, in general, with the "one God" theology that the strong profess, he does not agree with the implications that the strong glean from these principles—in fact, his argument in chapters 8–10 fleshes out his understanding of what it means to be one people under the one God. The unified God of Israel, who loves others selflessly—to the point of death (8:11)—calls believers to that same kind of selfless regard for others. That is the true theological meaning of the "one God" formula, which begins the entire section of argument. The entire ethical/ecclesiological discussion provides the clarification of the deeper meaning of that theological formula. Mitchell's rhetorical analysis, however, fails to make these connections.

Dunn takes a theological approach to 1 Cor 8:4–6.[10] In his view, Paul's intention is to maximize the force of the confession of God as one by affirming it in the face of other beliefs: it doesn't matter what others believe, because for us God is one.[11] Dunn finds Paul's adaptation of the Shema to be "astonishing" in that no sense of strain appears when Paul speaks of both Christ's lordship and God's oneness in the same breath: "Evidently the lordship of Christ was not thought of as any usurpation or replacement of God's authority, but expressive of it."[12] Paul left little doubt for his readers that he was attributing a role in creation to Christ, Dunn argues, and this formulation was a classic expression of wisdom Christology. For Dunn, however, the idea of preexistence communicated in 8:4–6 is not a "real" preexistence. Dunn draws a parallel between Paul's understanding of the preexistent Christ with the Jewish understanding of the preexistent Torah, where it was not so much that the Law was preexistent as that preexistent Wisdom was now to be recognized as the Law.

10. Dunn, *Theology of Paul*, 36–38, 252–55, 272–75.

11. Ibid., 37.

12. Ibid., 253.

Thus, for Paul, it was "not so much that Christ as Jesus of Nazareth had pre-existed as such, but that pre-existent Wisdom was now to be recognized in and as Christ."[13] It is hard to understand how, in Dunn's view, Paul could consider the *person* of Christ (as indicated in 1 Cor 8:6) to be preexistent in the non-personal and rather nebulous idea of Wisdom. Furthermore, the context of the argument connects God and Christ in contrast to pagan deities. This "us versus them" construct emphasizes the supremacy of the Jewish God, and yet Jesus is included within the description of that supremacy.

Overall, Dunn views Paul's exhortation in 1 Cor 8–10 as one that "counseled the avoidance of meals at which it was known beforehand that idol food would be served."[14] The crucial factor in determining social boundaries both within the church and with the outside world is the sense of responsibility for one another as members of the same body, Dunn argues.[15] While Dunn's analysis looks much more deeply at Paul's theology than many other discussions of 1 Cor 8:4–6, the connection between the confessional statement and the rest of the exhortation could be made more explicit. Why does Paul begin the entire section with a Christian version of the Shema? What role does this confession play in the discussion of whether one could eat meat in a temple, a private home, or elsewhere? What connection, if any, does this confession make to Paul's overall ethic to set aside one's rights in order to build up the community?

N. T. Wright also takes a theological approach to the passage. Wright is one of the few scholars who takes a close look at the monotheistic language of 1 Cor 8:4–6 and explains why these monotheistic beliefs were *central* to Paul's argument. Wright identifies a two-pronged battle that Jews and Christians fought in the pagan world: the battle against dualism (a rejection of the created order), and the battle against paganism (deification of aspects of the created order). The fight against paganism was the greater challenge during this period, Wright argues.[16] Monotheistic doctrine taught that Israel's God was the creator of the whole world (and thus everything in it is basically good), and that this God would eventually take his rightful place in the world, vindicating his covenant people and punishing Israel's oppressors. Since Paul was dealing with the question

13. Ibid., 274.

14. Ibid., 704.

15. Ibid., 706.

16. N. T. Wright, *Climax of the Covenant*, 125.

of how Christians should act in a pagan world, monotheistic doctrine is exactly the foundation to which he would turn.[17] For Wright, the one-God language helps to redirect the Corinthians to an understanding that they are the people of the one true God and that their new identity under this God involves "such security in the love of the true god that [they are] able to forgo all human privileges and rights to which [they] might otherwise lay claim."[18] The cross offers a fundamental challenge to paganism, which Wright sees as one of the key functions of monotheistic belief in the first century.

Wright's emphasis on Paul's monotheistic understanding as the interpretive key to 1 Cor 8–10 is correct. Wright, however, perhaps ascribes to Paul too much agreement with the Corinthians regarding the impact of idol foods. According to Wright, Paul in principle agrees with the strong that eating food in itself has no meaning: "Creational monotheism means that all meat is in principle edible by Christians."[19] On one level this is true: food on its own has no innate meaning before God. But Paul strongly maintains that food that has been part of an idolatrous sacrifice does have significant meaning—sacrificial meals involve communion with spiritual beings, and one cannot be partners of both the Lord and demons (10:20–22). It may well be that Paul's attitude toward food in general has changed (e.g., he no longer follows the Jewish Law regarding kosher foods), but when it specifically comes to food that has been sacrificed to idols, Paul draws the line firmly.[20] Wright acknowledges that, for Paul, "to worship in an idol's temple would therefore be to flirt with, or give the appearance of flirting with, the very powers that continue to enslave and distort human existence," and so, for the sake of the weak, one may be under an obligation to forgo the right to eat meat.[21] But Paul's argument is stronger than this. It is not so much because of wrong appearances that Paul exhorts the strong to put aside their rights for the weak, as it is because Paul believes they would be committing idolatry if they were to

17. Ibid., 125–26.

18. N. T. Wright, "One God, One Lord," 50–51.

19. Ibid, 54.

20. See Rom 14 and Gal 2:11–14, where Paul discusses eating a variety of foods. It is important to note, however, that in these contexts food in general is discussed—the context does not refer to food that has been sacrificed to idols, which in Paul's eyes is a different matter.

21. Wright, "One God, One Lord," 53–54.

participate in pagan rituals. In Paul's mind, the spiritual communion that occurs when taking part in any kind of sacrificial meal involves either the worship of the one true God, as is the case during the Lord's Supper, or the worship of demons, as in the case during pagan temple sacrifices. Idolatry is the key issue here. The conscience of the weak is also a concern, but the most important reason, in Paul's eyes, is the avoidance of idolatry.[22]

This brief discussion of some of the approaches to understanding 1 Cor 8:4–6 and the larger context of 1 Cor 8–10 has illustrated that many advances have been made in understanding the social situation in Corinth, the rhetorical style of Paul's argumentation, and the theological framework from which he operated. These concepts have helped to illuminate the difficulties Paul faced and Paul's style and rationale in addressing the problems in Corinth. None of these discussions goes far enough, however, in tying together Paul's underlying understanding of the relationship between Jesus and God and the function of the statements regarding that understanding in the immediate context. The nature of the connection between Paul's "Christian Shema" and the love ethic expressed in chapters 8–10 requires further exploration. Indeed, the nature of Paul's understanding of the relationship between Jesus and God itself needs to be explored further—while 1 Cor 8:4–6 is striking in this regard, it is hardly definitive. Other passages within 1 Corinthians—some less noticeable and some apparently contradictory—add further nuance to the discussion and cannot be ignored.

It is important at this point to offer an overview of Paul's argument in chapters 8–10; the overall picture enables a better understanding of the reasons for Paul's monotheistic language in verses 4–6. The entire section involves Paul's response to a query from the Corinthians regarding whether believers may eat meat that has been previously sacrificed to idols. In chapter 8, Paul assesses the Corinthian situation and the problems that have arisen as a result of some Corinthians invoking freedom to eat idol meats, a practice others find abhorrent. He discusses their right/authority, the basis for this right, their decision to invoke that right, the consequences of that decision, and then draws a conclusion. In chapter 9, Paul contrasts his own behavior with that of the Corinthians: he discusses his own rights/authority, the basis for that right, his decision not to invoke

22. Wright comes very close to this understanding. Our positions are very similar at this point, but I emphasize Paul's concern about idolatry somewhat more strongly than Wright.

that right, the consequences of that decision, and then he ends with an exhortation. The contrast may be illustrated in the following manner:

	The Corinthians	**Paul**
Right/Authority:	To eat or not eat as they see fit (8:8)	Right of apostles to receive support and to a wife (9:3–7)
Basis of the right as found in the Law:	Only one God exists (8:4–6; Deut 6:4)	• You shall not muzzle an ox treading grain (9:8–14; Deut 25:4) • priests eat offerings (9:13; Lev 6:26, Deut 18:1)
Use or not use the right?	Use (8:10)	Not use (9:12b, 9:15–18)
Consequences:	• Weak conscience is defiled (8:7) • Stumbling block (8:9) • Weak encouraged to eat idolatrous sacrifices and will be destroyed (8:10–11) • Sin against brothers, wounding their weak conscience (8:12) • Sin against Christ (8:12)	• Win more believers by enjoying the freedom to be all things to all people (9:19–22) • Share in the blessings of the gospel (9:23)
Concluding exhortation:	Better not to eat meat than to cause a brother to stumble (8:13)	Self-control leads to winning the race (9:24–27)

In what may seem to be an odd way to introduce his discussion of idol meats, Paul starts the entire section with a discussion in verses 1–3 of the role of love and knowledge in a believer's ethics, and he places greater weight on the role of love. This theme of love that builds up another person rather than oneself continues throughout chapters 8–10. The love language in 8:1–3 echoes the Deuteronomic call to love God and thus indicates that Paul already has in mind the language of the Shema, which he goes on to discuss in the following verses.[23] The love language is integrally connected to Paul's one-God language, and thus the monotheistic

23. Wright, "One God, One Lord," 47.

principles are at the center, rather than the periphery, of the ethical issues that Paul is addressing.

The contrast between the Corinthians and Paul in chapters 8–9 highlights their different approaches to these theological principles. The Corinthians focus on the knowledge that the Shema offers, and what that means for their personal gain, without considering the love command inherent in the understanding of the one God; Paul, on the other hand, understands that love and compassion for others underlie God's commands—whether the command involves an ox treading grain or the great truth about the oneness of God—and thus he is willing to forgo his "rights" for the sake of this love.

After Paul draws this contrast between the Corinthians's actions and his own, he turns to a slightly different argument in 10:1–13. Here he draws a comparison between the Corinthians and the Israelites in the wilderness. Paul emphasizes that the Israelites—all of them—received spiritual blessings: they all were under the cloud, all passed through the sea, all were baptized into Moses, all ate the same spiritual food and drank the same spiritual drink, and they were all drinking from the spiritual rock of Christ. Paul leaves no doubt that the Israelites were one people receiving God's blessings. But then he changes his tone: even though they were blessed, God was not pleased and most of them did not make it out of the wilderness. The reason, Paul explains, is that they desired evil things (10:6), and the Corinthians should heed this warning. They should not assume that because they are God's people they will not be held responsible for evil behavior. Just as the Israelites who practiced idolatry, who were sexually immoral, who tempted Christ, and who murmured were destroyed, so too will the Corinthians be judged if they give in to temptation.

It is at this point, in 10:14, that Paul brings the argument to a climax: therefore, flee from idolatry.[24] Here he directly addresses the question of idol meats and the spiritual reality of sacrificial offerings.[25] In 10:16–18

24. As Cheung states, "Eating idol food was considered the epitome of idolatry" (*Idol Food in Corinth*, 296).

25. In agreement with Gooch, who argues for continuity in Paul's treatment of eating in temples in chapters 8 and 10: "The tension between chapter eight's lack of condemnation of eating in an idol's temple *per se* and chapter ten's forbidding of participation in cultic meals is caused because Paul does not give his complete estimation of eating in an idol's temple in the first instance" (*Dangerous Food*, 84). Paul's strategy of persuasion is to start with the less offensive arguments in chapter 8 so that he does not immediately lose credibility with the Corinthian strong. See also Cheung, *Idol Food in Corinth*, 297.

Paul maintains that a spiritual union occurs between believers and God during sacrificial worship.[26] During worship that is not directed to the one God, worshippers become united with demons (10:20). Christians, because of their exclusive faith in the one God, must not allow themselves to become united with any spiritual being other than God (10:21–22). Although Paul does not explicitly use "one God" language here, he has in mind the statement from 8:4–6. In 10:19, εἰδωλόθυτον refers back to the discussion of chapter 8, as does the question whether an idol is anything. In 8:4 Paul agrees with the strong that an idol is "nothing," but here he clearly states that an εἰδωλόθυτον is actually sacrificed to demons. Although it may appear on the surface that Paul is inconsistent, the way he structures his sentences gives us a clue to his intent. After saying that idols are nothing in 8:4, Paul goes on to state in 8:6 that "for us" there is one God and one Lord. In other words, whatever the true ontological status of these other "gods" and "lords," Christians recognize only one God and one Lord as the God of all reality. Thus, 8:4 is actually a relational statement, not an ontological one. This is why Paul feels perfectly comfortable stating in 10:20 that behind these "nothing" idols lurk real spiritual powers. They are not "gods" in any sense of the Christian understanding—only one God has created the world and has the power to sustain it and rule over it. But nonetheless these demonic powers can influence Christians and so should be avoided. More than that, involving oneself in sacrificial worship to these demons—and thus partnering with these demons—rouses the jealousy of the Lord. Not only does this jealousy motif follow from the Shema, but also from the Decalogue, where Jews are told to have no other gods before Yahweh—for the Lord God is a jealous God (Exod 20:5).[27]

26. *Contra* Willis, *Idol Meat in Corinth*. Willis argues for a social emphasis on cultic meals in Corinth and disputes both sacramental (ingestion of the deity) and communal (sharing the meal with the deity) interpretations. His use of primary texts to affirm his social interpretation, however, could equally be used to affirm a communal interpretation. See, for example, his use of Plutarch and Athenaeus, both of whom decry a lack of popular regard for the deity at festivals (57–61). Although Willis suggests this means participants attended the meals for pleasure, clearly Plutarch and Athenaeus have an expectation of a significant religious experience in which the deity is present. Furthermore, Paul's own interpretation of the cultic meal is the central consideration here—and clearly Paul was concerned about fellowship with demons (1 Cor 10:20), not merely fellowship with the human participants in the ceremony.

27. Cheung argues that both Paul's theological framework and his practical instructions are grounded in the Jewish Scriptures. Cheung provides a number of examples from the Pentateuch that offer definitions of what constitutes guilt, similar to the types of examples Paul provides in 1 Cor 10:27–29 (*Idol Food in Corinth*, 300–302).

Paul concludes that if God is truly one God, the source of all things (8:6), then it is disloyal to give homage to other spiritual beings through the participation in and consumption of sacrificial offerings.

Paul thus argues throughout this section: do not let others be destroyed (8:7–13), do not let yourselves be destroyed (10:1–13), and do not provoke the Lord to anger (10:16–22), because commitment to the one God involves both love for others and exclusive love and loyalty to the one God.

Once Paul has come to the climax of his argument, he returns to praxis in 10:23–29a. He has just addressed the question of participation in pagan sacrifices, but now he must give instructions regarding those instances that could be considered gray areas. He clarifies the issue of marketplace meats and dining in private homes: eating meat in these contexts is permissible, unless the meat's origin as an idol offering is known. Willis offers an insightful analysis of these verses, arguing that verse 28 should not be restricted to the specific situation of verse 27. Rather, 10:28–29a qualifies all eating that is not explicitly forbidden as idolatrous. Thus, there are two classes of eating: tables of demons, which are forbidden, and other eating, which is permissible but which must always be qualified by considering others.[28]

In 10:29b–30 Paul anticipates the likely objections of the Corinthians who are currently eating idol sacrifices and see nothing wrong with the practice.[29] He responds to this objection by means of summing up his argument in 10:31–33: do all things for the glory of God, and this necessarily includes setting aside your own rights so as not to offend your brother, that he might be saved.[30] The argument has come full circle: Paul started in chapter 8 with a monotheistic understanding as the foundation of his love command, and he concludes in chapter 10 by again emphasizing that all actions ought to be for the purpose of glorifying the (one) God.

With this greater context in mind, we will now return to an examination of 8:4–6 and the verses immediately surrounding.

28. Willis, *Idol Meat in Corinth*, 244–45.

29. D. Watson, "1 Corinthians 10:23—11:1," 312.

30. See Willis, *Idol Meat in Corinth*, 254: "Living 'to the glory of God' is living with the highest regard for the needs of other people, seeking not to offend them."

1 CORINTHIANS 8:4–6

> Concerning the eating therefore of idol sacrifices, we know that an idol is nothing in the world, and that there is no God except One. For even if there are ones being called gods either in heaven or on earth, even as there are many gods and many lords, but for us there is one God, the Father, from whom are all things and we in him, and one Lord, Jesus Christ, through whom are all things and we through him.[31]

The section begins with the phrase Περὶ δὲ ("And concerning . . ."), which occurs elsewhere in 1 Corinthians (7:1, 25; 12:1; 16:1, 12) to introduce new topics. Paul may have used the phrase to address questions that the Corinthians raised in a previous letter to him (see 7:1),[32] although the use of the phrase only indicates that the topic is one with which both the Corinthians and Paul are familiar.[33] Paul addresses the topic of food sacrificed to idols (literally, "idol sacrifices") by using a term (εἰδωλόθυτων) that in Jewish thought has a strongly polemical tone;[34] later in Paul's argument (10:28) he uses the neutral term ἱερόθυτον.[35] Thus, at the outset, Paul's language offers a negative assessment of such meat. The possibility exists, however, that Paul uses the polemical term simply because the Corinthians may have used it in their letter to him.

Curiously, rather than immediately answering the question of whether such food could be eaten by Christians, Paul begins his response by offering a contrast between knowledge and love. He introduces the contrast with the phrase "we know that" (οἴδαμεν ὅτι), which seems to indicate that the following phrase, "all have knowledge," is actually a quote.[36] Whether this is a quote from the Corinthians's letter to Paul or simply a well-known cliché of the time is difficult to determine. It was

31. Author's translation.

32. See Barrett, *Corinthians*, 154.

33. See Mitchell, "Concerning Peri. de. in 1 Corinthians," for a convincing argument in this regard.

34. Büchsel, "εἰδωλόθυτον" This negative attitude is based on a Jewish resistance to any kind of religious syncretism; the refusal to eat idol meats was based on "a strict application of the first commandment and not on superstition . . ." (379).

35. In 10:28 Paul assumes the voice of a (presumably) Greek non-Christian, for whom the idea of idol meats would not be offensive, and thus the polemical εἰδωλοθύτων would not be appropriate.

36. Barrett, *Corinthians*, 189.

clearly a phrase with which the Corinthians were familiar, since Paul did not feel he had to explain the saying further.

The issue of knowledge is not new to Paul's letter. He spends a great deal of time in the first four chapters discussing the difference between the world's wisdom and the wisdom of God. Although Paul almost exclusively uses the term σοφία rather than γνῶσις in the opening chapters (but see 1:5), he does use the verbal form of γνῶσις in several instances (1:21; 2:8, 11, 14, 16; 3:20; 4:19). While γνῶσις and σοφία should not necessarily be equated, it is clear that one of the issues facing Paul in Corinth is the more general question of intellectual assent to various theological propositions, and the implications arising from this focus on the intellect. Certainly, in the surrounding Hellenistic culture, philosophy was highly regarded and having "knowledge" was a status symbol. Time and again Paul finds himself reminding the Corinthians that the knowledge of the world is not the prize they should be seeking (1:18–25). Even theological knowledge, based in Christian experience, can be misused, as Paul points out in 8:7–13.

Thus, it appears that the "knowledge" that all have is a basic understanding of Christian theological principles, a few of which are then spelled out in 8:4–6.[37] Paul responds to this question of intellect, which is tied to the question of idol meats, by trying to rearrange the Corinthians's priorities. Knowledge puffs up, he says, but love builds up. This contrast between an individual's being puffed up and the church's being built up figures strongly throughout the letter. (For the former, see 4:6, 18, 19; 5:2; for the latter, see 3:9–14; 10:23; 14:3–5, 12, 17, 26.) Paul discourages boasting, except in Christ (1:31). And so Paul begins this new section by

37. Yeo. *Rhetorical Interaction*, 185. *Contra* Newton, *Deity and Diet*. Newton argues that the complexity of views regarding cultic sacrifices is reflected in 8:1a: Paul is stating that everyone has their own knowledge about what occurs at festivals and which are the appropriate boundaries. Because of this wide range of valid individual interpretations, Paul was forced to turn to a "community consciousness" in order to resolve the conflict (275–76). Newton's interpretation, however, takes a very postmodern view of the ancient world. Paul would never have agreed that the variety of interpretations were all valid. His Jewish background prepared him for only one view: "Flee from idolatry!" (1 Cor 10:14). Paul spells out these prohibitions—believers must not eat in the temple (8:10; 10:20–22), nor may they eat meat which they know has been sacrificed to an idol (10:28); if they have no knowledge of the meat's origins, they are allowed to eat (10:25–27). Newton's analysis is also flawed in that he does not give enough weight to the fact that Paul spent eighteen months living in Corinth and surely would have been aware of the intricacies of interpreting what constituted εἰδωλοθύτων.

throwing down the gauntlet: the challenge is to build up the community in Christ, and this is done through love, not knowledge.

But he does not stop with a simple contrast between love and knowledge. He wants to drive his point home and to make it clear to those who espouse knowledge as the way of Christianity that knowledge is not enough. This seems to be the message of verse 2—"if anyone thinks he knows something, he does not yet know as it is necessary to know." True knowledge, like true wisdom (chs. 1–4), does not involve merely a worldly assent to theological or philosophical principles. This is where Paul's Jewish nature shines through. For the Jew, knowledge and action were not to be separated. To know God and to love God, for example, were one proposition—you couldn't have the one without the other. The foundational statement for Jews, the Shema, tied the two ideas together (see Excursus, below). For his mainly Greek audience, Paul is struggling to help them understand this Jewish way of thinking. And so he continues, in verse 3: "But if anyone loves God, this one has been known by him."[38] Paul's phrasing here may seem a bit odd—one would almost expect him to say, "If anyone loves God, he knows God." Instead, Paul places the focus on God's initiative in bringing us into relationship with him. Being known by God is not a reward for loving him; rather, loving God is a response to God's activity in one's life.[39] As Wright states: "The real *Gnosis*, Paul is saying, is not your *Gnosis* of God but God's *Gnosis* of you, and the sign of that being present is that one keeps the *Shema*: you shall love the Lord your God with all your heart."[40] Believers acknowledge God's activity through their loving response—knowing God and loving him are not two separate actions, they are one and the same.[41] Paul is trying to shift the emphasis here. The Corinthians are boasting in their knowledge, but Paul instead argues that love is the better aim. For our human knowledge is incomplete

38. P46 omits the reference to God, and Codex Sinaiticus retains the first reference to God but omits the reference to being known "by him." The vast majority of texts, however, retain the sense listed above. Given the connection in 8:6 with the Shema and the Shema's command to love God, it is likely that the majority retain an accurate sense of Paul's writing.

39. Barrett, *Corinthians* 190–91.

40. Wright, *Climax of the Covenant*, 127.

41. See also Ellis, "'Wisdom' and 'Knowledge.'" Ellis argues that Corinthian pneumatics have manifested knowledge apart from the fruit of the Spirit, specifically the fruit of love, and thus have only a distorted, fleshly, knowledge (97).

(8:2; see also 13:12), but God's perfect knowledge of us results in our love for him.

The rest of Paul's writing in Corinthians, especially in chapters 8–10, revolves around the concept of loving one another, of building up the church. It is crucial to understand that this focus on love as the primary ethos flows directly from Paul's Jewish monotheistic understanding. Loving God (i.e., knowing God and being known by God) and loving others are tied together (see the excursus on Deut 6:4–5 below). Paul understands the only great God, Yahweh, to be a God who loves his creation and calls humanity into relationship with him; the human response to God's calling is to aspire to love God as God loves humankind, i.e., by loving one another. Because one knows God's character, one loves others. Thus, the whole discussion that follows flows out of Paul's understanding of God's identity as a loving, relational God.

In the first three verses, Paul has laid down the framework for the discussion that is to follow—he has set his theme.[42] Paul even adds a "therefore" in the beginning of verse 4 to show that the preceding thoughts on love and knowledge are directly related to the question of idol meats. Love (which is a response to the one God's love) is the basis of all Christian action and is the ground for the ethical imperative Paul gives in the following verses and chapters.

Now he returns to the specific issue, again using περί to address the question of idol meats. Paul introduces a quote, possibly from the Corinthians's letter, of certain theological catchphrases that some of the Corinthians have used to justify their behavior.[43] He again signals that the expressions are quotations by using the phrase οἴδαμεν ὅτι: we know that "an idol is nothing in the world," and that "there is no god except one." It is important to note that Paul uses the first person plural verb form—he includes himself among those who have this knowledge,[44] and

42. Verses 1–3 "contain, expressed in general terms and in very compressed form, the blueprint of a deliberative argument," which is then explained in 8:7—9:27 (Smit, *About the Idol Offerings*, 74). In a similar manner, verses 4–6 provide another blueprint for the deliberative argument that takes place in 10:1–22 (77). I would add, however, that both sections are tied together by the one-God language: for Paul, a proper understanding of the one God leads to proper action, i.e., love of God necessarily involves love of others.

43. Fee, *Corinthians*, 365, 370.

44. *Contra* Fotopoulos, "Arguments Concerning Food," 611–31. Fotopoulos argues that Paul is already quoting the Corinthians when he says "we know," and therefore does not include himself as being among those who have such knowledge. He argues that

thus implicitly agrees with the theology of the statements that follow, even though he and the strong[45] disagree on the outworking of these propositions. Ultimately, Paul's understanding of the oneness of God differs from that of the Corinthian strong in that they have a truncated view of the character and implications of God's oneness, and this difference accounts for the variations in their approaches to Christian ethics.

So what does Paul mean when he agrees with the statement that "an idol is nothing in the world"? Does he mean that other gods do not exist at all? Or does he mean that such gods do exist but simply do not have any power compared with the only true God, the God of Israel? As noted in chapter 1, the Israelite religion appears to have developed from a more polytheistic understanding of the world (i.e., many gods exist and have power, although Yahweh is the God of Israel) into a more truly monotheistic understanding of God in post-exilic times (i.e., only one God exists, the God of Israel). When Paul agrees that an idol is nothing, therefore, he appears to be saying that idols such as Isis or Sarapis have no genuine reality in the world.[46] Thus they are not properly called "gods," even though this is how non-Christians (and non-Jews) would regard them. Paul clarifies later that nonetheless these idols are connected to demonic forces, which should not be taken lightly (10:20–22). Regardless of these other "gods," Paul affirms that for Christians "there is no God but one," meaning that only this one God is to be acknowledged and worshipped. While this may not appear, on the surface, to be a radical concept given that Greek thought in the first century proclaimed the existence of one high god who

---

Pauline refutations begin with an adversative followed by his own point of view in the second or third person. Yet Fotopoulos admits that Paul "does not reject the entirety of the theological content" of the quotations (627). This latter statement is closer to the truth: Paul and the strong agree, at least on the surface, to a number of theological propositions. The divisions in Paul's address are not as neat as Fotopoulos would have us believe. Even the statement in 8:6 begins with an adversative, and thus according to Fotopoulos's own reasoning, it could be considered part of Paul's refutation. Given this overlap, it is more likely that Paul is agreeing with the Corinthians in order to qualify their statements.

45. I use the term "strong" loosely, as a means of differentiating this group of Corinthians from the "weak" identified in 8:7ff. The term "strong," while present in Rom 15:1, does not occur in 1 Corinthians. Nonetheless, it is clear that there are indeed two opposing factions involved in the dispute, *contra* Garland, "Dispute over Food Sacrificed to Idols," 180. Although Garland is correct that Paul is concerned about a return to idolatry, this does not negate the emphasis throughout the letter on repairing divisions in the body of Christ. Paul has both concerns in mind here.

46. Fee, *Corinthians*, 371.

was over all the other gods,[47] the concept of worshipping only one God as *the* God, to the neglect of all the others, was a uniquely Jewish idea.[48]

But what does Paul mean in verses 5 and 6 when he uses the term "lord"? As discussed in chapter 1, this oft-used term has a wide range of meaning, but this did not prevent Paul from intentionally using Old Testament Yahweh texts in reference to Christ. But the question here is whether, in 1 Cor 8:4–6, Paul intends to use κύριος in this manner. The context here is very instructive. Since the situation addresses the question of God and Christ in opposition to idols, it is clear that Paul's use of the term "lord" here goes far beyond the master/servant analogy. The question is a religious one and involves the status of spiritual beings as "gods." Paul holds up the one as the true God—Yahweh and Christ together—in opposition to the false gods of the world, which are nothing. The oneness language here is all the more striking because Paul is contrasting Jesus and God with the "many" gods of verse 5. Somehow the Jewish Paul understands God the Father and the "Lord" Jesus to be one.

But before looking at the confession more thoroughly, it will be helpful to clarify the position of this statement within the larger argument. Although Paul does not begin this verse with οἴδαμεν ὅτι, the context suggests that Paul is again quoting one of the theological precepts of the strong in the Corinthian church, a precept with which Paul agrees and that he perhaps even taught the Corinthians in the first place. Rather than using οἴδαμεν ὅτι ("we know that"), Paul uses ἀλλ' ἡμῖν ("but for us"). Both this continuation of the first person plural and the position of the statement within the larger paragraph discussing Corinthian knowledge indicate that verse 6 is not a new Pauline idea for the Corinthians, but rather a continuation of the list of theological knowledge that the Corinthians profess (*contra* Dunn).[49] This is further made evident by the fact that verse 7 refers to the knowledge just mentioned in verses 4–6, and that not all people have this knowledge.

The parallel grammatical structure of the confessional formula describes God and Christ as having very similar—if not identical—functions:

47. See Nilsson, "High God and the Mediator," 101–20.

48. Mauser, "One God Alone," 262.

49. Dunn (*Christology in the Making*, 181) argues that it is difficult to recognize an earlier formulation behind Paul's statement in verse 6, and that Paul tailors his language to the specific situation found in Corinth.

ἀλλ’ ἡμῖν

εἷς θεὸς ὁ πατὴρ ἐξ οὗ τὰ πάντα καὶ ἡμεῖς εἰς αὐτόν

καὶ εἷς κύριος Ἰησοῦς Χριστὸς δι’ οὗ τὰ πάντα καὶ ἡμεῖς δι’ αὐτοῦ.

One interpretation of this language is that Paul does not so much equate Christ with God as describe Christ as the action of God; this would help to defer any tension within Jewish monotheism.[50] The context, however, excludes such a possibility. Paul's aim is to contrast Christian worship with polytheistic pagan worship—hence the focus on oneness. If Paul did not intend Jesus to be elevated to a status next to God, then in all likelihood he would have either deleted the reference to Jesus or reworded the language in such a way as to make it clear that the one God did not include Jesus. Paul could have said that the one God, who sent his Messiah, is over all things. But instead Paul uses language for Christ that is intentionally parallel (grammatically) with God. This indicates similarity with God, not difference. It also suggests that the "Lord" language is meant to be taken as a reference to divinity. Thus, if Paul were distinguishing between God and Jesus, he would be tending toward a polytheistic interpretation himself, especially in the minds of first-century Greeks. Rather, Paul uses the parallel structure to focus on the sameness, the oneness, of the object of Christian worship.

The text itself contains three prepositions which are used to define the relationships between God and the world and Jesus and the world. First, we are told that all things are from or out of (ἐκ) the Father. Most commentators take this to mean that God is the source of all things.[51] This conclusion can be supported by taking a closer look at Paul's use of the term. The preposition ἐκ can be used in a number of ways: to indicate source, separation, time, cause, means, and in a partitive sense.[52] Paul most frequently uses the term to indicate source. In theological contexts, ἐκ frequently refers to God as the source, whereas Paul almost never uses this term to indicate that Christ is the source (see 1 Cor 10:4 for a rare exception).[53] It appears most likely, then, that in 1 Cor 8:6 Paul is referring

50. Ibid., 182.

51. See, for example, Fee, *Corinthians*, 375; Bruce, *1 and 2 Corinthians*, 80; and Conzelmann, *1 Corinthians*, 144.

52. Wallace, *Greek Grammar*, 371.

53. These conclusions are the result of my own analysis of the use of ἐκ throughout the Pauline corpus.

to God as the source of all things. There is nothing that the one God has not created and sustained. Again, this is a very Jewish idea—there is one creator of all that exists; nothing exists which has its source in anything but God.

Next Paul says that we are in (εἰς) God. What exactly Paul means by being "in" God is not clear. The preposition can be used in numerous ways; Paul most frequently uses εἰς to indicate purpose, although when speaking of God he usually specifies the purpose of God's glorification. Thus, he could have the same meaning in mind here, although we should ask why Paul does not make his language more explicit. Paul could be using εἰς to indicate advantage, although he most often does so in reference to people, not to God—although Rom 11:36 provides a possible exception.[54] It is also possible that Paul intends reference/ respect; he does sometimes use εἰς to indicate reference/ respect to God and Christ, although he most often refers to people, e.g., the church or himself. If Paul uses εἰς in such a manner in 1 Cor 8:6, then the interpretation would literally read, "and we (exist) with reference to God." The sense of a referential use is to limit the action of the verb,[55] and thus Paul's intention here may be to remind the Corinthians that their existence is based on God's will and action; without God, we would not exist. Such an idea would parallel the preceding idea of God as the source of all things. All of these possibilities provide a very similar understanding of God: ultimately, the existence of the Christian is dependent upon the one God and fulfills God's plan.[56]

The first half of the theological statement in 1 Cor 8:6 seems to indicate that the one God whom Christians worship is the source of all that exists, and thus the believer's existence is based on the will and action of this one God. The statement itself seems to give the ground for why Christians worship this God: believers are, literally, nothing without him.

The second half of the statement, although parallel with the first half in almost every way, only uses the one preposition for the relationship between Christ, all things, and Christians. The term διά here refers to agency. Paul uses the agency category of διά to refer to human agents and

54. The εἰς in Rom 11:36 could also be taken in the sense of purpose—that everyone exists for God's purposes. Either way, it would be an unusual usage. See the further discussion of Rom 11:36 below.

55. Wallace, *Greek Grammar*, 203.

56. Hays offers a helpful summation when he argues that the statement about God "encompasses both origin and destination" (*First Corinthians*, 140).

to Christ; he rarely uses it to refer to God as agent. In at least two instances, however (Gal 4:7 and Rom 11:36), Paul refers to God directly as an agent in a manner similar to the way Paul refers to Christ as an agent.[57] In 1 Cor 8:6 Paul uses the term διά to refer to Christ as the agent through whom all things exist;[58] Paul then draws the further, more specific application that Christians (specifically, Paul and the Corinthians) exist through Christ's agency.

These observations suggest that Paul prefers using ἐκ of God and διά of Jesus, but at times he intermingles these. This may indicate that Paul is blurring the lines between Christ and God. While this may seem to be drawing too strong a conclusion from common prepositions, the context in which these prepositions occur communicates significant theological ideas that Paul would not take lightly. Rather, this former Pharisee would take great care in formulating arguments that are foundational for the rest of his gospel. Thus, this blending of terms—and thus the mingling of theological roles for Christ and God—indicates that Paul is already making significant claims regarding the unique divine identity. That these two sections of this statement are so similar suggests that Paul is intentionally making the same statement about both God and Jesus—they are the basis, foundation, source, reason, cause, means, etc., for all that exists; without them, creation would be, literally, nothing.[59]

It is noteworthy that Paul does not even use an explicit verb in this verse; εἰμί is implied throughout. Even more significant is the fact that

57. The language in both Gal 4:7–9 and Rom 11:36 has parallels to 1 Cor 8. As already noted, Rom 11:36 uses the same prepositions as 1 Cor 8:6 to describe God as over all things. In Gal 4:8–9 Paul discusses the knowledge of the Galatians, and says that their having known God is rather a matter of being known by God—an idea similar to that found in 1 Cor 8:3. God's agency is also seen in his calling (1 Cor 1:9; Gal 1:1), will (Rom 15:32; 2 Cor 1:1, 8:5), and glory (Rom 6:4). Note that Gal 1:1 and 2 Cor 1:1 are similar, but not identical, in that Paul opens his letters by claiming he is an apostle through (the will of) God.

58. BDAG interprets this as a description of "Christ as intermediary in the creation of the world" (225).

59. *Contra* Murphy-O'Connor, "I Cor. VIII, 6." He argues that the statement, a baptismal acclamation, is exclusively soteriological. But Murphy-O'Connor ignores the context of the chapter, in which cosmology is one of the key issues. The status of other "gods" over against the one God, and the cultic rituals of these "gods" are at the heart of the issue, not soteriology. Indeed, such a distinction between cosmology and soteriology is more complicated than the either/or question that Murphy-O'Connor presents. It is *because* the one God of Israel (both Father and Christ) is Lord over all creation that this same God is able to offer salvation to his people.

Paul does not change verbs when referring to Jesus. He does not explicitly state that all things exist in God but have relationship through Christ or that we exist in God but draw near through Christ; he uses the same phrasing as he uses for God—we exist/live/have our being through Christ. Certainly if Paul wanted to make a distinction between God and Jesus, he easily could have been more explicit and intentional. Instead, Paul chose to use parallel language for God and Jesus.

In talking about the relationship of the one God and one Lord with the rest of creation, Paul uses first-person plural language three times in verse 6; first, he uses it to introduce the "knowledge" that follows in the theological statement. But within the statement itself, Paul refers to "we" being in the Father and "we" existing through Jesus. The reference here is specifically to Christians; otherwise Paul would have needed to make a distinction between the ἡμῖν at the beginning of the verse and the ἡμεῖς later. Why does Paul feel the need to make an explicit statement about the status of Christians when, presumably, such status is already covered in the preceding and all-encompassing statement about *all* things? He simply could have said ". . . from whom are all things and all things are in him . . ." The reason can be found within the context of the "knowledge" that the Corinthians are professing. The Corinthians know that all things are from the Father and all things are through Jesus; even the Greeks would admit that the world itself exists as the result of some creative effort by the gods. But for Christians, their knowledge extends even further. Christians have the knowledge that their own individual being, their whole orientation toward life and the world around them, has its foundation in the reliance upon the one God for its very existence. The Christian life is an all-encompassing commitment, which has its background in the Deuteronomic call to love the Lord your God with all your heart, soul, and being.

Paul's doxology in Romans 11:36 may be instructive at this point. In that context, Paul uses the same three prepositions (ἐκ, εἰς, διά) as in 1 Cor 8:6, but in Romans God is the sole referent. This is perhaps to be expected, since the doxology concludes the discussion in chapters 9–11 in which Paul addresses the nature and efficacy of God's plan of salvation for Israel. Commentators here also see the text referring to God as the source and goal of the universe. Brendan Byrne, for example, maintains that "The three prepositional phrases bring together the sense of God's acting in creation ('from him'), redemption ('through him') and final salvation ('to him'). 'All things' . . . that is, both the entire creation in a static sense and the dynamic sweep of events, are gathered into the one supreme purpose—the 'glory of God' (v 36b)."[60] Paul is thus making a statement in Romans about the nature of reality and its ultimate relationship with and dependence upon the one God.

A slight variation occurs in Paul's formula in Romans in that the prepositions are listed in a different order. In Romans, all things are ἐκ God, διά God, and εἰς God, whereas in 1 Corinthians all things are ἐκ God, εἰς God, and διά Jesus. This could simply indicate that there is no set formula for describing God as the ultimate source of all reality. The fact that all three elements are present in both texts, however, is significant. Paul uses the same language of Jesus that he uses of God, and the Romans formulation suggests that his language for Jesus in Corinthians is not simply an addendum to the ἐκ/εἰς formula. Rather, the διά language is something that, within a few years of writing 1 Corinthians, Paul considers to provide an important description of God.[61]

The fact that such strikingly similar concepts are present in 1 Corinthians 8:6 and include Jesus as the one on whom, with God, everything depends makes a significant statement about Christ's identity.[62] Given Paul's theme of love in chapters 8–10, his use of this christological confession formula serves to emphasize that the one God on whom everything depends is also the one God who models self-giving love through Christ's death on the cross. Paul is trying to help the Corinthian strong realize that worshipping the one God necessarily involves a love commitment.

It is important to note that the formula Paul uses in verse 6 is not unique; Stoic thought also referred to all things as being from, to, and through God.[63] Was Paul's theology influenced by Stoic thought, or did

60. Byrne, *Romans*, 359–60. See also Fitzmyer, *Romans*, 635.

61. The short amount of time between the writing of 1 Corinthians and Romans is probably not significant for Paul's understanding of the relationship between Jesus and God. Certainly Paul does not suggest to the Romans that he had an important epiphany concerning this issue since he wrote to the Corinthians. In addition, if Galatians has an early date, then we have an example of Paul's using dia, language for God prior to writing 1 Corinthians (Gal 4:7, as noted above).

62. Bauckham sees the formulation of 1 Cor 8:6 as an intentional inclusion of Jesus within the divine identity because it assigns to Christ the role as instrumental cause of creation: "No more unequivocal way of including Jesus in the unique divine identity is conceivable, within the framework of Second Temple Jewish monotheism" ("Biblical Theology," 224).

63. See, for example, Pseudo-Aristotle [*Mund.*] 6; Philo *Cher.* 125–26; Seneca *Ep.* 65.8; and Marcus Aurelius *Medit.* 4.23.

he simply use language he knew might resonate with his Greek audience? For example, the Stoics maintained that God, or the Logos, "contains within himself the meaning of all things and gives meaning to all things."[64] A similar interpretation could apply to 1 Cor 8:6. The Stoics went further in such an interpretation, however, than Paul likely would have. Stoic thought was pantheistic, maintaining that everything is a part of one whole entity; for Stoics, God is to the universe as the soul is to the body.[65] Paul, however, was thoroughly grounded in Jewish theology. For him, God was the creator of all things but was nonetheless set apart from his creation; God is immortal and other.[66] Furthermore, other aspects of Stoic thought were also incompatible with Paul's theology. The Stoics did not believe in immortality, other than the soul temporarily surviving death before being consumed in the next great conflagration.[67] Paul certainly believed in life after death, as 1 Cor 15 indicates. Thus, although a monotheistic understanding of Yahweh as the ultimate creator and sustainer of all things could certainly use language which also appeared in Stoic writings, it could do so without necessarily embracing all that Stoic thought professes.[68]

Finally, the most difficult question that arises from this text is the question of how Paul can refer to the "one" God when he simultaneously exalts Christ as the "one" Lord, especially when the term κύριος is more than likely used here to connote the idea of deity. In verses 4 and 6, Paul is clearly referencing the great confession of Judaism, the Shema. More than that, he is rewriting the confession to include Jesus within its scope.[69] N. T. Wright states, "There can be no mistake: Paul has placed Jesus *within* an explicit statement, drawn from the Old Testament's best known monotheistic text, of the doctrine that Israel's God is the one and only God, the

64. G. Watson, *Greek Philosophy*, 44.

65. Bruce, *New Testament History*, 42.

66. See Rom 1:20.

67. Bruce, *New Testament History*, 45.

68. For recent discussion of Paul's relationship with the Stoics, see Engberg-Pedersen, *Paul and the Stoics*. Martyn provides an insightful response in "De-apocalypticizing Paul," 61–102. See also Engberg-Pedersen's "Response to Martyn." For other discussions of Paul and the Stoics, see Esler, "Paul and Stoicism," 106–24; and Paige, "Stoicism, ΕΛΕΥΘΕΡΙΑ," 180–93.

69. Moberly, "Toward an Interpretation," 141; and N. T. Wright, *Climax of the Covenant*, 121.

creator of the world."[70] So how can Paul rationalize this radical new understanding of the Shema? As discussed in chapter 1, although the Jewish theology of the first century had exalted figures, none provided a pattern that fully foreshadowed the exaltation of Christ to the level of deity.

If, as suggested above, Paul is not differentiating Christ from God but rather is uniting them in his argument against pagan deities, then it seems that Paul's understanding of Jewish monotheistic ideology does not focus on numerical oneness so much as on the uniqueness of this one God over against non-Jewish gods. This comports well with Bauckham's suggestion, noted in chapter 1, that Jews understood Yahweh to be the one God because of his unique acts in history, especially creation and rule. This understanding of divine uniqueness does not define God as unitariness (as in later Greek categories) and does not make distinctions within the divine identity inconceivable.[71] Rather, God's salvific acts in history reach their ultimate conclusion in the work of Christ, and cannot be separated from Christ. Thus, Bauckham sees Paul in 1 Cor 8:6 including Jesus within the divine identity: "Paul is not adding to the one God of the *Shema'* a 'Lord' the *Shema'* does not mention. He is identifying Jesus as the 'Lord' whom the *Shema'* affirms to be one."[72]

Bauckham's insight helps us to focus on the role of experiential knowledge. Israel's history was one of encountering Yahweh and learning anew about this God through these experiences.[73] In the encounters with Abraham, God was revealed as one who had chosen (the future) Israel to be his special people. In the exodus, God became known as a strong redeemer. In the establishment of the Law, God was disclosed as one who expected holiness from his people. In the defeat of enemies and entrance into the promised land, God was revealed as faithful to his promises. In the establishment of the throne of David, God was portrayed as one who

70. N. T. Wright, "One God, One Lord," 48.

71. Bauckham, *God Crucified*, 22.

72. Ibid, 38. See also Holtz, "Theo-logie und Christologie," 105–21. Holz also recognizes that God is revealed in his acts and argues that Jesus and God have equal standing in the confession of 1 Cor 8:6. He argues that the two are tied together because God is creator and Jesus is re-creator through the act of redemption.

73. In the list that follows, these lessons are not entirely new at each historical moment. For example, certainly the Israelites had experienced God as judge prior to the exile (especially in the sin and punishment motifs in the desert wanderings), but this aspect of God was further nuanced in the exile and thus added a more developed understanding of the identity of God.

intended an eternal kingdom. In the Babylonian exile, God was exposed as one who judges and yet promises to restore.

Just as Israel had come to know the one God by his actions, so too Paul had come to redefine his understanding of Yahweh based on his experience of the risen Christ.[74] Thus, his powerful Damascus road experience and the continuing influence of the Spirit enabled Paul to include Jesus within the divine identity.[75] Indeed, Paul's background as a Pharisee may well have laid the foundations for openness to this kind of change. The Pharisees were open to making new interpretations of Torah as new situations arose.[76] Consequently, Paul was predisposed to at least investigating new interpretations of Torah. When he met the risen Christ on the road to Damascus, therefore, Paul combined his experience with Scripture in coming to his new understanding about Jesus.

Bauckham's emphasis on the actions of God, as opposed to ontological status, thus provides a very helpful framework for understanding the transformation of Paul's theology. Although earlier I had noted a potential problem with Bauckham's rationale (remember Tertullian), it is precisely this experiential element which limits the identity of the one God and prevents the development of a new pantheon. Although a few sparse texts may indicate that Metatron or the angel Michael may at some point participate in judgment and rule, the lack of any experiential knowledge of such rule precluded the formulation of any cultic devotion.[77] Similarly, Wisdom, Glory, or other personifications of God were not experienced in such a manner as to promote their cultic worship. It appears that God chose not to reveal himself in such a way that these personifications would become deified. It is only in the person of Christ and the work of

74. To provide another example, the experience of the Spirit is what convinces many Jews that the Gentiles have now been accepted into the people of God (Acts 10:44–48 and 11:15–18). Paul, too, uses the argument of the experience of the Spirit to convince the Galatians that they have been accepted by God and do not need to be circumcised (Gal 3:2–5).

75. Fee similarly emphasizes the role of experience in Paul's theology in "Paul and the Trinity." Fee argues that "the key to Paul's new and expanded ways of talking about God as Savior—while at the same time rigorously maintaining his monotheism—is to be found in the *experience of the Spirit*, as the one who enables believers to confess the risen Christ as exalted Lord, and as the way God and Christ are personally present in the believer and the believing community" (51).

76. Ferguson, *Backgrounds of Early Christianity*, 516.

77. Notably, these texts deal with judgment in the end times, and thus suggest that any exaltation of these individuals occurs only in the future and is therefore limited.

the Spirit that experiential knowledge demands the inclusion of Christ (and the Spirit, although I have not focused on the Spirit in this work) within the identity of the one God.

Furthermore, this experiential knowledge was verified and limited by the Scriptures. The first Christians went back to Jewish foundations for their understanding of the identity and role of the Messiah. Yet the experiences of these Christians allowed them to radically reinterpret Scripture in light of what had occurred. Paul and others did not invent a new Torah, but rather took advantage of latent tensions within the Jewish Scriptures themselves, as Francis Watson has argued. Thus, Ps 110:1 now refers to the exaltation of Christ, Joel 2:28–32 now refers to the coming of the Holy Spirit at Pentecost, Isa 45:23 now refers to all people confessing the name of Christ, and Deut 6:4 now refers to Jesus as part of the unique divine identity of the one God.

Paul's experience and his reinterpretation of Scripture, therefore, led him to reconfigure traditional one-God language to include Christ. Yet this confession in 1 Cor 8:6 is not simply a cursory statement that Paul makes in order to reiterate the position of the Corinthian strong. Rather, Paul includes it in his discussion of knowledge and love because a proper understanding of the one God (who also includes Jesus Christ) serves as the foundation for the ethics that follow. Therein lay the problem. Although Paul and the Corinthian strong agree that Christians worship the one God, they somehow come to very different conclusions regarding what this means for Christian behavior. Either ethics and theology are completely separate—a notion foreign to Paul[78]—or the theology that Paul and the strong Corinthians appear to share on the surface has a deeper meaning, which Paul attempts to clarify in the following verses.

Paul begins his clarification by pointing out that not everyone in Corinth understands the oneness of God in the same manner as the "strong" Corinthians. The knowledge that all have (v. 1), not all have (v. 7). This may seem contradictory, but Paul is highlighting the idea that while Christians appear on the surface to have the same theological basis for their faith (8:4–6), their actions reveal distinct differences in their understanding of these theological principles (8:7–8).

In verse 8a Paul quotes the attitude of the Corinthian strong, and in some ways agrees with the statement (note the first person plural). This

78. See Rosner, *Paul, Scripture and Ethics*.

limited agreement[79] he spells out in verse 8b—one's standing, one's justification, before God is not a matter of whether one eats food. As he spells out elsewhere in his letters, a believer's ultimate position before God is determined by one's faith in Christ.[80] In fact, the strong may be misinterpreting the reservations of the weak, thinking the weak are trying to find righteousness before God through their works, when in fact their anxiety instead has to do with a foundational Jewish concern for avoiding idolatry and syncretistic worship (a concern with which Paul agrees in chapter 10). Here Paul implicitly rebukes the strong: the "weak," i.e., those who do not eat questionable food, are not lacking if they do not eat—they are not worse Christians than the strong. Similarly, the strong—those who eat of the fullness of the earth (10:26)—are not better Christians because they do eat. Paul rebukes the arrogance of the strong.[81]

In verses 9–13 Paul focuses on the "weak" brother and how the actions of the strong negatively affect the weak. In verse 10 he ironically describes the conscience of the weak as being "built up" so as to eat idolatrous sacrifices—this is the same term he uses in verse 1 to describe how love "builds up." Paul is drawing a negative comparison: the strong ought to build up the weak in love, but instead they build up the weak to sin.[82] Ultimately, the strong—because of the negative impact they have on their brothers—sin against Christ (8:12). For Paul, as for any Jew, the horizontal dimension of ethics, i.e., one's relationship to others, is interconnected to the vertical dimension of one's relationship with God (see the excursus below).

Overall, Paul describes self-sacrificing love as the ultimate ethic, the ultimate act of worship of the one God, rather than the freedom that the Corinthians flout. For Paul, love means that a person has more regard for

79. *Contra* Murphy-O'Connor ("Freedom or the Ghetto"), who states Paul fully adopts the conclusion of the strong that eating idol meats was legitimate, thus contradicting the apostolic decree. Paul encourages the strong to be patient with the weak, who are experiencing a time-lag between intellectual acceptance of the gospel and emotional assimilation of that truth. Murphy-O'Connor's analysis is seriously flawed, however, in that he fails to address Paul's strong anti-idolatry polemic in 1 Cor 10:1–22.

80. See, e.g., Rom 1:17, 3:22, 28; 5:1; Gal 2:16; 3:11, 24; Phil 3:9.

81. Still notes that if Paul were trying to correct the weak, we would expect him to say, "We are no worse off if we do eat, and no better if we do not" ("Paul's Aims," 337). Thus, the wording here underscores that Paul is calling the strong to relinquish their "right."

82. Dawes ("Danger of Idolatry," 90) argues that the sin which the weak commit is not merely acting against their conscience, but is the sin of idolatry which they commit by eating in pagan temples.

others than for oneself (9:19–23; 10:33; 13:4–7). Although Willis states that "love is perhaps the most important motif in 1 Cor 8–10, because many specific admonitions and encouragements in these chapters depend upon love,"[83] I would argue that it is important to recognize that this love is grounded in and flows from the understanding that God is the source and sustainer of all things. Thus, God's oneness is the most important motif in 1 Cor 8–10. The monotheistic language, then, is both peripheral to and crucial to the main argument. It is peripheral in the sense that the disagreement among the Corinthians does not concern Christ's identity in relation to God; it is crucial in the sense that ethics (which lay at the heart of the disagreement) flow from a proper understanding of the character of the one God.

The Corinthians who eat idol meats are focusing on the wrong aspect of their theology. Because only one God exists to whom they are answerable, the meats sacrificed to false gods have no significance and the Corinthians rejoice in their freedom to eat whatever they wish. Their focus is self-centered and not God-centered. But Paul says their focus should not be on their personal freedom; rather, if their focus is God-centered, then God's identity as one who loves his people and has concern for their welfare[84] must inform their actions. Thus, a one-God-centered focus leads to a one-people-centered focus. This in turn means that members of the community must take one another's needs and concerns seriously. By focusing on their new freedom and disregarding the concerns of others in the community, the Corinthians have unintentionally sinned against their brother, and thus sinned against Christ (8:12).

The language used here emphasizes a union between Christ and his church—in offending one, the Corinthians offend the other.[85] Paul assumes an understanding of the people of God and God as being closely tied together. This idea of divine fellowship is apparently missing from the Corinthian understanding of what it means to be the people of God. H. Wheeler Robinson has argued that the lines between the individual and the group in ancient Israel were more fluid than our understanding of individuality today.[86] God's covenant was with the nation, not with

83. Willis, *Idol Meat in Corinth*, 291.

84. Rom 8:28, Phil 4:19; 1 Thess 4:9; 1 Tim 5:4.

85. See also the unity language found in 10:17: ". . . we who are many are one body."

86. Robinson, *Corporate Personality in Ancient Israel*, 46.

individual Israelites except, as members or representatives of that nation.[87] Yet, as the prophets taught a stronger sense of individual salvation, the corporate personality was not lost. As a result, in Jewish ethics the corporate personality meant it was important for group members to be in right relationship with one another; the group protected its weaker members.[88] "The corporate personality of Israel could not stand in a right relationship with God unless it approached Him in this unity of internal and individual fellowship."[89]

Such an analysis sheds light on Paul's argument here.[90] The Corinthians's focus is apparently very individualistic; the Jewish understanding, and thus Paul's understanding, is more corporate in nature. Because of this lack of appreciation of a proper covenantal relationship with the one God, the Corinthians have been sinning by causing one another to stumble. Paul's exhortation in 8:7—11:1, then, is an explication of proper one-God theology and the meaning of that theology for Christian ethics. Although he does not use the phrase "one God" specifically after 8:6, he alludes to the theme of oneness (both the oneness of God and the oneness of the community) throughout the section. The oneness of the believer and Christ is attested in the statement that a sin against a brother is a sin against Christ (8:12). The oneness of the people of God is evidenced in Paul's missionary efforts to become all things to all people (9:19–23). The oneness of Israel is underscored in Paul's statement that the Israelites all received God's blessings (10:1–4). The oneness of salvation history is emphasized in the description of the preexistent Christ as the rock in the wilderness (10:4). The oneness of the believer and Christ in worship is articulated in the portrayal of a sacrificial meal as a communion with the Lord or with demons, and the command to flee idolatry (10:14–22). Finally, the oneness of God's rule is highlighted in both the description of the fullness of the earth as being of the Lord (10:26, quoting Ps 24:1) and the exhortation that all things should be done to the glory of

87. Ibid., 51.

88. Ibid., 42.

89. Ibid., 54.

90. Although Robinson's thesis has been rightly criticized for too great a dependence on a flawed sociological understanding of primitive man (see, for example, Porter, "Legal Aspects"; and Rogerson, "Hebrew Conception of Corporate Personality"), Robinson nonetheless demonstrates that the relationship between the individual and the surrounding community in Hebrew society had much stronger connections than in modern society. See also A. Johnson, *One and the Many*.

God, without offense to Jew or Greek or the church of God (10:31—11:1). Thus, the monotheistic language in these verses serves as the basis for the need for love-empowered unity among God's people. This theme of love-empowered unity continues throughout the Corinthian letter.

EXCURSUS: DEUTERONOMY 6:4–5

Deut 6:4–5 provided the "most fundamental of Israel's 'creedal' traditions" and entails not only a statement about God, but also a call for commitment to that God.[91] Indeed, the Shema was so important that devout Jews recited the words twice each day.[92] Lengthy debate has centered on the

91. C. Wright, *Deuteronomy*, 95. See also Horowitz ("Sh'ma Reconsidered"), who argues that the structure of the Shema follows the ancient pattern for suzerainty treaties; thus, its primary purpose is not to clarify the idea of God, but to establish and renew regularly the loyalty commitment between Israel and God. See also Stauufer ("θεός"), who argues that the monotheistic confession of the first Christians, including Jesus, emphasized this loyalty: "They are not to have any gods alongside him, whether mammon, the belly, idols, the forces of the cosmos . . . , local authorities, or the emperor in Rome. It is necessary to serve God, to give God what is His, to obey Him and to build on Him alone, to be faithful to Him through every threat even to the point of martyrdom" (3:101–2).

92. Recitation of the Shema, at least as early as the second century, included not just Deut 6:4–9, but also Deut 11:13–21 and Num 15:37–41. See Jacobs, "Shema, Reading of." Numerous sources indicate the importance of the oneness of God in the first century. Philo, for example, does not directly quote the Shema, but frequently refers to the "one God." He emphasizes both the contrast between the one God of the Jews and the plurality of gods found in other religions as well as the unique character of the one God as sole maker and ruler of the world (*Opif.* 171–72; *Leg.* 1.44, 51; 2.1–3, 51; 3.7–9, 82, 105, 126; *Cher.* 83, 109; *Sacr.* 64; *Plant.* 137; *Migr.* 134; *Her.* 236; *Congr.* 113; *Fug.* 114, *Mut.* 205; *Somn.* 1.229; *Mos.* 268; *Decal.* 64–65; *Spec.* 1.30, 52, 65, 67, 1.313, 331–32, 344; 2.257; 3.29; 4.159; *Virt.* 35, 40, 102; *Praem.* 123, 162; *Legat.* 115; QE 2.2). Yet, despite the emphasis on oneness, Philo occasionally delineates various powers. He refers to the Logos as the "second God" in *Deus.* 2.62, but note that within his argument Philo makes it clear that God nonetheless is above the Logos. Other powers are described in *Cher.* 27–28, where Philo states that the one God's "chiefest powers are two, even Goodness and Sovereignty. Through Goodness he begat all that is; through his Sovereignty he rules what he has begotten. And in the midst between the two there is a third which unites them, Reason, for it is through Reason that God is both ruler and good." See also *Somn.* 1.228–230, 238–40; *Her.* 205. In *Conf.* 169–171, 175; and *Fug.* 68–74, Philo states that God has various potencies that God allowed to assist him in creation. In these sections, Philo nonetheless affirms that there is but one God who is over all. Josephus also affirms the oneness of God (*Ant.* 3.91; and *Ag. Ap.* 2.167). The oneness of God (sometimes described in terms of "the only God" or "there is none beside thee") occurs in other writings during the Second Temple period as well, e.g., 1QH 15.32; 20:11; 4Q504 5:9; Sir 1:8; Ps.-Phoc. 54; *Let. Aris.* 132; 2 Macc 1:24–25; and *Sib. Or.* 3.10–34; 4.30–40. These passages also highlight God's unique wisdom, power, and rule.

precise translation of the Hebrew. The usual translation states, "Hear, O Israel: The Lord our God, the Lord is one," and originally may have meant that, unlike the pagan gods who appear in different guises and localities, God is one. The word "one" was also understood to mean "unique"—God is totally other than what paganism means by gods; he is the Supreme Being who is different from anything he has created.[93] For our purposes here, the major definitional questions involve: 1) the meaning of "one," and 2) the implications arising from the call to love this one God with all one's heart, soul, and strength.

Although many different types of "monotheism" have been described in the past three centuries, Christopher Wright is correct in pointing out that Deuteronomy emphasizes that Yahweh alone was in covenant relationship with Israel, and that this God had acted uniquely in Israel's history, doing "what no other god had done." This Yahweh was one and not many. Furthermore, it is Yahweh who defines what monotheism means, and not the other way around.[94] God's actions in history define who this Yahweh is, not some abstract philosophical idea about what "oneness" means. As noted earlier, this element of experience is crucial to Israel's—and Paul's—understanding of the identity of the one God. It is God's unique activity as creator and ruler over all creation that demanded the singularity of worship prescribed in the Shema.[95]

An additional nuance is important for this understanding of God. It is not only God's actions that make Yahweh worthy of worship, but it is also God's character. As J. Gerald Janzen states, ". . . in the Shema, *ehad* is to be construed as referring to Yahweh's integrity or moral unity. It is that moral unity which is the ground of the claim for Israel's loyalty (the Shema) . . ."[96] That God is faithful to his promises becomes key, not only for the Israelites as they experience oppression by foreign rulers, but also for Paul as he writes his letter to the Romans, as chapter 4 will discuss. Indeed, Jewish theology frequently emphasized God's actions and integrity over against the powerlessness and capriciousness of other gods.[97] As noted earlier, the question of numerical singularity within the divine identity came into discussion more forcefully during the rabbinic period,

93. Jacobs, "Shema, Reading of," 14:1372–73.

94. C. Wright, *Deuteronomy*, 97.

95. Bauckham, *God Crucified*, 9.

96. Janzen, "Most Important Word," 291.

97. See, e.g., Exod 8:10; 1 Kgs 18:16–39; Ps 86:8–10, 89:5–8; Isa 43:9–13.

when Judaism was responding to Christianity. It was only then that arguments about "two powers in heaven" caused upheaval. The initial emphasis on God's oneness, however, concerned Yahweh's unique relationship to Israel.

This unique covenant relationship demanded the response found in Deut 6:5: love the Lord your God with all your heart and with all your soul and with all your strength. Yet loving God is not simply a matter of affection; rather, the way that one loves God is to obey his commandments. As C. Wright points out, "the command to love is so often linked with the command to obey, in a sort of prose parallelism, that the two terms are virtually synonymous . . ." He adds that the fact that love can be commanded shows that this love is not merely an emotion, but is also a commitment to Yahweh, which results in action in line with his word.[98]

To put a finer point on it, obeying God's law necessarily involves care and concern for others, i.e., loving others, since much of the Law is concerned about appropriate relationships between people. Deut 10:14–22, for example, has links with the Shema, as Moberly has demonstrated: "It is not just that we have here a kind of combination of love of God and love of neighbor, but that speech about YHWH as supreme is inseparable from the call of Israel to be a particular kind of people."[99] Thus, if loving God means keeping God's commandments and keeping God's commandments necessarily involves loving others, then one loves God (at least in part) by loving others.

Indeed, the Shema has been connected with both the Decalogue and Lev 19:18, the specific call to love one's neighbor. Although the connection is not as visible or as frequent as one might expect, there are several places where the link occurs. In Deuteronomy itself, chapter 5 lists the Ten Commandments before making the call in chapter 6 to hear and obey. The Nash papyrus, which dates from the Hasmonean period, contains both the Shema and the Ten Commandments together. Rabbinic sources indicate that during the Second Temple period recitation of the Shema followed the recitation of the Decalogue. The *Testaments of the Twelve Patriarchs* contain several examples of the call to love both God and neighbor,[100] and Philo unites the ideas of piety (duty to God) and

98. C. Wright, *Deuteronomy*, 98.

99. Moberly, "How Appropriate Is 'Monotheism'?" 229. See also Moberly's "Toward an Interpretation," 124–44.

100. *T. Iss.* 5:2, "Love the Lord and your neighbor . . . ," and 7:6, ". . . The Lord I loved with all my strength; likewise, I loved every human being as I love my children"; *T. Dan*

humanity (duty to humankind) in several places.[101] This same division is also apparent in Philo's understanding of the Decalogue itself (which Philo considers to be a summary of the whole Torah)—the first five commandments concern one's obligation to God, while the second five concern one's obligation to humanity.[102] The importance of these commands can be seen in some of their rabbinic descriptions: the call to love God in the Shema was often considered a matter of putting on "the yoke of the Kingdom,"[103] while Rabbi Haninah called the Levitical command to love one's neighbor the decree upon which "the whole world is suspended."[104]

All of these connections point to an important understanding in Jewish religion: love of God should not be separated from love of neighbor.[105] To put it more strongly, the vertical dimension of loving the one God *necessarily* includes the horizontal dimension of loving one's neighbor. The oneness of God translates into the oneness of God's people. The exact composition of God's people was sometimes a matter of dispute,[106] but the call to love one another was understood to be an integral part of worshipping Yahweh.[107]

This understanding of the connection between the Shema and love of neighbor helps shed light on Paul's argument in 1 Cor 8:6. The Corinthian strong had a truncated understanding of God; on the surface, they and Paul

---

5:3, "Throughout all your life love the Lord, and one another with a true heart"; *T. Benj.* 3:3, "Fear the Lord and love your neighbor." It is, however, possible that the *T. 12 Patr.* are Christian in their present form. It cannot be ruled out, however, that the ideas concerning love of neighbor may nonetheless reflect their Jewish origins.

101. See *Virt.* 51, 95; *Spec.* 2.63; *Abr.* 208.

102. Allison ("Mark 12.28–31 and the Decalogue," 273) uses this connection to argue that the combination in the Gospels of the call to love God and love one's neighbor would have been understood as a synopsis of the Decalogue.

103. See, e.g., *m. Ber.* 2:2.

104. *'Abot R. Nat. B* 27:9–11, but note that *A* 16:33ff. the quote is attributed to Simeon ben Eleazar.

105. McBride states that the true servants of God are those who have acknowledged God's kingship over their lives and "accord their fellow subjects the same worth they themselves have received in abundance" ("Yoke of the Kingdom," 282).

106. "Neighbor" in early rabbinic Judaism was taken to mean one's fellow Jew or a proselyte; some rabbis included Samaritans, while others did not. See Neudecker, "'You Shall Love Your Neighbor,'" 499, 499 n. 9.

107. The reason for the command may also be important. Abrahams (*Studies in Pharisaism*, 18) argues that because humanity is made in the image of God, any disregard for others translates into a disregard for God.

could agree with basic theological affirmations of God's oneness. But at a deeper level, Paul argues that some Corinthians did not fully understand what it means to "know" the one God; they did not see the connection between God's oneness and the ethical imperative to put others lovingly before oneself. As a result, the church suffered from significant schisms that Paul was forced to address. Paul's response in chapters 8–10 indicates his Jewish understanding of the inseparability of love of God and love of neighbor. Those who confessed to loving God were not sufficiently aware of their ethical obligations, and so Paul offers a lengthy explanation of the ethical imperative required by the theological proclamation.

• • •

Overall, this examination of 1 Cor 8:4–6 has shown that although Paul is quoting the Corinthian strong when he uses "one God, one Lord" language, this monotheistic confession lies at the center of the disagreement between Paul and the strong. Whereas the strong presume to have knowledge of the one God, Paul hints even in 8:1 that true knowledge, true understanding of the oneness of God, involves something more than mere noetic assent to theological principles. Rather, a proper understanding of the one God necessarily involves love, not only in the vertical dimension of love for God, but also in the horizontal dimension of love for neighbor. Paul relies on his Jewish background, on the basic Deuteronomic call to love the one God with everything that a person is—heart, soul, and strength—as the foundation for this understanding. Because Yahweh is a relational God who loves his creation, those who are in relationship with the one God must also love the things that God loves, i.e., other people. The Corinthian strong are guilty of a self-centered philosophy that does not fully embrace what it means to be one people under one God. Paul corrects their mistaken theology by emphasizing the need to give up one's "rights" in order to build up the church body (8:7—9:27). In this way Paul strives to correct the horizontal relationships within the Corinthian community. Yet in his exhortation to flee idolatry Paul also warns against the destruction of the vertical relationship with God (ch. 10).

It is striking that the language of the formula is not the basis of the disagreement. Both Paul and the Corinthians agree that for Christians there is one God, the Father, from whom are all things and we in him, and one Lord, Jesus Christ, through whom are all things and we through him. This exclusive oneness language is set in opposition to non-Christian pluralistic "gods" and "lords." Christ is included in the "one" who is in opposition to the many. This structure, the parallel language, the use of "lord" in a religious context, the parallels with Stoic thought regarding one God/ one Lord as the origin and goal of all that exists, and Paul's ascription elsewhere of Old Testament Yahweh texts to Jesus, all indicate that Paul is indeed including Jesus within the divine identity, and that this theology is not new to the Corinthians. The synergy of Paul's own experience of the risen Christ and his reinterpretation of Jewish Scripture has led him to this conclusion.

This hypothesis, however, cannot be made in a vacuum. Elsewhere in 1 Corinthians Paul makes statements about the relationship between Jesus and God, although many of these are not as explicit as 1 Cor 8:6. Some of these statements appear to support a functional correlation between Jesus and God. Elsewhere, though, Paul appears to subordinate Christ to God. Can sense be made of these apparent discrepancies? It is to these passages that we now turn.

PASSAGES THAT IMPLY A FUNCTIONAL CORRELATION BETWEEN JESUS AND GOD

In order to fully understand the nuances of Paul's theology, we must consider what impact his one-God language has on the rest of his argumentation in 1 Corinthians. How does this strong monotheistic language influence the manner in which Paul describes God and Christ? Surprisingly, numerous passages in 1 Corinthians seem to place Jesus and God, in some way, on a level playing field; Paul makes very little functional distinction between the two. These passages include: 1:3, 23–24, 30; 6:11; 7:17–24; 8:4–6; 9:21; 10:4–9, 20–22; 12:4–6, and "Day of the Lord" passages, which include 1:7–8; 4:4b–5; 5:5; 11:26, 32; and 15:23–34. Some of these passages make very strong claims about Christ in relation to God, while others only implicitly make a connection.

The first of the passages we will examine is 1:3: "Grace to you and peace from God our father and the Lord Jesus Christ." The same word-for-word greeting appears in Rom 1:7b; 2 Cor 1:2; Gal 1:3; Eph 1:2; Phil 1:2; 2 Thess 1:2; and Phlm 1:3; nearly identical language is found in 1 Tim 1:2; 2 Tim 1:2; and Titus 1:4b.[108] In this greeting Paul derives grace and

108. In Colossians, where one might expect a functional correlation between Christ and God in the greeting, the text leaves out Christ: "Grace to you and peace from God

peace from both God and Christ. While it certainly is true that divinity is not a prerequisite for presenting either grace or peace to a person or community,[109] the fact that Paul presents God and Christ as functioning together without distinction is potentially significant. That this language appears within a rather formulaic introduction to the letter could indicate that Paul is taking it for granted and may not be aware of the theological implications of his language.[110] On the other hand, the fact that a formula exists at all would seem to indicate that the churches are quite familiar with this phrase and its close link between Christ and God.[111]

It may be helpful at this point to turn to the form of ancient letters for instruction. The basic opening phrase in the Greek letter has been expressed by the formula, "A to B χαίρειν," where A is the sender and B the recipient of the letter.[112] By the late second century BCE until the late first or early second century CE, the opening greeting was often combined with a wish for good health.[113] Even more important for this study is the observation that frequently in ancient near eastern cultures the sender of the letter invoked the gods to bring a blessing upon the recipient.[114] A similar pattern has been found in Aramaic letters, which can have greetings that are either religious (e.g., "May all the gods be much [concerned] for the well-being of my lord at all times") or secular (e.g., "Peace and life I send you").[115]

---

our Father" (1:2b). In 1 Thessalonians, the letter is addressed to the church: ". . . in God the Father and the Lord Jesus Christ; Grace to you and peace" (1:1). It is not clear whether Paul offers the grace and peace himself, or whether God and Christ are the implied source.

109. See, for example, Deut 20:10, where God instructs Israel to offer peace to its enemies (although here one could argue that God is ultimately the one who offers peace through his people Israel), and 2 Sam 10:19, where the Aramean kings made peace with Israel.

110. Bruce, for example, does not address Christology here, but simply says verse 3 is "a characteristically Christian greeting . . ." (*1 and 2 Corinthians*, 30). Barrett argues that Paul sees God as the source of grace and peace, with Jesus as the agent, yet Paul does not provide here any "ready-made doctrine" of God or Christ (*Corinthians*, 35).

111. Fee finds that "texts such as this one . . . make it clear that in Paul's mind the Son is truly God and works in cooperation with the Father in the redemption of his people" (*Corinthians*, 35).

112. Exler, *Form of the Ancient Greek Letter*, 23.

113. White, *Light from Ancient Letters*, 200.

114. White, "Ancient Epistolography," 9.

115. Fitzmyer, "Aramaic Epistolography," 34–35.

This general pattern Paul clearly follows, although he alters the formula to suit his specific purposes. John L. White observes that Paul replaces the traditional greeting (χαίρειν) with a combined blessing of grace and peace. "This expression is analogous to the opening blessing in certain ancient Near Eastern letters and is equivalent, in Greek, to a religious health wish. More significantly, perhaps, Paul Christianizes the expression by the addition of the words, '. . . from God our Father and the Lord Jesus Christ.'"[116] This suggests that by following the traditional formula and including a specifically religious health wish/blessing (as indicated by reference to God the Father), Paul may be intentionally making a statement about the exalted Christ when he invokes the name of Jesus—without further comment or any limitation—alongside God. Paul appears to be including Jesus within the sphere of that deity. Therefore, while the greeting may seem rather formulaic, based on Paul's repetitious use of the phrase, the underlying theology is perhaps quite deliberate and significant. Nonetheless, such a simple turn of phrase cannot by itself explain Paul's monotheistic beliefs; other passages in 1 Corinthians are required to offer further illumination.

The next passage for investigation is 1:23–24, and verse 30: "but we proclaim Christ crucified, a stumbling block to Jews and foolishness to Gentiles, but to those who are the called, both Jews and Greeks, Christ the power of God and the wisdom of God . . . He is the source of your life in Christ Jesus, who became for us wisdom from God, and righteousness and sanctification and redemption . . ." These verses once again raise the question of the place of Wisdom in biblical and extra-biblical Jewish literature. I concluded in chapter 1 that Wisdom in Jewish theology was a personification of God, not a hypostasis. The questions for interpreting 1 Cor 1:24 and 30, then, involve whether Paul intends to identify Christ with the personified Wisdom of God in these verses, and, if so, what this implies about Paul's theology.

The specific construction of the texts, however, suggests that personified Wisdom may not be the primary focus here. Rather, Paul appears to be emphasizing the paradox that Christ's scandalous death is the result of God's wise plan of salvation.[117] First, in both places where Paul

116. White, "Saint Paul," 437.

117. Weiss (*Der erste Korintherbrief*, 33–34) argues that the rejection by the Gentiles and Jews is sharply contrasted with the work Christ accomplished on the cross. The cross was not a defeat, but rather the wisdom of God through which salvation became possible.

identifies Jesus as the wisdom of God, he does so by using additional terms as well, terms that are merely attributive and do not approach the realm of personification. In 1:24 Jesus is the power of God as well as the wisdom of God, while in 1:30 Jesus is not only the wisdom of God, but also righteousness and holiness and redemption. These other descriptive terms have no parallel with potential personifications of God. Paul does not choose to describe Christ here in terms such as "Glory" or "Word," which could have indicated that Paul intended to identify Jesus with a well-known personification of God. Thus, the grammatical construction itself seems to indicate that here Paul intends something less than a reference to personified Wisdom.

Furthermore, wisdom material in general often appears in a context that emphasizes the importance of Jesus's saving death.[118] Birger A. Pearson affirms this emphasis: "Indeed Paul even goes so far as to suggest that true 'wisdom' is, in fact, nothing else than an understanding of the cross, the center of the Christian kerygma."[119] This is certainly born out in 1 Cor 1; Jesus is described in 1:24 as the "power of God"—a phrase which Paul used in 1:18 to describe "the message of the cross." It appears, then, that Paul intends to focus on the plan of salvation as God's wisdom.

The overall context of the discussion in 1 Cor 1 further affirms this conclusion. Paul is contrasting the non-Christian world with God; what Greeks value and consider "wise" is a far cry from the truth found in God's plan of salvation. Jesus is the epitome of that plan. Ultimately, Paul is arguing that the Corinthians should not be dividing themselves along party lines, boasting in those divisions and seeking status in Paul, Apollos, or anyone else. Status-seeking belongs to the non-Christian world and is foolishness. Rather, the gospel is about God turning the status-seeking, self-serving order of the Greek world on its head, so that no one may boast except in God (1:27–29). The language that closely unites Christ to God here is intended to contrast God's wise activity with the pseudo-wisdom of the non-Christian world.

It is possible, however, that by means of this contrast-oriented structure Paul intends to hint at a connection between Christ and personified Wisdom. In the wisdom literature, Wisdom is often contrasted with fool-

---

See also Dunn, who states that wisdom, for Paul, has "the sense of 'God's predetermined plan of salvation'" (*Christology in the Making*, 178).

118. Gray, "Wisdom Christology," 456.

119. Pearson, "Hellenistic-Jewish Wisdom," 57.

ishness, which itself is occasionally personified.[120] A similar contrast occurs in 1 Cor 1:18—2:16. Such a connection would be stronger, however, if Paul had included other aspects of personified Wisdom in 1:24 and 30, such as Wisdom's involvement in creation. While Paul emphasizes this elsewhere in his writing,[121] he does not choose to make the connection explicit here. Instead, he states that Jesus "became" (ἐγενήθη) wisdom. This is a different verb than those typically used to describe the emergence of wisdom prior to creation.[122] Rather, Paul here emphasizes that the crucifixion was the pivotal moment in history, at which time Christ became righteousness and sanctification and redemption through his atoning death.[123] This emphasis on the plan of salvation is further affirmed in 2:7, where Paul says that God had predestined this wisdom before the ages.[124]

An additional structural parallel is important here. In 1:31, Paul quotes Jer 9:23 (LXX). It is possible that Paul's argument in the preceding verses is an intentional parallel of Jer 9:22–23. In that text, the prophet warns against trusting in wisdom (σοφίᾳ), strength (ἰσχύι), or riches (πλούτῳ). Rather, the one who boasts should boast in the understanding and knowledge of God, who exercises kindness (ἔλεος), justice (κρίμα), and righteousness (δικαιοσύνην) on earth. Likewise, in 1:26–28 Paul argues in a triple formula that not many of the Corinthians were wise (σοφοί), powerful (δυνατοί), or noble (εὐγενεῖς). Just as the prophet refers to knowledge (γινώσκειν) of God, Paul refers to wisdom (σοφία), which he specifically identifies with Jesus. Then Paul offers a similar triple formula of positive characteristics: righteousness (δικαιοσύνη), sanctification (ἁγιασμός), and redemption (ἀπολύτρωσις). It is significant that in the Jeremiah text these characteristics describe God, while in Paul's version they describe Jesus.[125] Nonetheless, Paul is offering only

120. See, e.g., Prov 1:20–33; 9:1–18.

121. See the discussion on 1 Cor 10:4. In addition, the Christological hymns, e.g., Phil 2:5–11 and Col 1:15–20, do seem to indicate an intentional description of Christ's divine nature, pre-existence and presence at creation.

122. These descriptions include ἔκτισέν (Prov 8:22; Sir 24:8–9), γεννᾷ (Prov 8:25), and ἐξῆλθον (Sir 24:3).

123. For more on atonement, see my chapter 4. Collins states that Paul "views the death of Jesus as an event of cosmic proportions" (*First Corinthians*, 124).

124. Conzelmann, *1 Corinthians*, 62.

125. O'Day states, "Paul does not focus strictly on Yahweh's saving acts in the covenant, as Jeremiah does, but on God's saving acts in Jesus Christ. The positive triad in Paul thus reflects Christian soteriology: God through Christ to us" ("Jeremiah 9:22–23,"

a loose parallel. Although structurally the similarities are quite striking, linguistically the differences are numerous. Other than the quote in 1:31 which Paul introduces with the formulaic γέγραπται, only the terms wisdom (σοφία) and righteousness (δικαιοσύνη) are found in both texts. Another possible source for the structure also presents itself in 1 Sam 2:10 (LXX), where the wording is extremely close to that of Jeremiah. As Richard Hays argues, the context in 1 Sam 2:10 is more appropriate than Jeremiah for Paul's purposes: 1 Samuel records Hannah's prayer and the theme of reversal of fortune, whereas Jeremiah's exhortation occurs in the midst of a rebuke of Israel.[126] Nonetheless, the 1 Samuel passage uses the term φρόνιμος rather than σοφοί and thus does not make as direct a linguistic connection with 1 Corinthians.[127] Therefore, it may be appropriate to suggest that Paul is drawing upon Jewish Scripture traditions in general and may have both texts in mind.[128] As a result, it is difficult to draw with any certainty implications regarding the intersection of Paul's theology and Christology in regard to the Jewish Scriptures. At a minimum, however, Paul very closely connects the historical reality of Christ's actions with the wise plan of God. The understanding and knowledge of God (Jeremiah, 1 Samuel) is found in the activity of Christ. Thus, Christ's actions help to define who God is. Without Christ, one cannot properly know God.

Overall, Paul's main purpose in linking Christ and God in 1:24 and 30 is to show the difference, the separation, the ultimate distinctiveness of God's action in Christ over against the non-Christian world. In describing Christ as the wisdom of God, Paul is emphasizing God's plan of salvation and likely is not focusing on personified Wisdom. Certainly it is not *necessary* for the efficacy of this argument that Christ be equated with personified Wisdom and therefore God (and indeed the grammar indicates a different emphasis); the argument is just as effective when Christ is portrayed as part of God's wise plan of salvation. Nonetheless, through the contrast of wisdom and foolishness Paul may be hinting at a link between Christ and personified Wisdom. It simply does not suit the purpose

266). Capes (*Old Testament Yahweh Texts*, 133) goes further when he argues that this is an example of an OT text in which κύριος originally referred to Yahweh but now refers to Jesus.

126. Hays, *First Corinthians*, 34–35.

127. Although the term δυνατός is used for the powerful, just as in 1 Cor 1:26.

128. Hays, *First Corinthians*, 35.

of his argument, however, to make such an explicit connection. Paul is more concerned here with the prudence of God's surprising plan of salvation than he is with describing God's divine identity. Nonetheless, Paul's reference to the Jewish Scriptures and reinterpretation of them in light of Christ demonstrates that, for Paul, God's identity cannot be known apart from the actions of Christ.

The next passage that may shed light on Paul's understanding of the relationship between Christ and God is 6:11: "And this is what some of you used to be. But you were washed, you were sanctified, you were justified in the name of the Lord Jesus Christ and in the Spirit of our God." Here the spiritual status of the believer is transformed on the basis of both the name of Jesus and the Spirit of God. This raises the question of what it means for something to be done "in the name of" someone. This could simply denote that Jesus's name represents God's plan of salvation, and being "in" him (or doing something in his name) means an alliance with and active participation in God's plan.[129] Indeed, the reference to washing here may indicate a baptismal context, which would correspond to this concept of allying oneself with God.[130]

It appears, however, that there is a stronger, more one-to-one correlation between the salvific power of Jesus and God in this verse. Paul uses language here that is similar to his argument in 1:30. As just discussed, Jesus is the wisdom of God who was also righteousness, sanctification, and redemption (δικαιοσύνη, ἁγιασμός, and ἀπολύτρωσις). In 6:11, believers have been washed, sanctified, and justified (ἀπελούσασθε, ἡγιάσθητε, and ἐδικαιώθητε). Although redemption in 1:30 and washing in 6:11 have different etymologies, they nonetheless both convey a

129. Bietenhard, "ὄνομα," 5:273, states that Jesus's action is action in God's name. In addressing 1 Cor 6:11, Bietenhard argues that the fullness of Christ's saving work is contained in his name and is present to the community. The purification, sanctification and justification do not come in pronouncing the name but in the act of baptism, which means ultimately in the death and resurrection of Jesus Christ. Bietenhard does not address here the question of the relationship between the name of Jesus and the Spirit of God in this passage, but see n. 132.

130. It is possible that "in the name of the Lord Jesus Christ" here is simply a phrase used to qualify the rite of baptism and distinguish it from other rites, as suggested by Hartman, "Into the Name of Jesus." Nonetheless, the context suggests more is involved than a simple identification of a particular rite. Just as in 1 Cor 8:6, the context is one of contrast between God and the world. Paul argues that the Corinthians are no longer sinners because of their new identity achieved through Christ and the Spirit. The focus is on transformation, not on identification of a specific rite.

similar idea of leaving a less desirable state for that which is more desirable. Together, these terms all focus on the deliverance effected to the believer, who is now able to stand holy before God. Thus, once again, Jesus is the focal point of this transition. This is particularly significant since, in the Jewish Scriptures, it is God alone who can save.[131] That this power is now ascribed to Jesus suggests that Jesus is involved in judgment and rule, activities that (as Bauckham suggests) are key to divine identity.[132]

At the same time, in 6:11 the name of Jesus does not stand independently, but is closely linked with the Spirit of God. Yet the nature of this connection is ambiguous. At first glance there appears to be a distinction between the two, since "name" and "Spirit" are not phenomenologically the same. Nonetheless, Paul argues that the Corinthian believers are no longer sinners such as those mentioned in verses 9–10; they have been transformed, and the means of that change was both (the name of) Jesus and the Spirit of God.[133] This transformation is two-pronged—it is not solely by means of the name of Jesus, nor is it solely by means of the Spirit of God. The parallel grammatical construction (ἐν τῷ ὀνόματι . . . ἐν τῷ πνεύματι) indicates the parallel instrumentation (ὀνόματι τοῦ κυρίου Ἰησοῦ Χριστοῦ . . . πνεύματι τοῦ θεοῦ ἡμῶν).

Here again it is clear how thoroughly Paul's theology is intertwined with his Christology. What God has done by his name for Israel, i.e., delivering his people, Christ has done by his name and in concert with the Spirit of God for believers. When Paul speaks of God and God's redemptive activity in the believer, he cannot do so apart from Christ.

The next passage for consideration is 7:17 and 22–24: "However that may be, let each of you lead the life that the Lord has assigned, to which

131. See, e.g., 2 Kgs 19:19; Ps 54:1 (note that David asks God to save "by your name"); Ps 76:7–9; Isa 37:20; 45:20; Ezek 37:23.

132. Bietenhard states that "in the name" in the Old Testament appears most often in association with the name of Yahweh with the primary meaning of calling upon, invoking Yahweh by his name, that is, worshipping him in the cult ("Name," 2:650). In the New Testament, "the OT manner of speaking of the name of Yahweh has been transferred to Jesus and his name" (654). Furthermore, "the fullness of Christ's saving work is contained in his name (as Yahweh's saving work was in his) and is present in the church" (655).

133. Some interpreters do not find Trinitarian significance in this juxtaposition. For example, Bruce does not address the question (*Corinthians*, 62); Conzelmann comments that "the prevailing schema is that of tracing everything back to God" (*1 Corinthians*, 107); Soards states that the Corinthians's transformation comes "through the work of God's Spirit in Jesus Christ" (*1 Corinthians*, 125). Still others, however, find unconscious Trinitarian language; e.g., Fee, *Corinthians*, 246; Barrett, *Corinthians*, 143.

God called you. This is my rule in all the churches . . . For whoever was called in the Lord as a slave is a freed person belonging to the Lord, just as whoever was free when called is a slave of Christ. You were bought with a price; do not become slaves of human masters. In whatever condition you were called, brothers and sisters, there remain with God." Here God and Christ appear functionally the same: Christ assigns, God calls.[134] "Lord" here refers to Christ;[135] in both the preceding and following verses (12, 25) Paul uses "Lord" for Jesus when appealing to Christ's authority, and there is no indication of any shift in meaning here.[136] Furthermore, the parallel language within verse 22 indicates that Christ is the referent for Lord. Although it is possible that some distinction exists between the meaning of the two verbs (ἐμέρισεν and κέκληκεν),[137] no obvious differentiation occurs. Indeed, Fee comments, "It is difficult to escape the christological implications of this text, where the work of Christ is seen to be in union with the work of God. In Trinitarian terms, God the Father called; God the Son assigned. But both actions are the activity of the one God."[138]

Paul uses ἐμέρισεν elsewhere of God, not Christ. In 2 Cor 10:13, Paul refers to the area that God assigned (ἐμέρισεν) to him. In Rom 12:3, Paul exhorts believers not to think of themselves more highly than they ought, but to use sober judgment in accordance with the faith God has apportioned (ἐμέρισεν).[139] Thus, Christ in 1 Cor 7 is performing one of the tasks that elsewhere God performs.

The fact that Paul refers to both God and Christ here is important, since his argument does not hinge on any inherent connection between God and Christ. Paul just as easily could have referred to God alone

134. Conzelmann argues that Paul uses "apportion" and "call" as synonyms here, and alternates between the Lord and God as the giver: "The two ὡς-clauses are synonymous" (*1 Corinthians*, 126).

135. *Contra* Soards, who says Paul's usages here "are not sufficiently distinct to determine whether he means to name Jesus Christ or God as 'the Lord'" (*1 Corinthians*, 158). The fact that Paul does not clearly distinguish between the two is in itself significant.

136. The only clear references to God as Lord in 1 Corinthians occur in 3:20; 10:26; and 14:21, and are OT quotes (Ps 94:11; Ps 24:1; and Isa 28:11–12, respectively).

137. Fee (*Corinthians*, 310) distinguishes between the social situations in which the Corinthians found themselves (and which were assigned by Christ) and the salvation to which God called the Corinthians.

138. Ibid., n. 16.

139. Paul uses the verb elsewhere only twice (1 Cor 1:13 and 7:34), and then in the negative context of division, which thus does not apply to the meaning here.

throughout the argument, or to Christ alone. Since no specific reason is apparent for making the exchange between God and Christ here, it is possible that Paul is making an unconscious transfer. On the other hand, Paul may be intentionally using both referents as a means of signaling the unity between God and Christ. His Hebrew background, specifically the parallel language frequently found in poetry, may have influenced his writing here. If so, then in verse 17 "the place to which God has called him" is parallel to and further defines "the place to which the Lord has assigned him."[140] Although this may seem to argue in favor of κύριος referring to God in verse 17, the parallelism within verse 22 suggests that there it is Christ who is κύριος. Regardless of whether Paul refers to Christ or God in verse 17, it is undeniable that the entire passage strikingly unites the action of God and Christ throughout.

The next passage for consideration is 9:21: "To those outside the law I became as one outside the law (though I am not free from God's law but am under Christ's law) so that I might win those outside the law." Here Paul affirms that he is not outside of God's law (he is not lawless) by appealing to the fact that he is within Christ's law.[141] While this does not provide a direct correlation between Christ and God (for example, the terms "Law of Moses" and "Law of God" do not equate Moses with God!), it is important that Paul considers being within Christ's law to be equivalent to being within God's law. The parallel here is not crucial to Paul's argument—he is simply describing his missionary zeal and clarifies his own righteousness by means of the God and Christ language. Yet on another level Paul desires to emphasize the continuity between the old and new covenants: God has not changed the rules in the middle of the game. God is not arbitrary in sending Christ, but rather fulfills his plan by sending Christ. Paul is not suggesting the existence of a new law—but rather, that Christ is the norm.[142]

Since this passage raises the question of the continuity of salvation history, a question that will come to the fore in the study of Galatians and

140. Although this passage is not typically defined as poetry, the similar language and structure in each verse, and the occasional alliteration (e.g., v. 17), suggest a possible stylistic correlation.

141. For similar Pauline phrases, see Rom 8:2 and Gal 6:2. In Rom 8:2, the law of the Spirit of life in Christ sets the believer free from the law of sin and death; in Gal 6:2, bearing one another's burdens fulfils the law of Christ.

142. Conzelmann, *1 Corinthians*, 161.

Romans in the following chapters, I will not spend a significant amount of time here discussing these issues. At this juncture, however, it may be helpful to look briefly at the specific term used in 1 Cor 9:21, since Paul does not use the precise phrase ἔννομος Χριστοῦ elsewhere. Does Paul have a specific codified law in mind?[143] Or does he consider the "law" of Christ to be a more general term referring to a Spirit-filled life?[144] Paul does not directly argue for the establishment of a new law and only infrequently refers to commands from Christ, although in 1 Corinthians he does do so occasionally.[145] In addition, as noted previously, Paul relies heavily on the Jewish Scriptures for many of his arguments. Thus, he has not divorced himself completely from his Jewish background. Rather, he has reinterpreted the Scriptures in light of his experience of the risen Christ. His new hermeneutic, based upon his experience, is what allows him to make the paradoxical statement in 1 Cor 7:19 that circumcision (itself a command of God) is nothing, but what counts is keeping the commands of God. Because Paul saw that the Spirit had come upon those who were not circumcised, Paul reinterpreted the role of circumcision as a rite that had been devalued under the reign of Christ (Gal 3:2–5).

Clearly, Paul's understanding of what comprises the decrees of God is different after his conversion experience, even though many of his ethical exhortations still mirror the Jewish Scriptures, e.g., the command to flee idolatry. As I will argue in the following chapters, Paul has de-emphasized the ritual aspects of the Law, while still maintaining the ethical aspects. In 1 Cor 9:19–23, then, Paul can describe himself as becoming a Jew in some instances, e.g., observing food laws, while becoming a Gentile in other instances; he is not ἄνομος but ἔννομος Χριστοῦ.[146] Ultimately, for Paul, believers have received the Spirit and thus are able to live in a manner that is consistent with the Law through the fruit the Spirit bears (Gal 5:22–23).

143. Dodd, e.g., maintains that ἔννομος Χριστοῦ implies the existence of a νόμος Χριστοῦ ("ἔννομος Χριστοῦ," 137). Dodd cites a number of allusions in Paul's writing to sayings of Jesus, and argues that Paul treats these maxims as if they were elements of a new Torah. Following Christ is thus more than a matter of simply walking in the Spirit, but involves following the precepts that Jesus handed down to his disciples (147).

144. Winger ("The Law of Christ," 548), e.g., notes that Paul almost never invokes a command of Jesus, which one would expect if the commands were central; rather, love is a matter of the Spirit. Paul is deliberate in avoiding definition of the law of Christ.

145. 1 Cor 7:10, 9:14.

146. Thielman, "Coherence of Paul's View," 245.

Therefore, although Paul considers Christ's death and resurrection to have transformed the necessity of various requirements of the Law, Christ has not completely superseded the Torah. Christ is not in competition with God, but rather fulfills God's plan. Thus, when Paul uses parallel language of Christ and God in discussing the Law, he expresses an understanding of continuity in God's plan of salvation and Christ's place within it. The importance of this unity for Paul's thinking cannot be overestimated. As I will argue below, Paul considers it crucial to affirm that Christ has not established himself in a position above God. Paul does not see himself as founding a new religion, but rather as explaining the fullness of God's plan of salvation for all humanity.

Another important passage for consideration is 10:4, 9: "For they drank from the spiritual rock that followed them, and the rock was Christ. . . . We must not put Christ to the test, as some of them did, and were destroyed by serpents." This is the only place where Paul directly reads Christ back into an Old Testament event. His purpose here is to use the Israelites's desert experience as an illustration of the negative effect of falling into sin. The reference to the rock in verse 4 probably derives from a combination of traditions. First, Exod 17:1–7 and Num 20:1–13 record Moses striking a rock with his staff at Massah/Meribah and water pouring forth for the Israelites to drink. The second tradition appears in Pseudo-Philo and the rabbinic writings and may explain Paul's use in 10:4 of the term ἀκολουθούσης. In this tradition, the rock followed the Israelites in the desert and served as a perpetual spring from which they drank.[147] In addition, Philo identifies the rock in the wilderness with Wisdom,[148] as does Wis 11:4.

The question to consider here is precisely how Paul intended his reference to Christ to be interpreted. Clearly Paul does not mean that Jesus was a literal rock, "as though preachers should solemnly seek to determine whether Christ was igneous, metamorphic, or sedimentary."[149] Rather, Paul uses the language of typology within this section, specifically in verses 6 (τύποι) and 11 (τυπικῶς). The question, then, revolves around the precise nature and extent of this "type."[150]

147. *L.A.B.* 10:7; 11:15; *Sifre* on Num 11:21; Tosefta *Sukkah* 3:11; see also *Mekilta* Exod 17:6.

148. *Leg.* 2.86, 88.

149. Hays, *First Corinthians*, 161.

150. Goppelt defines τύπος as "type" in the sense of "advance presentation" ("τύπος," 8:258). For further discussion, see Goppelt's *Typos*.

It is possible that when Paul refers to Christ as the rock, he is already drawing the comparison between the type (the rock) and the antitype (Christ) for his argument.[151] If this is the case, then Paul does not link Christ with preexistent Wisdom. Rather, he simply argues that as God provided spiritual sustenance for Israel in the desert, so Christ provides spiritual sustenance for the Corinthian community.[152]

But the structure of the passage itself argues for a different interpretation. The verbs (ἐγενήθησαν and συνέβαινεν) emphasize the *occurrence* of events, which suggests that Paul indeed intends a typology and not an allegory.[153] It is important to note that verses 1–5 serve as the type, and it is only in verse 6 that Paul signals the beginning of the antitype with his statement that ταῦτα δὲ τύποι ἡμῶν ἐγενήθησαν. That Paul's identification of Christ as the rock in the wilderness occurs within the type itself (i.e., the record of the historical event) suggests that Paul understood Christ to be the preexistent one who provided for Israel.[154] Paul also may have been drawing on the Song of Moses in Deut 32:4, 15, 18, 30–31, in which Yahweh is the rock of Israel. In addition, as noted above, a first-century tradition existed linking the rock with Wisdom. Paul is likely taking advantage of this tradition in order to draw an even closer connection between God and Christ than that which he conferred in 1:24

151. Dunn, for example, argues that the rock only represents Christ: "as water from the rock, so spiritual drink from Christ" (*Christology in the Making*, 183). Dunn understands Paul's hermeneutic here to specifically involve a typological allegory. Paul does not find it necessary to identify Moses as the type of Christ (since the parallel is obvious), but he does feel the need to clarify that the rock, a less obvious type, was Christ (ibid., 184). Oropeza (*Paul and Apostasy*, 105 n. 157), however, has pointed out that it is difficult to see how Christ is both Moses and the rock simultaneously.

152. In contrast, Lietzmann draws a comparison between Moses and Christ: "Wenn mann den typologischen Ausführungen des Apostels gefolgt, versteht man leicht, wieso sich an Moses für die Israeliten das Heil ähnlich knüpfte wie für die Christen an Christus" (*An die Korinther 1–2*, 45).

153. Goppelt, "τύπος." Typology focuses on historical events, whereas allegory focuses on metaphorical meanings apart from any historical connection. Furthermore, Paul uses the imperfect to describe Christ as the rock, not the present tense as one would expect in an analogy (Oropeza, *Paul and Apostasy*, 105 n. 157).

154. See also A. Hanson, *Studies in Paul's Technique*, 151. For a more in-depth discussion, see Hanson's *Jesus Christ in the Old Testament*. Although Hanson sees Christ as pre-existent in this text, he denies that a typology exists. I would argue, on the other hand, that both are possible simultaneously. Christ was indeed present with Israel in the desert, but it is the Israelites's sin and punishment that Paul uses as a type for the current Corinthian situation.

and 30.[155] Although it did not serve Paul's purposes there to explicitly identify Jesus as part of the divine identity, it does serve his purposes here. Paul strongly wants to discourage the Corinthians from having anything to do with idols, and he does so by showing how God has dealt with his people who have sinned in the past.[156] He links Christ and God to show continuity; the Corinthians will receive the same harsh punishment if they go astray. If Christ and God are distinct, or if Christ had nothing to do with punishing the Israelites in the desert, the Corinthians might say, "That was how God dealt with his people then, but Christ will deal with us differently." Paul emphasizes the unity of God and Christ here to allow the Corinthians no room for rationalizing away sinful behavior. Paul's argument will lose its effectiveness if the Corinthians fail to see the intrinsic connection between God and Christ throughout history.

Verse 9 is not as clear-cut a case of reading Christ into the Old Testament as verse 4, since a textual variant exists which could possibly replace "Christ" with "Lord." In an Old Testament context, "Lord" would more likely refer to God. "Christ," however, is generally considered to be the preferred reading.[157] Nonetheless, the parallelism between Christ and God is not as obvious since the word "Christ" is not repeated after the statement "as some of them tempted." One could thus read the text: "Let us not tempt Christ as some of them tempted (God) and were destroyed by the serpents." The analogy, then, would not be a direct parallel—although a functional correlation between Jesus and God would still be implicit. Given Paul's explicit reference to Christ in the desert in verse 4, however, we must consider the possibility that Paul intended Christ to be read into the Old Testament story here as well.

What, then, does it mean to tempt Christ? In the Old Testament, one tempted God by failing to acknowledge his power and will to save, and expressed this temptation/testing by complaining against God's guidance, and failing to see God's glory or signs and wonders: "To test God is thus to

155. It is unclear, however, whether the Corinthians would have been aware of Jewish traditions connecting the rock with Wisdom; the subtle reminder here that God's wisdom is different than the world's may have been lost on them.

156. See, for example, Sandelin, "Christ as the Nourishing Rock." Sandelin notes parallels between the sacrament in the desert and the Lord's Supper, but nevertheless argues that Paul's intention in this section is to warn against idolatry.

157. P46 and numerous other texts contain "Χριστόν" and other manuscripts (including Codex Sinaiticus) contain "κύριον," whereas only a few later texts contain "θεόν."

challenge Him. It is an expression of unbelief, doubt and disobedience."[158] The testing of God alluded to in 1 Cor 10:9 involves the story of Num 21:4–9, in which the Israelites again grumbled against God in the desert (even after they had received manna and water) and God in return sent venomous snakes among the people. Psalm 78 also relates the various instances of grumbling in the desert; it is striking that the psalmist also takes up the motif of God as Rock (77:35)—a verse in which God is not only described as Rock, but also as Redeemer. It is likely, then, that Paul fully intends for Christ, as Rock and Redeemer, to be read into the Old Testament story here as well. The Israelites tested God/Christ by complaining and not appreciating the miraculous provision; they challenged the idea that God was leading them to a better place (Num 21:5). Paul warns the Corinthians not to fall into the same sins (1 Cor 10:6–10), one of which is to test Christ by calling into question his plan of provision and salvation. It is fitting that the reason for the Israelites's grumbling was that they were not happy with their food; the Corinthian strong are grumbling because they are not happy with their food, either—they want to be free to eat more than the weak think is proper. Paul warns, in essence, that their appetite may lead to their destruction;[159] by eating meat sacrificed to idols, they are participating in the table of demons (10:20–21).

Thus, Paul's references to Christ's presence in the Israelite desert wanderings serve to emphasize the continuity between the effects of sin, specifically idolatry, in the old and new covenants. What happened to the Israelites when they challenged God/Christ is no less a danger for the Corinthians, who face the same God in Christ; they must flee from idolatry. That Christ can be tested, with the same results as the testing of God, indicates a strong emphasis on the unified action of Christ and God. Furthermore, it implies that Christ will judge in the same manner as God. Thus, Paul once again describes Jesus in roles (preexistent provider, redeemer, and ultimate judge) that are traditionally reserved for the divine. This passage demonstrates that Paul's one-God language in 8:6 does not preclude identifying Christ with God.

The next passage for consideration occurs only a few verses later. In 10:20–22 Paul argues: "No, I imply that what pagans sacrifice, they sacrifice to demons and not to God. I do not want you to be partners with de-

158. Seesemann, "πεῖρα."

159. Phil 3:19.

mons. You cannot drink the cup of the Lord and the cup of demons. You cannot partake of the table of the Lord and the table of demons. Or are we provoking the Lord to jealousy? Are we stronger than he?" These verses continue Paul's line of thought and his concern to link Christ and God so that the Corinthians will not wander into sin. In verse 20 a contrast is presented between the demons and God as the object of the sacrifice; in verse 21 the contrast is between demons and the Lord. "Lord" here clearly refers to Jesus and not to God,[160] since verse 16 states that the cup (the same term used in verse 20) is a sharing in the blood of Christ. The parallel is all the more significant because the first part of verse 20 is an allusion to Deut 32:17. The Song of Moses theme, begun in 10:1–11, continues here. The Israelites turned away from their rock and sacrificed to demons instead of to God; Paul warns the Corinthians not to do the same, lest they rouse the Lord's jealousy (v. 22). But here the "Lord" is Jesus, and nowhere in this passage does Paul make any attempt to distinguish between Jesus and God; rather, he lets stand the implicit comparison of Christ to God.

As noted earlier, Jewish monotheistic belief in the first century was concerned with fighting against paganism and dualism. In this passage, Paul is essentially equating Christ and God, in opposition to the demons. Since this text deals with the question of idol worship, an issue that goes to the core of Jewish beliefs about worshipping the one God (Exod 20:4; Deut 6:4; etc.), it is significant that Paul refers to Christ in opposition to demon worship.[161] This brings Christ within the scope of the one God, the "us" versus the "them" of the non-Christian world.

Another passage implying a functional relationship between God and Christ is 12:4–6: "Now there are varieties of gifts, but the same Spirit; and there are varieties of services, but the same Lord; and there are varieties of activities, but it is the same God who activates all of them in everyone."[162] Paul is again very concerned with unity in this section. He does not repeat the "one God" language (here it is the "same" God), but rather he takes it for granted; the discussion in chapters 8–10 has already set the stage

160. Conzelmann, *1 Corinthians*, 174 n. 39. Cf. Barrett, *Corinthians*, 238, who states that "Lord" in v. 22 refers to Christ.

161. Bauckham recognizes the significance of Paul's argument: "The implication for Jewish monotheism and Christology is remarkable: the exclusive devotion that YHWH jealously requires of his people is required of Christians by Jesus Christ. Effectively Jesus assumes the unique identity of YHWH" ("Biblical Theology," 223).

162. The NRSV translation here does not preserve the language at the end of v. 6 that God works "all in all."

for such a theological understanding. The oneness language here focuses instead on the one body (vv. 12, 13, 20), the one Spirit (vv. 11, 13), and the individual members of the body (vv. 8, 18, 26). After discussing the variety of gifts, Paul encourages the Corinthians to pursue love and to seek those gifts that build up the church (14:1–5). This entire section of the letter, chapters 12–14, begins with the unity language found in 12:4–6. Although one could argue that "Lord" in verse 5 refers to God, the previous reference to Jesus as Lord only two verses earlier strongly suggests that Jesus is the referent here as well. Certainly Paul gives no indication that he has changed his word usage. Paul is clearly drawing a parallel between the Spirit, Jesus, and God. His intent is to promote concord within the church, and he starts this process by underscoring unity within his understanding of the one God. The very reason that the Corinthians should not be in competition with one another is that they have all received their many blessings from the same God—that is, the same Spirit, Lord, and God.[163]

New Testament scholarship has long been wary of finding the Trinity in the New Testament. Certainly it is accurate to say that Paul does not purposefully set out in the extant letters to describe an organized doctrine of the Trinity. Nowhere does he formulate a Nicene-style definition of ontological divinity. But this does not mean that he had not contemplated God's identity in light of the Christ event. Rather, what Paul emphasizes here in 1 Cor 12:4–6 is an extremely close connection between the Spirit, the Lord, and God. The parallelism in these verses suggests that Paul "*experienced* God as Trinity."[164] Paul is thus describing a complexity within the oneness of God.[165] Throughout chapter 12, this interrelationship becomes apparent. The Spirit mediates a variety of gifts to believers (12:7–11); the Corinthians, who are recipients of these diverse gifts, together comprise

163. Barrett argues that "the Trinitarian formula is the more impressive because it seems to be artless and unconscious. Paul found it natural to think and write in these terms" (Barrett, *Corinthians*, 284). Conzelmann, however, does not find the language as compelling, and states that the order of the sequence is still free and is adapted to the context; it is not yet possible to speak of a Trinity (Conzelmann, *Corinthians*, 207; cf. n.4). Fee, in agreement with Barrett, states that one must note the "clear Trinitarian implications" of these verses; these passages are the "stuff" from which later Trinitarian thought is constructed. In addition, Fee argues that Paul ascribes full deity to both Christ and the Spirit in this passage (Fee, *Corinthians*, 588).

164. Hays, *First Corinthians*, 210.

165. As opposed to simple oneness. I am indebted to Stephen Barton for his suggestion of the term "complex oneness."

the body of Christ (12:12–13, 27), and God arranges all the parts (12:18, 24, 28). It is only as the Spirit, Christ, and God work together that a complete picture emerges, in which God works all in all (12:6). The point of the "all in all" language at the end of verse 6, which is echoed elsewhere in Paul's thought,[166] is not to place God over Christ and the Spirit, but to affirm that the one unique God, of whom Jesus and the Spirit are a part, is the source of all reality.[167]

The function of the introduction in 12:4–6, then, is to show the theological basis for unity within the church, a theme construed throughout the section. Although vast variety exists, all are joined in Christ (12:12–13). Paul focuses on the combined efforts of the Spirit, Lord, and God; he describes a complex oneness. Although some distinctions may occur between the Spirit, Lord, and God, together they ultimately work "all in all." Thus, the church ought to reflect this accord.

In this context, then, Paul's monotheistic understanding of God underscores the manner in which Yahweh, through Christ and the Spirit, provides the foundation for loving cooperation within the community of believers. The diversity within the divine identity does not detract from God's oneness, but enhances it.

The next set of passages that connect God and Christ functionally are the "Day of the Lord" passages, namely 1:7–8; 4:4b–5; 5:5; 11:26; 11:32; and 15:23–24. These texts, which either explicitly or implicitly speak to the Day of the Lord, give insight into Paul's eschatology. This, in turn, helps explain Paul's theology in light of the Christ event. 1 Corinthians suggests that, for Paul, the Day of the Lord involves the coming of Christ, the resurrection of the dead, revelation of hidden things, judgment of the wicked and the righteous, and the reign of God and Christ. Passages in Paul's other writings confirm these aspects of the Day of the Lord, as well as fill in some of the details (e.g., God's wrath, boasting in the holy church, and the suddenness of the Day's arrival).[168]

It is crucial to recognize that in these passages Paul uses "Lord" to refer to Jesus, and not to God.[169] Paul has, in effect, taken language

166. Cf. 1 Cor 8:6; Rom 11:36; Eph 4:4–6.

167. See Bauckham, *God Crucified*, 39, for comments on 1 Cor 8:6 and Rom 11:36 in this regard.

168. See, for example, 1 Thess 1:10; 2:19–20; 3:13; 4:15–17; 5:2, 23; 2 Cor 1:14; 5:10; Phil 1:6–10; 2:16; Rom 2:5–6, 16, 18; 13:12, 16:20.

169. The only passage where it is not entirely clear that Jesus is the referent is 1 Cor

that was used exclusively of Yahweh in the Old Testament and applied it to Christ. Yet the basic understanding of what that day would entail remains the same. For the prophets of the Old Testament, the Day of the Lord meant that at some point in the near future Yahweh would punish the enemies of his people, but also punish his people for breaking the covenant. Then, either through a new king/messiah or directly, Yahweh would establish his own kingdom.[170] The descriptions of the coming of the Lord recur throughout the variety of prophecies: the proud will be humbled and the Lord exalted, idols will disappear, men will be seized in fear and will hide in caves, the stars will not show their light, the sun will be darkened and the moon will turn to blood, God will punish the wicked and he himself will reign.[171] Gerhard von Rad describes the prophets's understanding of the Day of the Lord as one of holy war—yet this war will now affect all nations, including Israel, and will even affect the fixed orders of creation: "The event has been expanded into a phenomenon of cosmic significance."[172]

These themes, especially those of judgment and the coming and reign of God, are clearly basic to Paul's understanding of the eschaton. On one level we should expect this, given Paul's Jewish background. On another level, however, the application of these themes to Jesus as the one who comes in judgment is a significant new step.[173] Paul uses the same language of Christ's judgment as is ascribed to Yahweh in the Jewish Scriptures. Nowhere does Paul argue for a distinction between a time in which Christ will judge and a time in which God will mediate a different judgment; rather, such language appears to be interchangeable for him. Thus, the Day of the Lord (Yahweh) has become, for Paul, synonymous with the Day of the Lord Jesus Christ.[174] In fact, the specific titles that

---

4:4–5. Given Paul's descriptions elsewhere of Jesus coming and judging on the Day of the Lord, the natural reading is that "Lord" here too refers to Jesus.

170. Hiers, "Day of the Lord."

171. See, for, example, Isa 2:11–21; 13:6–22; 24:21–23; 34:1–4, 8; Jer 46:10; Ezek 30:3; Joel 1:15; 2:1–11; Amos 5:18–20; Zeph 1:7–8, 14–18; Zech 14:9.

172. von Rad, *Old Testament Theology*, 124.

173. Capes affirms that Paul "deliberately applied to Jesus these Old Testament concepts [Day of the Lord, the Second Coming, and judgment] originally reserved for Yahweh" (*Old Testament Yahweh Texts*, 88).

174. Kreitzer, *Jesus and God*, 129. Kreitzer argues that "a referential confusion and conceptual overlap between God and messianic representative is frequently present in those Pauline passages which speak of the Day of the Lord and are reliant upon theo-

Paul uses for Christ may be significant in this regard. Capes argues that "one reason for Paul's use of κύριος as a christological title was to apply to Jesus concepts and functions originally reserved for Yahweh in the Old Testament. No other christological title could serve to associate Jesus so closely with Yahweh."[175] As I have argued previously, if Paul had wished to distinguish between Jesus and God or to clearly define that Jesus did not share in the divine identity, he could have used other terms to describe Jesus. The fact that he uses a title that is so theologically heavily loaded, especially within this specific eschatological context, suggests that Paul intends to ascribe divine attributes to Jesus.

Furthermore, the Jewish view that God is known through his unique acts of creation and rule, combined with the fact that Paul understands Jesus as coming as the final judge, argues for the inclusion of Jesus within that unique divine identity. On the other hand, as noted previously, it is true that judgment in and of itself is not entirely unique to the divine identity. Paul even argues in 1 Cor 6:2–3 that the saints will judge both the world and angels.[176] Indeed, the closest analogy between Paul's understanding of Christ in Jewish literature might be found in statements about the Son of Man in the Enochic Similitudes. Is it not possible, then, that Paul is equating Christ with, for example, a figure like the Enochic Son of Man, and thus does not quite consider him uniquely divine?[177]

While it is certainly possible that Paul was aware of a Son of Man tradition as expressed in the Similitudes, and while such ideas may very well have influenced his understanding of Messiah, Paul's eschatological language more closely parallels Old Testament writings. He frequently uses "Day of the Lord" language,[178] an expression that is used extensively in the

---

centric Old Testament texts which have been christologically reinterpreted" (113). In his conclusion, Kreitzer states that the conceptual overlap occurs to such a degree that "Christ is specifically identified with God." However, he says that Paul clarifies and qualifies this identification by the means of the subordination of Christ to God (165). For a discussion of the role of subordination texts in 1 Corinthians, see pages 91–102.

175. Capes, *Old Testament Yahweh Texts*, 89.

176. See the discussion on pages 7–9 and 59–61.

177. Although the Son of Man is worshipped in the Similitudes (e.g., 62:9), this does not necessarily mean that he is considered to be uniquely divine with God. There is no evidence of any kind of cultic veneration of the Enochic Son of Man in Judaism, which (as Hurtado maintains) is an important indicator of monotheistic beliefs.

178. Paul's usage varies between "Day of the Lord," "Day of the Lord Jesus Christ," "Day of Christ," etc.

Old Testament but occurs in the Similitudes only once. Considering the frequency of judgment themes in *1 Enoch*, the lack of the phrase "Day of the Lord" is striking.[179] Thus, the continuity with Old Testament language and themes seems to indicate the Paul is drawing a comparison between Christ and God when he uses "Day of the Lord" imagery. Were he intending to compare Christ with the Enochic Son of Man, he likely would have used language more directly parallel with that text, rather than focusing on the "Day of the Lord."

Overall, then, these eschatological passages in Paul's letters suggest that his one-God theology nonetheless makes room for Christ within the divine identity. Christ performs the same functions as God and is referred to by the same title. Paul does not describe a two-stage judgment in which Christ is the lower court judge and God provides the final court of appeals. Rather, Paul's language about the judgment in the last days parallels that of the Jewish Scriptures and suggests that he understood Christ to perform the very acts of God.

As this variety of passages throughout 1 Corinthians has suggested, Paul's use of one-God language in 8:6 does not preclude him from drawing parallels between Jesus and God in a variety of ways. Several texts appear to focus on the continuity of salvation history and Jesus's role in God's plan (1:24, 30; 6:11; 9:21). In these texts, it is possible that Christ is being equated with God, but the argument does not necessarily hinge on such an understanding. Nonetheless, Paul emphasizes that God's redemption of humanity takes place in the Christ event; he cannot speak of one without discussing the other. God and Christ, through their activities, help to define one another.

In two places (1:3 and 7:17–24), Paul closely unites Christ and God in a manner that is perhaps unconscious. In the former he includes Christ within the scope of the deity, to whom a formulaic religious health wish is made, whereas in the latter he uses interchangeable language of God's calling/appointment. Paul does not feel a need to explain such language, which may indicate that his understanding of Christ's functions are already well developed and have been expressed to the Corinthians previously.

179. *1 En.* 60:24. In 61:5 the author uses the phrase "the day of the Elect One," but otherwise the references to the "day" describe the judgment itself rather than the figure who executes the judgment: e.g., "the great day of judgment" (22:11; 54:6; 84:4; 98:10), "the day of tribulation" (1:1), "the day of the great conclusion" (16:1), "the day of burden and tribulation" (45:2).

The most significant passages underscore the need for unity in the church, basing this exhortation on the unity of God (12:4–6), and also present a unified God over against pagan pluralism (10:20–21). Despite this emphasis, Paul does not hesitate to ascribe to Christ roles that in the Old Testament were reserved for God (10:4, 9; the "Day of the Lord" passages). He both ascribes preexistence to Jesus and proclaims that Jesus will be the final judge. Ultimately, God's actions and plans are so intrinsically connected to the person of Christ that Jesus cannot be separated from God without damaging the identity of the one God.[180]

PASSAGES THAT APPEAR TO IMPLY A HIERARCHY BETWEEN JESUS AND GOD

Despite the significant claims above, three passages in 1 Corinthians strongly suggest that a hierarchy exists between Jesus and God (3:21–23; 11:3; 15:27–28). Although they may not explicitly describe where the differences lie, these passages focus on distinction rather than on unity between Jesus and God. We cannot properly assess Paul's understanding of the relationship between Jesus and God and the function of his monotheistic language without taking these passages into consideration.

The first of these passages occurs in 3:21–23: "So let no one boast about human leaders. For all things are yours, whether Paul or Apollos or Cephas or the world or life or death or the present or the future—all belong to you, and you belong to Christ, and Christ belongs to God." This passage appears in the midst of Paul's response to the division regarding church leaders. On the surface, verses 22b–23 seem to indicate a hierarchy, with God at the top, then Christ, then the church, and finally all things. Indeed, commentators frequently make a distinction between soteriology and ontology in these verses, arguing that Christ is functionally subordinate to God, while ontologically he is still of one essence (to use a Nicene term) with the Father.[181] It is important to recall, however, that first-century Jews like Paul would not have thought in terms of ontological and functional distinctions.[182] Hierarchical constructions may reflect Hellenistic rather than Jewish thought; the Greeks tended to regard the

180. This does not mean that the two are the same "person," but rather that in their distinct persons they mutually define one another through their interdependent actions.

181. Barrett, *Corinthians*, 97–98; Fee, *Corinthians*, 155; Soards, *1 Corinthians*, 83.

182. Bauckham, *God Crucified*, 78.

supreme God as "the summit of a hierarchy of divinity, or the original source of a spectrum of divinity," but the Jews tended to accentuate "the absolute distinction between God and all else as the dominant feature of the whole Jewish worldview."[183]

So is Paul being influenced by Hellenistic philosophy here? Or is his intent actually quite different? On the face of it, his argument is rather perplexing. His point is to keep the Corinthians from boasting, but to keep them from boasting, he gives them more to boast about: all things are theirs! So what does Paul mean here?

A good place to start in answering this question is to consider the nature of the relationship between "all things" and the Corinthians. Paul includes three antithetical sets within his definition of all things: 1) the church (as represented by Paul, Apollos and Cephas) and the world, 2) life and death, and 3) the present and the future. A similar list occurs in Rom 8:37–38, although the list there is longer and not strictly paired—it includes death and life and present and future, but also adds angels and demons, powers, height and depth, and anything else in creation. In Romans, Paul's point is that nothing can separate believers from the love of God in Christ Jesus. The list is meant to demonstrate the all-inclusiveness of "all things." A similar emphasis can be seen in the 1 Corinthians text: when Paul refers to "all things," he is not just limiting his discussion to the things of the church. He truly means *all* things. The difficulty lies in the fact Paul does not use a verb other than ἐστιν to clarify his meaning. If the genitive here is a simple possessive, then how is it that all things (including both believers and the unbelieving "world") belong to the Corinthians in the same manner that Christ belongs to God? If Christ is subordinate to God and the Corinthians are subordinate to Christ, then how are all things—including Paul, who elsewhere claims his authority as an apostle[184]—subordinate to the Corinthians? A strict subordinationist hierarchy does not make sense of these intricacies.

It is necessary to keep in mind that these verses follow upon the contrast between the wisdom of the world and the wisdom of God; in fact, Paul revives this idea in the verses directly preceding (3:18–20). When he warns against boasting in human leaders, then, he is again addressing the wisdom of the world and calling it foolishness. In the Old Testament, boasting (in the negative sense) is regarded as the basic attitude of the

183. Ibid., 16.

184. 1 Cor 1:1; 9:1–2.

foolish and ungodly; it involves a person trying to stand on his or her own feet and build on what they themselves can accomplish and control, rather than depending on and trusting in God.[185] For Paul, the only legitimate boasting is in Jesus Christ.[186] Paul faults the Corinthians for depending on their associations with things of the world, for depending on the status found in associating with a particular leader.[187] The ultimate value, the ultimate reality that gives a person boasting rights is the attachment to the one true God ("Let the one who boasts boast in the Lord," 1:31.) Yet, paradoxically, the one true God in whom the Corinthians ought to boast is the same God who revealed himself in Jesus's humiliating death on a cross. Jesus's exaltation, and thus boasting rights, came through humility. Rather than the Corinthians foolishly boasting in their leaders and thus falling victim to the "wisdom" of the world, the world ought to boast in the Corinthians, since they are associated with Christ, who is associated with God.

Paul develops some of these ideas further in 2 Cor 5:16–21, when he again contrasts human knowledge with a more full knowledge of Christ. In verse 19 Paul explains that God was reconciling the world to himself through Christ. In addition, Paul explains that he is an ambassador for Christ. Thus, again this sense of association or relationship is apparent; it begins with God, is mediated through Christ to believers, and ultimately spreads to the world. This parallel is instructive for interpreting 1 Cor 3:21–23. Paul is trying to impress upon the Corinthians that their boasting is misplaced if it relies on the reputations of mere men. Ultimately, the world can be reconciled to God; it is for this reason that Paul says the world is theirs—because the final status and fate of the world depends on whether or not the world receives the true wisdom from the Corinthian believers. 1 Cor 6:2–3 further reminds the Corinthians of their high position (even if it may seem lowly to those with human "wisdom"): the saints will judge the world, and even angels. Even Paul and his work will be judged on the basis of the Corinthians themselves (1 Cor 3:12–15). Further evidence of these themes in Paul's thinking appears in the great Christ hymn of Phil 2:5–11. In that text, Paul uses Christ's humility to demonstrate that selfish ambition is not the way of the cross. Contrary to

185. Bultmann, "καυχάομαι," 3:646.

186. Ibid., 649.

187. Note the similar genitive construction in the Corinthians's claims to be "of Paul" or "of Apollos" in 1:12 and 3:4.

the demands of the Greco-Roman culture, it is only in the act of servanthood that one is truly exalted, and even this is to the glory of God the father. Paul even brings this idea of servanthood to the fore in 1 Cor 4:1, when he describes himself and the other leaders of the church as servants of Christ and stewards of the mysteries of God.

In 1 Cor 3:21–23, then, Paul is trying to remind the Corinthians that they no longer belong to the world. No longer are they under the control of the world, influenced by its every whim. Rather, the fate of the world belongs to the Corinthians, who belong to Christ, who belongs to God. Hence, even though the world is in the hands of the Corinthians, the Corinthians must keep in mind that true boasting involves humility—it involves trusting God and not oneself. The Corinthians thus should not put themselves above Christ, just as Christ would not put himself above God.

Indeed, the whole of chapter 3 is very theocentric. In 3:5–10, for example, Paul tries to quash leadership rivalries by ascribing all growth to God. He refers to the Corinthians as the temple of God (3:16–17), and in 3:19–20 affirms God's wisdom. This entire passage focuses on God as the source of the Corinthian church. The seemingly hierarchical language of 3:21–23, then, serves to check Corinthian pride by reminding them of the proper order of creation—all things are ultimately grounded in God. While it may seem presently that the world holds the key to status, it is really the message of the cross (and the humility it espouses) that provides the blueprint for the proper foundations of right relationships. Paul's focus is not on delineating the specific relationship between God and Christ. Rather, the theological statement supports his ethical exhortation regarding boasting and emphasizes the necessity of keeping one's pride within certain boundaries. Paul's language, therefore, should not be interpreted as portraying a strict hierarchy between Christ and God. This is neither his motivation nor his intent. Rather, he aims to realign the Corinthians's priorities by reminding them that their definitive status is only achieved by their relationship with the one God.[188]

In the second passage for consideration, 11:3, Paul states, "But I want you to understand that Christ is the head of every man, and the husband is the head of his wife, and God is the head of Christ." This pas-

188. Note that the interpretation outlined here fits better with the Jewish emphasis on the distinctiveness of God over against pagan idolatry; it thus avoids the pitfall of importing Hellenistic philosophical categories into Jewish thought.

sage introduces a section on propriety in worship, a section in which the meaning of the word "head" (κεφαλή) fluctuates.[189] The overall argument in verses 2–16 addresses the question of head coverings; Paul states that men should not cover their heads during worship, while women should. He cites a number of reasons, but for this study the most important lies in his emphasis on the nature of creation, which he sets up through this apparently hierarchical language. The reason for the head coverings lies in the relationship between man, woman, Christ, and God. These relationships appear to be roughly parallel; at least, Paul does not state that God being the "head" of Christ is any different than man being the "head" of woman.

In order to understand Paul's argument, it is necessary to determine what he means by "head." In the vast majority of uses of the term κεφαλή in the Greco-Roman writings, the term refers to a literal, physical head.[190] Indeed, that is the meaning in a number of places in chapter 11.[191] Nonetheless, in several instances the term appears to have a metaphorical meaning.[192] But does the metaphor *necessarily* imply a hierarchy of authority? The use of the term elsewhere in Greek writings suggests that in some cases the term can imply a hierarchy, while in others it can refer to a source or origin.[193] For a variety of reasons, delineated below, the interpretation of "head" that makes the most sense here is "source." Christ is the source of *every* man—not just Christians—because Christ is the ground of all humanity (Col 1:16).[194] Man is the source of woman in the sense that she was created from his flesh (Gen 2:18–23). Paul emphasizes this again in verses 8 and 12. God is the source of Christ in that Christ comes from God and fulfills his purposes.

189. For discussion on the various interpretations of κεφαλή in the New Testament, see Grudem, "Does κεφαλή ('Head') Mean 'Source' or 'Authority'?"; Bilezikian, "Appendix"; Mickelson, "What Does *Kephale* Mean?"; Cervin, "Does κεφαλή Mean 'Source' or 'Authority Over'?"; Grudem, "Meaning of kephalē"; Fitzmyer, "*Kephale* in 1 Corinthians 11:3"; and Perriman, "Head of Woman."

190. This is one of the few points on which Grudem and Bilezikian agree.

191. The first reference in v. 4, the first reference in v. 5, and vv. 7 and 10.

192. The three references in v. 3, the second reference in v. 4 and the second reference in v. 5.

193. Grudem does not allow for any uses which imply "source or origin," although Bilezikian ("Appendix," 221–33) notes several instances in which Grudem's interpretation is skewed and does not allow for the possibility even where it is warranted.

194. Barrett, *Corinthians*, 249.

Although it may appear on the surface that Paul argues for a hierarchy, a number of factors call this into question. In verse 7, for example, Paul seemingly argues for a hierarchy based on the priority of origin, a common ancient ideology.[195] But even if this was a common argument, it does not necessarily follow that Paul is using the priority of origin here. Elsewhere in the letter, being first is not necessarily a good thing: in Adam all die, but in Christ all will be made alive (15:22). In addition, what is omitted from verse 7 is just as important as what is included: man is the image *and* glory of God, whereas woman is *only* the glory of man—she is not the image of man, because she, too, is the image of God.[196] This fact makes subordination difficult to justify. It is also important to note that the structure of 11:3 does not support a hierarchical interpretation. If Paul were seeking to introduce a strict hierarchy, then logically one would expect his argument to flow as follows: God is the head of Christ, Christ is the head of man, and man is the head of woman. But Paul's approach is not so linear, and this suggests that an alternate interpretation may be preferable.

The current investigation into 8:6 is helpful in this regard. There it was clear that Paul referred to God as the source of all things, and he used the preposition ἐκ to make this statement. In 11:12 he uses the same preposition to state that all things are of God. Once again, God is the source. Yet this is precisely the place in which Paul is explaining that the woman is ἐκ the man. Man is the source of the woman. The LXX makes this connection when Adam describes Eve as being made ἐκ man (Gen 2:23). In contrast, Paul uses the term διά to describe man's relationship to woman. He is not ἐκ woman, because she is not the source in the Genesis account. Rather, in childbirth, the man is born through the agency of a woman. Thus, the specific terms Paul uses here speak to origins, not to hierarchy.[197]

Even so, Paul here emphasizes the distinctions—man and woman are not the same, and so the requirements for head coverings are not the same. The cultural context of honor and shame helps to explain these

195. Martin, *Corinthian Body*, 232, 295 n. 14.

196. Bruce, *Corinthians*, 105.

197. Although there is not have space here to flesh this out more fully, Paul's treatment of women elsewhere in his letters suggests that he considers them to be equals. His references to women as deacons, coworkers, and apostles argue against a hierarchical interpretation of the relationship between men and women.

differences: a male finds honor, in part, by protecting the purity of the women within his sphere of protection, whereas women maintain their purity "by thwarting even the most remote advances to or invasion of their symbolic space."[198] The head covering was a symbol of such purity; when a married woman publicly removed her veil, for example, she was stating that she was promiscuous.[199] Given this context, Paul appears to be wary of the potential mixed messages a woman would signal if she prayed or prophesied with her head uncovered. Although she has freedom in Christ, this freedom does not nullify the messages communicated by certain actions within Greco-Roman culture. Paul also may be suggesting the possibility that women who pray or prophesy publicly expose themselves to male erotic fantasies; thus, they should wear a head covering to signify that the male/female relationship, in terms of *eros*, is superseded in Christ.[200] Therefore, this passage focuses on the proper way, culturally speaking, of focusing on God and not the individual during worship. Furthermore, the passage focuses on the interdependence of men and women, rather than on a hierarchical or egalitarian structure.[201] Although the body of Christ brings about a new unity, this does not mean that men and women are independent of one another or that their actions no longer reflect upon one another. Instead, believers need to be aware of the statement that their actions make within the larger culture. In addition, this argument for interdependence makes more sense of the almost circular Christ–man/man–woman/God–Christ structure than does a hierarchical perspective.

In a similar manner, the angels also provide cause for a woman to cover her head (11:10). This phrase probably refers to two traditions. First, a number of Qumran texts suggest that angels are present during worship.[202] Second, both Gen 6:1–2 and *1 En.* 6–16 record the story of

198. Malina and Neyrey, "Honor and Shame in Luke-Acts," 42. Note the language of shame (καταισχύνει, αἰσχρόν, ἀτιμία) in vv. 4–6, 14.

199. Winter, *Roman Wives, Roman Widows*, 93.

200. F. Watson, "Authority of the Voice," 532.

201. In agreement with Watson. He errs, however, in identifying 11:3 as containing unmistakable "hierarchical conceptuality," but he argues that the role of this verse is "remarkably limited" ("Authority of the Voice," 529).

202. See Fitzmyer, "Feature of Qumran Angelology," 198. Some scholars, such as Barrett (*Corinthians*, 254), suggest that Paul is encouraging the women to veil the glory of man (which then brings focus on the glory of God), and thus conform to the created order. This prevents giving offense to the angels who are present during worship. Under this interpretation, however, it is difficult to see how uncovered female heads bring glory

angels who sinned by coming to earth and impregnating human women. In this context, Paul's use of "head" to indicate "source" makes a great deal of sense. Angels have a potential sexuality and thus could fall into temptation because of women—especially women who appear sexually available because of their lack of head covering. This defies the natural order of things: man and woman were originally one,[203] with God creating woman from man (her source); God intended that the two come together again and become one flesh (Gen 2:24). Thus, woman was meant for man and not for angels. By veiling herself, the woman both hides her beauty from the angels who are present during worship, thus decreasing angelic temptation, and she also places "authority" over her head—in effect, she declares that she is off limits to the angels and is intended for man.[204]

Indeed, Stuckenbruck affirms that the worldview of Paul and the Corinthians was one in which humans and angels shared social space. Because angels were often depicted in terms of male sexuality and women were assumed to be particularly vulnerable to invasion, Paul offers a "warning that more than just social relationships between men and women are at stake; ultimately, wearing veils is a matter of maintaining the cosmic order. The head coverings are prophylactic in the sense that they protect this order by helping to draw boundaries between distinct, yet sometimes socially overlapping, spheres more clearly."[205]

The apparently hierarchical language that begins this section, then, is crucial for Paul's argument. Yet the hierarchy is not so much one of authority as it is one of derivation. God has made man and woman for one another (v. 12), but even more so, their existence is grounded in Christ and God. In worship, then, believers need to reflect these realities and be careful not to communicate a different message. Women should not unintentionally imply that they are promiscuous or independent of their husbands; rather, a woman should cover her head as a symbol of her purity and fidelity. Women should also be aware of the potential for

---

to men; rather, it would bring shame upon men to have the women of their household suggesting they are sexually promiscuous.

203. I am not arguing that Adam was originally androgynous or bisexual, although strains of such an idea have been found in ancient Jewish thought (see Barrett, *Corinthians*, 255).

204. Such a declaration then would be similar to today's custom of wearing a wedding ring. If a married woman walked into a nightclub full of single men, she would be making quite a statement if she "unveiled" herself by slipping off her wedding ring.

205. Stuckenbruck, "Why Should Women Cover Their Heads?" 231.

eros, encountered by both men and angels, which offers the possibility of distraction. Thus, the head covering makes a statement to those angels present that the woman is respecting the natural order of things. It also makes a statement to the men present that male/female relationships are superseded in Christ; the distinctions between men and women, which have not been erased, are recognized—as is the interdependence of men and women.

In a setting in which schisms are frequent, Paul's focus on interdependence once again underscores unity. The interdependence of Christ and God provides a model for Paul to use in promoting interdependence among the worshippers at Corinth. What may thus appear on the surface to be a passage separating Christ and God is in reality a passage meant to describe their close relationship. The establishment of a hierarchy would only serve to defeat Paul's purposes in the letter, because it would only increase the schisms within the church. But for Paul, the close relationship between God and Christ provides the perfect example for promoting peaceable relationships in Corinth. God and Christ are not independent of one another; they cannot do whatever they want without regard for the other. In a similar manner, the Corinthian women must be aware of the honor/shame implications of their actions. Their freedom in Christ does not provide a warrant for actions that, in the larger cultural setting, would bring disgrace to the church of God.

The final passage for consideration is 15:27–28: "For 'God has put all things in subjection under his feet.' But when it says, 'All things are put in subjection,' it is plain that this does not include the one who put all things in subjection under him. When all things are subjected to him, then the Son himself will also be subjected to the one who put all things in subjection under him, so that God may be all in all." This passage speaks the loudest for a relationship of subordination between God and Christ. The language arises because Paul is addressing the question of the resurrection of the dead, and he argues forcefully that Christ has been bodily raised from the dead. In describing Christ's triumph, Paul states that all things—except God—will be subjected to Christ.[206] Paul overturns the argument of those who say there is no resurrection of

206. Kreitzer (*Jesus and God*, 159–60) finds rough parallels in Eph 1:10 (all things will be brought together under one head, Christ) and Col 1:18 (that in everything Christ might have supremacy). But he notes that in neither passage is there any subordinating phrase comparable to that in 1 Cor 15:28c.

the dead by arguing that if this is so then Christ is already at the bottom of the hierarchy—he is food for worms, as will be the rest of the believers. But Paul says the opposite is true: rather than Christ being at the bottom, he is at the top—he rules over all things, and will finally destroy death itself. To reinforce his argument, Paul quotes Ps 110:1 (the Old Testament passage most often quoted in the New Testament) in verse 25 and Ps 8:6 in verse 27. In Psalm 110, sitting at the right hand of the Father is a significant concept. Martin Hengel describes it as "the transference of divine authority and judgment; at the same time it is the most intimate relation of one who is chosen by God with God himself. He who sits at the right hand of God participates directly in his reign."[207] Paul's intentional use of this scripture, therefore, suggests that he understands Jesus as uniquely participating in God's divine acts of judgment and rule; Christ shares in the divinity of the one God.

Yet as soon as Paul makes this statement, he immediately clarifies it by maintaining that Christ's work does not displace God as supreme ruler.[208] Here as elsewhere Paul is keen to emphasize the proper order of things—everything has its own distinct place in the universe.[209] This is his argument in 15:39–41, for example, where he discusses the varied glory of heavenly and earthly bodies.[210] As much as Paul wants to declare the new covenant and the changes that Christ has wrought, he is careful not to state that the entire order of creation has changed. Rather, Paul argues that, for all of the newness found in Christ, these events are still part of God's overall design and order for the universe. Paul underscores this in verse 34, when he argues that those who deny the resurrection are sinning and are ignorant of God. Just as in chapters 8–10, Paul connects a proper knowledge of God to right action.

As we know from the disputes of the second century, Paul was right to be concerned about the development of a wedge between God and Christ. Less than one hundred years after Paul wrote to the Corinthians,

207. Hengel, *Studies in Early Christology*, 185.

208. Indeed, Barrett argues that these verses describe "the moment of the establishing of the kingdom of God. The apocalyptic scheme of thought takes God as the rightful king of the universe" (*Corinthians*, 356–57).

209. For the Pauline emphasis on order in this section, including the political overtones of such ordering, see N. T. Wright, *Resurrection of the Son*, 335–38.

210. The argument in these verses concerns the difference between physical and spiritual bodies; nevertheless, Paul's argument is that each kind of body has its own unique place—"God gives to each the body he has chosen" (v. 38).

Marcion's distinction between the God of the Old Testament and the God of the New caused great distress among the early churches. Although gnosticism was not fully formed until the second century, the roots of these ideas may have had some influence in Paul's time.[211] It appears that Paul was able to envisage the potential trajectories of his opponents's theology. As he described the way in which the Law's role had changed since the advent of Christ,[212] perhaps Paul was concerned that the God associated with the giving of that Law would similarly diminish in importance.[213] As a preemptive response, then, the apparently hierarchical language serves not to separate God and Christ but, paradoxically, to join them together. When Jesus hands the kingdom over to God at the end, it is an affirmation that the God of the Jews has indeed accomplished all that he promised; the original plan has been fulfilled.

Yet Paul could not allow himself to end with the idea of Christ handing over the kingdom to God. This would leave unanswered the question of what happens to Christ at that point, and could even imply that Christ hands over the kingdom and has no further involvement with God. But for Paul, Christ and God cannot be separated,[214] and so he adds the statement that Christ will subject himself to God. By subjecting himself, Christ is returning to the source from which he came. Christ confirms in his subjection that his sphere of reality belongs within God's sphere of reality—there is no separation between the two.[215] He is, in a sense, returning home. And thus, God is found to be "all in all." This is true not

211. Conzelmann, *1 Corinthians*, 15.

212. See, e.g., Rom 7:4–6; 2 Cor 3:6–18; Gal 3:23–25.

213. Orr and Walther suggest that the subjection statement "seems so obvious that it may perhaps hint at some confusion in Corinth that Paul perceives as a dangerous misunderstanding of the relation of Christ and God." They further argue that Paul does not intend a subordinationist Christology, but rather he "is determined to set forth God as *the all in all*" (*1 Corinthians*, 334).

214. By this I do not mean to imply they are one person, for they clearly are distinct. Rather, I'm arguing that Christ and God are unified in their will and purposes. They share in the divinity of the one God.

215. See also Bruce, who argues that this passage emphasizes the oneness of God: the kingdom of Christ merges into the kingdom of God, and in this way the promise that the Messiah's kingdom will know no end is fulfilled. Christ then subjects himself to God, "but since the Son is the image and revelation of the Father, 'Father and Son are really one in this activity'" (*Corinthians*, 148). In the final statement, Bruce quotes from Cullmann, *Christology of the New Testament*, 293.

only because Christ finds his fullness in communion with God, but also because God cannot be all in all without Christ.

The exploration of these three passages suggests that when Paul uses language about Christ and God that appears hierarchical, it occurs in contexts where he emphasizes the created order. That is, Paul feels the need to encourage the Corinthians to remember that God is ultimately the source of all things. Those who boast ought to boast in God, not man, for the ultimate fate of the world is in God's hands. Those who pray and prophesy must recognize and proclaim in culturally appropriate ways their interdependence, which is modeled by Christ and God. Those who question the resurrection of the dead need to comprehend Christ's ultimate triumph over death, a triumph which is part of God's plan and does not supersede it.

In none of these passages is Paul's primary focus to define the relationship between God and Christ, although even within these apparently hierarchical texts Paul describes Christ as functioning in divine roles alongside God (15:25). Rather, Paul uses the relationship between God and Christ to illustrate further principles within the larger argument. The unity of God and Christ promotes unity among the church. God is the source of all things, including Christ; Christ without God is not Christ, but equally, God without Christ is not "all in all."

CONCLUSIONS CONCERNING THE FUNCTION AND COHERENCE OF PAUL'S ONE-GOD LANGUAGE IN 1 CORINTHIANS

Paul's purpose in using one-God language is not primarily to correct Corinthian convictions about the numerical oneness of God. Rather, Paul's language assumes they are in agreement about the inclusion of Christ within the divine identity. Paul's own experience of the risen Christ and his reinterpretation of the Jewish Scriptures led him to this realization, a conclusion that must have been part of his original teaching to the Corinthians since he feels no need to explicitly justify it in his letter. Paul thus describes a complexity within the oneness of God: the one divine identity is expressed in the work of both God and Christ.

Furthermore, the one-God language is central to Paul's argument regarding the eating of idol meats. Paul aims to correct the ethical inferences the Corinthians have drawn from their monotheistic conviction; namely, Paul seeks to heal divisions by teaching the Corinthians about self-sacrificing love. For Paul, love of the one God is inextricably bound together with love of others. The Corinthians have not made this connection, and so Paul must correct their theology in order to correct their ethics.

The language about God and its impact on the language about Christ throughout the rest of the letter on the surface seems erratic. But because of the different ethical contexts throughout the letter, the purpose of the monotheistic language varies from discussion to discussion and serves to support the larger argument. In those contexts where Paul is eager to emphasize the created order of the world and God's ultimate control over that order, he tends to use one-God language that on the surface appears hierarchical (3:23; 11:3; 15:28). Paul is very concerned to respect the uniqueness and authority of the one God; this one God creates, rules, and designs the order of the universe. Paul in no way wants to imply that Christ has created an entirely new reality or that he is separate from God the Father. Believers are new creations in Christ (2 Cor 5:17), but Christ's work is part of the overall divine plan (Rom 8:28–30). Furthermore, this unified action of Christ and God helps Paul to underscore the interdependence of believers in their interactions with one another. They are not independent of each other, but must continually be concerned about how their actions influence those around them. Paul's apparently hierarchical language thus is not intended to diminish Christ in any way, but to affirm God's design throughout salvation history. God is the source of all reality. Hence, Christ is not and cannot separate himself from God—the incarnational Christ returns to the source of all that is, to the one who, with Christ, is "all in all."

Furthermore, throughout 1 Corinthians and despite the one-God language, Paul frequently describes God and Christ as functioning in a similar manner (1:3; 1:23–24, 30; 6:11; 7:17–24; 8:4–6; 9:21; 10:4–9, 20–21; 12:4–6; and "Day of the Lord" passages). Often these passages emphasize unity, especially unity of the one God over against the pagan world. Jesus and God together are one, as one God and one Lord.[216] The oneness they share is the source of all things; it is wisdom, it has authority. The new revelation in Christ is not to be compromised with non Christian beliefs in the surrounding Hellenistic culture, because Christ is a fulfillment of

216. Paul would also include the Spirit, although the Spirit has not been the focus of this particular investigation.

the one God's plan. Not only does Christ fulfill the plan, but Christ was present (i.e., preexistent) in the "old" plan; Christ and God are one. As one, Christ and God are worshipped. As one, God and Christ were with Israel in the desert. As one, they offer grace and peace and wash, sanctify, justify, call, and gift the believer. Both who God is and what God does are inextricably linked to who Christ is and what Christ does.

Therefore, Paul's one-God language, while on the surface appearing unreflected and inconsistent, nonetheless maintains a strong undercurrent of coherence. Paul is not thinking systematically when he uses monotheistic language, but this does not mean that he has no fundamental convictions about the oneness of God. For Paul, God's unique divine identity involves God as the source of all things, creator, ruler, and coherent designer. The new revelation in Christ represents the fullness of God's overall scheme to draw his people to himself. To be sure, some things said of Christ are not, strictly speaking, said about God: Christ is God's wisdom (1:24, 30), he is the Passover Lamb (5:7), he was the rock in the wilderness (10:4), he is the last Adam (15:45–49). But rather than stressing Christ's distinct identity, Paul emphasizes continuity in salvation history. God and Christ, through their distinct and mutual actions, define one another. For this reason Paul can describe Christ as the source, with God, of "all things" (8:6), and he can use "Day of the Lord" language in reference to Christ (1:5–8; 5:4–5). Thus, Paul underscores the role Christ has always had and will continue to have in God's grand design. Christ and God together are all in all.

3

The Superior Mediator

Galatians 3:20

INTRODUCTION

PAUL'S USE OF ONE-GOD language in Galatians is vastly different from his use in 1 Corinthians. Here there is no explicit reference to Christ, no side-by-side language of the unity of God and Christ. Rather, within the argument contrasting the promise and the Law, Paul makes an obscure comment about mediators and the one God. Because this reference is difficult to comprehend, many commentators have dismissed the significance of Paul's monotheistic foundations. I will argue, however, that the theme of oneness is intertwined throughout the entire section; what appears to be simply an aside instead is integral to Paul's argument.

It is perhaps ironic that a text describing God's oneness should have innumerable interpretations. Indeed, scholars have consistently struggled to uncover Paul's intended meaning in Gal 3:20. A suitable way to begin this section, then, is to present a brief survey and critique of some of the more common expositions of this text. Many of these interpretations are very similar and overlap to some extent, but the nuances vary.

First, some scholars maintain that Paul argues the Law is inferior to the promise because God gave it indirectly, both through angels and by a mediator, whereas God gave the promise directly to Abraham. Dunn, for example, takes this approach. He argues that the association of the Law with angels was not unfamiliar in Jewish thought, and that as such it was an unthreatening motif. Paul is not denying that the Law originated with God; the angels's role is simply mediatory.[1] Paul's argument at first seems to be an attempt to find support in the Jewish concept of monotheism, Dunn argues, but the "real point is that God does not need an intermediary." Paul is thus contrasting the Law given through intermediaries and the promise given by God directly to Abraham.[2] This viewpoint, however, does not adequately take into account the overall positive view of mediation that existed in Jewish thought.[3] Mediation was an integral part of the Jewish belief system, and Moses was held in high esteem because he was God's mediator to the people. Thus, mediation itself is not likely to be the issue.

Second, some scholars focus on the distinction between direct and indirect intervention, but they especially emphasize the theme of oneness in Paul's thought. Hans Dieter Betz, for example, states that in Paul's reasoning the Torah is inferior to the promise because it was not given directly but through "subaltern divine beings."[4] This inferiority is not due to the angels themselves, but to the fact that mediation itself involves a plurality of parties: "Paul argues that anything that stands in contrast to the oneness of God is inferior. Since the concept of mediator presupposes by definition a plurality of parties, it is inferior and, consequently, renders the Torah inferior."[5] Betz cites some evidence in Jewish tradition that God's direct proclamation is superior to mediation (e.g., 1QH 6.13 and *Pesiq. Rab.* 21.5). Betz concludes that Paul implies "the process of divine redemption requires conformity to the oneness of God"—a soteriology reflected throughout Galatians by Paul's focus on one God, one redeemer Christ, one gospel, one church, and one fruit of the Spirit.[6] Betz's view suffers from similar problems as the first argument, in that he does not consider the overall positive view of mediation in Judaism. Prophets, priests, and kings were all God's mediators, yet

1. Dunn, *Epistle to the Galatians*, 191. See also Dunn, *Theology of Galatians*.

2. Dunn, *Epistle to the Galatians*, 191. See also Mussner, *Galaterbrief*; Barrett, *Freedom and Obligation*, 34; and Barclay, *Obeying the Truth*, who notes that Paul contrasts the direct address of the promise with the indirect gift of the Law; he finds that even though Paul tries to distance God from the Law, "he does not quite deny that God is the ultimate author of the law" (91 n. 41).

3. See this chapter's discussion on "The Mediator."

4. Betz, *Galatians*, 169–70.

5. Ibid., 171–72.

6. Ibid., 172–73. See also Longenecker, who argues that the law is inferior because it was received indirectly, "whereas God's redemptive activity is always direct and unilateral in nature, reflecting the oneness of his person" (*Galatians*, 143).

these same prophets, priests, and kings fully affirmed God's oneness. Their status as mediators did not inherently place them in opposition to God's oneness. In addition, the sources Betz cites are not as convincing as he suggests. 1QH 6.13 refers to men not needing a mediator to reply to God; the context thus does not apply to mediation of the Law. Also, although *Pesiq. Rab.* 21.5 does refer to God giving the Law directly to Israel, it is important to realize both that this is a late text and that the argument nevertheless includes Moses's role as mediator of the Law to the people. Thus, mediation itself cannot be the issue.

A third argument also affirms a contrast between indirect and direct origins of the Law and the promise, but focuses more explicitly on God's grace as the reason that the direct approach is better. Ronald Y. K. Fung argues that Paul defines mediation as involving a plurality of parties who must both agree to the terms of the contract in order for the contract to be effective. Under this understanding, Paul argues that the promise is superior because it is "a unilateral disposition dependent solely on God's sovereign grace."[7] Donald Guthrie develops this concept further. He notes the importance of God's direct address of the promise: the means indicates the esteem with which a thing is held. For example, a difference exists between a king who sends an ambassador to negotiate a treaty and a king who negotiates the treaty himself: "The peace would be the same, but the importance of the mission would be differently construed."[8] Paul's focus here is thus on the numerical unity cited to support the superiority of the promise over the Law. Guthrie concludes, "God consulted with no others when he made the promises to Abraham. They were his own supreme declarations. But the law was different, because this was essentially a contract which depended on the good faith of both parties concerned, and if one party failed a mediator would be necessary. But with a promise it is all in the hands of one person, i.e., the giver."[9] This interpretation, as the others, errs in its presuppositions about mediation. Jewish mediators did not act as a neutral third party who brought two parties together; rather, they acted as God's spokesman. Mediation was a matter of explaining God's will to the people—not negotiating with them. When viewed in

7. Fung, *Epistle to the Galatians*, 161–62.

8. Guthrie, *Galatians*, 105.

9. Ibid., 106.

this light, the contrast between the Law and the promise collapses. God's grace is involved in both.

Fourth, some scholars perceive the identification of an *angelic* mediator as the key that will unlock the meaning of the passage. F. F. Bruce, for example, looks carefully at the grammar of 3:20 in order to determine the identity of the mediator. The term "mediator" does not necessitate two pluralities, he argues; a mediator can just as easily mediate between two individuals, between an individual and a plurality, or between two pluralities.[10] The solution to determining the identity of the mediator and thus uncovering the meaning of the passage, he argues, is the logical relation between the ἑνός in the first clause and the εἷς in the second. "If a mediator is not 'of one,' whereas God is 'one,' it follows that the mediator to whom Paul refers here is not God's mediator."[11] Although some scholars have suggested that Moses is representing the angels, Bruce agrees with A. Vanhoye[12] that the angel of the presence who was with Moses in the wilderness was the mediator on behalf of the angels just as Moses was the mediator on behalf of the Israelites. Vanhoye compares the situation to David and Goliath, who represented their people for war; here, the mediators represented their respective parties for communication. Bruce considers Vanhoye's interpretation to be "the best solution of the problem."[13] Bruce's analysis rightly investigates the nuances of Paul's grammatical choices and highlights the contrast between the mediator and God in verse 20. Yet this evaluation does not ultimately solve the interpretive problem. If the angelic mediator is not of God, then the Law is not of God; elsewhere, however, Paul affirms the holiness of the Law.[14]

10. Bruce, *Commentary on Galatians*, 179.

11. Ibid.

12. Vanhoye, "Un mediateur des anges en Ga 3,19–20."

13. Bruce, *Commentary on Galatians*, 179.

14. See, e.g., Rom 7:12. Francis Watson argues that Paul believed Torah was derived from multiple angelic sources, and this is the reason for the apparent contradictions within the Law itself: one angel provides one teaching, while a different angel provides a contrary teaching (*Paul and Hermeneutics*, 520). Under this view, however, it would appear that the oneness of God is threatened. If the one God allows his angels to provide contradictory advice to his people, then either God's supervision over his messengers is lax (or ineffective), and he is not truly Lord over all, or he is unconcerned about the harmful effects of such teaching on his people, in which case he is hardly worthy of worship.

A fifth approach, which is similar to Bruce's perspective but much more negative, finds a great divide in salvation history. This conclusion is based on the interpretation that God was not involved in the giving of the Law, and thus the Law is one of the cosmic powers (στοιχεῖα) which enslave humanity. J. Louis Martyn takes this position, arguing that the Law was instituted by angels in God's absence.[15] The stunning implication of God's absence (and the temporary nature of the Law) is that the "nomistic election of Israel seems to be placed in question, if not excluded."[16] Martyn does not argue that Paul denies the election of Israel (he cites Rom 4, Rom 9–11, etc.), but states that if Galatians were the only letter we had from which to extract Paul's views, we might conclude Paul did not believe in the divine election of Israel. Martyn's argument, however, downplays the language of 3:19, in which the verbs προσετέθη and διαταγείς imply divine ordination.[17] Martyn admits the verbs can be taken this way, but argues that because Paul does not use traditional verbs for the "giving" of the Law, he intends to imply in Galatians that God did not give the Law himself. It is clear, however, from both Galatians and elsewhere that Paul does not intend to denigrate the Law to this extent. Paul's ethics continue to be grounded in the standards established by the Law (e.g., Gal 5:14, which quotes Lev 19:18); if Paul truly regards the Sinaitic Law as "the cursing and enslaving voice . . . that does not speak for God,"[18] then

15. Martyn, *Galatians*, 357, 366. See also Martyn's *Theological Issues in the Letters of Paul*. Albert Schweitzer makes a similar argument in *Mysticism of Paul*. In Schweitzer's view, Paul maintains "that the Law was given by Angels who desired thereby to make men subservient to themselves, and that by the death of Jesus their power has already been so shaken that the Law has now no more force" (69). For Paul, the obedience which Jews rendered to the Law "was rendered not to God but only to the Angels" and this obedience meant that humanity was placed under the world elements until Christ set humanity free (70). Schweitzer's interpretation is flawed in that it fails to consider Paul's terminology in reference to angels. As the "Angels" section below will point out, Paul almost always uses the term ἄγγελος in a positive manner, or if he intends to refer to a demonic angel, he limits the term in some obvious way. His usual manner of referring to evil spiritual beings is to employ one of a variety of alternative terms.

16. Martyn, *Theological Issues*, 172.

17. N. T. Wright, *Climax of the Covenant*, 161. Delling comments on διατάσσω and the Law in Gal 3:19, noting that "the fact that it is not ordained directly by God in its details does not mean for Paul that it was not instituted by God in intention . . ." ("διατάσσω").

18. Martyn, *Galatians*, 368.

why does Paul so frequently quote it in his ethical exhortations?[19] In fact, Jewish literature of the time would not support the argument that God was absent at Sinai—although the literature does support the view that angels were present at the giving of the Law, and even that angels themselves gave the Law on God's behalf (see below).

A sixth interpretive solution does not regard the mediator question as the key to the interpretation of 3:20, but instead focuses on the issue of the continuity of salvation history, in stark contrast to Martyn. L. Ann Jervis, for example, contends that Paul's argument centers on the desire to show God's faithfulness throughout salvation history. Jervis rightly criticizes scholars who interpret 3:19–20 as deprecatory to the Law; such an explanation runs counter to Paul's larger argument, which aims to show that God is faithful and has not changed his mind since he gave the promise to Abraham. If God were absent at the giving of the Law (if the angels alone were responsible for the giving of the Law), she argues, then God's faithfulness would be undercut—and what good would the promises of such a God be?[20] Jervis calls attention to the Old Testament narratives of the giving of the Law, all of which describe God speaking directly to Moses and do not refer to angelic presence (except Deut 33:2). Paul's purpose in referring to the Shema in 3:20, Jervis argues, is "to underscore his point that his gospel is continuous with Judaism. This is the same function that reference to the Shema (God is one) plays in Rom 3:28–31—to stress that Paul's gospel is the outworking of Judaism, even of God's giving of the law."[21] While Jervis offers an important overview of Paul's purpose, her analysis fails to explain the contrast between the mediator of 3:19 and God in 3:20. If Paul emphasizes continuity, then why does he contrast the mediator of the Law with God?

A seventh approach suggests that mediation as such is not the issue; rather, the problem revolves around Moses as the specific mediator of the Law. N. T. Wright takes this approach, arguing that God's oneness is a central theme throughout the passage. Paul argues that God's oneness demands one family, but the ethnic boundaries inherent in the Law separate people into multiple groups and thus preclude this one family from being

19. See Rosner, *Paul, Scripture and Ethics.*

20. Jervis, *Galatians*, 98.

21. Ibid., 103.

realized.[22] Paul's point in 3:20 is that Moses is not the specific mediator through whom this one family is brought into existence—he cannot be, because he mediated revelation to Israel only.[23] This interpretation, however, would not provide an adequate response to the Galatian Judaizers,[24] who would likely reiterate their belief that the one family *is* the Jewish family. Anyone who wants to be part of God's family must simply convert to Judaism. Thus, Paul and the Judaizers would remain at an impasse in their argument.[25]

As this brief survey shows, a variety of nuances color the multiple interpretations of Gal 3:20. Scholars generally approach the issue from the vantage point of trying to discover Paul's understanding of the role of the Law. While this is certainly an important query (and one that will be explored in a limited manner below), few scholars seriously address the question being asked here: What is the function of Paul's monotheistic language in this passage? Some of the questions requiring investigation in order to arrive at an appropriate conclusion include: 1) What did Paul envision as the role of the angels at Sinai? Does their presence depreciate the Law's value or increase it? Were the angels friendly or hostile? Which angels were they? Do they relate to the angels of the nations? How does the fact that the MT does not explicitly record angelic participation in the giving of the Law affect the strength of Paul's argument? How would the Galatians have interpreted Paul's argument? How would his opponents have interpreted it? 2) What does Paul mean by "mediator" here? What status does a mediator have? Who is the mediator in 3:19? Is the mediator in 3:20 the same mediator as in 3:19? 3) What exactly is meant by the concept of oneness here? Does it have any relation to the oneness mentioned elsewhere (3:16 and 3:28)? Why does Paul mention the Shema and what is the function of this language?

Accordingly, most of this chapter will address these three major and interrelated issues: angels, mediators, and oneness. Before tackling these

22. Wright, *Climax of the Covenant*, 166.

23. Ibid., 169.

24. I use the term "Judaizers" of those Christians who argue that a Gentile believer must live according to Jewish customs in order to be considered truly part of the people of God.

25. For further discussion of this point, see the section "Oneness and the Exegesis of Gal 3:20" below.

concepts, however, it will be helpful to identify the overall context by reviewing Paul's view of the Law and the specific argument of Gal 3.

Given that the entire letter to the Galatians is concerned with the relationship between faith and the Law, it is important to understand Paul's concept of justification. If Paul radically condemns his former Jewish heritage as a legalistic religion based on human striving, then how can he simultaneously affirm his Jewish belief in the one God? How can this one God be trusted if he deserts Israel and the Law he gave to them?[26] Or is there another way of understanding Paul's negative critique of the Law which nonetheless preserves its monotheistic underpinnings? If God is truly one, then how is the work of Christ continuous with the work of the Law? The Law-faith dichotomy so strongly present in both Galatians and Romans is intertwined with the oneness of God because it calls the character of this one God into question.

Indeed, no other subject in Pauline studies has stimulated more discussion in the last thirty years than the "New Perspective" on Paul. Commencing with E. P. Sanders's work, *Paul and Palestinian Judaism*, scholars have continued to debate whether Judaism was a legalistic religion in the first century, whether Paul misunderstood Judaism, and whether interpreters throughout the centuries have incorrectly analyzed Paul's references to "works of the Law."[27] I will begin with a brief overview of Sanders's views and the development of the New Perspective, as well as the response of various critics. Then I will propose an understanding of Paul's arguments regarding the Law and faith in Galatians (and elsewhere), and continue to interact with various scholarly opinions as I draw the paradigm.

Sanders has suggested that "covenantal nomism," as he termed it, maintained a distinction between "getting in" and "staying in" the covenant.[28] Jews understood that entrance into the covenant was by God's gracious election, whereas staying in was a matter of faithful law observance:

> God has chosen Israel and Israel has accepted the election. In his role as King, God gave Israel commandments which they are to obey as best they can. Obedience is rewarded and disobedience

26. For more on this question, see chapter 4.

27. Examples of these various positions will be provided in the discussion below.

28. Sanders, *Paul and Palestinian Judaism*, 236.

> punished. In case of failure to obey, however, man has recourse to divinely ordained means of atonement, in all of which repentance is required. As long as he maintains his desire to stay in the covenant, he has a share in God's covenantal promises, including life in the world to come. The intention and effort to be obedient constitute the *condition for remaining in the covenant*, but they do not *earn* it.[29]

In comparing Judaism and Pauline Christianity, Sanders notes that "righteousness" has different meanings. In Judaism, righteousness involves Torah obedience and repentance, whereas in Paul, righteousness involves salvation by Christ. Righteousness in Judaism involves maintaining one's status in the covenant, whereas in Paul the term involves transfer into the covenant: "Thus when Paul says that one cannot be made righteous by works of law, he means that one cannot, by works of law, 'transfer to the body of the saved.'"[30]

Additional differences exist between Judaism and Paul's Christianity, according to Sanders. Unlike Judaism, repentance does not play a large role for Paul. Also, his view of sin most often involves sin as a power from which one must be freed, whereas in Judaism sin simply involves transgression. Perhaps the biggest difference is Paul's "participationist eschatology." Everyone, whether Jew or Gentile, must transfer into the body of Christ and participate in Christ's death and resurrection—everyone must come under a different lordship. Thus, for Sanders, the antithesis between Judaism and Pauline Christianity lies not in the difference between grace and works, but in the type of religion they represent.[31] Paul believed that salvation came only through Christ, and thus any other path to salvation is misguided: "What is wrong with Judaism is not that Jews seek to save themselves and become self-righteous about it, but that their seeking is not directed toward the right goal . . . They do not know that, as far as salvation goes, Christ has put an end to the law and provides a different righteousness from that provided by Torah obedience . . ."[32] Sanders

29. Ibid., 180. Sanders argues that this viewpoint holds true regardless of the sect of Judaism. Essenes as well as Pharisees had characteristics consistent with covenantal nomism. Thus, even extreme apocalyptic viewpoints did not alter the basic understanding of covenant election by grace.

30. Ibid., 544.

31. Ibid., 546–48.

32. Ibid., 550.

argues that, for Paul, ultimately the problem with Judaism was that it was not Christianity.[33]

Dunn has added his own nuance to the debate by arguing that although "works of the law" refers to all that the Law requires, in the context of Israel and the nations, certain laws come to the forefront: namely, those laws that operate as boundary markers by separating Jew from Gentile (e.g., Sabbath and dietary observances, and circumcision). Paul's pre-Christian zeal for the Law suggests that Paul's conversion was from Pharisaic Judaism, "a Judaism which kept itself separate from other Jews, not to mention Gentiles."[34] Thus the post-conversion Paul was very concerned with the boundary-defining role of the Law, i.e., that it separated Jew and Gentile. For Dunn, this separation of people groups lies at the heart of the Law-faith dispute.

N. T. Wright presents a different but complementary version of the New Perspective. He understands Paul as having a focus in covenant theology: the first-century Israel was still under the curse of the exile. In Christ, God was doing for his people exactly what he had promised, but this was different than what Israel had been expecting. Paul's understanding of what God had done in Christ changed his perception about the nature of Israel's plight. Israel's sinfulness, which had resulted in the pride of national righteousness, ultimately led to Israel's rejection of God's Messiah.[35] Yet all of this was part of God's plan for the world as a whole. The end of the exile had arrived with Christ: "The renewed people of God *was* the new temple . . . The word of the Lord *was* now going out to the Gentiles. All this and more is to say: Israel's destiny is now fulfilled."[36]

Wright argues, *contra* Sanders, that justification is not about "getting in" the covenant, but rather it involves God's declaration that one is already in. For Paul, the gospel is about declaring that Jesus is the Messiah; justification is an affirmation of those who believe that Jesus is Lord.[37] It is a matter of God declaring forensically that a person is in the right, i.e., that a person's sins have been forgiven and that the individual is part of

33. Ibid., 552.

34. Dunn, *Theology of Paul*, 353.

35. Wright, *Climax of the Covenant*, 261–62.

36. Ibid., 262.

37. Wright, "New Perspectives on Paul," n.p.

the new family of God. For Wright, this vindication follows one's calling, but they are not the same thing.

Clearly there is variation among New Perspective proponents. Nonetheless, it may be helpful to summarize some of the key issues. In general, those who advocate the New Perspective argue that Jews in the first century understood that God had chosen Israel based on his graceful election, and not based on any works. Thus, getting in the covenant is not based on a legalistic works-righteousness. New Perspective proponents vary in their assessment of exactly what Paul was responding to in his polemic against works of the Law,[38] but in general the issue surrounds the ethnic distinction between Jews and Gentiles. Identity, not personal striving, lay at the heart of Paul's concern. Nationalistic pride and ethnocentrism were at issue when Jews boasted in their works, a boasting that Paul condemned. Grace offered an inclusivity that boasting in works did not. God's concern, in Paul's mind, was to include in the people of God peoples from all races, not just from the Jews. This is what "justification by grace" was designed to show.

Although many scholars have agreed with Sanders even as they present variations, others have offered sharp critiques. One of the more recent responses to Sanders comes from Stephen Westerholm, who argues that the rabbinic texts that Sanders uses to support his claims are not as unequivocal as Sanders asserts. Rather, they convey a mix of God's grace and Israel's lawkeeping as a means of receiving covenant blessings. "If Judaism did indeed preach that salvation is by grace, it is remarkable that the rabbis seldom, if ever, got around to saying anything of the kind . . ."[39] Furthermore, the rabbis do not appear to be troubled by the mix of merit and grace in their writings regarding election. For Westerholm, Paul's defense of justification by grace involves an understanding that the righteousness of God found in Christ operates apart from the Law: "Those who continue to pursue the righteousness of the law mistakenly attribute to the works of their unredeemed flesh a role in securing divine approval."[40]

Simon J. Gathercole has also taken issue with New Perspective proponents. He has reviewed Jewish literature from the Pauline period and

38. Some scholars simply maintain that Paul misunderstood Judaism when he contrasted grace and works. See, for example, Räisänen, *Paul and the Law*, 178.

39. Westerholm, *Perspectives Old and New*, 350.

40. Ibid., 429.

argued that Jewish theology included a belief that the final vindication of God's people would be based on their obedience.[41] In a related concept, Gathercole suggests that the cause of the Jewish confidence (i.e., boasting) before God lies not only in covenant election, but also in Jewish obedience.[42]

An assessment of the primary sources is needed to properly evaluate these varying theories. Although an extensive review of texts is not possible here, a sample of Jewish texts will be considered. In the Jewish Scriptures, for example, Ps 119 offers a lengthy praise of God's Law, but also argues that God's precepts "are to be fully obeyed" (v. 4). Indeed, the Deuteronomic blessings and curses are handed down based on whether Israel observes the Law (Deut 30:15–18). Yet, at the same time, forgiveness and restoration are part of God's provision (Ps 51:7, 17). The entire sacrificial system suggests that sins do not put one out of the covenant if repentance occurs (Lev 16:29–34).

Other texts illustrate this diversity as well. *Jub.* 23:16 requires that all of God's commands are to be observed without turning aside to the right or left. In 23:10 Abraham is praised since he "was perfect in all of his actions with the Lord . . ." In addition, the author looked forward to a time when Israel would be perfectly obedient (1:22–24; 5:12; 50:5). But at the same time, *Jubilees* has numerous passages that refer to God's election of Israel (1:17, 25; 2:21; 19:18). *1 Enoch* suggests a dire outcome for sinners on the day of judgment (22:9–13). *Psalms of Solomon* also suggests that the righteous and wicked will receive the just reward for their deeds (2:34–36). *4 Ezra* is arguably the most negative of these writings, stating that the ungodly will perish because they have not performed God's works (7:22–24), and only a few will be saved (8:1–3).[43] Yet, other texts focus more on repentance and God's merciful grace. The *Prayer of Manasseh*, for example, praises God for his forgiveness of sins.

The Qumran community also expressed an understanding of the need for strict obedience. The *Rule of the Community* frequently calls on all those who enter the community to "do what is good and right" (e.g., 1QS 1:1–10). A member must "order his steps {to walk} perfectly in all the ways

41. Gathercole, *Where is Boasting?*

42. Ibid., 194. He cites a variety of texts to support this claim, including 2 Macc 8:36; *2 Bar.* 48:22b; CD 7; and Wis 15.

43. Sanders (*Paul and Palestinian Judaism*, 409) argues that 4 Ezra shows the consequences of the collapse of covenantal nomism.

commanded by God concerning the times appointed for him, straying neither to the right nor to the left and transgressing none of his words . . ." (1QS 3:9–11). But the same document also praises God for his grace in forgiving sins (1QS 11:10–15). Other Qumran texts emphasize the strict demands of the Law (CD 2:15; 4Q174 1:6–7). God's judgment, in which all are rewarded according to their deeds, is also emphasized (1QM 11:14; 1QpHab 7:15—8:1). Yet, other passages emphasize God's grace and election (1QH 12:34–37; 15:15–20).

Philo also records his view that God requires strict obedience—one must not turn to the right or the left, but follow the Law (*Deus.* 162; *Abr.* 269; *Post.* 102). Yet Philo also takes up the concept of God's mercy. He states that God "ever prefers forgiveness to punishment" (*Praem.* 166). God thus provides atoning sacrifices (*Spec.* 1.235–241; 1.188–190; 2.193–196) and heals those who repent (*Abr.* 19; *Spec.* 1.187–188; *QG* 1.84; *Mut.* 124; *Somn.* 1.91).

Thus, it appears that a mix of grace (i.e., the unearned mercy and forgiveness of God) and Law obedience appears within a first-century Jewish understanding of righteousness before God. Neither Sanders's viewpoint nor the traditional stance can be fully maintained. Nonetheless, Sanders's research has offered a necessary corrective to the traditional understanding of first-century Judaism. Judaism can no longer be perceived as a completely legalistic religion in the way in which some scholars have argued.[44] God's grace—both in choosing Abraham and his descendants before they had any opportunity to earn God's favor, and in offering a means of forgiveness—was an integral part of the reason Israel worshipped Yahweh. But the expectation of lawkeeping was simultaneously an integral part of the covenant. The distinction between "getting in" and "staying in" proposed by Sanders presents too sharp of a dichotomy.

The full impact of this must be taken into consideration when considering Galatians. Paul emphasizes the temporary nature of the Torah. The Law was added on account of transgressions (3:19), i.e., the Law pointed out and defined transgression (Rom 7:7).[45] Ultimately, the Law

44. See, for example, Bultmann, *Theology of the New Testament*, 2:240.

45. F. Watson observes. "Paul's antithetical hermeneutic claims to have uncovered a deep tension within the law itself, between an 'optimistic' voice that assumes that its commandments can and should be obeyed, and a 'pessimistic' voice that holds that this project of bringing righteousness into human life is doomed to failure" (*Paul and Hermeneutics*, 66).

showed humanity that even though God required holiness, no one was able to keep all its commandments.[46] Thus, the Law itself made provisions for atonement, cleansing, and forgiveness. The very fact that the Law makes such provision suggests both that strict adherence was required and that God's gracious forgiveness was necessary to wipe away humanity's inevitable transgressions.

The Torah, then, served both to point out transgressions (the moral law) and to provide a means of atonement (the cultic law).[47] For Paul, the Law changed when Christ came. Because Christ's death on the cross was equivalent to initiating a sacrifice of atonement,[48] and this one a final and permanent sacrifice, the cultic sections of the Law are no longer necessary. God has offered, in Christ, the final cultic offering. To reject Christ, then, is to reject the ultimate provision for humanity's sin. Thus, what was once *not* legalistic now becomes legalistic if a Jew continues to offer a sacrifice that is no longer valid—the Jew thus offers a "work" in place of God's grace. Because Jesus has provided "definitive atonement" on the cross, the Old Testament sacrifices no longer have the power to atone.[49] Furthermore, the symbolism of Torah itself has forever changed: "Apart from Christ, the law is reduced to legal obligation and a standard of performance for Paul. The law's ethnic component becomes merely an ethnic distinction and nothing more; it is no longer a sign of God's

46. This is the implied point of the "curse" discussion in Gal 3:10–14.

47. Even though the Law itself does not delineate these distinctions by these terms, one is able to separate those laws that direct human relations (moral law) from those laws that direct temple worship (purity laws, cultic rituals, etc.).

48. Andrew Das (*Paul, the Law*, 143), however, argues that Paul does not understand the Old Testament sacrifices to have salvific efficacy. He prefers the image of the scapegoat as providing substitutionary representation. Thus, Christ remains the agent of deliverance. Although Das argues that granting salvific power to the OT rituals would negate the need for Christ, this overlooks Paul's idea that the OT rituals were meant as a temporary provision until Christ came. Their inferior nature can be seen in the need for the annual repetition of the sacrifice of atonement, as opposed to Christ's single and eternal sacrifice. Stuhlmacher takes this latter position: "The cultic celebration of the Day of Atonement is abolished and superseded by virtue of this act of God, because the atonement granted definitively by God in Christ once and for all renders superfluous further cultic atonement ritual" ("Recent Exegesis on Romans," 104).

49. Schreiner, *Law and Its Fulfillment*, 44. Das (*Paul, the Law*, 188) similarly argues that now that Christ has come, the entire gracious framework of Judaism has collapsed for Paul.

grace."[50] The Torah still provides instruction by pointing out the need for Christ, but Paul argues that the end (Christ) should not be replaced by the means (Torah).

Therefore, in response to the question of what Paul finds wrong with the Law, it appears that Paul is reacting against (what is for him) a Jewish misunderstanding of the role of the Law. Whereas non-Christian Jews understood the Law to be the ultimate gift of God, a gift that brought redemption, Paul argues on the other hand that the Law is temporary[51] and cannot give life. It is only through the death and resurrection of Christ that the believer is able to receive life. Through his death Christ has dealt with sin; through his resurrection, Christ's Spirit (Gal 4:6–7) empowers believers to live a holy life—the kind of life required by the (moral) Law, but which previously followers of God were unable to emulate due to human sin. Paul emphasizes this in Rom 8:3–4—what the Law was powerless to do God did by sending his Son to be a sin offering; now the Law can be fully met by those who live by the Spirit. What the Law could not bring—life[52]—comes through the Holy Spirit, which is given to those who believe in Christ. Thus, Christ's death offered atonement; Christ's resurrection offered transformation.[53]

For Paul, then, the Law has been transformed by a decisive apocalyptic event. Christ has fulfilled the Law; because Christ offered himself as the ultimate sacrifice of atonement,[54] the Law—especially in regard to its cultic components—is no longer necessary. By the Holy Spirit, which Paul emphasizes in Galatians, the believer is empowered to fulfill the moral intent of the Law.[55] What was once the centerpiece of Judaism—the Law—

50. Das, *Paul, the Law*, 188.

51. In one sense, the Law is also eternal for Paul, in that Christ is the fulfillment of the Law and this fulfillment is eternal. What is temporary is the prominent position of the Law in pre-Christ Judaism.

52. Gal 3:21.

53. See Rom 4:25.

54. See Rom 3:25 and the discussion, "Rom 3:30 Within the Context of 3:21–31," in chapter 4.

55. F. Watson's conception of Paul's antithetical hermeneutic is helpful at this point. Paul, unlike most of his Jewish contemporaries, highlights the parts of Torah, such as Deut 32, which spell out the curse and the death which came with the Law as well as God's own provision for redemption. I would add that as Paul searched the Jewish Scriptures to make sense of this provision, the experience of the risen Christ helped him to focus on the eschatological promise of the outpouring of God's Spirit, which Paul interprets in Gal 4:6 as the Spirit of Christ (see the section, "Christ's Exalted Status," below).

has now been replaced by the promised fulfillment of that Law—Christ. Christ must now become the focal point.[56] To continue to observe the Law in the same manner and for the same reasons, therefore, amounts to a rejection of Christ and thus a rejection of God's covenant grace.

But if one takes Acts 16:3 to be historical, then the portrayal of Paul's understanding described above may indict Paul himself, who circumcised Timothy. The context of Acts 16:3, however, suggests Paul's intention was not to guarantee Timothy's salvation. Directly following the apostolic council, Paul hardly would have changed his position while he traveled to area churches disseminating the council's decision! Rather, a distinction must be made between Timothy—who was partly Jewish via his mother's ethnicity—and the Gentiles, who had no ethnic connection to Judaism. Paul did not object to Jewish Christians "practicing their ancestral religion so long as it was understood that doing so was not *necessary* for salvation, either for them or for Gentiles."[57] The text states that Paul circumcised Timothy "because of the Jews who lived in that area, for they all knew that his father was a Greek." Thus, Paul was following the principle of being all things to all people.[58] For missionary purposes, Paul was willing to have Timothy circumcised. Timothy was a test case, a demonstration that Paul was not trying to lead Jews away from Judaism.[59] Thus, Paul was not being hypocritical, because he was not observing the Law in the same manner and for the same reasons as he had done prior to his Christian conversion. Rather, the mark of Judaism that Paul placed on Timothy was a mark of ethnicity but not a mark of election; the meaning of circumcision had shifted focus. That is, where formerly circumcision signified one's membership in the elect people of God, now the Spirit signified one's membership in the elect people of God. But, through the circumcision of Timothy, Paul is affirming that retaining one's Jewish identity is still important under the new covenant. As he will argue in Rom 9:4–5, the heritage of the Jews is full of great blessings, including the promise and its fulfillment in Christ; Paul's actions here confirm that one's Jewishness, and

56. Hays makes a similar statement: "Moses and the Law of Sinai are assigned a temporary supporting role, not the lead, in the drama of God's redemptive purpose. Thus, the Torah is neither superseded nor nullified but transformed into a witness of the gospel" (*Echoes of Scripture*, 157).

57. Witherington, *Acts of the Apostles*, 474.

58. 1 Cor 9:19–23.

59. Witherington, *Acts of the Apostles*, 475.

therefore one's witness to God's faithfulness throughout history, should continue to be embraced.

A further question can be raised regarding Paul's own claim to have been "blameless" under the Law (Phil 3:6). How could Paul argue in Philippians that he was blameless, when in Romans he contends that all (Jew and Gentile alike) have sinned (3:23)? A close look at Phil 3:6 will reveal that Paul is referring to his pre-Christian view of himself. Paul wanted to assure the Philippians that if he, who had at one point considered himself blameless and thus equal with any current Judaizing proponent, could nonetheless turn away from his previous understanding of the Law, then the Philippians should not hesitate to do so as well.[60] It is clear that in Phil 3 Paul moves away from any boasting in his status. In 3:7–11 he strongly argues that he counts all of his status as loss for the sake of knowing Christ. All of his previous reasons for boasting mean nothing to him now in the face of true righteousness—a righteousness not derived from the Law but from faith (3:11).

Paul's understanding of the purpose of the Law helps to explain his vitriolic attitude toward circumcision in Galatians. Circumcision stood as the key marker of one's acceptance of the Law. But to force a Gentile to accept a mark of the old Law, the temporary Law, the Law which has been fulfilled in Christ, was tantamount to forcing the Gentiles to reject the gracious sacrifice of Christ! This is why Paul in 4:9 condemns the Galatians for wanting to return to the weak and beggarly principles of the world: by following the Law, they would be returning to the former age.[61]

Paul, therefore, has not set out to establish a new religion. He does not believe he is forsaking his Jewish heritage. He has not abandoned Yahweh, the one God of Israel—nor does he believe that Yahweh has abandoned his people. Rather, the death and resurrection of Christ has brought a new age in which the former symbols have radically changed their meaning. Yet this meaning is consistent with the promise God originally gave to Abraham, as Paul argues in Gal 3.

Paul's argument in 3:20 falls within the larger section spanning 3:1—4:7. In 3:1–5 Paul introduces the crux of the argument. The evidence shows that the Galatians have clearly received the Spirit (3:2, 3, 5). He emphasizes that their receipt of the Spirit was the result of their belief in the

60. Westerholm, "Righteousness of the Law," 260 n. 19.

61. See the discussion of στοιχεῖα in the "Angels" section below.

gospel, and not the result of any works of the Law. But now the Galatians have turned to another gospel (1:6); although they started with the Spirit, they have now turned to "the flesh" (3:3).

After this initial argument, Paul turns to Abraham to support his contention that receipt of the Spirit comes through faith and not works.[62] This is the argument found in 3:6–22. More specifically, in 3:6–9 Paul argues that the sons of Abraham are those who have faith, just as Abraham had faith. He then contrasts in 3:10–14 those who have faith with those under the Law. In 3:10–12 he explains that those under the Law are under a curse, whereas in 3:13–14 he states that Jesus is the answer to this curse. God had promised Abraham that the nations would be blessed through him (3:8); it is in Christ that the blessing of Abraham comes, and that blessing is the promise of the Spirit (3:14). Thus, already in this section Paul is uniting the concepts of the Abrahamic blessing of the Gentiles, the coming of Christ, the receipt of the Spirit, and faith as the means of receiving all these things.

In 3:15–22 Paul turns to the illustration of a will and inheritance. He argues that just as a will cannot be added to or set aside, neither can God's promise be altered by the advent of the Law. Paul emphasizes that the promise was made to Abraham and to his *one* seed (ἐφ' ἑνός), Christ. Paul emphasizes the continuity of salvation history: Jesus is not a new idea or new addition—rather, he is the fulfillment of the original plan.

But Paul's argument raises two very important questions.[63] First, if God's plan is ultimately realized in the fulfillment of the promise, then what was the point of introducing the Law? This is the question Paul attempts to answer in the cryptic passage 3:19–20. Second, is the Law, as an addition, thus opposed to the promises of God? Paul attempts to answer this question in 3:21–22.[64] Both answers are tied to the question of sin—παραβάσεων in 3:19 and ἁμαρτίαν in 3:22. Does Paul state here that

62. For a recent discussion of Paul's use of Abraham as an example of faith, see Calvert-Koyzis, *Paul, Monotheism*.

63. I maintain that both the question of 3:19 and the question of 3:21 are spurred by Paul's larger argument. 3:21 is *not* a response to the argument of 3:19–20, as some scholars have argued (see, e.g., Wright, *Climax of the Covenant*, 168; and Duncan, *Epistle to the Galatians*, 116). The οὖν in v. 21 refers not only to 3:19–20, but to the larger argument of 3:6–20.

64. Just as Paul used the Shema in 3:20, he continues to use Deuteronomy to underscore his argument in 3:21. Heckl ("Ein Bezugstext für Gal 3:21B") observes that Paul alludes to Deut 6:24–25 when he describes the promise of life for those who do the Law.

the purpose of the Law is to increase sin?[65] Or does he merely state that the Law makes humans aware that they are sinful and cannot achieve righteousness without God?[66] The latter interpretation makes more sense of Paul's arguments about the Law elsewhere (e.g., Rom 7:7–12). The Law served an important purpose in pointing out humanity's need for redemption and thus prepared humanity to understand the meaning of Christ's sacrifice. Yet the Law was only temporary and was unable to give life. This, however, is the very thing that the Spirit, received through faith, *is* able to do.[67]

Paul continues this argument in 3:23—4:7. He uses yet another illustration to emphasize the temporary nature of the Law. Just as a pedagogue in the first century reared a child, offering education and discipline, so the Law also taught and disciplined the Jews.[68] But just as a pedagogue is no longer needed once the child becomes an adult, so it is with the Law. Now that Christ has come, the teacher is relieved of his duties (3:23–25).

In 3:26–29 Paul returns to the "son" language which first arose in 3:7. The sons of God are the sons of Abraham, and on the same basis—through faith. The whole oneness question now comes full circle—the one seed of 3:16 has become the one body of 3:28. Those who believe in Christ are now the one seed of 3:16 because they are "in Christ," the one seed. As such, the members of the body are heirs of the promise. And what is the promise? That the nations would be blessed through Abraham—and that blessing is the receipt of the Spirit (4:6–7), who gives life.

Paul reiterates his argument in 4:1–7, but changes the metaphor from seed to heir. The heirs of the promise, while minors, are no better than slaves (and are under the temporary guardianship of their pedagogue, the Law); but when the heirs became adults, i.e., when Christ arrived, the slaves received their inheritance: they became children of God crying out by the Spirit, "Abba! Father!"[69]

65. As Betz suggests in *Galatians*, 165.

66. Longenecker, *Galatians*, 128; Dunn, *Epistle to the Galatians*, 189–90; Matera, *Galatians*, 128; Burton, *Galatians*, 188.

67. Gal 6:8; Rom 8:2, 6, 11, 13; 1 Cor 15:45; 2 Cor 1:22, 3:6, 5:5; 2 Thess 2:13; Titus 3:5.

68. See Lull, "'Law Was Our Pedagogue.'"

69. It is interesting that the minors become "adults" in a sense, i.e., they have received their inheritance, but the inheritance results in becoming a child!

Overall, the whole of this argument centers around the receipt of the Spirit.[70] The Galatians are clearly part of the body of Christ, as evidenced by the work of the Spirit in their midst. But Paul emphasizes time and again, through various related illustrations, that this promised Spirit was a promise received through faith. His whole argument is designed to show that the promise (the blessing of the Spirit who brings life and who is received through faith) is superior to the Law. Whereas the Law is temporary and instructs humanity regarding their sinfulness, the Spirit gives life and adoption as children of God, with all the blessings that entails. Thus, 3:19–20 must serve this larger purpose of showing the inadequacy of the Law in comparison with the promise. Furthermore, the theme of oneness is intertwined throughout Paul's argument: the promise was made to Abraham and his one seed, the mediator is contrasted with the one God, and believers are heirs because they are one in Christ.[71]

ANGELS

As a precursor to what he will say in verse 20, Paul states in verse 19 that the Law was put into effect "through angels" by a mediator. This rather oblique statement regarding angels could have a bearing on the interpretation of verse 20, and so Paul's angelology needs to be investigated. It would be impossible here to offer a complete description of the range of beliefs regarding angels during the Second Temple period; it is necessary, however, to provide some overview of both Paul's angelology and the Jewish tradition concerning the presence and participation of angels at Sinai. Only then will it be possible to evaluate the interpretive possibilities regarding Paul's statement about the Law and its relation to the one God in Gal 3:19–20.

When investigating the various traditions regarding the giving of the Law at Sinai, it is striking to observe that the MT of the Old Testament nowhere explicitly uses the term ἄγγελος to refer to the presence of angels at Sinai. In the stories of the giving of the Law (Exod 19, Deut 9–10), God speaks directly to Moses without any angelic mediation. Nonetheless, a reference to angelic presence likely occurs in Deut 33:2, where it is said

70. See Cosgrove, *Cross and the Spirit*; Fee, *God's Empowering Presence*; and Lull, *Spirit in Galatia*.

71. We will explore the significance of this oneness more fully in the section "Oneness and the Exegesis of Gal 3:19–20," below.

God came to Sinai with "myriads of holy ones," although the term "angel" is not specifically used. In addition, the various descriptions of the natural phenomena that accompanied the giving of the Law (lightning, thunder, clouds, fire, etc.) imply the presence of angels; these phenomena, in fact, were frequently interpreted as angels or the work of angels.[72] Furthermore, later rabbinic tradition viewed Ps 68:18 as important for indicating a large number of angels accompanying God at Sinai.[73] A clearer reference to angels at Sinai occurs in the LXX of Deut 33:2, which states specifically that angels from God's right hand accompanied him. But there is no mention of the angels themselves *mediating* the Law.

The author of the *Book of Jubilees* (late second century BCE) describes Moses's meeting with God on Mt. Sinai, when "the Lord revealed to him both what (was) in the beginning and what will occur (in the future), the account of the division of all of the days of the Law and the testimony" (1:4).[74] God speaks to Moses and says, "And you write down for yourself all of the matters which I shall make known to you . . ." (1:26). At this point, however, God tells the angel of the presence to "write for Moses from the first creation until my sanctuary is built in their midst forever" (1:27). The angel, identified as the one who went before the camp of Israel, then takes the tables of the divisions of the years and dictates to Moses what he should write. Although this opening passage is thus rather ambiguous since both God and the angel seem to speak to Moses, in several places the angel mentions the "laws" that he has written down for Moses.[75] Thus, *Jubilees* offers a precedent for the idea that God spoke to an angel who then, in turn, mediated some aspect of the Law to Moses. It is important

72. Callan, "Pauline Midrash," 551. Callan cites Ps 104:4; *Jub.* 2:2; and *1 En.* 60:11–24.

73. See *Midr.* Ps 68:18, where the rabbis discuss the number of chariots and angels which descended upon Mt. Sinai at the giving of the Law. Rabbi Abdimi said 22,000 chariots of ministering angels accompanied God; Rabbi Tanhum bar Hanilai said, "There were as many chariots as only an accountant can imagine—a thousand thousands of thousands, and myriads of myriads" (Braude, *Midrash on Psalms*, 1:544–45).

74. The translation is by Wintermute in Charlesworth, *Old Testament Pseudepigrapha*.

75. See 6:22; 30:12, 21 (here the term "ordinances" is used), 50:6, 13. Other verses do not specifically refer to the law which the angel made known, but refer to the Sabbaths the angels have made known to Moses (e.g., 50:1–3); in 50:4, e.g., the angel takes credit for *ordaining* the year-weeks and the years and the jubilees.

to note that the author of *Jubilees* does not conceive of this angelic mediation as undermining the authority of Mosaic law.[76]

Philo refers to the angels as mediators at Sinai in *Somn.* 1.140–44. The function of angels is "to convey the biddings of the Father to His children and report the children's need to their Father" (1.141). They act on behalf of the people as mediators (1.142) because the Jewish people shudder in dread at God's exceeding might. Philo then refers to Exod 20:19, where the people asked Moses, rather than God, to speak to them, but in Philo's version the Israelites asked "one of those mediators," i.e., one of the angels, to speak to them. The reason they ask for a mediator is that, "should He, without employing ministers, hold out to us with His own hand, I do not say chastisements, but even benefits unmixed and exceeding great, we are incapable of receiving them" (1.143). Thus, in Philo's view, the glory of the Law demanded the use of angelic mediators; since it was such an "exceeding great" blessing, the Israelites could not bear to receive it directly. It is significant that in this interpretation mediation does not decrease the status of the Law (see below), but rather, is necessary for the protection of the people. If anything, angelic mediation is an indication of the supreme greatness of the Law.

Josephus in *Ant.* 15:136 records a speech of Herod's in which he addresses the recent murder of Jewish ambassadors and describes the impiety of the act. Herod says that the Jews "have learned the noblest of our doctrines and the holiest of our laws from the messengers sent by God. For this name can bring God to manifestation for men and reconcile enemies to one another." Unfortunately, the phrase δι' ἄγγελων could refer either to prophets and priests or to angels.[77] Nonetheless, a careful

76. Najman, "Angels at Sinai," 318.

77. Davies ("Note on Josephus") argues that "prophets" or "priests" provides the best interpretation. He bases his decision on five arguments: 1) the context involves human envoys who can be killed, and this is not a characteristic of angels; 2) elsewhere in *Antiquities* Josephus does not refer to angelic mediation at Sinai; 3) a similar passage in *Ag. Ap.* 1.37 refers to prophets; 4) Josephus elsewhere at times avoids the use of the term "angel" where it would be appropriate (e.g., *Ant.* 5.277, where Josephus uses φάντασμα instead of ἄγγελος, even though both the MT and the LXX refer to angels); and 5) the term ἄγγελος in the LXX can sometimes refer to prophets and priests (e.g., Hag 1:13, Isa 44:26, 2 Chr 36:15). See also Walton, "Messenger of God." Walton argues that the use of ἄγγελος for the high priest may occur as early as the late fourth century BCE. Walton rightly admits that his argument is hindered both by the third-hand fragment and by the fact that the fragment does not record the description of a Jewish author, but rather the report of a Greek author trying to describe his understanding of the Jewish religion. For

evaluation of the text suggests that it is more likely that ἄγγελοι refers to angels. The superlative nature of the phrases "the noblest of the decrees" and "the holiest things in the laws" indicates the extreme importance of these parts of Law (and thus intensifies Herod's argument that ambassadors are to be honored and not harmed—15:137: "What greater impiety could there be . . . ?"). If the presence of angels serves to heighten the glory of an event, then the parts of the Law that are most glorious would likely include some angelic presence and not merely human actors. In addition, the noblest of the decrees are likely to be those handed down on Sinai, the epitome of holy law-giving.[78] Finally, the phrase that follows ("For this name[79] can bring God to manifestation for men and reconcile enemies to one another") seems to indicate angelic activity, since angels mediate God's presence to his people and are sometimes confused with God (e.g., Gen 16:7–14; Exod 3). Thus, Herod's speech uses angels as an example of the holiness of envoys in general. The Jews have learned to give the utmost respect to ambassadors because they have experienced heavenly envoys. Just as the Greeks consider ambassadors to be "sacred and inviolable" according to their customs, so too, Jews consider ambassadors to be sacred

a response to Davies and arguments in favor of angels, see Bandstra, "Law and Angels." On Davies's first argument, Bandstra responds that Josephus's point is to indicate the high regard in which envoys are held by both Greeks and Jews. It would, in fact, undermine Herod's argument to his troops if he were referring to prophets who can be killed, because the Israelites frequently did kill the prophets; Herod thus would not want to give warrant for the Arabs killing the Jewish envoys! Bandstra describes Davies's second contention as an argument from silence, and counters it with another argument from silence: although Josephus uses ἄγγελος to refer to messengers in general, he never uses the term to refer to the canonical prophets. Third, Bandstra convincingly shows that the alleged parallel between *Ant.* 15:136 and *Ag. Ap.* 1.37 is not grammatically parallel after all. Fourth, while Josephus does occasionally omit references to angels, he does not hesitate to mention angels when it suits his purpose and understanding of their role and function. Fifth, Bandstra agrees that in the LXX ἄγγελος can be used for prophet or priest, but he argues that this alone is not enough to prove the use here. In addition, Bandstra also investigates the phrases "the noblest of the decrees" and "the holiest things in the laws." He maintains that both phrases refer to the most central and authoritative parts of the law, which for Josephus meant God's retributive justice. When Josephus does refer to angels, it is usually in appearances prior to the giving of the law; the angels reveal God as one who blesses virtue and condemns vice. In addition, these angels are sometimes able to reconcile enemies to each other, as Josephus asserts in *Ant.* 15:136. Bandstra concludes that Josephus does intend to refer to angels in this passage, but that he does not intend an explicit reference to the giving of the law on Mt. Sinai.

78. *Contra* Bandstra, "Law and Angels."

79. "This name" refers to the idea of an ambassador or mediator (πρέσβεις).

and inviolable because the angels provide a key example of the important role of mediators.

Rabbinic texts also provide evidence for the belief that angels were present at the giving of the Law at Sinai. Various descriptions of angelic activity emerge in these interpretations. One strand describes the angelic presence positively: angels honored the Torah and Israel for accepting it, and threatened to destroy those who would not accept the Law.[80] On the other hand, some rabbis held a negative view of the activity of angels at Sinai, arguing that angels coveted the Law and/or did not want humanity to receive it.[81] The value of rabbinic evidence is tainted, however, by its late date. It is likely that the rabbis were responding to Christian descriptions of the role of angels at Sinai; thus, the rabbinic texts must be regarded with caution in that they may not be representative of pre-Christian Jewish beliefs. Indeed, Hindy Najman identifies three exegetical strategies employed by some rabbis to circumvent the idea of angelic mediation at Sinai: the outright rejection of angelic mediation, the elimination of angels even where explicitly mentioned in the Hebrew text, and the portrayal of angels at Sinai as obstacles to the giving of the Law.[82] She concludes that "the general tendency of the rabbis is to inherit second temple traditions emphasizing the unique immediacy of the revelation to Moses, and thus the unique authority of Moses, rather than second temple traditions portraying Moses learning the law from angels."[83]

Overall, it is apparent that some Jewish traditions affirm that angels were present at Sinai. The extent of the role of these angels is certainly open to interpretation, but evidence exists that at least some Jews understood angels to have played a mediatorial role in the giving of the Law. The presence and participation of angels was an indication of the great glory of the event. It appears that only later, and perhaps in response to Christian interpretation, the participation of angels was considered to be a negative factor.

In order to understand the range of possibilities for interpreting Paul's reference to angels in Gal 3:19, it is necessary to begin with a brief

80. *Pesiq. Rab.* 10.6; 21.7, 8, 33.10; *Šabb.* 88a; *Cant. Rab.* 4.4.1; *Num. Rab.* 16.24; *Tanḥ. B ytrw* 14; *Pesiq. Rab. Kah.* 12.22; 16.3; *Midr. Ps.* 68.10; 103.8.

81. *Deut. Rab.* 7:9; 8:2; *Exod. Rab.* 28:1; 51.8; *Šabb.* 88b; *Pesiq. Rab.* 20.4; 25.3; *'Abot. R. Nat. A* 2; *Midr. Ps.* 8.2; *Cant. Rab.* 8.11.2.

82. Najman, "Angels at Sinai," 326–331.

83. Ibid., 331.

investigation of Paul's cosmology overall. Such an inquiry is not easy; although Paul only uses the term ἄγγελος ten times,[84] he frequently uses other language to refer to spiritual powers, including ἀρχαί, ἐξουσίαι, δύναμις, στοιχεῖα, δαιμόνιον, and σατανᾶς.[85] Although some early Jewish literature gives evidence of increasing fascination with heavenly beings, their roles, names, and histories, Paul does not appear to share the same fascination. He never makes it a priority to explain systematically his understanding of the heavenly realms or the traditions upon which he draws to achieve this understanding. We must piece together what we can from his references.

From Paul's use of ἄγγελος alone certain nuances are apparent. That angels hold a high status for Paul may be inferred from Gal 1:8 and 4:14. Yet these angels do not hold a higher status than redeemed humans (Rom 8:38, 1 Cor 6:3). Furthermore, angels can be either good or evil (2 Cor 11:14 and 12:7). Although Paul does not address the role of angels directly, he implies that at least one of their functions is to watch humanity (1 Cor 4:9; 11:10). Another possible role includes speaking and preaching as mentioned in, respectively, 1 Cor 13:1 and Gal 1:8. Overall, it can be said that Paul generally has a positive view of angels; when he takes a negative view, the term is specifically qualified, for example, by a reference to Satan (2 Cor 12:7).

When we begin to explore the other language Paul uses for the spiritual realm, the picture becomes more unclear because the terms can have a variety of meanings and can be either impersonal or personal in nature.[86] The first observation to make, however, is that Paul consistently argues that Christ is superior to all powers and authorities.[87] Second, these spiritual powers nonetheless have some amount of influence in the present world, and even affect those in Christ. For example, Paul wanted to visit the Thessalonians but was stopped by Satan (1 Thess 2:18), Paul's thorn in

84. Rom 8:38; 1 Cor 4:9; 6:3, 11:10; 13:1; 2 Cor 11:14; 12:7; Gal 1:8; 3:19; 4:14. In the disputed letters, see Col 2:18; 2 Thess 1:7; 1 Tim 3:16; 5:21.

85. In the disputed letters, additional language includes κυριότητες, θρόνοι, κοσμοκράτορας, πνεύματα, and διάβολος. For specific nuances for these various terms, see Reid, "Principalities and Powers."

86. For a summary of the various schools of thought regarding Paul's angelology, see O'Brien, "Principalities and Powers."

87. See, for example, Rom 8:38; 16:20; and 1 Cor 15:24. In the disputed letters, see Eph 1:21; Col 1:16; 2:10,15, 20.

the flesh is "a messenger of Satan," (2 Cor 12:7), and he warns believers not to be tempted (1 Cor 7:5) or outwitted by Satan's schemes (2 Cor 2:11).[88] Even though this sense of conflict between good and evil powers exists in Paul's writings, at times Paul refers to these evil powers as serving a good purpose, such as in 1 Cor 5:5, where Paul urges the Corinthians to hand over the sinner to Satan so that the man's sinful nature may be destroyed and his spirit saved on the day of the Lord.

But from where do Paul's ideas originate? It is possible that Paul's understanding of the spiritual realm was influenced by Hellenistic ideas about astrology and fate.[89] If this were the case, then his understanding of spiritual powers may have focused more on impersonal forces.[90] In some cases, we do see Paul referring to impersonal forces such as "sin" and the "flesh."[91] Nonetheless, Paul likely does not rest his entire understanding of spiritual powers on merely these forces, since his Jewish background included an understanding of evil spirits as personal beings who wage war against the one God.[92] As I have argued, Paul was firmly tied to his Jewish roots and believed Christ's redemptive activity was the fulfillment of God's plan for salvation. It would be difficult to imagine him maintaining this continuity while simultaneously (and without further explana-

88. See also Gal 4:9; Eph 6:12; 1 Tim 3:7; 4:1; 5:15; and 2 Tim 2:26.

89. MacGregor, for example, suggests that Paul is influenced by Gnostic astral religious beliefs that the stars, which determined fate, were more hostile than friendly. Thus, Paul views demonic intelligences as cosmic spiritual forces. Yet MacGregor ("Principalities and Powers," 17–28) denies any dualism in Paul's thought, because of Paul's belief in Christ's pre-existence and victory; Christ both created all things and has made all things subject to him, even though the final consummation is still in the future. See also Lee, "Interpreting the Demonic Powers," 54–69.

90. O'Brien takes issue with this viewpoint, and ultimately concludes that Paul's "powers" are not purely evil structures, but that the powers of evil are personal, spiritual agencies. Social structures can themselves become demonic, but to limit the powers to structures alone falsely restricts Satan's range of opportunities ("Principalities and Powers."

91. See, e.g., Rom 6–7; Gal 5:17. Walter Wink argues that Paul was actively demythologizing the spiritual powers by referring to them in impersonal terms, such as flesh, sin, death, etc. Wink describes the powers as "*the inner aspect of material or tangible manifestations of power*," which he compares to a "mob spirit," in that the spirit does not exist outside of the mob and suddenly enter it, but is actually constituted when the crowd reaches a flashpoint of excitement and frustration (*Naming the Powers*, 104–5).

92. E.g., Gen 6:1–4 and *1 En.* (*Book of Watchers*) suggest that demons are angels who have rebelled against God and thus are personal beings, not impersonal forces.

tion) completely restructuring the foundational understanding of the spiritual realm.

We should consider, then, the Jewish traditions that may have influenced Paul's concept of the spiritual realm. One such view involved the "angels of the nations"—that is, the belief that each nation had its own angel watching over it.[93] Sir 17:11–18, for example, records that God placed a ruler over every nation, but God reserved Israel for himself. Similarly, Philo writes that God "set boundaries of nations according to the number of the angels of God" (*Post.* 91). *Jub.* 15:30–32 expresses a comparable idea, but with a negative twist: God placed "spirits" over the nations to lead them astray, but no angel presides over Israel—God alone is their ruler. Hence, this tradition suggests that even though wicked nations may rage against Israel, behind those evil structures lie very real spiritual powers.[94]

Lloyd Gaston has considered the tradition regarding the angels of the nations and applied it specifically to Gal 3:19–20.[95] He argues that the Torah was offered to all nations, but only Israel accepted it. But because the Torah was identified with Wisdom, it therefore was considered to be eternal. Thus, because God is one, it is this same Torah which governs the entire world. The angels of the nations administered the law among the Gentiles; that was their charge. This explains Paul's reference in Gal 3:19, Gaston argues. "The problem with the angels of the nations is that there are seventy of them; they are not unique, and they cannot fulfill the promise of God to Abraham and his 'one seed' concerning the Gentiles."[96] But in Christ, all are made one. Gaston's argument, however, is questionable

93. See Stuckenbruck, "Angels of the Nations."

94. Cullmann (*Christ and Time*, 191–210; esp. 198), for example, refers to this tradition and states that when Paul refers to powers and rulers and authorities, he means *both* the human instruments and the spiritual powers behind those human actions. Because of Christ's victory on the cross, these powers have now lost their evil character and stand under the Lordship of Christ. Their perceived power is only an illusion, Cullmann argues; it is as though these powers are bound to a rope and thus are still active in the world, but are not truly free. See also Caird (*Principalities and Powers*), who argues that "the belief in national angels was a courageous proclamation of the universal sovereignty of God" (7). Caird argues that the fall of the angels was not pre-cosmic, but rather the result of human sin (e.g., the Watchers tradition of Gen 6). He describes Satan as the accuser who protects God's justice. Because humans have sinned, Satan accuses humanity and continues to do so, even though God's justice is secondary to his eternal purpose of grace. Satan treats that which is secondary as if it were the absolute will of God.

95. Gaston, *Paul and the Torah*, 35–44.

96. Ibid., 43.

on several levels. First, he denies that any tradition exists of angels mediating the Law, a conclusion controverted above. Second, Paul would never use an argument based on the eternity of the Torah in a section where he argues precisely the opposite: the Torah was only temporary and has now been superseded in Christ! Third, as noted above, when Paul refers to ἄγγελοι, he retains a generally positive perspective; if he intended to refer to the angels of the nations, he likely would have used a more negative term, such as στοιχεῖα.[97]

Another Jewish perspective, and one which is more promising for understanding Paul's angelology, is that of Jewish apocalyptic eschatology.[98] The revelation of heavenly mysteries that characterizes apocalyptic often occurred through a heavenly intermediary; frequently this revelation involved a discussion of a new age breaking into the current age. At that time, God would finally conquer his enemies—both those opposing governmental forces in this world and those evil supernatural beings in

97. I do not mean to imply that στοιχεῖα in 4:3, 9 refers to the angels of the nations; rather, this phrase has a distinct negative connotation. If Paul meant to denigrate the Law based on the angels of the nations, he likely would have used a more deprecatory term. See Ps 82 for God's judgment on these angels for failing to promote justice among the nations.

98. *Contra* Carr (*Angels and Principalities*), who argues that although Jewish angelology developed considerably during and after the exile, such ideas were nonetheless only peripheral to Jewish beliefs. Carr downplays the significance of the angels-of-the-nations tradition, and says that the idea of cosmic battle was not prevalent in Paul's time. He finds no evidence of astrological beliefs or fear of evil, hostile forces in the first century or in any of the geographical areas in which Paul's churches grew. These only became significant in the second century and later, he argues. The powers and principalities in Paul generally refer to the heavenly host and serve to emphasize Christ's glory. In dealing with Eph 6:12, the most blatant description of hostile spiritual forces, Carr concludes that the text is a later interpolation. Arnold rightly criticizes Carr's approach in "'Exorcism' of Ephesians 6:12." He argues that Carr does not give enough attention to Jewish pre-Christian ideas, such as those found in the Qumran literature. The most blatant example Arnold cites is the War Rule (1QM), which describes the struggle between the Spirits of Light and the Spirits of Darkness. See also 1 QS 3:18–25; 4:9, 20, 23; CD 2:18; 12:2; and 11QMelch, in which Melchizedek is a warrior who will slaughter the powers of darkness. In addition, Carr ignores key New Testament texts—specifically, all of the Gospel traditions regarding demons and spiritual powers (see, e.g., Matt 9:34; 12:24; 25:41; Mark 3:22; and Luke 11:15). Furthermore, Arnold argues that Asia Minor was a center for magic during Paul's time, and astrological beliefs were far more prevalent than Carr admits. Arnold criticizes Carr's interpretative logic, especially on Eph 6:12; Carr's interpolation claim finds no support in either textual traditions nor in any variations among the church fathers. Certainly Carr's interpretation cannot bear the weight of Arnold's astute criticisms.

the spiritual world.[99] This element of war against both structures and personal supernatural beings fits well with what we find in Paul's writing: at times Paul refers generally to "powers" and "principalities," while at other times he refers to specific evil spirits, namely "Satan."[100]

With respect to the Galatians, Paul argues that "we" were once under the στοιχεῖα (4:3), and he worries that although they have been freed through Christ (4:4–7), they now seem to be returning to these "weak and beggarly" στοιχεῖα.[101] The "we" that Paul uses includes both himself, as a Jew, and his Gentile audience before they were believers. Thus, the Law itself cannot be the στοιχεῖα here, despite the reference in verse 5.[102] Verses 8–9 are highly suggestive of demonic activity; before their conversion, the Galatians were enslaved to beings that were not gods. Paul's language is reminiscent of 1 Cor 8:4 and 10:20, in which he understood pagan idolatry to be a partnership with demons. In Gal 3:8–9, he argues that the Galatians, by wanting to be under the Law, are instead returning to these στοιχεῖα.[103] His chronological emphasis in these verses is sug-

99. See Aune, "Apocalypticism," as well as the further discussion in chapter 4 of this book.

100. Neyrey argues that Paul is like the others in his world in perceiving evil heavenly powers as personified: "Twentieth century Westerners describe night as the absence of light, death as the absence of life, and evil as the absence of good. Not so Paul and his world. They perceive Night as a somebody, not an absence of something" (*Paul, in Other Words*, 161). Furthermore, Paul does not consider his personifications of Sin and Death to be simple figures of speech. Neyrey argues that the wealth of terms Paul uses suggests a well-populated heavenly realm; these figures constitute a "formidable army waging deadly combat against God's holy ones" (162). Thus war and conflict on heaven and earth is one of the major themes in Paul's understanding of the heavenly realms. See also Stewart ("On a Neglected Emphasis"), who argues that this sense of cosmic battle is important in the New Testament, and the emphasis is one that has been largely lost in modern scholarship. Although ascertainable human forces resulted in Christ's death, Stewart argues that in the New Testament these human forces always appear as mere agents of sinister spiritual powers. While I agree that Paul understands much of the spiritual battle to be against personal supernatural beings, I do not think this is *always* the case for Paul. In some instances, his language intimates that impersonal forces are at work (although, perhaps, in concert with spiritual beings).

101. For an overview of the various theories regarding Paul's understanding and use of στοιχεῖα, see Reid, "Elements/Elemental Spirits."

102. Paul refers to being "under the Law" eleven times, five of which are in Galatians. He refers to slavery under the law in several instances (Rom 6:14; Gal 3:23; 4:5), while in other places he specifically refers to Jews by this term (1 Cor 9:20—four times; Gal 4:21).

103. Arnold ("Returning to the Domain") argues that Paul used the apocalyptic category of demonic powers, equivalent to "principalities and powers," in his arguments

gestive of the apocalyptic view of two ages. Formerly, the Galatians were enslaved; with the advent of Christ, they are free. But by returning to "the Law," something that Paul has just argued is only temporary, the Galatians are suggesting they want to return to an age dominated by false gods. This is Paul's point. He is not making a distinction between personal or impersonal spiritual beings.[104] Rather, he is addressing the old age, in which all humanity (whether Jew or Gentile) was enslaved to sin and in need of redemption, in contrast to the new age in which nothing has authority over Christ. Nonetheless, it is striking that in Paul's view of the new age inaugurated with Christ, the Torah *as an end itself* has become something that is "not god" on par with pagan idols!

Overall, several observations regarding Paul's angelology can be made at this point: 1) Paul is not concerned as such to delineate his understanding of the angelic realm, but rather draws ad hoc on this or that tradition without further comment; 2) Paul understands the cosmic realm to be populated by a range of powers, many of which are wicked personal spiritual beings, while others are impersonal forces;[105] 3) Paul's language about the spiritual realm more often addresses evil beings and powers rather than "good angels" or angelic beings subservient to God; 4) when Paul refers to *evil* spiritual beings or abstractions, he almost always uses terms other than ἄγγελος; 5) Paul consistently argues that regardless of the influence of spiritual beings on the heavenly and earthly realms,

about the Law. The στοιχεῖα in Gal. 4:3, 9 are demons who try to lead humans astray by encouraging people to continue to observe the Law, even though it is now obsolete in Christ. These angelic beings, however, are *not* the angels of Gal 3:19, he concludes.

104. In agreement with Dunn (*Galatians*, 212–13).

105. For an insightful analysis, see Forbes, "Paul's Principalities and Powers" and "Pauline Demonology and/ or Cosmology?" He argues that Paul considers the spirit world to be populated both by personal spirits and by personified hypostatized abstractions; Paul's terminology is deliberately abstract and impersonal. Forbes disagrees with scholars who try to demythologize Paul's apocalyptic language; rather, Paul is not substituting terms for angels and demons, but he is adding the idea of impersonal forces to the catalogue of Satan and other personal beings ("Paul's Principalities," 85). This continuum of pure abstractions, personifiable abstractions, literary personifications, and actual spiritual beings has its root in Middle Platonism. Thus Paul is "working creatively" with both his Jewish and Hellenistic backgrounds ("Pauline Demonology," 73). Forbes's viewpoint perhaps does the most justice to the variety of Pauline terminology for the spiritual world. Those who err on the side of either strict personifications or pure abstractions miss the intricacy of Paul's descriptive language.

Christ has subjected these powers and angels and is ultimately victorious, even if the full effects of this victory are not manifest now.

This brief overview of Paul's angelology suggests the following implications for the interpretation of Gal 3:19–20: 1) Paul's description of the angelic mediation of the Law is likely peripheral to his argument, since angelology rarely figures at the forefront of Paul's thought; 2) the fact that Paul uses the term ἄγγελοι in Gal 3:19 rather than another term, such as ἀρχαί or στοιχεῖα, suggests that Paul understands the angels to be good angels; 3) the glory that the good angels add to the experience at Sinai is nonetheless subordinate to the glory of God's definitive revelation in Christ.

Outside of Galatians, the New Testament writers refer only three times to angelic presence at the giving of the Law. In Acts 7 Stephen addresses the Sanhedrin. He states that Moses "was in the congregation in the wilderness with the angel who spoke to him at Mount Sinai, and with our ancestors; and he received living oracles to give to us" (v. 38). Clearly, in this reference, the idea that an angel spoke with Moses is not considered derogatory. Rather, the Law is considered to be "living oracles" that the Israelites refused to obey.

At the end of his speech, Stephen accuses the Jews of murdering Jesus and addresses them: "You are the ones that received the law as ordained by angels, and yet you have not kept it" (v. 53). In this instance, the angelic mediation of the Law only seems to increase its glory—Stephen implies that the Israelites ought to have obeyed something so special as to be given by angels.

Finally, the author of Heb 2:2–3a asks, "For if the message declared through angels was valid, and every transgression or disobedience received a just penalty, how can we escape if we neglect so great a salvation?" Again, the angelic message is not considered derogatory.[106] Just two verses earlier the author calls angels "ministering spirits sent to serve those who will inherit salvation." It is also clear, however, that the message of salvation that Christ brings is superior to the angelic message.

It is impossible to know the origin of the tradition expressed in these verses. Paul's own teaching could be the source just as easily as a wider

106. Koester argues that angelic mediation of the Law stresses its exalted status: "Hebrews argues that if angelic mediation shows how great the Law is, then the message proclaimed by the Son of God must be even greater, since he is greater than the angels" (*Hebrews*, 205).

tradition found in Judaism. Regardless, it appears that some of the first Christians were aware of the idea that angels participated in the giving of the Law at Sinai, but this participation did not necessarily lend a negative overtone; in fact, the presence of angels may have served to increase the respect with which the Law was held. It is surprising that in the earliest Christian records the tradition is not more negative.[107]

This study of angels in Gal 3:19–20 has revealed the existence of a Jewish tradition which maintained that angels mediated the Law on Mt. Sinai. This appears not to be the primary tradition regarding the giving of the Law; nonetheless, the presence and mediation of these angels in this tradition served to heighten the glory of the event. The importance of the Law itself and the significance of this moment in salvation history were marked by the participation of supernatural messengers of God.

Paul's reference to angels here thus may also serve to heighten the glory of the event. Had Paul wanted to argue that the presence of the angels depreciated the Law, he likely would have used a different term than "angels." The Law was given for a good purpose and was not evil or demonic; it has, however, served its purpose. As important and magnificent as the event on Sinai was, it is no match for the fulfillment of the one God's promise to Abraham.

THE MEDIATOR

The concept of a mediator ties verses 19 and 20 together. Paul describes the Law as having been given "by the hand of" a mediator, a phrase in which the Greek translates literally the Hebrew idiom meaning "through." Paul then goes on to state that the mediator is not "of one" in verse 20. But Paul never specifically clarifies who this mediator is, and we are left to guess at his view of mediation. Does he consider mediation, generally, to be a positive or negative concept? Do the specific circumstances at Mt. Sinai warrant a positive or negative view of mediation? Does the specific identity of the mediator provoke Paul's critique? These questions require further investigation if we are to understand Paul's argument.

To begin, we will consider the idea of mediation in the Greco-Roman world. The Hellenistic usage of the term μεσίτης can be seen as early as

107. Later Christian interpretations take a more negative view. See, e.g., Origen's commentary on Song of Songs, in which Origen discusses Song 1:2 and considers the Law to be inferior to the direct revelation of Christ.

the third century BCE, and at its basic level means "one in the middle."[108] Oepke provides three basic meanings: the neutral who both sides can trust, an intermediary (in a spatial sense), and a mediator or negotiator who establishes a relation that would not otherwise exist. The first of these meanings has a variety of nuances which generally reflect the term's usage in a civil legal setting: an arbiter, a witness to a transaction, the neutral with whom an object of dispute is temporarily left, a pawnbroker, or a guarantor. Thus, when Paul uses this specific term, it is possible that he is calling to mind such legal imagery, especially for the mostly Gentile church to which he is writing. Since the context involves the giving of the Law, a civil legal meaning could indeed be intended here.

In addition, the concept of mediation is prevalent within Gentile religion. Deities can act as the guarantor of human relationships; this concept is evidenced by the practice of making oaths in the name of a particular deity. In addition, various religions viewed the cosmos as one universal body; the deity occupied the center of this body and both held together the various parts and maintained separation between warring factions of this body. Mithra, for example, is in the middle between heaven and the underworld; he mediates between day and night.[109] Thus it is clear that civil legal meanings are not the only way of interpreting the term μεσίτης. Cosmic overtones may be involved as well.

In Jewish thought, the word μεσίτης is used in the LXX only in Job 9:33, and in a different sense than that which is found in non-Jewish Hellenistic usage.[110] Thus, if a word study provided the only evidence of mediation in Jewish thought, it would seem that mediation does not figure prominently in Jewish Scripture.[111] At least, the Hellenistic civil litigation term does not appear in the Old Testament. But when the larger concept of mediation is examined, it becomes clear that mediation is an integral

108. Oepke, "μεσίτης" 4:599.

109. Ibid., 4:603–5.

110. See Becker, "μεσίτης." He states that Job 9:33 refers to the μεσίτης as one who listens to prosecution and defense arguments and restores the law by dealing with the guilty party; thus, arbitrating between two parties is not in view here.

111. Becker states that "we cannot find the concept of mediator in the OT." He qualifies this statement, however, by noting: "Where the term appears, it means something quite different from the concept in the Gk. world. The . . . priest and . . . prophet were mediators between God and his people, though never in the role of a neutral third party" (ibid.).

part of Jewish thought: "Though the word is not used, mediatorship is at the heart of OT religion."[112]

If we consider the wider concept of a mediator as someone who stands between two parties, it is clear that the Jewish Scriptures are rife with mediatorial figures. These include priests, kings, prophets, and angels, and were commonly accepted mediators in the first century.[113] This definition should be nuanced further, however. The mediator did not simply negotiate between two parties of equal standing; rather, the mediator presented God's viewpoints to the people and thus acted more as a spokesman than as any kind of neutral third party.[114] The necessity for a mediator comes out of the Jewish idea that even though the God of Israel could be known personally and individually, he was nonetheless transcendent—no one could see God and live. Thus, mediation was necessary, and took place in such forms as the priest and offering.[115]

112. Oepke, "μεσίτης," 4:614.

113. Chester, "Jewish Messianic Expectations." Chester finds evidence of the proliferation of Jewish mediatorial figures in Philo, *Apoc. Ab.*, *P. Jos.*, *Apoc. Zeph.*, *Jos. Asen.*, 11QMelch and other Qumran texts, Ezek. Trag., *1 & 2 En.*, and *T. Mos.* Although Chester is correct that mediation is evident in a number of these sources, the evidence does not always support his conclusions. For example, he cites The *Exagoge* of Ezek. Trag. as a remarkable text in which Moses is elevated to God's throne. Bauckham ("Throne of God," 55–57), however, has noted that the text records a dream of Moses in which the metaphor of a throne is used to symbolize power and leadership; it does not provide a picture of the *reality* of a human figure on a throne. Nonetheless, Chester does show that a variety of mediatorial figures, from personified concepts (e.g., Wisdom and Logos in Philo), to exalted human figures (e.g., Abel, Abraham, Adam, Enoch, Jacob, Melchizedek, and Moses), to angelic figures (e.g., Michael) played important mediatorial roles in Judaism during the first century.

114. Wilson argues that the Mosaic prophet was seen as "the only legitimate channel of communication between Yahweh and the people. God speaks directly to the prophet, who, like Moses, clearly and accurately perceives the Word of God . . . and repeats it to the people. In addition, the people are to go to the prophet when they want to approach Yahweh with questions or requests" (*Prophecy and Society*, 162). The role of the Mosaic prophet is to speak only God's words, and not to add to or take away from the divine message. Thus, "a word from a Mosaic prophet is a word directly from God" (164).

115. De Lacey, "Jesus as Mediator," 103–4. He notes other forms of mediation as well, including other human and angelic mediators. He concludes that Paul plays on the various meanings of mediation in Gal 3:19–20. Whereas Moses is a go-between (chosen as mediator by both God and the people) who ensures the two parties do not meet, Jesus is the kind of mediator who brings the two parties together—he is the means by which we enter the presence of God himself (116–17).

The key example of such a mediatorial figure in the Old Testament was Moses; he is "the absolute mediator to later ages."[116] Moses is unique and fulfills many roles—as spokesman, as lawgiver, as intercessor, as the one who stands between Yahweh and the people. The other great Old Testament mediator figure is the Servant of Yahweh in Deutero-Isaiah. This figure intercedes and suffers for the people.[117]

Jesus, of course, is the great mediator of the New Testament.[118] Mediation, however, was viewed differently with the coming of Christ. P. G. Davis states that "the covenant itself was the center of gravity in the predominant forms of Palestinian Judaism; generally, mediators were significant not in themselves but because of what they mediated, namely, the covenant relationship with God . . . In Christianity, Jesus the mediator himself tended to eclipse or absorb the substance of what he mediated."[119] Thus, it appears that even though the term μεσίτης appears rarely in either the Old or New Testament, both Jews and the first Christians embraced mediation as integral to their faith.

116. Oepke, "μεσίτης," 4:611.

117. Ibid. For one analysis of the various kinds of mediators, see Davis, "Divine Agents." Davis uses chronology to sort the various mediators into categories of legacy, intervention, and consummation. The legacy pattern consists of the work of an individual mediator which remains in force for later generations. Abraham, David, and Moses fall into this category. The intervention pattern involves mediation in the present; the mediator makes possible some form of interaction between God and humanity. Priests, shamans, and magicians fall into this category, as do angels. The consummation pattern describes a mediator who will come in the future to play a role in fulfilling or restoring God's relationship with his people. Elijah provides the key example here. Davis concludes that Christ uniquely fills all three patterns simultaneously; Enoch provides the closest parallel in Jewish literature, but nonetheless this does not explain the rise of the worship of Christ. Davis's analysis is helpful in highlighting the breadth of the mediatorial concept in Judaism, although his decision to use time as the basis for defining his categories seems somewhat arbitrary. Angels, for example, potentially cross the various categories because of their eternal nature. In addition, the members of Davis's categories may display wide differences from one another. For example, a mediator figure would be viewed very differently if he were mediating teaching or assurance or judgment or redemption. Yet Davis's time-based categories do not recognize these differences. The intervention pattern, for example, would include both priests who make temple sacrifices and Gabriel's appearance in Daniel, where his activity is primarily that of a teacher/interpreter. It seems inadequate that a single category could contain such vast differences.

118. De Lacey argues that "the concept of Jesus Christ as mediator is a central and powerful one" for Paul ("Jesus as Mediator," 102).

119. Davis, "Divine Agents," 501–2.

Nonetheless, at least some Jews seem to have viewed mediation as an indication of inferior status. This strand of Judaism appears most clearly in the rabbinic material. One very early text, however, also provides insight into the question of the value of mediation. A Midrash on the Passover Haggadah from the third or early-second century BCE comments that the Lord brought Israel forth from Egypt "not by means of an angel, nor by means of a seraph, nor by means of a messenger; but the Holy One, blessed be He, Himself, in His glory . . ." The writer quotes Exod 12:12 and comments on it: "'I will go through the land of Egypt,' I, and not an angel; 'And I will smite all the first-born,' I, and not a seraph; 'And against all the gods of Egypt will I execute judgments,' I, and not a messenger; 'I am the Lord,' I am He and no other."[120] This passage occurs within the historical context of the debate between early Pharisees and Sadducees, and thus the prominence of angels was a matter of frequent debate. This Midrash was written against the belief in angels as God's intermediaries, and indicates the text was written "before the Pharisaic Order had attained sufficient power to prevent an opinion contrary to the tenets of the majority of its members being introduced into a liturgical service."[121]

The early date of this material is important for understanding the impact of its teachings about mediation. Paul declared himself a Pharisee, and he clearly affirmed the existence and activity of angels. Thus, it is highly unlikely that Paul would affirm the kind of negative view of intermediaries expressed in this text—a view specifically opposed to Pharisaic beliefs. If Paul did have a negative view of mediation, then most likely he would have drawn such a view from other textual traditions.

But the Passover Haggadah is not the only text to cite an instance in which God deals directly with his people and refuses to use a mediator. *Sipre Zuta* on Num 12:8, for example, clarifies that God spoke with Moses

120. Finkelstein, "The Oldest Midrash," 296–97. Finkelstein finds this denial of the angelic participation of the Exodus extraordinary because it contradicts Scripture (Num 20:16). He also notes that *y. Sanh.* 2.1,20a and *Hor.* 3.2,47a probably refer to the Passover Haggadah when they deny angelic participation in the Exodus.

121. Finkelstein, "Oldest Midrash," 311–12. Finkelstein finds additional evidence of the debate between early Pharisees and Sadducees in the text where it cites the "visible manifestation of the Divine Presence." This phrase relates to how the high priest should enter the holy of holies. The Pharisees believed the priest should not light the incense until inside the holy of holies, because God was not visible, whereas the Sadducees believed the high priest must light the censer first so that the cloud of smoke would protect him from laying eyes on the visible manifestation of God (310).

directly, not by means of an angel. *Sipre*, Deut 325 states, "I personally will exact punishment from them, not through an angel, not through a messenger."[122] *Sipre*, Deut 42, which comments on Deut 11:14 ("I will give the rain of your land in its season"), says, "'Then I will give': I—not by means of (by the hands of) an angel and not by means of a messenger."[123] *Mek.* (Pisha 7) on Exod 12:12 states that the Lord smote the first-born, "not by means of an angel, and not by means of a messenger." *Mek.* (Pisha 13) on Exod 12:29 is very similar. In addition, *Mek.* (Shabbata 1) on Exod 31:12–13 says, "'And the Lord said to Moses': Not through an angel nor through a messenger."[124]

In another instance, the people want to hear directly from God. *Mek.* (Bahodesh 2) records comments on Exod 19:9b in which the rabbi quotes the people as saying, "'We want to hear directly from the mouth of our king. Hearing from the mouth of an attendant is not the same as hearing from the mouth of the king.' Said the Omnipresent, 'Give them what they want, so that the people may hear.'"[125] It is interesting that this comment runs contrary to Exod 20:19, where the people ask Moses to intervene, since they cannot bear to hear God directly. This positive view of mediation is reflected in another rabbinic text, *Exod. Rab.* 34.1: "We will never find God's strength [fully] displayed toward any of His creatures, for He does not visit His creatures with burdensome laws, but comes to each one according to his strength. For know thou, that if God had come upon Israel with the full might of His strength when He gave them the Torah, they would not have been able to withstand it, as it says, 'If we hear the voice of the Lord our God any more, then we shall die' (Deut 5:22)."[126]

In contrast, other sources also denigrate human transmission of God's teachings. *Song Rab.* 1.2, 4 records Rabbi Judah as saying that when God spoke the Ten Commandments the Israelites's knowledge of the Torah was firm, but when Moses became their mediator they were liable to forget what they had learned; just as Moses, a human being, is transitory, so is his teaching transitory.[127] This passage certainly indicates

122. Neusner, *Sifre to Deuteronomy*, 2:368.

123. Goldin ("Not By Means of an Angel and Not By Means of a Messenger") looks at this latter Midrash and finds that a grammatical ambiguity necessitated the explanation.

124. Neusner, *Mekhilta*, 2:253.

125. Ibid., 2:51.

126. Freedman and Simon, *Midrash Rabbah, Exodus*: 425.

127. Ibid., *Song of Songs*: 21–22.

a preference for God's direct dealing. It is interesting that just prior, in 1.2, 2, Rabbi Johanan relates a tradition in which an angel carried the words on Mt. Sinai from God to each Israelite in turn, asking if they would receive it; when they replied positively, the angel kissed them on the mouth. Immediately following Rabbi Johanan's interpretation, other rabbis suggest that "the commandment itself" went to each Israelite to ask whether they would receive it, and when they replied affirmatively, the commandment kissed them on the mouth and taught them Torah. Thus, this section of *Song Rab.* suggests a disagreement regarding the directness of the transmission of the Torah and the resulting effect.[128]

A distinction should be made, however, between a *preference* for God's direct activity and a negative view of mediation as a whole. Rather, these texts indicate that in a specific instance God may have preferred to act directly; in other contexts, an intermediary may have been quite acceptable. The question arises, then, as to whether the giving of the Law at Sinai was one of these specific cases of God's direct involvement. Most interesting for our study here is ʾ*Abot. R. Nat.* B, chapter 2: "Moses received Torah from Sinai. Not from the mouth of an angel and not from the mouth of a Seraph, but from the mouth of the King over the kings of kings, the Holy One, blessed be He, as Scripture says, 'These are the statutes and ordinances and laws which the Lord made between him and the people of Israel on Mount Sinai be (sic) Moses. (Lev 26:46).'"[129] ʾ*Abot. R. Nat.* A, chapter 1, states, "The Torah which the Holy One, blessed be He, gave to Israel he gave only by means of Moses, as it is said, '. . . between himself and the children of Israel.' Moses had the merit of serving as the messenger between the children of Israel and the Omnipresent."[130] These

128. Callan ("Pauline Midrash," 557–58) also cites *Yal.* to Jer 31:32 (2.317) and to Isa 54:13 (2.479): "In this world Israel learned the Torah from flesh and blood; therefore they forgot that which was given through Moses who was flesh and blood. Even as flesh and blood pass away, so also do its teachings." *Tanḥ. 'hry* 36a expresses a similar sentiment. Callan takes these texts to indicate a denigration of mediation. This, however, goes too far. The texts denigrate *human* teaching, but this does not necessarily exclude angelic mediation. Thus, the argument cannot be made that mediation itself is a negative concept in these texts. In addition, Callan cites the *Midr. Pss.* 31:2 and 50:3 in support of his argument. Yet it must be noted that the rabbinic comments on these two psalms discuss the difference between human and divine redemption, not human and divine teaching. Thus they do not apply to the transmission of the Law, as Callan implies.

129. Neusner, *Fathers According to Rabbi Nathan, Version B*, 25.

130. Ibid., 4.

rabbinic sources react strongly against the idea of angelic mediation at Sinai, *yet they clearly affirm Mosaic mediation of the Law to Israel.* Thus, for many of the rabbis, mediation itself was not the issue at Sinai. Rather, their polemic concerned the *identity* of the mediator.

Non-rabbinic, earlier sources also contain some texts that may indicate a negative attitude toward some kinds of mediation. Philo in *QG* 1.55 states that God did not use a mediator to exhort him to give others a share of incorruptibility. Callan takes this to suggest "that for God to make use of an intermediary would be a less perfect way of acting than to act directly."[131] In *Her.* 19 Philo says, "Now wise men take God for their guide and teacher, but the less perfect take the wise man; and therefore the Children of Israel say 'Talk thou to us and let not God talk to us lest we die' (Exod 20:19)." Yet Philo also states that a mediator was necessary at the giving of the Law, as indicated in *Somn.* 1.143, where he says that the people "are incapable of receiving even benefits unless he employ ministers." Perhaps in Philo's mind direct communication would have been preferable but nevertheless was impossible.

Josephus records in *Ant.* 3.89 that before he gave the Ten Commandments, Moses made the people approach to hear God so that "the excellence of the things said might not be impaired, being feebly transmitted to their knowledge by human tongue."[132] In addition, the LXX of Isa 63:9 reverses the order of the MT so that "not an angel but the Lord himself saved them." Whether this transposition is significant is debatable. Certainly other texts exist, even within the MT itself, that suggest at times God chooses not to use a mediator (e.g., an angel or dream or vision) and speaks with his people directly (e.g., Gen 2:16–17; 6:13—7:4; 12:1–3, 7; Num 12:8.). At Qumran mediation is also mentioned. 1QH 14:13–14

131. Callan, "Pauline Midrash," 556. Callan's article, while helpful, often goes too far in its claims. For example, he cites Philo's *Deus.* 109–10 and *Decal.* 176–78 as evidence for a negative view of mediation. The former, however, has nothing to do with mediation, while the latter supports the idea that God uses mediators in certain instances. In this case, God allows a subordinate power to deal with evil, and Callan takes this to indicate a denigration of mediation. But the reverse is not necessarily true—because something is mediated does not necessarily mean that the people are receiving less than God's best. Callan also cites *Sipre Deut* 221 in support of "direct communication," yet the text describes a negative view of the prophet using an additional mediator! The mediator himself should speak to the people "directly." This seems to indicate that when the mediator (the prophet) is speaking, God IS speaking directly to Israel.

132. Note that such a statement does not exclude angelic tongues.

suggests that in the future, among those who are saved, there "shall be no mediator to [invoke Thee]/ and no messenger [to make] reply." It is not clear, however, whether this text is making a negative statement about mediation or simply describing the future state of the community.

In assessing these texts, however, we should be wary of taking isolated passages and turning them into proof texts for a negative attitude toward mediation. One line in Philo, for example, does not countermand other instances where angels clearly have an acceptable mediatory function (e.g., *Somn.* 1.143). The most that can be said is that in certain instances God is depicted as preferring to act directly rather than through an intermediary. Goldin picks up on this theme, stating, "It may be of some significance that the emphasis of not by an angel and not by a messenger occurs in the following contexts: (1) God's redemption of Israel from Egyptian bondage; (2) God's punishment of Israel; (3) God's providing for Israel on its Land; (4) God's revelation of the Law to Moses at Sinai; (5) Moses's communication to Israel of the Sabbath as covenant-sign . . ."[133] This emphasis is indeed striking, and the date of the rabbinic material itself forces the question of whether this emphasis is a reaction to Christian proclamations that Jesus now fulfilled these roles rather than Moses or even God. According to this new teaching, Christ was the rock in the wilderness (1 Cor 10:4), and was thus part of that redemptive process. Christ sits on the judgment seat (2 Cor 5:10), Christ provides for his people (Heb 1:3), Christ is the mediator of the new covenant (Heb 9:15, 1 Cor 11:25), and Christ offered new teachings regarding the Sabbath (Mark 2:27–28). Thus, a strong possibility exists that the rabbinic emphasis on God's refusal to use a mediator is a polemical reaction to Christian teaching.

Overall, it is clear that mediation was integral to Jewish beliefs.[134] The concept is remarkably different from the civil litigation definition found in Greek culture. Rather, God's mediators were sent from God with God's message to God's people. The sense of a "neutral third party" who represents both sides in a dispute does not portray an accurate picture. Instead, the mediator is a mouthpiece of God.[135] Certainly Moses was not neutral;

133. Goldin, "Not by Means," 424.

134. Wilson's investigation of the sociological function of prophets in Israelite society concludes that "the prophet was thus considered a central figure in Israelite society, for he was the only legitimate means of communication between God and the people" (*Prophecy and Society*, 251).

135. Gottwald makes virtually the same statement in regard to prophets: "The prophet

he did not present the Law to Israel, then gather suggestions for change, then present these to Yahweh, and so on, as a neutral third party might do in order to achieve a compromise. In the Jewish understanding, God's mediator is a more one-sided representative who offers God's interests to the people for acceptance or rejection. It is not a negotiation of terms. At times, however, a more two-sided role is observable. Occasionally the prophetic mediator also intervenes on behalf of the people; both Moses and the Servant of Yahweh, for example, ask God to forgive Israel's sins. In addition, the role of the priest is to intervene on behalf of the people and offer expiation of sins through sacrifice. Yet even in these circumstances, the priests must intercede according to specifically prescribed methods. When Nadab and Abihu try to perform their priestly duties inappropriately, for example, they are punished by death (Lev 10:1–2). The two-sided priestly intermediary role is constrained by God's requirements. Thus, the primary role of the law-giving or prophetic "mediator" in Jewish thinking is to bring God's word to his people. This positive emphasis will be important for any interpretation of Gal 3:20.

As noted in the introduction to this chapter, a number of possibilities exist regarding the specific identity of the mediator in 3:19–20. The most likely options include an angel, Christ, or Moses. I will discuss the likelihood of each of these possibilities in turn. Before doing so, however, an important observation will aid in critiquing these options further: the grammar of the text indicates that verse 20 provides an explanatory comment on the mediator of verse 19. The presence of the article in verse 20 suggests that the mediator in verse 20 is the same mediator as in verse 19. This is the anaphoric use of the article, in which the article denotes previous reference.[136]

The existence of the article does not in itself, however, require the noun to be interpreted as an *individual* mediator. One could take the article to be a generic article, indicating the *class* of mediators in general. In this interpretation, Paul would be making a statement about the inferiority of mediators generally because of their lack of oneness, that is, the fact that they represent more than one party. To suggest that Paul rejects the idea of mediation, however, assumes a Hellenistic definition of a mediator as a neutral third party who represents multiple parties. Yet this is not

---

is the mouthpiece or spokesman of God. The pith of Hebrew prophecy is not prediction or social reform but the declaration of divine will" (*Light to the Nations*, 277).

136. Wallace, *Greek Grammar*, 217–20.

the kind of mediator that Paul has in view here. Given what we have just seen regarding the nature of mediation in Judaism (specifically, that the mediator acts primarily as God's mouthpiece), it can hardly be said that Paul would offer a negative critique of this kind of mediation as a whole.[137] Rather, it is more likely that Paul has a specific mediator in mind.

With this grammatical construction in mind, it is time to turn to the various possibilities. First, Paul could be referring to an angel. He has just said that the Law was ordained through angels, and finishes the thought with "by a mediator." The proximity of the term "angels" thus suggests the possibility that an angelic mediator may be in view here. As argued above, when Paul uses the term "angel" without further limitation, he generally has good angels in mind, i.e., those who are aligned with God's plan and purposes. Thus, if the reference is to an angel, then the mediator is probably *not* a demonic power.[138] The Law is not being denigrated on the basis of a "hostile takeover."[139]

The question could involve, then, a "good" angel who represents the other angels present at the giving of the Law. Nonetheless, this does not appear to be the best option. Given that this angel is one who promotes the purposes of God, it would be difficult for Paul to criticize the messenger without criticizing God. Yet this is precisely what the language of verse 20 appears to do. Paul makes a sharp contrast between the mediator and the one God by alluding to the Shema of Deut 6:4.

More importantly, Paul's argumentative strategy falters severely under this interpretation. Numerous Jewish texts describe God's *direct* dealing with Moses.[140] While some Jews maintained that angels mediated the Law, as noted above, this was certainly not the only belief or even the primary belief about the giving of the Law. Certainly Paul would have been aware of this—his knowledge of the MT and LXX was extensive,

137. In addition, elsewhere in the early Christian tradition, mediation is not seen as negative: 1 Tim 2:5; Heb 9:15. In these texts, of course, Christ is the mediator *par excellence*.

138. *Contra* Martyn and Schweitzer, as argued in the first section of this chapter.

139. Although one could argue that this is precisely Paul's rationale in Rom 7:8–11, Paul does not refer to angels in that text—rather, it is "sin" that seizes the opportunity afforded by the introduction of the Law. Furthermore, Paul concludes in Rom 7:12 that the Law itself is holy, just, and good.

140. See in the MT alone, for example, Exod 20:1, 22; 31:18; 34:32; Lev 7:38; 26:46, 27:34; Num 9:5; Deut 5:24–26; Neh 9:13.

as evidenced by his citation of various texts throughout his letters.[141] It is not likely that, without offering a more detailed explanation of his point of view, Paul would base his argument on an idea that could be so easily countered by multiple Scriptures. It is precisely when Paul argues something controversial that he relies heavily on Scripture; when the issue is generally agreed upon, he provides fewer scriptural allusions.[142] Thus, if the focal point of Paul's argument were a controversial interpretation of angelic mediation at Sinai, he would offer more than a passing comment in support of his contention.

The second option is that Christ is the mediator of 3:19–20a. Many earlier interpreters declared that Christ was the mediator referred to in verse 19. John Calvin, for example, concluded that God's communication with humanity has always been through Christ: in the wilderness experience, Christ was the angel of the presence, and at Sinai, Christ was the mediator. Christ was not the mediator of one, because he brought both Jews and Gentiles into the covenant, not just the Jews. The reference in verse 20 to the Shema indicates God's consistency—he has not changed his mind or his contract with his people.[143] This interpretation, however, does not have much basis in the Pauline letters. The only other place where Paul reads Christ back into the Old Testament experience is in 1 Cor 10:4, where Christ is identified as the rock in the wilderness.[144] But here in Galatians Paul's purpose is very different: he wants to emphasize the *distinction* between the promise and the Law, and he has already linked Christ with the promise in 3:16. Thus, to identify Christ as the mediator of the Law in 3:20 would run contrary to Paul's larger argument. In fact, this is the primary difficulty with any interpretation that identifies Christ as the mediator of verse 20a.[145] Bruce is right in asserting there must be a

141. See Rosner (*Paul, Scripture and Ethics*, 24) who argues that the Hebrew Scriptures are "a crucial and formative source for Paul's ethics."

142. Gal 3 itself provides a prime example. The faith vs. works question was controversial, and thus Paul repeatedly appeals to the Old Testament to support his new understanding. See also Rosner (ibid., 190–91), who argues that 80 percent of Paul's scriptural quotations are found in places where his theology "departs most dramatically" from Judaism.

143. Calvin, *Epistles of Paul*, 62–63.

144. Paul also reads Christ back into history in Gal 3:16 when he refers to Christ as Abraham's one seed, but the reference here does not place Christ directly into the Israelite experience in the same way as 1 Cor 10:4 does.

145. See also Luther (*Lectures on Galatians*), who identified Christ as the mediator of v. 20 (although he identified Moses as the mediator of v. 19). Luther argued that v. 20a

logical relation between the ἑνός in the first clause and the εἷς in the second: "If a mediator is not 'of one,' whereas God is 'one,' then it follows that the mediator to whom Paul refers here is not God's mediator."[146] Bruce goes too far in stating the mediator is not God's mediator (Paul does not want to divorce the Law from God), but Bruce is correct in pointing out that a stark contrast is intended. It is highly unlikely, therefore, that Christ is the mediator referred to in verses 19–20.

If neither an angel nor Christ is the specific mediator, then perhaps Moses fits the description.[147] Indeed, this provides the best solution to the quandary. Although the Old Testament never actually uses the term "mediator" for Moses, Jews clearly understood Moses to be the mediator of the Law, as previously noted. He was the one who consistently served as God's mouthpiece through the giving of the Law. Yet he also occasionally intervened on Israel's behalf. When the appearance of God was too great for Israel to behold, Moses stepped in; when Israel's sin caused God to threaten to destroy Israel completely, Moses interceded and assuaged God's anger.

Furthermore, Moses's own mediation between God and the people is often viewed as God's direct dealing with Israel. In several passages, God is referred to as the one who spoke the Law, even though it was Moses who actually spoke the words to Israel. The fact that Moses has mediated the message does not change Israel's perception that God has spoken to them.[148] Moses is God's mouthpiece.[149] Even in the New Testament we see this overlap of ideas—in Mark 7:1–23, Jesus contrasts the "command-

states, "An intermediary implies more than one," meaning that the mediator is "one who mediates between an offender and the one who has been offended" (325). The people are the offenders, God is the one offended, and Christ mediates the situation. "God is one" refers to the fact that God had not offended anyone and thus does not need an intermediary—in contrast to humanity, which certainly does. Luther's interpretation suffers from a poor translation of the Greek in v. 20a. Literally, the Greek says, "The mediator is not of one, but God is one." Paul emphasizes a stark contrast between the mediator and God. The mediator, then, could not be Christ since Paul consistently portrays Christ as being unified with God, rather than contrasted with God.

146. Bruce, *Galatians*, 179.

147. As argued by Dunn, Longenecker, Betz, Fung, Guthrie, Jervis, F. Watson, and N. T. Wright.

148. Exod 19:7–8; 24:3, 7; Deut 5:27–28.

149. The understanding of the Israelite prophet "has always included the notion that the prophet was an intermediary through whom God spoke directly to Israel . . ." (Wilson, "Prophetic Books," 213).

ments of God" (7:8) with the "teachings of the elders" (7:5). As he further explains this contrast, he cites what "Moses said" (7:10) in comparison to what the Pharisees themselves say. Moses's words *are* the commandments of God.

In addition, the phrase "by the hand of," used by Paul here in Gal 3:19, had become almost idiomatic of Mosaic mediation.[150] This simple grammatical cue would call to mind a very specific mediator. If Paul had intended another mediator, he would have needed to distinguish that mediator from the one implied by his language. Since no distinction appears, we can assume that Paul intends to imply that Moses is the unnamed mediator.

This presents a problem, however: if Moses is God's mouthpiece and faithfully transmitted God's Law, then how can Paul criticize Moses without simultaneously disparaging the God who speaks directly through him? The answer to this question can only be discovered as we explore the issue of oneness below.

Overall, the concept of mediation was integral to the Jewish faith. The context was not the same civil-litigation context of the surrounding Hellenism, but rather involved God's use of humans and angels to communicate his Word and will. God regularly used mediators—whether priests, prophets, or kings—to communicate with His people. The term "mediator" was almost never used, but the concept was interwoven throughout Jewish tradition. In addition, it was a fairly one-sided concept: the mediator was a spokesman for God, representing God's interests to the people. Occasionally the mediator would bring Israel's interests before God (as in the case of intercession or in the specific role of the priest), but the primary job of a non-priestly mediator was to communicate God's point of view.

Thus, in general, mediation was not considered a negative idea. Rather, it was God's normal means of dealing with Israel. Moses was considered the mediator *par excellence*. At times, however, it appears that God may have preferred to act directly rather than through a mediator. The texts are not always in agreement regarding which of these events were direct and which involved intermediaries. Mediation, in general, was accepted; simply because something was mediated, then, does not *necessarily* imply that it was of inferior status.

150. Betz, *Galatians*, 170.

The text of Gal 3:19–20, however, looks at a very specific instance and a very specific mediator. Although numerous theories have been expounded, neither an angel nor Christ fit the identity of the mediator. It is unlikely that Paul would have based his argument on an angelic mediator without further explanation when this was hardly a normative interpretation within Judaism. Moses was the much more likely candidate as mediator in Jewish thought. The contrast between God and the mediator rules out an interpretation of Christ as the mediator in verse 20; Paul consistently emphasizes the unity of Christ and God, not their differences. Furthermore, the anaphoric use of the article in verse 20 indicates that Moses is the specific mediator in both verses. Thus, the interpretation that mediation in general causes Paul's negative contrast must be ruled out. Such an interpretation is not consistent with the overall positive view of mediation in Judaism. Therefore, the evidence suggests that it is the specific mediator, Moses, who is at the heart of the contrast with God.

ONENESS AND THE EXEGESIS OF GALATIANS 3:20

So far this investigation has led to the conclusions that neither the angels nor mediation *in general* were the issue when Paul made his perplexing statement in 3:20. Before we can fully understand how Paul's one-God language functions in this argument, however, it is necessary to clarify further what Paul meant by the specific language he uses.

The English translations of Paul's argument in 3:20 do not do justice his intentional structure. This configuration is very instructive:

ὁ	δὲ	μεσίτης	ἑνὸς	οὐκ	ἔστιν,
ὁ	δὲ	θεὸς	εἷς		ἐστιν.

The parallel language clearly indicates that Paul intends a strong contrast between the mediator (Moses) and God. But Paul's grammar is not what we would expect—why is the "oneness" in the genitive case in 20a, but in the nominative case in 20b? Unfortunately, the genitive causes various interpretive possibilities to arise. Does ἑνός refer to the mediator, or does it stand alone? Should we read the text: "The mediator of one is not" and then ask, "Is not what?" Or should we read it: "The mediator is not of one" and then ask, "Not of one what?" The first reading would identify Moses as mediator-of-one who is not something else. The second reading would identify Moses as not part of the unity (oneness) of something or someone.

Starting at the end of the verse and working back to the first part may clarify the issue. Paul is clearly using the Shema in verse 20b,[151] and is thus making a statement about God's identity as the unique Lord over all.[152] The fact that the statement is exactly parallel to 20a except for the genitive case of "one" (and, of course, the οὐκ) suggests that Paul intended the first part of the verse to be read in a similar manner, thus highlighting the contrast: "The mediator is not (of) one, but God is one." Thus, we must investigate the answer to the question, "not of one" what?

One possibility, as noted above, is that the mediator is not a representative of one party. Although I argued against such an interpretation by stating that the prophet serves primarily as a mouthpiece of God, it is true that *at times* the mediator intercedes on behalf of the people. It is this potential for divided loyalties that may cause a problem. Some rabbinic sources, for example, suggest that when Moses brought the Ten Commandments down the mountain, he saw Israel's sin; knowing the Law he carried would condemn them to death, he broke the stone tablets before the condemnation could take place. In this way, Moses, as representative of both the people and God, faced divided loyalties. If Paul is referencing this tradition, he may be contrasting Moses's mixed allegiances with God, who does not have this problem.[153]

It is unclear, however, how this interpretation explains the purpose of 3:19–20 within Paul's larger argument in Gal 3. Under such an explanation, the fact that Moses has divided loyalties seems to somehow stain the Law itself, whereas the promise—because God gave it himself—is not subject to such derision. But ultimately such an interpretation does not solve the problem. Whether the Law was mediated or given directly, it is nonetheless the Law of God. Would the content of the Law have changed had God spoken the words directly to the people? Probably not—God himself wrote the stone tablets of the Ten Commandments, and so there was no room for error. Yet the people still disobeyed. Would the people

151. *Contra* Lightfoot (*St. Paul's Epistle to the Galatians*, 145–146), who says the statement is "quite unconnected" to the Shema even though it resembles the Shema in form.

152. Note the lack of introductory formula here. This suggests that Paul expected the recipients of the letter to be familiar with the text. This, in turn, suggests that the Shema was part of Paul's previous teaching to the Galatian church.

153. Callan reaches this conclusion ("Pauline Midrash," 567).

have been empowered to obey the Law had they heard the words from God himself? Perhaps they would have remembered the experience more vividly, but the nature of the Law was such that the Spirit was not given through it.[154] Yet it is receipt of the Spirit, according to Paul, which is necessary for holy living. In fact, Paul consistently argues that the problem with the Law is that it did not have the power to give life (2:21; 3:21). The logical conclusion arises, that if the Law itself were no different regardless of who gave it, then it is not the *means* of receiving which lies at the heart of the problem, but the Law itself.

Another possible explanation is that Moses is not the mediator of the one people of God, since the Torah was given to the Jews only and thus the promise to bless the Gentiles remained unfulfilled. This interpretation exploits the inherent difficulty between the universality of the promise and the restricted scope of the Law. God promised to make one family of believers; because the Law was given only to Israel, however, the promise could not be fulfilled. Only in Christ is the covenant universal enough to fulfill God's promise. Thus, the mediator, Moses, is not the mediator of one family, whereas God is one and requires one family comprised of all peoples. Paul sees Christ as the answer to the problem—through Christ, all peoples can enter the one family of God.[155]

But if this is the case, then how would the Judaizers in Galatia have responded to Paul's argument? I suspect their answer would have been that the Torah is for all people—the various peoples simply must become Jews (who believe in Christ), and then they would be included in God's one special family.[156] Ultimately, for the Judaizers, the blessing of the nations *is* the blessing of Judaism. Christ is the Jewish Messiah. To be non-Jewish is to reject the Messiah, who himself embraced the Torah.[157] The Law thus becomes universal as Gentiles are initiated into (Christian)

154. Not to mention that despite witnessing the parting of the Red Sea, the Israelites turned to idolatry shortly thereafter. Witnessing God's mighty acts was not enough to thwart sin.

155. Mauser ("Galater III.20") suggests that the promise of universal salvation motivates Paul's language in Gal 3:20; Moses is the mediator of the Law, which is restrictive and not universal, and therefore the Law is inferior to the promise. See also N. T. Wright, *Climax of the Covenant*, 157–74, and the discussion in the first section of this chapter.

156. Evidence exists that Jews were concerned to fulfill their call to be "a light to the Gentiles" through evangelism and proselytization; see, e.g., Matt 23:15; Acts 2:11; 6:5; 13:43. See the further discussion of this point in chapter 4, in the second section, "The Jewish Perspectives: Salvation History and the Gentiles."

157. Although in his teaching Jesus certainly interpreted parts of the Torah very differently than many of his contemporaries.

Judaism and accept the Torah.[158] God's oneness is not endangered. Under this interpretation, then, Paul is not really defeating his opponents with the argument of Gal 3:19–20. The Judaizers say the universal blessing comes through Christ-plus-Torah, and Paul says it comes through Christ, but the dispute is not resolved.

There must be another answer to the question then. The mediator is "not of one" what? "Not of one party" has been ruled out, as has "not of one family." Perhaps at this point it will be helpful to look more closely at the genitive construction in verse 20 and the interpretive possibilities that such a construction presents. Rather than looking at all the possibilities, however, I will focus on the most promising.[159] One could argue that ἑνός in verse 20 is simply a descriptive genitive and should be translated, "The mediator (Moses) is not characterized by oneness." This could imply that two parties are involved in any act of mediation and Moses represents more than one interest.[160] As noted above, however, this interpretation does not adequately explain why the Law itself (not the mediator) is inferior to the promise.

Another possibility arises if we interpret the term as a partitive genitive and translate, "The mediator is not a part of one." This in itself could be interpreted in a couple of different ways. It could imply that the mediator is neutral and is not a part of one party or the other in the dispute, and thus reflects a Greco-Roman understanding of civil-litigation-style mediation. Such an interpretation, however, contradicts the understanding of Jewish mediators as the mouthpiece of God. A second interpretation of a partitive genitive in 3:20 might read, "The mediator is not a part of [the] one [God], but God is one." Under this interpretation, Paul would be distancing Moses from God. A similar interpretation is possible if one were to take ἑνός as a genitive of source: "The mediator is not sourced in

158. The same can be said of Christianity. While Christ brings universal salvation, it is nonetheless salvation for those who have faith in Christ; those who do not have this faith remain outside the one family. Barton comments on Paul's concern for unity in Galatians: "The difference is not between universalism and particularism, but between one kind of particularism and another" ("Unity of Humankind," 245).

159. Unfortunately, 3:20 is so unspecific as to allow an interpreter to fit the genitive into almost any category. For example, ἑνός could be a genitive of production: "The mediator is not produced by one," meaning it takes two parties in dispute to produce the need for a mediator. While such an interpretation is possible, other categories make more sense of Paul's statement.

160. As Callan has argued ("Pauline Midrash," 567).

[the] one [God], but God is one." Such an interpretation would need to be finely nuanced—it is difficult to imagine Paul ever saying that Moses was not sent from God. Paul could hardly call himself a Jew if this were the case! But if Paul were making an ontological observation, this interpretation might make more sense. Moses is not sourced in the one God in the sense that Moses is not divine; he is merely a man. Perhaps Paul is worried that the Judaizers's veneration of the Torah included veneration of Moses to an inappropriate level.[161]

Another, similar, possibility lies in the interpretation of ἑνός as a genitive of subordination: "The mediator (Moses) is not over one." Once again, this still provides more than one possible interpretation. First, it could mean that the mediator Moses is not over one of the parties in the sense of forcing one of the parties, i.e., Israel, to accept the covenant. It could also mean that Moses is not superior to the one seed, Christ. Or it could mean that "the mediator is not over [the] one [God], but God is one." In this case, Paul would be clearly putting Moses in his place: the Law of Moses is not superior to the promise of God. Rather, the former is subject to the latter.

While some of these interpretations appear more likely than others, it is important to note that no single construction is convincing in and of itself. The argument for the best interpretation of Gal 3:20 does not stand or fall on grammatical considerations alone. The text simply does not give enough clues to rule out the varying interpretations.

Given these considerations, it may be helpful to ask why Paul did not supply a more specific noun to explain his thoughts further—why simply refer to "of one" without further clarification? It is important to note that this grammatical construction is extremely unusual throughout the New Testament, the LXX, and early Jewish literature. The use of ἑνός together with ἔστιν and without any further clarification (i.e., of one what?) is extremely rare.[162] Ps 13:1, 3 (LXX); Ps 52:4 (LXX); and Luke 10:42 are the

161. For a discussion of Jewish traditions regarding Moses's heavenly enthronement, see Meeks, "Moses as God and King." Although Meeks does cite various references in Philo, the strongest statements regarding Moses are found in the much later rabbinic documents.

162. When ἑνός is used elsewhere, the genitive is frequently used as the result of a preposition which requires a genitival use. In addition, the "one" is always clarified by the immediate context (e.g., "one cubit" or "one of the columns," or "twenty-one years," etc.) See, for example, Deut 18:6, "from one of the cities"; 1 Kgs 6:24, "the wing of one cherub"; 1 Macc 8:16, "all were obedient to that one."

only texts that come close to such a construction, but they are not precise equivalents. The three Psalm texts are identical: οὐκ ἔστιν ἕως ἑνός.[163] These texts clearly refer to the preceding phrase, in which "there is no one who does good." Thus, they respond to the question, "no one *what*?" with the answer, "No one who does good" (literally, "There is not up to one [who does good]"). Furthermore, the ἕως forces the use of the genitive here. No such conjunction or preposition exists in Gal 3:20. The Luke passage does not provide much help, either. Luke 10:42 states, ἑνὸς δέ ἐστιν χρεία ("But there is need of one"), and clearly refers back to the "many things" Martha is worried about in 10:41. The genitive here is not forced by a preposition, and thus is closer to the grammar of Gal 3:20. Luke uses a simple descriptive genitive: "Martha, Martha, you are worried about many things, but there is need of (only) one." Thus, this construction may look somewhat similar to Gal 3:20, but it does not in fact provide a parallel. Perhaps the best conclusion that can be gleaned from these examples is that authors who use the genitive for "one" generally have a referent in mind within the text.

What, then, is the referent in Paul's mind? The immediate sentence does not provide a further clue, yet the larger argument of Gal 3:1—4:7 does. In 3:20, Paul basically says, "Moses is not ἑνός." But Paul has already told us in 3:16 who *is* ἑνός: Christ. This partially explains Paul's odd use of the genitive in verse 20: he is specifically using it to call to mind the reference to Christ in verse 16, which was in the genitive. Thus, Paul's point in 3:20 is that Moses is not Christ. For all of the glory of the Law, as evidenced by the angelic presence, the mediator Moses does not compare with the mediator Christ.

Yet Paul's statement does not end here. Rather, he contrasts the mediator Moses, who is not Christ, with the one God. Indeed, the whole point of the verse is to make a stark contrast between the mediator (Moses) and God. Paul wants to emphasize that Moses is not at all like the one God. The genitive ἑνός serves a dual purpose here. At the same time that it refers to Christ (i.e., Moses is not the one seed of verse 16), it also separates Moses from God. Moses is not "of" the one God in that he is not divine, he is not unique, he is not Lord. Such a statement seems a bit jarring—a bit out of place. Why does Paul feel the need to introduce a contrast here between

163. Paul is clearly aware of these constructions, since he quotes these psalms in Rom 3:12.

the mediator of the Law—that is, God's mediator, God's mouthpiece—and God himself?

Perhaps the larger context will reveal the answer to this question. How might God's oneness, as opposed to Moses's non-uniqueness, convince the Galatians that the promise was superior to the Law? Throughout the section Paul is comparing the Law and the promise. This comparison continues in Gal 3:20 when Paul states that the mediator of the Law is not ἑνός, i.e., he is not the mediator of the promise. Paul is making an implicit comparison between Moses and Christ; he uses the one-God language to argue that Christ is the superior mediator. Moses was the mediator of the old covenant; Christ is the mediator of the promise, of the new covenant. In fact, Paul has already hinted at this earlier in his argument: in 3:13–14, Christ is the one who redeemed believers from the curse by becoming a curse himself. In this sense, Christ picks up the role that occurs only secondarily in Moses, that of intercessor. Christ takes the curse upon himself in order to save from the curse those who believe. Ultimately, the purpose of Christ's mediatorial intercession is to bring the blessing of Abraham to the nations *by Christ Jesus*. This blessing is the promise of the Spirit, which is received through faith *in Christ Jesus*. Although Paul does not specifically use mediator language here, the idea of a mediator is clear. But Paul's concept of Christ as mediator goes beyond the Jewish idea of the prophetic mouthpiece of God who proclaims both God's covenant promises and the rule for remaining in the believing community. Christ's mediatorial role certainly includes this prophetic element, but for Paul the primary role of this new mediator is priestly. It is both redemptive and dispensary: Christ offers himself as the curse and thus mediates punishment by taking it upon himself, and he also dispenses the promised Spirit to those who believe. Thus, Christ encompasses both prophet and priest but takes on a new role as well, and thus provides the life that the Law could not offer.

In other parts of Galatians, as well, Paul emphasizes Christ's mediatorial role, in the sense of Christ acting as the mouthpiece of God. Christ revealed the gospel to Paul (1:12), and Christ—along with God—sent Paul to be an apostle (1:1). Even Paul's language about the gospel bears an interesting parallel to the Law. Whereas the Law in Jewish tradition is referred to as the Law of Moses (i.e., the Law mediated by Moses), the gospel for Paul is the gospel of Christ (1:7). Moses and Christ are both mediators; the two, however, mediate different covenants. Thus, to turn back to the Law of Moses is to turn away from the covenant in Christ (5:4). Such a comparison may also help to explain why Paul uses the phrase "law of Christ" in 6:2; the phrase carries an implicit contrast with the Law of Moses. The law of Christ involves the life in the Spirit, a life that is not possible under the Law of Moses.

It is this contrast which lies at the heart of Gal 3:20. The Law was added because of transgressions, ordained through angels by the hand of the mediator Moses. But Moses is not "of one," whereas God is one. The old covenant was a temporary teacher mediated by one who was not "of one"; the new covenant, the lasting promise that gives life through the Spirit, was mediated by the superior mediator, Christ. Furthermore, the old covenant was given to Moses in great glory—multitudes of angels were present at Sinai—yet the glory of the new covenant is even greater. What is greater than the angels? God himself. The implication in the contrast between the old and new covenants, between Moses and Christ, is that while Moses was not "of" the one God, Christ *is* part of the one God of the Shema. And that is why he is the superior mediator. The power to obey the Law can only come from God himself, but Moses—since he was not God—could not offer that kind of power. Christ, on the other hand, brought the power to obey God's will because he was part of the one God. Christ fulfills the promise because anyone who believes in Christ receives the Spirit, and it is the Spirit who brings life. Paul makes it clear that it is by *Christ's* Spirit that the Galatians can now cry out, "Abba! Father" (4:6). Thus, Paul's argument has come full circle. Gal 3 began with the evidence of the Spirit manifested in the Galatian church, and the argument concludes with that same Spirit—and it is the spirit of Christ.

One may wonder why Paul would bury such a profound Christological statement in obscurity. First, the Shema itself was hardly obscure. The lack of introductory formula suggests Paul knew his readers would be familiar with the saying. Clearly Paul intended to call to mind thoughts about the identity of the one God. Second, the following verses, which many commentators describe as an early baptismal formula,[164] would likely call to mind thoughts about a believer's initial baptism and the related catechetical teaching. Although not much is known today about this teaching, the Galatians certainly knew much more. It is possible that Paul is referencing his own previous instruction about Christ's relationship to God, and he is

164. See, for example, Betz, *Galatians*, 181–85; Longenecker, *Galatians*, 154–59.

using here a few catchphrases to call to mind that instruction. Rather than reiterating the catechism, he may simply be using a bit of shorthand so as not to distract from the larger argument. As I argued in chapter 2, the Corinthian church was certainly aware of this connection between God and Christ, since they cited the formula to Paul. It is not outrageous to think that the same teaching is operative here. Nonetheless, the ontological implications of Christ's identity are not the primary issue in Gal 3, and so Paul does not go into greater detail. Rather, he wishes to focus on the faith/law question and its relationship to receipt of the Spirit. Granted, such an argument is based on silence, but it nonetheless offers a plausible explanation of why Paul did not feel the need to be more explicit in 3:20. He was not writing to a confused twenty-first century audience, but to a group of believers who had recently received his own instruction regarding God and Christ.

It is important to consider also the links of this christological idea of "oneness" with the other references to "oneness" within the argument of Gal 3:1—4:7.[165] Both 3:16 and 3:28 emphasize the importance of oneness. In the first instance, Paul performs lexical acrobatics in order to emphasize that Christ is the *one* seed of Abraham. It is clearly important for Paul to affirm the continuity of salvation history. Christ's mediation was part of God's original plan; it was not an addition, and it certainly did not come after the Law. Thus, Paul emphasizes the *single plan* of God. Then in 3:20 he emphasizes the *unity* of this one seed with God. Christ is the superior mediator who is both prophet and priest, and, through his unity with the one God, is able to dispense the promised Spirit. Finally, in 3:28, Paul emphasizes the one *unique people* that comes through the one seed. In fact, the one people (the "sons of God" in 3:26) is Abraham's seed (3:29), which in 3:16 was identified as Christ! This is possible only because the new people are *in Christ* (3:28) and *of Christ* (3:29), who is Abraham's seed. It is significant that the wording in 3:28 (πάντες γὰρ ὑμεῖς εἷς ἐστε) is very similar to 3:20b (ὁ δὲ θεὸς εἷς ἐστιν); just as God is one, now the believers are one by virtue of their being *in Christ*. Just as God is unique and superlative, so the new community is unique and surpasses any previous kind of community.[166]

165. Not many commentators discuss links between 3:16, 20, and 28. Wright (*Climax of the Covenant*) provides a notable exception.

166. There is no gnostic sense of deification of the believer; Paul does not say that believers are ἑνός ("of one") in the way that he implies Christ is ἑνός and thus part

CHRIST'S EXALTED STATUS

The argument for Christ's superiority and unity with God is not explicitly stated in 3:19–20, but the hints of Paul's exalted view of Christ found elsewhere in Galatians support this conclusion. In addition, other New Testament passages view Christ as the mediator in a sense similar to what I have argued here.

From the beginning of Galatians, Paul indicates that Christ is more than human. In 1:1 and 1:12 Paul takes great care to emphasize that he was not sent by man, nor was the gospel he received taught to him by any man. Rather, Paul's authority comes from Christ and from God. In 1:1, Christ is clearly included in the category of divine, not human, revelation.[167] The reference in 1:12, however, is not so clear-cut. In that passage, "a revelation of Jesus Christ" could be either a subjective or objective genitive. If the former, then Paul is referring to the divine revelation he received from Jesus. If the latter, then Paul is referring to a revelation about Jesus; if this is the case, then God is the implied sender and nothing is implied about Jesus's divinity. In verses 15–16 Paul states that God called Paul and revealed his Son to him. Thus, in verse 1 Paul is sent by divine origins, both God and Christ, and in verse 15 he has a divine revelation sent from God. Nonetheless, verse 16 refers to Jesus as God's Son, denoting a special relationship with the one God.[168] Within this first chapter, then, Paul makes a very close connection between Christ and God. Even though his description varies slightly from verse to verse, Paul describes the divine origins of his gospel as coming from both Christ and God.

---

of the one God. Rather, they are εἷς—they are a unity. Paul has already described the nature of this unity in the first part of 3:28—it is a single people in which ethnic, class, and gender distinctions do not define the community. It is Christ Jesus who defines this unique new community. For a similar emphasis on the unity of the one people of God, see Eph 2:14–16. Barton comments that "at its most profound, the vision of the unity of humankind is *grounded in the vision of the oneness of God*. It is essential, therefore, that our understanding of what it means to be human, both as individuals and corporately, flows from our faith in the sovereignty of God in creation and the love of God in redemption" ("Unity of Humankind," 254).

167. Matera states that in 1:1 "Jesus is accorded the honor of being associated with God" (*Galatians*, 38). See also Morris, who argues that Paul takes it for granted that the Galatians agree "that Jesus Christ was more than a mere man" (*Galatians*, 33 n. 5).

168. For further discussion on the phrase "son of God," see the section "Other Passages in Romans" in chapter 4.

This emphasis is a result of the Judaizers's attacks on Paul's authority—Paul wants to make it clear that he answers to no one but God. Hence, he distances himself from the rule of Jerusalem. He did not go to Jerusalem at first (1:17), and when he did go later, he only saw Peter and James (1:18–19). Then, when he finally met with all the leaders, it was in a private conversation (2:3), and his ministry was affirmed (2:7–10). No additional requirements were added to his teaching (2:6). Paul does not intend to completely break with the Jerusalem church, for he values their ministry, as evidenced by his desire elsewhere to support the poor in the Jerusalem church (Rom 15:25–26). But he wants to distance himself from Jerusalem so that the Galatian Judaizers cannot say, "If your authority is from Jerusalem, then why do you not hold to the teachings of the men from James?" Therefore, when Paul emphasizes the source of his ministry, and thus the authority with which he teaches, he makes it clear that God is the ultimate authority. Yet he includes Christ within the scope of this authority.

Furthermore, in Gal 4:4, Paul uses the verb ἐξαπέστειλεν to state that God sent his Son. Although "sending" itself is not a unique concept, the specific verb here is unusual. It is found in Paul's letters only here and in verse 6. Rather than using the much more common verb ἀπέστειλεν, Paul uses a term that possibly adds the nuance "sending from," and thus may imply Christ's preexistence with God in heaven.[169] Nonetheless, not all scholars agree that such an implication can be derived from this verb.[170] By itself, the verb in 4:4 is not conclusive regarding Christ's preexistence. The possibility is strengthened, however, by the designation of Christ as God's Son. Furthermore, when we consider Paul's other statements on the matter, such as Phil 2:5–11, it becomes more plausible that in this instance Paul also has preexistence in mind.

More telling is Paul's language about the Spirit in Galatians. Frequently he refers to the Spirit by itself, but in 4:6 he says, "Because you are sons, God sent the spirit of his son into our hearts, crying, 'Abba!

169. Ridderbos argues that the term "comprises two thoughts: the going forth of the Son from a place at which He was before; and His being invested with divine authority" (*Epistle to Galatia*, 155). See also Matera, *Galatians*, 150; and Hansen, *Galatians*, 118.

170. Rengstorf argues that ἐξαπέστειλεν is interchangeable with ἀπέστειλεν and adds no specialized meaning ("ἀποστέλλω"). See also Williams, who states that the verb "does not necessarily bear the concept of preexistence. After all, scripture can use that language about prophetic messengers who were hardly thought to have preexisted their birth . . ." (*Galatians*, 112).

Father!'" Here the empowering, miracle-working Spirit is clarified as the very spirit of Christ.[171] Yet Paul writes elsewhere that the Spirit is God's Spirit.[172] Paul does not envision two different spirits, but rather one Spirit which indwells and empowers the believer to live a holy life. But the description of this spirit is interchangeable: sometimes it is the Spirit of God, while at other times it is the Spirit of Christ. This is most clearly seen in Rom 8:9–11.[173] What is remarkable about this language is that in the Old Testament, it is undeniably Yahweh who sends his Spirit upon his people;[174] yet for Paul, this Spirit is now the Spirit of Christ. The reason he makes this connection here is because he argues that believers are now children of God; since the Spirit of the *Son* resides within them, then they, too, can call God, "Abba, Father." It is the Spirit of Christ, the spirit of sonship, that unites the believer to God.

The concept of the Spirit is itself crucial for understanding Paul's arguments in Galatians. As mentioned above, the problem with the Law, in Paul's view, was that it could not bring life. Paul draws on his Jewish heritage in linking the ideas of righteousness and life,[175] and uses this idea of giving life almost synonymously with the idea of being made righteous: if the Law could bring righteousness, then Christ died for nothing (2:21). The implication is that Christ alone brings righteousness and thus life. Paul makes a similar statement in 3:21: if a law was given that was able to produce life, then indeed righteousness would have come through the Law. Rather, it is through the Spirit that one receives life (6:8)—and one receives the Spirit through faith in Christ (3:5). Throughout this letter, then, Paul closely ties these concepts of God, the Spirit, and Christ. That Christ is highly exalted is evidenced by the fact that Yahweh's Spirit and Christ's Spirit are, at times, interchangeable.

171. Fee notes, "The Spirit of God is also the Spirit of Christ (Gal 4:6; Rom 8:9; Phil 1:19), who carries on the work of Christ following his resurrection and subsequent assumption of the place of authority at God's right hand" (*God's Empowering Presence*, 837).

172. Rom 8:9; 1 Cor 7:40.

173. For a discussion of this passage, see the section "Other Passages in Romans" in chapter 4.

174. See, e.g., Exod 31:3; Isa 42:1; 44:3; 59:21; Ezek 36:26–27; 37:14; 39:29; Joel 2:28–29.

175. Deut 30:15–16; Prov 10:2, 16; 11:4, 19; 12:28; 21:21; Ezek 14:14, 20, 18:21–22, 27–28; 33:14–16, 19; Zeph 2:3.

Another passage of interest occurs in 4:14: "... though my condition put you to the test, you did not scorn or despise me, but welcomed me as an angel of God, as Christ Jesus." Paul makes an emotional plea, reminding the Galatians of their initial love for Paul and how they willingly received him even though he was ill. The Galatians did not despise or loathe Paul, but they received him with as much honor as they would have received an angel of God, or even Christ Jesus himself. The language Paul uses provides a progressive intensification. They did not reject Paul; better, they received him as if he were an angel; best, they received him as if he were Christ himself.[176] Paul is not arguing for the deity of Christ here—that is not his purpose. Rather, he uses the assumption of Christ's exalted status in order to present a hyperbole: he is reminding the Galatians of how extremely welcoming they were to him in the beginning of his ministry.[177] But this escalation of descriptive terms illustrates that Paul considers Jesus to hold more honor than the angels.

In 6:14 Paul makes another striking comment. As we saw in 1 Corinthians, Paul frequently makes use of the Old Testament exhortation to boast only in the Lord—which, of course, in the Old Testament, meant boasting only in Yahweh. Yet in 6:14, Paul uses the same language to state that he will boast in the cross of Christ. For Paul, boasting in the crucified and risen Christ is equivalent to boasting in Yahweh. What God has done in the Christ event is what makes him worthy of praise. The actions of Christ help to define who God is and that he is worthy of boasting. The strength of Paul's statement here is also instructive. He does not say that he will boast in God *and* in the cross of Christ. Rather, the cross of Christ is the *only* thing in which he will boast. For Paul, Christ's death is the moment that defines God himself.

The veracity of the interpretation of Gal 3:20 presented here is strengthened by the recognition that among the traditions of the early church stood the view of Christ as the mediator *par excellence*. This, of course, does not necessarily mean that Paul instigated the tradition or

176. Dunn argues that the "typical understanding" of the one sent is that the messenger speaks with the authority of the sender himself (*Galatians*, 235). Thus, "as Christ Jesus" simply refers to Jesus as the one who sent Paul. Such an interpretation has merit but does not nullify the implications of divinity, since (as noted in 1:1) Paul considers the divine origins of his message to have come from both Jesus and God. Furthermore, the intensification in 4:14 implies that Jesus is greater than the angels.

177. Hansen (*Galatians*, 134) argues that Paul uses "two exaggerated comparisons" to demonstrate how welcoming the Galatians had been.

that he was even aware of it. It does, however, affirm that the interpretation of Gal 3:20 offered here is not out of line with the faith of first-century Christians.

The closest parallel can be found in 1 Tim 2:5–6: "For there is one God and there is one mediator between God and men, the man Christ Jesus, who gave himself as a ransom for all, as was attested in its own time." It is interesting that in this passage, the emphasis lies on Christ's humanity.[178] Whether the letter is Pauline or not, scholars agree that it was written by someone within the Pauline school of thought. Thus, the idea of Christ as mediator was not foreign to Paul and may have been promoted by him.

The concept of Christ as the superior mediator is also clearly found in Hebrews. Christ is the high priest (3:17; 4:14–15; 5:5–10; 6:20, 7:24—8:7; 9:11–14; 10:21), and thus a mediator to God's people. He is the mediator (μεσίτης) of the new covenant (9:15; 12:24). Christ's deity is also clearly a component of the letter—the author makes every effort to portray Christ as being higher than the angels (1:4–14; 2:9).

These two letters provide the clearest parallels for the concept of Jesus as the supreme mediator. Of course we should keep in mind that, regardless of their authorship, they are later letters than Galatians and thus do not represent concurrent ideas. They could themselves be influenced by Paul's letter to the Galatians, or they could represent a separate tradition. Nonetheless, the existence of this concept of Christ as mediator verifies that the interpretation of Gal 3:19–20 presented here is not novel, but rather is consistent with the theology of the early churches.

CONCLUSIONS

In conclusion, this study of Gal 3:19–20 has investigated the cryptic references to angels, mediators, and oneness. It is clear that a tradition existed that embraced the presence and participation of angels in the giving of the Law at Sinai. It is also clear that Paul's own view of angels was quite positive. Thus, Paul does not intend to disparage the Law based on angelic mediation; if he were to intend a negative connotation, he likely would have used a term other than "angels" to describe the Sinai event. It appears

178. Mounce (*Pastoral Epistles*, 88) argues that the description of Christ's humanity is not a denial of his divinity, but rather serves as an emphatic assertion of the incarnation.

his reference to angels serves as a simple description of the events at Sinai and falls within the Jewish tradition of recounting angelic presence in order to increase the glory of the event.

Paul's account of the origin of the Law in 3:19 leads to his enigmatic contrast in 3:20 between the Law's mediator and God. This study has found that mediation was integral to the Jewish religion, where mediators acted as the mouthpiece of God. The overall positive attitude towards mediation suggests that the issue of mediation in general was not at the heart of Paul's problem with the Law.

In addition, the grammar of 3:19–20 suggests that the mediator in verse 20 refers to the specific mediator of verse 19 rather than to the concept of mediators in general. This study dismissed the possibilities of an angel or of Christ as the mediator in verse 19, finding instead that Moses provides the best interpretive option. In many respects he is the obvious choice: Jews regarded Moses as the mediator of the Law (even though they did not often use the specific term "mediator"), and they frequently used the term "by the hand of" Moses. Thus, when Paul uses similar language in 3:19–20 without any further clarifying remarks, it is extremely likely that he has Moses in mind. Moses was the mediator *par excellence*—that is, until Christ came.

Within Paul's larger purpose in 3:1—4:7, verses 19 and 20 play a significant role. Throughout the section Paul argues that the Galatians have received the Spirit through faith, and not by works of the Law. He continually emphasizes the promise God made to Abraham, and identifies Christ as the one seed to whom the promise was made. Thus Christ was part of the original plan and was involved prior to the advent of the Law. Paul wants to underscore that God has not changed his mind; the one God is not fickle or capricious, but rather intended from the beginning to bless Abraham's descendants through the promise, not the Law. Paul explains that the Law, which cannot give life, was a temporary addition intended to point out humanity's sin and need for redemption, a redemption which came through Christ's saving activity and the Christian's subsequent faith. The promised blessing, then, is the receipt of the Spirit, which is the spirit of Christ. Those who have received the Spirit comprise a single unique and superlative community in Christ. Oneness language flows throughout the argument and emphasizes the continuity of God's plan throughout salvation history.

Within the context of this argument, Paul uses 3:19–20 to explain the purpose of the Law as a temporary but necessary step in the process. The contrast in verse 20 highlights the inferiority of Moses compared to the implied mediator of the new covenant, Christ. Yet the grammar in this cryptic text does not make such an interpretation obvious. This study noted, however, that in other texts where the ἑνός construction is used in conjunction with a "to be" verb, some kind of clarification invariably exists. Paul did not provide a similar clarification within verse 20, but instead used the genitive construction to refer back to verse 16. Moses is not ἑνός; that is, he is not Christ, the one seed. The genitive construction has a second purpose as well. It describes Moses, the mediator of the Law, as not being "of" the one God; as such, he was inferior to Christ, the mediator of the covenant of the promise, who is "of" the one God. Whereas the mediator Moses primarily served as the mouthpiece of God, Christ primarily serves in a redemptive and dispensary role, bringing salvation to the people and sending forth the Spirit.[179] Thus, Christ the superior mediator brought the promised blessing of the Spirit and brought life, something Moses and the Law were incapable of accomplishing. Christ was able to accomplish this precisely because he was "of" the one God in a way that Moses was not; that is, Christ participates in God's deity.

Elsewhere in Galatians there are hints of Paul's view of Christ's exalted status as well. It is surprising that Paul does not state his views more directly, but this may be due to the fact that Paul wanted to emphasize the question of faith versus works and felt he did not need to reiterate the kind of statements that the Galatians likely had heard in their early catechetical teaching.

To summarize the various facets of Paul's argument in Gal 3:19–20, then, the discussion could be restated in this way: "What was the purpose of the Law? It was added temporarily to highlight humanity's transgressions (and the need for God's grace) until the seed should come to whom the promise (that is, the blessing of all nations—specifically, the receipt of the life-giving Spirit through faith) was made, that is, Christ. The Law was ordained gloriously by angels through the hand of the mediator Moses. But the mediator Moses is not Christ; he is not (part) of the one God, and although he brought the Law he could not bring life. Thus, Moses is

179. Technically, it is God who sends forth the Spirit in 4:6; nonetheless, it is the spirit of "his son." Thus, even though God is ultimately responsible for dispensing the Spirit, Christ is part of that activity.

inferior to the superior mediator, Christ, who is part of the one God and thus is able to bring redemption and life through the Spirit."

Thus the one-God language in Gal 3:20 functions to highlight the contrast between the old and new covenants. In 3:19 Paul explains the Law's good purpose—but in 3:20 he is quick to explain that even if the Law was good, the promise is better. The one-God language here does not serve as an argument for the deity of Christ—Paul assumes his audience is in agreement with him on that point. Hence, questions of ontology are not at the center of the argument. Rather, Paul uses these previously agreed-upon christological ideas to support his argument that the promise is superior to the Law.

Once again, then, I would argue that Paul's one-God language is not the primary focus of his argument. Rather, this is one of the few subjects on which there appears to be agreement, because Paul does not offer any remedial instruction on the divine identity of Christ within his letter. Even though Paul's focus is not on delineating oneness theology, this theology is essential to his overall argument. Whereas in 1 Corinthians Paul used the one-God language to focus on ethics, in Galatians Paul uses the Shema to underscore his view of salvation history. Because God is one, he has a single plan and has not changed his mind. Furthermore, Christ was a part of the plan from the beginning. The reason that Christ is superior to Moses is because he participates in the deity of Yahweh and thus is able to bring life through the Spirit. Not only is this implied in 3:19–20, but Paul's interchangeable references to the Spirit of God and the Spirit of Christ throughout his letters suggest as much. This observation is consistent with what I argued in 1 Corinthians: Paul can and does speak about Christ in the same manner, and with the same functions, as he speaks about God. The activity of Christ is what defines who God is. Thus, Paul's one-God language is integrally connected to his Christ language. Speaking of the one God, then, is not an aside or an afterthought. Rather, it provides the foundation for Paul's argument that the promise is superior to the Law. The one God made a promise long before the Law ever arrived and, in Christ, this God has been faithful to his promise.

4

The People of the One God

Romans 3:30

INTRODUCTION

THUS FAR THIS STUDY has explored how Paul used his understanding of the one God in two very different contexts. In 1 Cor 8:6, Paul was concerned to promote a love ethic within the body of Christ. His monotheistic statement was not the central issue—the Corinthian Christians and he agreed that there is one God, and agreed that Christ is included within the divine identity. Although at times it appeared that Paul vacillated on the question of Christ's inclusion within the divine identity, I argued that the context shaped Paul's use of monotheistic language. When he wished to emphasize God's control over the created order, Paul's language appeared hierarchical but was intended to establish proper boundaries. That is, Christ does not exceed God; rather, all things are part of the one God's plans and purposes. When Paul wished to emphasize the unity of God, especially over against the pagan world, Paul emphasized the equality of Christ with God. Much of Paul's language indicates he believed that Christ shared in the functions and attributes of God. Thus, in 1 Cor 8:6, a context which inevitably involves a contrast with pagan deities, Paul emphasized the oneness of God and Christ. Nonetheless, his use of this one-God language was intended as part of a correction of the Corinthian understanding of the ethical implications of God's oneness. The Corinthians had neglected the horizontal dimension of loving one another, a dimension that for the Jewish Paul was integral to the vertical dimension of loving God with all of one's heart, soul, and strength.

When Paul used one-God language in Gal 3:20, the context was very different. There he wished to contrast Moses with Christ as the superior mediator of God's promises. Although the verse is surely one of the most difficult passages among Paul's writings, I concluded that Paul held a positive view of both angels at Sinai (their presence heightened the glory of the Law) and of mediators in general. Many Jews did not question the use of a mediator, who in essence acted as the mouthpiece of God. This was an accepted part of their religious life. Thus mediation itself did not pose the central issue for Paul. These conclusions, in addition to the unexpected grammatical construction, suggested that Paul's concern lay with the *specific* mediator involved in the giving of the Law—Moses. This mediator was then contrasted with the one God. Moses was not "of" the one God. Given the context of the argument—the contrast between the Law and the promise—this implied that the mediator of the promise, Christ, was "of the one God" whereas Moses was not. Once again Paul was assuming an understanding of the equality of Christ and God—he did not take the time to explain it fully to the Galatians, who had heard his teaching previously. Rather, he used their common monotheistic understanding to underscore his point: the freedom that the Galatians have experienced, the life in the Spirit, is superior to the old way of life under the Mosaic covenant. Thus, the Galatians must not turn back toward circumcision or other aspects of the Law, because the Law has been fulfilled in Christ. The oneness of God was crucial to Paul's argument because it emphasized the unity of salvation history; Christ was not a new addition, but rather was part of God's plan from the beginning.

Paul's letter to the Romans provides us with yet another context in which to explore his usage of this most basic of Jewish principles. The immediate context of Rom 3:30 suggests that the ethnic issue of Jew-Gentile relations is at the heart of Paul's discussion, yet we must consider how this issue plays out within the larger argument of Romans. What is the significance of the one-God language in this context? Does it lie at the heart of Paul's argument, or does it make only a peripheral point? What function does the concept of the one God play in Paul's overall argument? Does Paul allude to God's oneness elsewhere in Romans to support his contentions? How does Paul describe the relationship between God and Christ in this letter? Does his strong monotheistic language regarding God result in an increase of hierarchical language about Christ? In response to these questions, I will argue that although one-God language appears explicitly only infrequently, this emphasis nonetheless lies at the heart of Paul's letter—and indeed, at the heart of his soteriology. Paul is not as concerned here with numerical oneness, but with the character and identity of the one God. It is because this one God is both impartial and faithful to his promises that both Jew and Gentile alike are justified on the same basis: faith in Jesus Christ. The unity that Paul tries to promote among the Jews and Gentiles is the logical outgrowth of Paul's understanding of the one God. Thus, the God of the Jews is necessarily the God of the Gentiles; yet because this God is faithful, he has not turned his back on his promises to the Jews. It is important, then, to emphasize that the God of the Gentiles is still the God of the Jews. Both Jews and Gentiles will be blessed through God. This blessing is the result of the death of Christ, and it is this action of Christ that defines God's faithfulness. Jesus and God thus mutually define one another. In addition, rather than finding one-God language that subordinates Christ to God, we instead discover that Paul more often speaks of God and Christ as having similar functions and roles. Indeed, he calls Christ "God" in 9:5 and certainly implies as much throughout the rest of his letter. Ultimately, it is because of this interdependent relationship between Christ and God that Paul is able to argue for the unity of Jews and Gentiles.

In order to understand Paul's rationale for writing 3:30, it will be helpful to investigate Paul's purpose in writing the letter as a whole. Paul's intention in offering a more theologically reflective letter may have been to address a specific controversy (e.g., the nature of justification or the inclusion of the Gentiles), to solicit support for his planned trip to Spain, or simply to prepare the way for his upcoming visit—all of these possibilities may be considered as potentially having an impact on our understanding of why Paul wrote Rom 3:30. In this verse, Paul assumes certain characteristics about the one God, such as his impartiality, which will be discussed below. Paul's rationale for the inclusion of such language is important for understanding his larger argument. But unlike Paul's other letters, e.g., Galatians, where the reason for Paul's writing is abundantly clear, Romans presents a variety of possible directions to travel, and the signposts leading to the appropriate destination are not always obvious.[1]

1. Donfried states that although some scholarly consensus has been reached, a number of issues concerning Paul's purposes in writing Romans remain unresolved, especially the question of Paul's theological intention (*The Romans Debate*, lxix–lxxii).

Indeed, it is clear that Romans presents a different situation for Paul; unlike his other letters, he is not writing to a church he has founded or previously visited (1:13). All of Paul's information about the Roman church comes secondhand—from Priscilla and Aquila, for example, who spent time with Paul in Corinth after they were forced to leave Rome by the Claudian edict (Acts 18:1–3).[2] Although Paul's reasons for writing Romans may seem clear enough from chapters 1 and 15, the issue of which such reasons are operative in the heart of the letter is less clear at any given point.

The more comprehensive discussion of the gospel in Paul's letter suggests the possibility that Paul is writing his version (albeit a brief one) of a systematic theology. He outlines his gospel, discusses what he believes to be the pertinent theological motifs, and finalizes his letter by adding a few personal greetings in chapter 16. Some scholars, such as Krister Stendahl and Günther Bornkamm, thus find themselves convinced that Paul's focus remains steadfastly on his own theology and that he does not address the specific concerns of the Roman church.[3] Such an omission is perhaps to be expected when Paul himself had not been involved previously with the church in Rome. Although it is certainly accurate that the structure of the letter to the Romans reflects a greater depth and breadth of thinking than presented elsewhere in Paul's writings, the letter nevertheless retains a similar pattern to Paul's other letters. His typical greeting, thanksgiving section, body, and concluding greetings suggest that Paul is not intending to offer a different pattern for understanding what follows.[4] Like his other

2. See Suetonius *Life of Claudius* 25:4. Many scholars (e.g., Dunn, Fitzmyer, Barrett, Byrne) think Suetonius's reference to "Chrestus" is a misspelling of Christ, and thus refers to Jewish-Christian disputes resulting in the expulsion of Jews from Rome in 49 CE. Nonetheless, it is impossible to determine the extent of the expulsion—did it include all Jews, Jews who lacked Roman citizenship, or only those involved in the dispute? For more on this issue, see n. 11 below.

3. Stendahl, (*Final Account*, ix); Paul's letter is the "final account of his theology and mission" (ibid.; see also 12). Bornkamm, "Letter to the Romans," 27–28. Bornkamm argues that Romans is, in effect, Paul's last will and testament—a message that summarizes the themes of his ministry in a more universally valid manner. Nonetheless, it is not a "timeless theological treatise." Bornkamm grants that the letter is situated within the historical situation, but suggests that the situation reflects Paul's history and experience, and not the history and experience of the Roman church ("Letter to the Romans," 21).

4. Certainly it would be possible for Paul to offer a theological treatise within his usual style, but it is more likely that he would indicate a change in pattern. The unusual negative tone in the letter to the Galatians, for example, is made clear by the lack of thanksgiving section in the opening of the letter.

letters, he intends to offer specific instruction to the Roman church. What makes this letter out of the ordinary is that it is addressed to a church that Paul had never before visited. Furthermore, in several places, Paul delineates his personal concerns as they intersect with the Roman congregation: e.g., he wishes for their prayers as he heads to an uncertain future in Jerusalem (15:31), and he desires to visit the congregation (15:32). In addition, the Jew-Gentile question, which has been prominent in Paul's churches, also figures as a significant theme in Romans. Rom 3:29–30 addresses this very question. Clearly, contemporary circumstances influence Paul's writing, not merely a quest for an intellectual legacy.

It is necessary, then, to consider these specific circumstances and determine if one or more provide the main thrust for Paul's letter, and specifically which purpose is operative in Paul's discussion at 3:30. Three main possibilities emerge from Paul's writing: he hopes the Romans will send him off as he intends to travel to Spain (15:23–24, 28–29), he is eager to visit the Romans and share his gospel with them (1:10–15), and he wishes for Roman support (in prayer, at least) as he travels to an unknown future in Jerusalem (15:30–32).[5] At first glance these desires do not appear to intersect directly with Paul's one-God language in 3:30. As will be explained below, however, these interests work together to shape Paul's entire letter, as well as his argument in 3:21–31.

Since Paul mentions these interests only very briefly, and Romans is quite a long letter, these purposes may seem inadequate to explain such an in-depth letter.[6] As far as we know, Paul did not write lengthy introductions of himself to other churches he visited.[7] Why, then, did Paul write to the *Roman* church? Paul could have written such a letter to any Christian church that he himself had not founded—so why Rome? I wish to suggest that although the purposes Paul indicates in his letter may appear only

5. Morris (*Romans*, 17–18) notes these three main purposes as well.

6. This is precisely the question asked by Byrne (*Romans*, 13). He turns to a rhetorical-critical explanation of Romans and suggests that Paul's design is not merely to remind the Romans of the gospel which he and they hold in common, but to bring about a "deeper sympathy for and conformity to the specifically Pauline contours of the gospel: most notably the inclusion of the Gentiles as equal citizens in the eschatological people of God" (19).

7. Of course, most of the cities Paul visited did not have already established churches. Rather, it was Paul himself who founded them. Nonetheless, some churches were indeed established by others and did not receive introductory letters from Paul, as far as we know. The Jerusalem church provides but one example.

briefly, they indicate very strong motivations that are not distinct from one another, but rather are intertwined.[8] Furthermore, they are integrated as a result of Paul's focus on the unity of the church.

Throughout the letter, Paul addresses the relationship between Jews and Gentiles (see table below). Certainly evidence of this theme appears in Paul's other letters as well—most obviously in Galatians and Philippians. Paul's intent to visit Rome on his way to Spain may also reflect this unifying purpose, since it is not ultimately *necessary* that Paul stop in Rome in order to achieve his goal of reaching Spain. He could simply go to Spain, continue to make tents to support himself, and avoid relying on churches to provide for his needs (or at least, rely on his already established churches). In some ways, such self-reliance was preferable to allowing any misunderstanding of potential patron-client relationships.[9] The fact that Paul reaches out to the Roman church in an effort to establish a base of operations suggests that he is concerned to maintain relationships and communications among the various churches.[10] While Paul's interest in the Spanish mission suggests a reason for his writing to the *Roman* church (i.e., Rome provides a logical geographical base for his mission), this rationale alone does not explain the length of Paul's letter, or indeed some of the issues he addresses. For example, if Paul is merely writing an introductory letter as he seeks to establish a base of operations, why would he include a discussion regarding the weak and the strong in chapters 14–15?

Part of the answer may lie in Paul's mention of the desire he has to share *his* gospel with the church at Rome. By addressing specific issues within the Roman church, he can demonstrate in practical ways to the Romans the contours of his own understanding of the gospel message. Indeed, it seems quite important to Paul that the Roman church understand his missionary philosophy. He indicates that he wishes to reap a harvest among them (1:13), and the length of the letter itself emphasizes Paul's interest in communicating his understanding of the gospel message. As mentioned above, throughout the letter Paul addresses his concern for the inclusion of both Jews and Gentiles within the fledgling

8. Most scholars argue that Paul does not have merely a single purpose in mind when writing to the Romans. See, e.g., Guerra, *Romans and the Apologetic Tradition*, 41–42; Dunn, *Romans 1–8*, liv–lviii; and Fitzmyer, *Romans*, 79–80.

9. 2 Cor 11:9; 12:13.

10. Stuhlmacher, "Purpose of Romans," 237.

Christian church. From Paul's contacts with Priscilla and Aquila and others, he may well have heard disturbing reports about ethnic conflicts within the Roman church. The historical evidence suggests that the expulsion of the Jews from Rome in 49 CE may have caused a vacuum in church leadership.[11] Prior to the edict of Claudius, Jews were the majority in the Roman Christian church, believers met in synagogues, and their socialization was mainly Jewish. But because of the controversy between Jews and Christians, Emperor Claudius forced at least some Jews (and by implication, Jewish Christians) to leave Rome. Gentile Christians may have been allowed to remain, as the government may not have identified them with the Jewish Christians. As a result, the constituency of the Roman church changed dramatically. During the five years the Jews remained outside Rome, the Gentiles began meeting in houses rather than synagogues. Gentiles now became the leaders in the churches. And new Gentiles became converted to Christianity without the Jewish acculturation that the first "God-fearers" in the Christian church had received. As a result, when Jewish Christians returned to Rome in 54 CE, they returned to a church where everything had changed; they no longer were the leaders in the church, and their specifically Jewish customs were no longer being observed. They likely felt very out of place and now had to choose between their Jewish cultural identity and their Christian faith. Meanwhile, the Gentiles were boasting that they were the true church and that God had left the Jews behind. Paul's whole argument in Romans centers on emphasizing the righteousness of God, with the inevitable corollary that a righteous God could not dismiss his promises to the Jewish people.[12] Thus, the discussion in 3:30 comes into focus as being a central

11. See Lampe's discussion in *From Paul to Valentinus*, 11–16. Lampe argues persuasively for a 49 CE date but suggests not all Jews were forced to leave; rather, only the key figures of the conflict were expelled. As a result, the fledgling Christian sect began to separate from the Jewish synagogues. Even if Lampe is correct that only key leaders were expelled, these would include the Jewish Christian leaders of the early Christian church in Rome. Thus, those left behind to lead the Christian church would be mostly Gentile Christians and possibly a few Jewish Christians who previously had declined to take any strong leadership role within the church. These Jews would not be likely candidates to step forward boldly in defense of Jewish practices; at any rate, they would be outnumbered.

12. This position is argued by Walters in *Ethnic Issues in Romans*. See also N. T. Wright, "Romans and the Theology of Paul"; and F. Watson, "Two Roman Congregations." Wright agrees that the shifting leadership as a result of the Claudian edict caused tension, but suggests Paul's missionary strategy also influenced Paul's purposes. Watson argues

component of Paul's message: the one God is sovereign over both Jew and Gentile and is faithful to *all* his people.

This ethnic component becomes all the more poignant when we consider Paul's third purpose for writing, his upcoming trip to Jerusalem. He is preparing to deliver the collection from the Gentile churches for the poor in Jerusalem. In his letter to the Romans, Paul indicates that he is concerned that both his life and his effectiveness as an apostle are at stake in Jerusalem (15:30–32). If the Jerusalem church accepts the Gentile offering, then it is a mark of acceptance of Paul and his mission to the Gentiles. The approval of the Jerusalem church—as the "mother church"—would be crucial for Paul's continuing ministry. What could provide a better endorsement for Paul than to have one of the key Gentile churches—the one located in the center of Roman power—support him in his ministry? Indeed, Jacob Jervell argues that Paul wanted to represent *all* of the Gentile churches when he was in Jerusalem, and thus he wished to include Rome: "Such an influential and recognized congregation is certainly invaluable as a partner in battle and witness to the apostle of the Gentiles."[13]

Furthermore, since this church lay in the heart of the Roman Empire, the emperor would be watching closely the relationship between Jews and Christians. As a result of such scrutiny, the conflicts that led to the Claudian edict must have been very disturbing to the Jerusalem church. Christians were in a precarious position, especially if they no longer received the same protections as non-Christian Jews, and the church throughout the empire could be in grave danger.[14] Thus, when Jewish Christians who returned to Rome following the lapse of the Claudian edict became disgruntled with the Gentile leadership of the Roman church, the Jerusalem church had cause for concern. As a result, if the Jerusalem church continued to hear about conflicts between Jewish and Gentile Christians in Rome, and if these conflicts raised the ire of the new emperor,[15] Paul may have feared

---

that Paul urges a primarily Jewish Christian church in Rome and a primarily Gentile Christian church in Rome to set aside their mutual suspicions and worship together as one Paulinist church (which observed freedom from the Law).

13. Jervell, "Letter to Jerusalem," 64.

14. Of course, such danger presented itself only a decade letter during the latter part of Nero's reign.

15. It is likely that the original dispute that resulted in the Claudian edict was a controversy between non-Christian Jews and Christians (probably Jewish Christians, although Gentiles may have been part of the dispute as well), whereas the potential for conflict being explored here is between Christian Jews and Christian Gentiles. Thus, the

that the Jerusalem church would have denied his ministry to the Gentiles as an act of self-preservation. These intra- and inter-church politics help to explain Paul's emphasis on the unity of Jew and Gentile believers. His appeal to foundational principles in 3:30 thus underscores his attempt at the unification of the church and the ultimate support of his ministry.

Overall, then, it appears that while Paul had a variety of purposes in mind when he wrote Romans, the Jew-Gentile question was coming to a head within the fledgling church. Because of this crisis, Paul wrote to the influential Roman church to ask for their support. He spelled out his theology at length, emphasizing the priority of the Jews as well as the inclusion of the Gentiles, so that the church might be drawn together and the situation defused as much as possible. Once Paul had accomplished this, he hoped to continue expanding the church in the west, using Rome as a base of operations. Despite Paul's efforts at unification, his journey to Jerusalem resulted in his arrest and imprisonment.[16]

This context helps to clarify Paul's use of one-God language in 3:30 and elsewhere. I would tentatively suggest that Paul inserted his understanding of Israel's one God as a means of unifying the church, to bring Jew and Gentile into a shared understanding of God's universal plan for salvation. By appealing to the character of the one God, specifically God's impartial judgment which places both Jew and Gentile on equal footing, Paul hoped to strengthen the foundation for the unity he so desperately sought among the members of the new Christian churches.

In addressing the question of the proper emphasis to place on 3:30, and indeed, on 3:21–31 as a whole, we need to take a closer look at where this section fits within Paul's overall structure. While some elements of

---

potential for the degree of controversy may be significantly less. Nonetheless, the government in Rome would have a significantly lower threshold for tolerating a new religion once it had already been proven controversial and disruptive to public order—and the emperor would not likely care whether the disputes were between Christians and Jews or other Christians. Even under a different emperor, those in power in Rome would be keeping a much closer eye on the new religion.

16. One could argue that Paul's reception by the Jerusalem leaders in Acts 21:17–25 indicates that Paul received a warm reception (v. 17) and thus refutes any hypothesis that the Jerusalem leaders were about to reject Paul. It is clear, however, that regardless of the initial reception offered by the Jerusalem leaders, they were quite concerned about the reaction of the "many thousands of Jews" who had believed the Gospel and yet remained "zealous for the law" (v. 20). The leaders were quick to ask Paul to make a vow to show his loyalty to Judaism. Despite these actions, Paul's presence caused an uproar in Jerusalem, which led to his arrest.

the Pauline organization are easier to identify (e.g., chapters 9–11), other sections pose more of a conundrum. Specifically, the relationship of chapter 5 to the rest of the material is difficult to identify. It seems clear that one section is formed by chapters 1–4 and another section ends at 8:39;[17] it is uncertain, though, how chapter 5 fits into these sections.[18]

One possibility is that chapter 5 may conclude the first section. Numerous "backward links," including the theme of righteousness from faith, potentially suggest that chapter 5 provides the finishing touches to the preceding line of thought.[19] In considering Paul's writing style, however, it is apparent that one of the hallmarks of his writing is that he expertly ties together his themes throughout his work. He frequently looks both backward and forward simultaneously. Certainly the arguments of the preceding chapters are related to what Paul is about to argue, but nonetheless a significant shift in focus occurs in chapter 5. As Fitzmyer notes, in 1:16—4:25 Paul focuses on Jews and Greeks, who are not mentioned in 5:1—8:39. Rather, the Holy Spirit is mentioned in 5:4, a topic which will be developed extensively in chapter 8. Also, 1:16—4:25 emphasizes juridical, forensic notions, but Paul focuses in 5:1—8:39 on ethical and mystical concepts.[20] Hence, chapter 5 appears to begin a new section that ends at 8:39.

Another difficulty in reconstructing Paul's structure lies in the question of the originality of chapter 16. Manuscript evidence suggests the possibility that three different forms of Paul's letter to the Romans circulated during the early years of the church—a short form, ending with chapter 14, a form which includes chapter 15, and the longer form including all of chapter 16. The question of the integrity of the letter is an important one—if Paul originally wrote his letter as a general circular, as some scholars have suggested,[21] then it is inappropriate to draw significant inferences from the historical situation in Rome. The immediacy and intensity of the Jew-Gentile question and its implications could then be called into

17. See, for example, Byrne, *Romans*, 27; Moo, *Romans*, 32.

18. Fitzmyer (*Romans*, 96–97) outlines four main views concerning the function of chapter 5: 1) it concludes the first section; 2) it introduces the second section; 3) 5:1–11 ends the first section, whereas 5:12–21 introduces the second section; and 4) it stands as an independent unit.

19. Dunn, *Romans 1–8*, 242.

20. Fitzmyer, *Romans*, 97–98.

21. See, for example, Lake, "Shorter Form of Romans."

question. The problem with the shortest form of Romans, however, is that such a hypothesis cuts short Paul's discussion of the strong and the weak, which overflows into the first thirteen verses of chapter 15.[22] It seems unlikely that 15:1–13 was added to the discussion only later. Furthermore, Paul's lengthy greetings in chapter 16 can be explained by the itinerancy of some members of the Roman congregation as a result of the Claudian edict. Despite never having visited the Roman church, Paul probably had run into several of its members during their travels. Paul likely would have heard reports about members of the Roman church from Priscilla and Aquila and others; thus, sending personal greetings to those he had not yet met would be a means of endearing himself to the church even before his arrival. Chapter 16 is thus likely original.

Given these considerations, the following structure seems to fit best with Paul's purposes:[23]

1:1–17	Introduction
1:18—4:25	The human situation and God's solution
1:18—3:20	Wrath of God (for both Gentiles and Jews)
3:21–31	Righteousness of God through Christ
4:1–25	Abraham's example as confirmation
5:1—8:39	The old and the new; death and life
9:1—11:36	The righteousness of God and the problem of Israel
12:1—15:13	The practical outworking of this new life
15:14—16:27	Conclusion: Paul's plans and greetings

As this brief outline suggests, 3:21–31 is the hinge on which Paul's argument swings.[24] After making it clear in chapters 1–3 that God is impartial and is not pleased with either Jew or Gentile because both have

22. Fitzmyer, *Romans*, 56.

23. For a very similar structural arrangement, see Fitzmyer, *Romans*, 98–101.

24. Stuhlmacher (*Romans*, 57) comments that 3:21–26 is the heart of the letter to the Romans. See also Reumann ("Gospel of the Righteousness of God," 432), who says 3:21–31 is "the most significant passage" in Romans. He notes that 3:21–31 is related to the theme in 1:16, contrasts with 1:18—3:20, and is the section out of which chapters 4–11 grow and chapter 12 depends.

sinned, and must therefore face his wrath, Paul provides the divine solution in 3:21 and following: a new righteousness from God has been made known, a righteousness through faith in Jesus Christ, a righteousness given to all who believe, Jew and Gentile alike. Thus, the entire tone and direction shifts radically in 3:21–31; up to this point, Paul has emphasized the righteousness of God as impartial wrath against sin, but at 3:21 Paul emphasizes the righteousness of God as impartial grace made available through Christ.[25] The rest of Paul's letter explains this new revelation and delineates the consequences of God's action in Christ. That the "one God" language of 3:30 occurs within this key section is therefore significant to the rest of the letter; indeed, it is significant to Paul's entire argument. Drawing on this structural understanding, I will investigate below the impact of Paul's one-God theology throughout his letter.

THE JEWISH PERSPECTIVES: SALVATION HISTORY AND THE GENTILES

Before investigating Paul's logic in 3:27–31, a passage that seems aimed at Jews and arguing for the inclusion of the Gentiles within the new Christian community, it will be helpful to consider how first-century Jews in general understood their relationship to the Gentiles. Specifically, we will consider the variety of Jewish understandings of salvation history

25. For alternative constructions of 1:18—4:25, however, see Hays, "Psalm 143"; and Stowers, *Rereading of Romans*. Hays argues against the division of chapters 1–4 into distinct pericopes "as if they had no relation to one another, as if, for example, the meaning of δικαιοσύνη θεοῦ in 3:22 could be determined without reference to its meaning in 3:5" ("Psalm 143," 109). Although he rightly identifies the issue as the question of God's integrity (109), this thematic consistency between subsections does not negate the change in focus in 3:21. God's integrity means that he must deal justly with all who have sinned and, as v. 20 points out, *all* have sinned; 3:21, however, shifts away from the negative effects of sin in order to explain the positive and yet unexpected manner in which God preserves his righteousness. Stowers delineates two subsection in chapters 1–4, 1:18—3:9 and 3:10—4:25 (see 174–75). Nonetheless, he himself notices a distinction in the materials in precisely the section I have identified above: "Whereas 1:18—3:21 argues *that* God by his nature must treat gentiles equally, 3:21—4:2 announces *how* God has now in fact acted impartially toward gentiles and thus made known his righteousness" (203). Such thematic shifts provide stronger support for a structural break than Stowers's rhetorical argument that the section continues because of an ongoing dialogue with the interlocutor. An ongoing dialogue can nonetheless have distinct subsections within the discussion.

and what this meant for the Gentiles.[26] This will help to evaluate Paul's own views in light of the surrounding Jewish cultural milieu.

Jewish beliefs were rooted in their understanding of the one God, Yahweh, who had chosen Israel to be his special people. God had called Abraham to follow him and had promised to make Abraham into a great nation—"and all peoples on earth will be blessed through you" (Gen 12:3). God had affirmed his covenant with Israel and asked them to respond by their obedience to the laws that God gave to Moses at Sinai. If they followed the Law, Israel would be blessed—"the Lord your God will set you high above all the nations on earth" (Deut 28:1)—but if they disobeyed God's commands, Israel would be cursed. Israel's history involved a long journey of obedience and disobedience, blessings and curses.[27] Overall, Israel receives special blessings from God, including distinctive responsibility, as a result of being chosen to be God's special people. By the first century CE, however, the historical situation in which Jews found themselves differed markedly from these promises. Jews were subject to Roman rule, and more Jews lived outside the promised land than in it.

As a result, Jewish apocalyptic eschatology gained popularity. Although apocalyptic views are complex and varied, in general they involve the revelation of divine mysteries through visions or other forms of immediate disclosure of heavenly truths.[28] A variety of characteristics are found in apocalyptic literature: transcendentalism, mythology, a cosmological survey, pessimistic historical surveys, dualism, division of time periods, numerology, and descriptions of fallen angels, God and Satan, life

26. Nickelsburg argues that "Jewish attitudes about the salvation of the Gentiles vary widely, from exclusivity to inclusivity" (*Ancient Judaism*, 78). Nickelsburg is right to emphasize the variety of attitudes within first-century Judaism. Nonetheless, as I draw my conclusions below, I will try to paint a broad picture that will give a general overview of these attitudes.

27. Martens (*God's Design*) argues that God's design for Israel involved four concepts: deliverance, community, an ongoing relationship with God, and blessings from God. Similar concepts occur in N. T. Wright's discussion, although he expresses them differently: "There is one creator God, who has chosen Israel to be his people, giving her his Torah and establishing her in his holy land. He will act for her and through her to re-establish his judgment and justice, his wisdom and his *shalom*, throughout the world" (*New Testament and the People of God*, 279). Childs (*Old Testament Theology*, 240–46) also describes the promises of God, noting several branches of the varied concept, including judgment and salvation, the messianic kingdom and its messiah, the land, and eternal life.

28. Rowland, *Open Heaven*, 70.

after death, heaven and hell, and judgment.[29] Nonetheless, the eschatological dimension of apocalyptic should not be over-emphasized. Generally, the apocalyptic authors were more concerned with human history as it led up to the new age. The birth pangs of the age to come would allow the community to identify the transition and not despair about God's apparent absence from history.[30]

The apocalyptic perspective regarding Gentiles, who appear to be in control in this era, and the promise of God to make things right for the Jews, is therefore important to consider. Jewish apocalyptic eschatology generally outlined that at the end time, in Yahweh's great Day of Judgment, God would redeem Israel from her oppressors and judge the heathen nations. Gentiles would no longer reign over Israel, but would receive the just reward for their abuse of God's people.[31] God would judge Jew and Gentile alike by their deeds. In some apocalyptic writings, distinction is made between the righteous and the wicked on purely ethical grounds (e.g., *1 En.* 91–105, 108), but the tendency in most Jewish apocalyptic writings is to equate the righteous with true Jews and the wicked with sinful Jews and Gentiles,[32] although each work approaches this differently. *Jubilees*, for example, makes it clear that the uncircumcised will be destroyed (15:26). Similarly, the *Testament of Moses* portrays Moses as gleefully awaiting the destruction of Gentile nations (10:7). In addition, the Qumran community had a very restrictive understanding of Israel: only members of the Essenes were elect (1QS 11:7–9; CD 1:13—2:1; 1QpHab 2:1–4). Thus, even non-Essene Jews faced the wrath of God (1QS 2:4–9; 3:13—4:1).[33]

Nonetheless, some apocalyptic writings tended to have a more universalistic view in which the Gentiles who acknowledged God would

29. These are the categories proposed by Russell, *Method and Message*, 105.

30. Rowland, *Open Heaven*, 188–89.

31. See, e.g., *1 En.* 38:4–5; 46:4–8; 48:8–10; 53:1–7; 54:2; 62:1–12; 63:1–12; *2 Bar.* 40:1–4; 72:2–6; Dan 2:44; 7:11–27; *Pss. Sol.* 17:22–25, 30; *Jub.* 23:30; 24:28–33; *As. Mos.* 10:7; 4Q174 1:3–6; 1QM 1:9–15.

32. Russell, *Method and Message*, 297.

33. J. Collins remarks, "The 'Sons of Darkness,' also, were not simply the Gentiles but evil-doers, and from the perspective of the sect many ethnic Israelites fell into this category. Consequently, the texts vacillate between the traditional distinction between Israel and the Gentiles and attempts to define the opposition in non-nationalistic terms" (*Apocalypticism*, 91).

share in the blessings of Israel.[34] Indeed, some Gentiles found the Jewish religion attractive and converted; that Jews even allowed conversion into their religion by those who were not ethnically Jewish is significant and indicates that foundationally Judaism involved recognition of the one true God, Yahweh, and his promises and plans for Israel.[35] Other Gentiles, who were not willing to make a full commitment to Judaism, nonetheless followed some of its requirements and thus were called "God-fearers." That Jews allowed these God-fearers into their synagogues also indicates that at the basic level, being Jewish meant acknowledging Yahweh as the one true God.

In addition, Jewish law itself commanded Israelites to have mercy on the Gentiles. Exod 23:9; Lev 19:33; Deut 10:19 and 23:7, for example, enjoin Jews from oppressing the alien, because Jews know what it was like to be a foreigner in Egypt. Ps 146:9 records that "God watches over the alien . . ." Other passages also demonstrate God's concern for the Gentile, often in contrast to the views of the Jews themselves. The book of Jonah serves as perhaps the most significant example. God sent Jonah to the Ninevites so that they might repent of their wickedness. Jonah runs away from God precisely because he does not want the Ninevites to come to repentance. In Jonah's mind, he prefers that the Gentiles face destruction. The book closes with God's chastisement of Jonah for his hatred of the Ninevites. God expresses his concern for these Gentiles in 4:11: "And should I not be concerned about Nineveh, that great city, in which there are more than 120,000 people who do not know their right hand from their left, and also many animals?"

The book of Isaiah also affirms that Gentiles will be blessed and thus contains a universal outlook; other elements, however, suggest that the nations ultimately will submit to Israel's rule and thus suggest a certain hierarchy in regard to Jews and Gentiles. Van Winkle argues that "the tension between universalism and nationalism may be resolved by recognizing that for Deutero-Isaiah the salvation of the nations does not preclude their submission to Israel. The prophet does not envisage the co-equality of Jews and Gentiles. He expects that Israel will be exalted, and that she will become Yahweh's agent who will rule the nations in such a way that

34. See, for example, *1 En.* 10:21; 50:2–5; *T. Benj.* 9:2; 10:5–6, 9; 11:2; *T. Levi* 5:7; 18:9; *T. Naph.* 8:3.

35. This, of course, is what Paul argues in Rom 9:6–8, although he uses the argument to refer those who believe in Christ as the one true Israel.

justice is established and mercy shown."[36] This is an important observation. Whatever blessing the Gentiles would receive, as promised by God to Abraham, was interpreted by Jews in a hierarchical manner. The Jews were to reign as the people of God, and God would only dispense the blessing to the Gentiles *through Israel*. The priority of the Jews as the elect people of God was sacrosanct. This attitude will become important for the interpretation of 3:27–31 (see the section "Rom 3:30 Within the Context of 3:21–31," below).

The extent to which first-century Jews were concerned for the Gentiles is open to debate.[37] Nonetheless, various evidence suggests that at least some Jews were involved in significant missionary activity. For example, famous converts are recorded in Jewish writings.[38] The Jewish population significantly increased.[39] Jewish literature describes Gentiles

36. Van Winkle, "Relationship of the Nations," 457.

37. On one side of the spectrum, McKnight argues that "Judaism never developed a clear mission to the Gentiles that had as its goal the conversion of the world." (*Light among the Gentiles*, 116). Although he admits that a few missionaries may have been scattered throughout Jewish history, McKnight concludes that Jewish missionary activity was not aggressive. Nevertheless, he acknowledges that the Jewish belief that God was creator of all things meant Jews believed that humanity, at some level, was a unity and God showed concern for all people. Thus, the Jews generally had a favorable attitude toward the Gentiles (13). This did not preclude them, however, from maintaining their exclusivistic national identity. Proselytism was generally viewed favorably, but conversion needed to be total commitment. Overall, McKnight concludes that Jews maintained "a serious openness" to Gentile participation in Judaism, but that the predominant means of witnessing was not zealous missionary activity but rather the good behavior and lifestyle of the Jews (117). For a similar conclusion, see Goodman, *Mission and Conversion*. On the other side of the spectrum, Feldman (*Jew and Gentile*, 445) argues that Jews of the first century were indeed zealous missionaries. His work emphasizes that first-century Judaism was strong, not weak and lachrymose as sometimes depicted. Jews were effective in resisting Hellenistic influences and seemed to be universally observant of the Torah, despite many of them living in the Diaspora. He notes that some syncretism is attested in Egypt, but that Jews in Asia Minor did not appear to assimilate foreign ideas. Rather, Jews were influential on their neighbors: Feldman argues that the various expulsions of Jews from Rome were due, at least in part, to Jewish missionary activity. Many aspects of Judaism were appealing to the Gentiles, including its antiquity, the greatness of Moses, and Jewish virtues. Although Feldman admits there is no single item of conclusive evidence proving Jews were active missionaries, he argues that the cumulative evidence is considerable.

38. For various examples, see Feldman, *Jew and Gentile*, 324–32.

39. Ibid., 293. Feldman may make too much out of this evidence, however; a variety of factors could account for the increase in Jewish population, and it is impossible to determine precisely how much of this increase might be due to conversion.

coming to know God in the end times.[40] The Hebrew Scriptures were translated into Greek.[41] In addition, the New Testament suggests Jewish missionary activity was prevalent in the first century.[42]

Nonetheless, the evidence should not be overstated.[43] Although Jewish missionaries were probably not going to extreme lengths to proclaim the blessings of Torah, a great deal of evidence exists that many Gentiles were attracted to Judaism and were encouraged to join the religion. That some Gentiles became proselytes suggests more than disinterest on the part of the Jews who helped these Gentiles join the people of the one God. Thus, even though clear distinctions existed between Jew and Gentile, the Jews

40. See, e.g., Isa 2:2–4; Mic 4:1–3; Tob 13:11; 14:6; *1 En.* 10:21; 50:2–3.

41. McKnight (*Light among the Gentiles*, 60) acknowledges that sometimes LXX renderings were used to promote Gentile understanding or at least to make the text compatible with Hellenism, and *in that sense*, one could say that literature was used for proselytizing. Nonetheless, he argues that this does not prove that the Septuagint was designed to convert Gentiles or even that copies were given to Gentiles in order to convert them. But McKnight significantly downplays the influence the LXX would have had on the Gentiles. Had the Jews wanted to promote isolation from the Gentiles, they surely would not have put their sacred texts into the lingua franca of the first-century Roman Empire. In addition, evidence exists that some Greeks in the first century were familiar with the LXX (Feldman cites Pseudo-Longinus and Pseudo-Ecphantus in the first century, as well as others from other centuries; see 312–13). Clearly, the translation was not intended for Jews only.

42. Matt 23:15; Acts 2:11; 6:5; 13:43.

43. Both Feldman and McKnight skew the evidence in favor of their arguments. For example, Feldman cites *T. Levi* 14:4: "... the light of the law which was granted to you for the enlightenment of every man," and interprets "enlightenment" to mean the Jews had a "burning" missionary concern (*Jew and Gentile*, 294–95). This is an unwarranted extrapolation. The passage nowhere suggests that missionaries actively converted Gentiles. It is simply not that specific. Rather, it could merely imply that the Law could be read by Gentiles, who would receive enlightenment from their own reading. McKnight (*Light among the Gentiles*) treats the evidence with a similar prejudice. For example, he suggests that the names of famous converts appeared in Jewish writings either by accident, or as the result of so few converts that the names were easily remembered. He is willing to admit that Jews had a favorable view toward proselytes, but he denies any significant missionary activity. We must ask, however, where these proselytes learned about Judaism and who convinced them to convert if there were no missionaries. McKnight may simply define missionary activity too narrowly—he is willing to admit that good behavior and the Jewish lifestyle encouraged proselytism, yet he does not acknowledge that these factors are part of missionary outreach. For McKnight, "aggressive attempts to convert Gentiles" (48) seems restricted to those who travel to the far corners of the world shouting the Torah from the rooftops. He does not consider that serving as a missionary may involve a Jew in his or her own home, neighborhood, or marketplace aggressively attempting to convert one's neighbor.

were concerned to share their knowledge of Yahweh. Their exclusivist practices did not mean an exclusivist religion. They encouraged Gentiles to understand the covenant promises, acknowledge the faithfulness of the one God, and observe Torah. Gentiles who made such steps were welcomed into the covenant.

Another source to which we can look for our understanding of the Jewish attitude toward Gentiles is the rabbinic writings concerning the interpretation of Lev 19:18b: ". . . love your neighbor as yourself." The earlier writings considered "neighbor" to refer only to the fellow Jew and also proselytes. Non-Jews were not covered by this commandment.[44] Some texts advocate hating those whom God hates, i.e., the apostate and heretic (*'Abot R. Nat.* A 16). Although some texts suggest that the command to love one's neighbor is in some way connected to the universal idea of humanity, it is not clear whether these texts actually envision kindness toward all of humanity.[45] Neudecker concludes that "R. Akiva and Ben Azzai, as well as Hillel, had only fellow Jews in mind in those contexts where the sources record their attitudes to Lev 19,18 and thus relate the commandment directly only to fellow Jews."[46] Nonetheless, he does not discount the possibility that these rabbis, had they specifically been asked about non-Jews, would have included non-Jews within the commandment to love one's neighbor. Thus, while the rabbinic sources offer only tentative evidence, it is reasonable to conclude that Jewish ethical concern was primarily directed at other Jews. It was debatable whether Gentiles should receive the same consideration as Jews.[47]

44. Neudecker, "'And You Shall Love Your Neighbor,'" 499. We need to keep in mind, however, that even the "early" rabbinic interpretations are generally later than the first century. Thus, it is difficult to determine whether the documents accurately portray pre-Christian sentiments, or if these documents simply reflect the increased negative sentiments toward Gentiles following the destruction of the Jerusalem temple in 70 CE.

45. Ibid., 502.

46. Ibid., 512.

47. Bassler (*Divine Impartiality*) finds evidence in a late rabbinic document that God's impartiality implied equality between Jew and Gentile. *Tanna debe Eliahu* contains several passages in which the rabbi argues that God treats Gentiles the same as he treats Israel. This universality applies to the benefits of the Aqedah, the efficacy of repentance, and the presence of the Holy Spirit, all of which are bestowed upon deserving Jews and Gentiles. She notes that the document may reflect the influence of Gal 3:28, for the language is similar: "Do I show partiality? Whether Gentile or Israelite, whether man or woman, whether male slave or female slave obeys a commandment, the reward for it is immediate" (*S. Eli. Rab.* [13] 14, quoted in *Divine Impartiality*, 65). Bassler concludes,

On the other hand, Jewish theology contained elements which clearly applied to all people, regardless of nationality. Jews believed that the Noahic covenant, for example, applied to all of humanity. Part of that covenant, the prohibition against murder, was based on the understanding that all people are made in the image of God (Gen 9:6). Thus it did not matter whether the victim was a Jew or a Gentile—the value of life remained the same. In addition, God's promise not to destroy the world again by flood was a promise not just to the Jews, but also to the Gentiles.[48]

Jews clearly understood Yahweh as a God who ruled over the entire world. He was not merely a national deity whose only sphere of influence fell upon the Israelite people. Rather, the one God was creator, sustainer and impartial ruler over all the world—even if God's favor rested uniquely on the Israelite people.[49] Paul clearly exploits this Jewish theology within the argument of Rom 3:29–30. Jews would not deny that God is God over everything—to do so would be to deny the oneness of Yahweh. Yet Paul uses his understanding of the character of the one God to state that the One who is not capricious or arbitrary in his rule over all people justifies by faith both Jews and Gentiles. As a result, God is God over the Gentiles, too. (The implications of this statement will be explored below.)

Overall, then, the Jewish attitude toward Gentiles in the first century was determined by the Gentile attitude toward the one God. Those

---

"Although the *Tanna debe Eliahu* is unique among Jewish writings in developing this aspect of impartiality, it does demonstrate for us that the ramifications of impartiality which Paul perceived in the letter to the Romans were latent in the doctrine and not solely the result of Paul's Christian faith or missionary career" (76). Nonetheless, the document is so late (tenth century) that it is impossible to determine whether these views reflect earlier traditions.

48. See, e.g., Ross, *Creation and Blessing*, 207: "The sign of the covenant [the rainbow] was to all flesh. It was a token of God's pledge to all humankind." See also the Babylonian Talmud (*Sanh.* 56a, and Pseudo-Phocylides *Sentences*), which describes several stipulations that are binding on all humanity, e.g., the imperative to recognize government, the command to avoid blasphemy and idolatry, and the command to avoid bloodshed. Sanders (*Paul and Palestinian Judaism*) has considered such rabbinic evidence regarding Jewish views toward Gentiles in general, and has argued that no systematic view regarding the salvation of Gentiles is presented in the rabbinic materials. Rather, different rabbis held different views. He concludes, "Even those who were of the view that righteous Gentiles would have a place in the world to come do not specify what a 'righteous Gentile' is. However, the later view, that he is one who keeps the seven Noachian commandments, is probably not too far off the mark" (210). See also Bockmuehl, *Jewish Law*.

49. See, e.g., Gen 1:1—2:25; Ps 33:6–11; 90:2; 102:25–27; Job 38–41; Isa 40–46.

Gentiles who embraced Yahweh would not receive the same sentence of judgment that the wicked Jews and the (non-believing) Gentiles in general would receive. On one level, Jews had a respect for all humanity and understood that Yahweh was the Lord over all people, not just the Jews. Nonetheless, for Gentiles to be included in the blessings of God, they needed to draw near to God via Jewish practices and distinctives, such as the requirement that proselytes be circumcised. Thus, the issue was not based on purely ethnic distinctions. Ultimately, whether one received the blessings of God depended on whether one responded positively to God, which Jews believed necessarily involved the observance of Torah. Thus, a certain hierarchy was involved in that any blessings the Gentiles received would come through Israel and through adherence to the revelation that God had given to his special people.

In line with other Jews, Paul would agree that whether one received the blessings of God depended on whether one responded positively to God. But for Paul, unlike for non-Christian Jews, the response to God involved believing that Jesus was the "righteousness from God," the decisive sacrifice of atonement.[50] His argument in Rom. 3:21–31, especially in verses 24–26, emphasizes that righteousness is only effected through faith in Christ. Without responding to God in this way, even Jews would be excluded from the blessings of God.

OVERLAPPING THEMES

The themes that Paul addresses in Rom 3:30, namely the Jew/Gentile question, law and faith as they relate to justification, and the oneness of God, are neither new nor unique to 3:21–31. Rather, they are interwoven throughout Paul's letter. Thus, in order to address with precision Paul's meaning in 3:30, it is necessary to survey similar language within the rest of the letter in order to determine Paul's larger purpose.

Paul's discussion of Jew/Gentile relations forms a remarkable pattern in Romans. Chapters 1–4 contain numerous references to Jews and Gentiles, as do chapters 9–11 and chapters 15–16. But chapters 5–8 and chapters 12–14 are entirely devoid of any *specific* mention of Jews and Gentiles.[51] That this pattern flows along the lines of major sections within

50. For a discussion of the meaning of the term ἱλαστήριον, see the section, "Rom 3:30 Within the Context of 3:21–31," below.

51. Certainly some reference may be *implied* in these chapters, such as in 7:1, "I am speaking to men who know the law . . . ," or even on the question of weak and strong in

the epistle, as noted above, provides evidence for the aptness of that structure and is indeed quite instructive, as illustrated below:

Section and Theme	Jew/Gentile Language[52]
1:1–17 / Introduction	1:5, 13–14
1:18—4:25 / The human situation and God's solution	1:16; 2:9, 10, 14, 17, 24, 28, 29; 3:1, 9, 29, 30; 4:9, 11–12, 16
5:1—8:39 / The old and the new: death and life	None
9:1—11:36 / The righteousness of God and the problem of Israel	9:3–5, 6–8, 24–29, 30–31; 10:1–3, 12, 16–21; 11:1–2, 7, 11–24, 25–32
12:1—15:13 / The practical outworking of the new life in Christ	None in chapters 12–14; the only references occur in 15:8–12
15:14—16:25 / Conclusion: Paul's plans and greetings	15:16, 18, 27; 16:3

As this chart suggests, when Paul emphasizes the distinction between Jew and Gentile as denoted by Israel's election through the old covenant, his language reflects this distinction. But when Paul focuses on the qualities of the new life of the Christian, a life marked not by distinction but by unity, his language no longer sharply emphasizes such features. Paul begins the letter by addressing the tensions between Jew and Gentile, by addressing the question of boasting. As he compares the two groups, he argues that both are under the same judgment from God (3:9, 3:23). Once he reaches this conclusion, his language no longer emphasizes distinctions, but unity. He discusses the life of the believer—a life based not on distinction between Jew and Gentile, but on their same faith in the one God. Thus, the Jew/Gentile language does not appear in this section. Yet as Paul reaches the pinnacle of his description of this new life—that nothing can separate a believer from the love of God (8:38–39)—the ob-

chapters 14–15. Nonetheless, Paul's focus in these sections remains on the unified state of sin or grace for *all*, and the unified call to holiness for *all*, and thus he does not feel compelled to name specific distinctions between Jew and Gentile. In fact, to do so would be patently against his purposes in these sections.

52. This includes such references as "circumcised," "uncircumcised," etc., which clearly refer to the distinction between Jew and Gentile.

vious question must be asked: if God loves the faithful, then why do God's promises to Israel seem to remain unfulfilled? How can such a God be trusted? The very righteousness of God is brought into question, and the issue focuses on ethnic Israel because the new revelation in Christ seems to deny Israel's election. Hence, the Jew/Gentile language reappears. Once Paul addresses this question, the language again fades into the background as he discusses the new life of the believer and exhorts various behaviors that conform to the will of God. The Jew/Gentile language reappears only at the end of the hortatory section as Paul emphasizes the unity required between Jew and Gentile. It is as if his argument has come full circle: he recognizes distinctions, argues for grace and new life which are not based on these distinctions, and then acknowledges that the ethics of the new community in some ways still do not reflect this new reality and must therefore change.

Overall, Paul's language regarding Jews and Gentiles occurs throughout the letter, signifying that the question of Christian unity in Rome is of major concern to Paul. Thus, when investigating his meaning in 3:30, it is important to remember that the statement is in no way an aside or a parenthetical element. Rather, the oneness language occurs within the heart of Paul's argument.

Another theme which recurs throughout Paul's letter to the Romans is that of justification, and the question of how Torah fits into God's plan of salvation. In chapter 3, I extensively discussed Paul's view of the Law, and therefore I will not repeat those arguments here. Rather, we will briefly explore how Paul's view of justification influences his argument in Romans, especially in Rom 3:29–30.

An important passage for understanding Paul's view of the Law in Romans is found in chapter 10. The argument occurs within the larger section, chapters 9–11, where Paul defends the righteousness of God and his ultimate faithfulness to Israel. In 10:3, Paul explains that the problem non-Christian Jews face is that they do not know "the righteousness that comes from God." The righteousness from God, Paul has already told us in 3:21–22, comes through faith in Jesus Christ. Because the Jews did not accept Christ, they "sought to establish their own" righteousness (10:3b). Paul thus argues that Judaism was not a legalistic religion (in the sense of trying to earn God's favor through human striving) until the Jews failed to "submit to God's righteousness." This is why Paul says in 10:4 that Christ is the end of the law—he is its fulfillment.[53] Christ is not the end of the Law in the sense of its erasure; if that were the case, then how could Paul justify his constant use of the Law to support his arguments? Rather, the Torah no longer stands as the identifying feature of (true) Judaism—Christ does. Through the Holy Spirit, given through faith in Christ, the believer is now empowered to live the kind of life that is pleasing to God (Rom 8:13).

As a result, the cultic demands (including boundary markers) of the Law no longer have the same meaning. They are marks of the past—they are marks which look forward to God's redemption. But since that redemption has come in Christ, to continue to employ such "boundary markers" as symbols of membership in the elect people of God would be deceptive because they imply that God's definitive work has not yet occurred. With Christ's exaltation, the Spirit has become the new mark of the people of God. Nonetheless, when Paul refers to "works of the law," he refers to more than boundary markers.[54] For Paul, anything which is not based on faith in Christ has become a work of the law. God's grace is offered in Christ and nowhere else—to reject Christ is to reject grace, and thus forces one to rely on works which, ultimately, can never achieve righteousness. This is why Paul calls Christ the "stumbling stone" in 9:32–33. The ones who trust in Christ will never be put to shame, but the ones who reject him, and thus reject God's grace, are now pursuing righteousness by works.

All of these concepts come together in the argument of Rom 3:21–31. As noted in the structural analysis above, 3:21–31 provides a key passage within the epistle. It is here that Paul spells out the answer to the problem of 1:18—3:20 (that Jew and Gentile alike are sinful and must face God's just condemnation). In verse 21 Paul says that a righteousness from God *apart from law* has been made known—yet this righteousness does not nullify the Law, but rather upholds it (v. 31). This righteousness, Paul quickly clarifies, comes through faith in Jesus Christ (v. 22).[55] More specifically, Christ is a "sacrifice of atonement"; thus Paul uses the language of the Law to describe what Christ has done in dying on the cross.[56]

53. See Badenas, *Christ the End of the Law*.

54. *Contra* Dunn, *Theology of Paul*, 358.

55. See below for discussion of the "faith in/of Christ" issue.

56. See the section below, "Rom 3:30 Within the Context of 3:21–31," for discussion of the specific meaning of the term. For the OT context, see Exod 30:10; Lev 9:7; 16:10, 17–19, 30, 34; 17:11; 23:26–28.

Nonetheless, the sacrifice of atonement justifies "those who have faith in Jesus" (v. 26). Thus, we have another example where Paul uses the Law itself to support his contention that justification is apart from the Law.

Now that Christ has arrived, the distinctions between Jews and Gentiles have different significance. Jewish ethnicity is still important in the historical sense that it is through Jews that God has brought salvation to all people. In both 3:1–2 and 9:4–5 Paul highlights the importance of God's blessings upon the Jewish people through the covenant and the Law.[57] Nonetheless, those aspects of the Law that testified to the coming promise have now been superseded by the fulfillment of that promise: Christ. Hence, when Paul asks rhetorically whether God is God of only the Jews in verse 29, and refers to the Shema in verse 30, his language derives not only from the Jewish understanding of the one God, but also from his conviction that salvation ultimately rests on God's grace and stands apart from the Mosaic law. Nevertheless, it stands apart from the Law only because that grace has fulfilled the Law and accomplished its purposes (v. 31). Despite what appears to be an inconsistent plan, Paul argues that the one God has purposed the redemption brought by Christ from the beginning. In order to prove his point, he uses the example of Abraham to show that righteousness always came from believing in the one God "who gives life to the dead and calls things that are not as thought they were" (4:17).

Jew-Gentile relations and justification are not the only themes present in 3:30 that recur throughout Paul's letter. The oneness theme itself appears elsewhere (although not quite as explicitly), and forces the question of the relationship between Christ and God. The central text of 3:21–31 ties Christ and God together—God's righteousness is expressed in the activity of Jesus Christ. Yet Paul does not here explicitly spell out the dynamics of this relationship. He does not, for example, use a Christianized Shema as he does in 1 Cor 8:6. Rather, he draws on the traditional Shema. Yet Romans is a later epistle. Has Paul changed his mind? Or does the context of this epistle require a different emphasis?

Certainly Paul's language about God dominates the letter in a way incomparable to his other epistles. Fitzmyer notes that the word θεός occurs 153 times in Romans, whereas Χριστός occurs 66 times. In fact,

57. See also Esler, "Ancient Oleiculture." Esler argues that Paul is concerned in Rom 11 to maintain the distinctive identities of Jew and Gentile (including Jewish priority) while at the same time insisting on their overall unity.

θεός is the word found most frequently in the epistle: "Significantly, Paul is clearly preoccupied with the activity of God in human history."[58]

An analysis of Paul's references to God and Christ shows distinct emphases in Romans.[59] Paul's abundant use of God language emphasizes both God's will (God's providence, his predestination, and his role as director of human history)[60] and God's judgment, with special emphasis on God's wrath.[61] These are clearly the dominant themes. Nonetheless, Paul also describes such attributes as God's encouragement, peace, kindness, and mercy.[62] God as father figure also appears, although significantly such language is focused in chapter 8, where the bulk of the language regarding the Spirit also appears.[63]

Paul's language about Christ, on the other hand, emphasizes mainly his atoning death and resurrection.[64] Paul also emphasizes the blessings that come through Christ's agency, which include peace, righteousness, and life.[65] In addition, participation in or belonging to Christ is key to a believer's identity.[66]

Although this analysis may suggest a strict separation between God and Christ, other passages in the epistle hint at an overlap between the two. We will explore these more thoroughly below, but I will mention them briefly here. In the beginning of the letter (1:1–9), Paul describes Christ by means of the language of sonship, and contrasts Christ according to the flesh and Christ according to the spirit of holiness. We will consider what Paul meant by these phrases, and how he defined Christ's relationship with God. The closeness of the relationship comes into question again in 5:8, where *God's* love is demonstrated through *Christ's* actions. This is further emphasized in 8:3, where God sends his Son. What does this imply

58. Fitzmyer, *Romans*, 104.

59. The following is the result of my own analysis.

60. 1:10, 24–28; 2:18; 8:20, 27–33; 9:11, 15–23, 29; 10:19; 11:2–8; 12:2; 13:1.

61. 1:18; 2:2–7, 13, 16; 3:5–6, 19–20, 25–26; 4:5–8, 24; 8:30, 33; 9:28–29; 11:1–2, 21, 33; 12:19; 14:3, 10–12.

62. E.g., 2:4; 9:16, 23; 11:22; 11:31–32; 12:1; 15:5, 13.

63. Believers as sons, children and heirs appears in 8:14, 16, 17, 19, 21; 9:8, 26. God as "father" appears in 6:4 and 8:15. References to Christ as God's son occur in 1:3, 4, 9; 5:10; 8:3, 29, 32.

64. 1:4; 4:24–25; 5:6, 8, 10; 6:4–10; 7:4; 8:11, 32, 34; 10:7–9; 14:9, 15.

65. 1:7; 3:22, 24; 5:1, 9, 11, 17, 21; 6:4–5, 8, 11, 23.

66. 1:6; 6:4–8; 7:4; 8:10; 12:5; 14:8, 14; 16:2–3, 7–9, 11–12, 22.

about the relationship between God and Christ? Does it imply Christ's preexistence? In 8:9 and 11, an interesting dilemma appears, in that Paul refers to the Spirit as both the "spirit of God" and the "spirit of Christ." Is the same Spirit intended here, and if so, what does that say about the relationship between Christ and God? When we turn to 8:31–39, we find Paul stating that believers are more than conquerors "through him who loved us"—yet, is that Christ as in 8:35, or God as in 8:39? Even the manuscript evidence attests to the variation in thought. A similar problem occurs in 14:1–12. Paul uses κύριος language, but it is unclear whether he intends to refer to Christ or to God. The most hotly debated of these passages is 9:5 where, depending on the punctuation, Paul may be referring to Christ as θεός. But the confusion continues—10:6–13 provides an interesting parallel to 3:30 in that it emphasizes the Lord's impartiality by referring to the same Lord over both Jews and Gentiles, yet here Christ is in view rather than God. In 11:36, however, Paul offers a doxology to God in which there is no mention of Jesus. Christ's position is also quite different in 15:6, where Paul refers to God as the God of Jesus Christ. Finally, Paul ends the letter in 16:27 with a concluding doxology, which could be addressed to God or Christ or both.

Thus, even though Paul attributes specific and distinct roles to God and Christ in his letter to the Romans, in several places he nonetheless appears to leave his language ambiguous. We will ask whether this language is innocuous, or whether Paul intends to make specific theological statements through these word choices. To this we will return.

ROMANS 3:30 WITHIN THE CONTEXT OF 3:21–31

In order to consider Paul's intent in using the one-God language of 3:30, we will first consider his overall argument in 3:21–31. In 3:21–26, Paul expands his thesis statement from 1:16–17, explaining the revelation of the righteousness of God in Christ; 3:27–31 then resumes Paul's diatribal discussion with his interlocutor and discusses the implications of this newly revealed righteousness.[67]

As noted earlier, verse 21 marks a new subsection. Previously Paul argued that both Jew and Gentile have sinned and, because God is impartial, both face God's wrath (a theme he reiterates in v. 23). In the following verses, Paul explains how, despite humanity's sinfulness, God's

67. Dunn, *Romans*, 183; Käsemann, *Romans*, 91; Johnson, *Reading Romans*, 51; Witherington, *Romans*, 99.

righteousness is revealed, and this revelation comes in an unexpected way: apart from the Law. Nonetheless, the Law and the prophets testify to this righteousness. Paul is concerned here to emphasize that although God's provision may be unexpected, it nonetheless has been part of God's plan from the beginning.[68]

Starting in verse 21, Paul repeatedly emphasizes that the "righteousness of God" has been made known through the Christ-event. Although we cannot fully review the debate regarding the meaning of this phrase,[69] it is important to note that Paul nowhere fully explicates his understanding of the phrase—even though he is writing to a church that has no first-hand experience of his teaching. This probably indicates that Paul and the Roman church shared a common understanding of the "righteousness of God," and thus Paul did not find it necessary to explain himself.[70]

The most likely source of such a common understanding, given Paul's Jewish background and the likely Jewish foundations of the Roman church, is the Old Testament witness. Various emphases occur throughout the Jewish Scriptures, such as God's deliverance or salvation in Isaiah, and covenant love, faithfulness, and trustworthiness in the Psalms.[71] Indeed, it is possible to see a development of ideas within the Jewish Scriptures. In

68. See Hays, "Three Dramatic Roles," for a discussion of Paul's understanding of the Law as oracular witness.

69. In this long-standing theological debate, scholars have argued variously that the expression refers to: 1) human righteousness as valued by God (e.g., Ridderbos, J. C. O'Neill); 2) God's own righteousness (e.g., Kümmel, Barrett); or 3) the gift of righteousness that originates with God and is given to humans (e.g., Bultmann).

70. Williams, "'Righteousness of God,'" 260.

71. Ibid. 260–263. In his analysis of Paul's letters, Williams further narrows this definition and concludes that Paul's understanding of the righteousness of God means that God is faithful to the promises he made to Abraham to gather all nations into the people of God. Williams's analysis, however, produces a definition that is too specific. Certainly God's righteousness includes his trustworthiness in keeping his promises to Abraham, but this is not *all* that it involves. If God is trustworthy, then he must be faithful to all his promises, not just to the promise regarding blessing the nations through Abraham. God must be held true to his word when, for example, he promises to bless Israel if the people obey his commands and curse Israel if they fail to keep God's law (Deut 30:15–20). Indeed, Paul sees the issue as larger than simply the question of Abraham (and implicitly, larger than simply the inclusion of the Gentiles). Chapters 9–11 serve to answer the question of whether God can be trusted, since it appears that the promises to Israel (and these are the larger promises than simply the blessing of all the nations through Abraham) have not come to fruition. Thus, a broader understanding than what Williams presents is necessary.

the postexilic period, God's righteousness concerned the "quality whereby God acquits his people, manifesting toward them a gracious, salvific power in a just judgment."[72] Later the idea developed and included the concept of fidelity and steadfast mercy.[73] This broad sense of God's righteousness fits the Pauline context well. The argument in 3:21–26 includes questions in the judicial/forensic context (justification of sinners, grace, salvation) and questions of faithfulness to God's revealed scriptures (v. 21). Thus, when the "righteousness of God" is revealed in 3:21–26, it involves the illumination of God's just judgment and his fidelity to all his promises;[74] for Paul, this clearly comes about in the Christ-event (vv. 24–25).

Paul explains in verse 22 that this revelation of God's righteousness is based on faith, a faith that is specifically linked to the death and resurrection of Jesus, although here Paul focuses on the death of Jesus. At this point, however, a significant ambiguity arises in the Greek. If πίστις Χριστοῦ is a subjective genitive, then Paul is referring to Christ's faithfulness. If the phrase is an objective genitive, however, then the believer's faith in what Christ has accomplished is in view.

The first option, that Paul wants to emphasize Christ's faithfulness, is attractive because it highlights the obedience of Christ.[75] Thus, Jesus is able to fulfill the commands of God and simultaneously provide a model for believers to emulate. Certainly the Jewish Scriptures laud those who keep God's statutes and seek God with all their hearts (Ps 119:2). The πίστις Χριστοῦ would thus provide a remarkable example of that which pleases God.

The question, however, is whether such an interpretation fits the context here. Paul's argument concerning Abraham in chapter 4 is instructive in this regard. When Paul speaks of Abraham's faith, he emphasizes that this faith was a matter of believing that the promise God had made

72. Fitzmyer, *Romans*, 106.

73. Ibid. Fitzmyer warns that the concept should not be equated with the idea of mercy—righteousness must include the judicial/forensic context (107).

74. See also Beker ("Faithfulness of God"), who correctly emphasizes the faithfulness of God as a key issue for the entire letter.

75. Hays argues strongly for the subjective genitive in *Faith of Jesus Christ*. Hays concludes that the faith of Jesus Christ "may be understood as a reference to the faithfulness of 'the one man Jesus Christ' whose act of obedient self-giving on the cross became the means by which 'the promise' of God was fulfilled. (This interpretation should not be understood to abolish or preclude human faith directed toward Christ, which is also an important component of Paul's thought.)" (161).

would come true. This trust in God was prior to any act of circumcision or other act of obedience. In verse 24, Paul states that Abraham's faith is an example for us—if we trust God in the same manner, then we, too, will receive righteousness. It is important to note that in verse 24 it is a matter of believing in God, "the one who raised our Lord Jesus from the dead." Once again the close relationship between Jesus and God is apparent: πίστεως Χριστοῦ (3:22, 26) is interchangeable with πιστεύουσιν ἐπὶ τὸν ἐγείραντα Ἰησοῦν τὸν κύριον ἡμῶν ἐκ νεκρῶν (4:24). In both statements, this faith results in the believer's justification. For Paul, believing that God is true to his promises is ultimately synonymous with believing that in Christ these promises have been fulfilled.

At first glance, it almost appears that the concepts implied by both objective and subjective genitives are present.[76] Abraham trusts in God, and this trust involves the belief in God's faithfulness to his promises. Yet it is not Abraham's obedience/faithfulness that is in view, since there is no command for Abraham to follow at this point.[77] Thus, the objective genitive seems to be more appropriate for describing Abraham's faith. This is an important observation, because the logic of chapter 4 shows that Abraham provides a type for *believers* to exemplify; he is not a type of Christ.[78] It would seem, then, that a believer's faith *in* Christ provides the proper parallel to Abraham's faith in God. Abraham believed in the God who can bring life to that which was dead, and 4:24 clearly refers to the believer's faith in God.[79] Thus, Paul's emphasis in this section appears

76. Indeed, Hays criticizes Dunn for making a sharp distinction between "trust" and "faithfulness." Instead, Hays argues that both concepts are included in the term πίστις (*Faith of Jesus Christ*, 295). Hays is right to underscore this affinity; nonetheless, as he himself has observed, πίστις is not a univocal concept for Paul (161). Thus, we must uncover Paul's emphasis in each instance. See Matlock, "Detheologizing the ΠΙΣΤΙΣ ΧΡΙΣΤΟΥ Debate," 6.

77. Dunn ("Once More, ΠΙΣΤΙΣ ΧΡΙΣΤΟΥ," 265) points out that an emphasis on Abraham's faithfulness would be more destructive to Paul's argument than helpful, since Paul's opponents likely used Abraham as an example of faithfulness to the commands of God both when he was circumcised and when he offered up Isaac.

78. As argued by Dunn, *Romans*, 166. See also idem, "Once More," 265, where Dunn argues that Paul emphasizes Abraham's *trust* (not faithfulness) in "the life-giving power of God" in 4:22–24, rather than Abraham's faithfulness as a prefiguration of Christ.

79. Gathercole argues, "It is Abraham's belief that God will give life to his and Sarah's bodies that makes his belief an archetype of Christian belief . . . The crucial point is that Abraham's belief in the God who gives life to the dead is witness to Christian faith in that same God, who is identified as the one who raised Jesus from the dead" ("Justified by Faith," 164–65).

to be on the believer's faith in what Christ has accomplished on the cross, not on Christ's obedience itself.

To this discussion another observation should be added: as is commonly recognized, Paul makes very little reference to Jesus's life, teaching, or miracles. Presumably Christ's faithfulness was not a one-time event, but rather a lifelong disposition of faithfulness toward God. Although Paul emphasizes repeatedly the importance of Christ's death, he does not discuss the historical details themselves or describe in any depth the steps that Jesus took in his earthly life to be faithful to God. Such a lack of explication is hard to fathom if Paul had wanted to emphasize Jesus's faithfulness![80] Not only this, but if the phrase πίστις Ἰησοῦ Χριστοῦ was a technical term that Paul used specifically to describe Jesus's faithfulness (and as a result of Paul's exegesis of Hab 2:4, as Hays argues), we would expect to find the phrase in such passages as the Christ hymn of Phil 2:5–11. Although Paul emphasizes Christ's obedience there (ὑπήκοος, verse 8), nowhere do we find a description of Christ's πίστις.[81] In addition, a number of Pauline passages indicate the importance of the believer's trust in Christ, such as Phil 1:29 and Rom 10:12.[82]

When we turn to Rom 3:22, however, it is still possible that Paul has the subjective genitive in mind, since the sentence contains a redundancy ("διὰ πίστεως Ἰησοῦ Χριστοῦ εἰς πάντας τοὺς πιστεύοντας . . .") that could be resolved by supplying a subjective genitive meaning in the first instance and an objective genitive meaning in the second ("through the faithfulness of Christ to all who believe . . .").[83] Nonetheless, the context suggests that an alternative interpretation is preferable. Paul intentionally uses the redundancy to emphasize that God's righteousness is available to *all* who believe in Christ: "The usage in 3:22 is simply part of

80. Dunn notes that Paul fails to emphasize Christ's faithfulness, even in those arguments where it might be expected, such as Rom 5:15–19, "where the antithesis ἀπιστία/πίστις would have been very natural, had Christ's faith been a factor in his thought . . ." (*Romans*, 166).

81. Clearly there is a strong connection between obedience and faithfulness, but the two cannot be strictly equated. The point here is that if Paul used a specific phrase to signal this aspect of his theology, then it is remarkable that the Christ hymn lacks that phrase.

82. See also Col 2:5. Dunn states that the key issue for Paul is "how God's righteousness operates, the means by which or 'terms' on which he acts on man's behalf . . ." (*Romans*, 166).

83. This is argued by Hays, *Faith*, 158.

a sustained motif."[84] Indeed, Paul's entire argument here sustains the idea that all, both Jew and Gentile, now have access to God by the same means. But more importantly, verses 22b–23 explain the point that Paul is trying to make in 22a: there is no distinction (between Jew or Gentile, implied) since *all* have sinned; likewise, *all* believers are justified equally on the basis of faith in Christ.

The redundancy could also be the result of a possible insertion of pre-Pauline material.[85] Certainly verses 24–26 contain unusual language; Paul does not normally speak of the Christ-event in sacrificial terms, and the terms used here (e.g., ἀπολυτρώσεως, ἱλαστήριον, ἔνδειξιν, πάρεσιν) are also rare in the Pauline letters.[86] For our purposes here, the origins of Paul's language are not as crucial as the final form that Paul uses.[87] Certainly, the language Paul uses here "is scarcely foreign to Paul or outside his range."[88] While it may be convenient to explain Paul's redundancies in terms of an attempt to incorporate pre-Pauline material, we nonetheless need to deal with Paul's finished formulation. He clearly intended to repeat certain concepts, including the righteousness of God, faith in (or of) Christ, the impartiality of God, and concerns about how all of this relates to the Law. If Paul were redacting an earlier formulation and did not intend such an emphasis, then he likely would have edited the redundancy out of his argument.

Before drawing final conclusions regarding the meaning of πίστεως Ἰησοῦ Χριστοῦ in this section, it will be helpful to look more closely at the context of 3:21–26 to clarify the use of the genitive in this case. The sacrificial context of 3:21–26 is instructive.[89] As has been frequently

84. Dunn, "Once More," 264.

85. Scholars disagree on whether the inserted material begins in v. 24 or 25.

86. See, e.g., Käsemann, *Romans*, 92–99. Various scholarly interpretations have resulted from the hypothesis of pre-Pauline material: either Paul is introducing a pre-Pauline fragment in order to establish common ground with the Romans whom he has never met, even while inserting his own emphases in places (Dunn, *Romans*, 164); or he is taking over the tradition and inserting new language in order to correct the Romans's theology (Reumann, "Gospel of the Righteousness"); or perhaps the language is Paul's after all (Das, *Paul, the Law*, 134–35).

87. As Johnson states, "In its present form, the passage is clearly and completely the result of Paul's fashioning. Whether some portion of it may have had some antecedent form is of less importance" (*Romans*, 51).

88. Ibid., 52.

89. *Contra* Stowers (*Rereading of Romans*, 211), who finds little evidence of atoning sacrifice in this passage. Stowers argues that the blood of Jesus refers to the means of his

noted, ἱλαστήριον is used in the LXX to refer to the mercy seat, and as a result also refers to "means of expiation."[90] The term, and the idea of blood, would call to mind the slaughtering of the goat on the Day of Atonement.[91]

It is also possible, however, that the term refers to an apotropaic ritual, in this case, one that involves substitutionary symbolism. As part of the Day of Atonement, the high priest symbolically placed the sins of the people upon the scapegoat before sending it off into the wilderness.[92] This imagery would highlight Christ as the effective agent of the removal of sins.[93] Nonetheless, the scapegoat ritual, even though it was connected with the Day of Atonement, does not itself involve blood; Paul's clear reference to blood indicates that he likely had the primary sacrificial ritual in mind here. As Fitzmyer states, "God has set forth Christ Jesus on the cross as the 'mercy seat' of the new dispensation, the new means of expiating (= wiping away) the sins of human beings. Jesus's death, then, surpasses and supersedes the ritual of expiation in the Temple of old . . . Christ's blood has achieved for humanity once and for all what the Day of Atonement

death and not to the blood of sacrifice. Furthermore, he argues that blood itself had no atoning power in Jewish theology. Dunn offers an excellent response: "Since Jesus's death was not particularly bloody in the earliest traditions, the notice of the blood here is to be explained precisely by the association of ideas within Jewish traditions, 'blood sacrifice'—the manipulation of blood being a crucial part of the ritual, particularly of the Day of Atonement sin offering . . ." (*Romans*, 171).

90. E.g., Barrett, *Romans*, 77–78; Dunn, *Romans*, 171. Whether these sins are expiated or propitiated has been a matter of extensive debate. In the former instance, Paul would be arguing that sins are cleansed, whereas in the latter case, Paul would be arguing that God's wrath has been averted. See, e.g., C. H. Dodd's defense of expiation, in *Bible and the Greeks*, and Nicole's defense of propitiation in "C. H. Dodd and the Doctrine of Propitiation." It is possible, however, that both ideas are included within the Pauline terminology. God's wrath clearly was in Paul's mind, as 1:18—3:20 indicates, but it is also true that Paul depicts God as the one who offered the sacrifice, rather than the object of the sacrifice (Dunn, *Romans*, 171). The sin offering dealt with sin in that the death of the spotless sacrifice removed the sin of the sacrificer; the one without sin dies so that the sinner may live (ibid., 172).

91. Dunn (*Romans*, 171) also notes similar language in 4 Macc 17:22, although he does not consider the parallel to provide an alternative to the view that Paul understood Jesus's death as a sacrifice in terms of the Day of Atonement.

92. Lev 16:1–34.

93. Das states, "The Lord's death is effective, for Paul, in a way that the OT rituals were not; otherwise, his death would not have been necessary (Gal 2:21, 3:21)" (*Paul, the Law*, 143).

ritual symbolized each year for Israel of old, the wiping away of human sins."[94] As discussed previously, Paul argued that Christ's death fulfilled the promise in a way that Torah did not. From the Jewish perspective, proper sacrifices to God brought forgiveness; Paul takes up this idea and uses sacrificial terminology in order to make his point that Christ has provided the definitive sacrifice under the Law, and thus has redeemed believers from their sins.

This sacrificial understanding may suggest the possibility that both the subjective and objective genitive meanings of πίστεως Ἰησοῦ Χριστοῦ are intended in 3:22. Numerous Old Testament texts suggest that obedience is an important part of sacrifice and, ultimately, is more important than the act of sacrifice itself. The sons of Eli[95] and Saul,[96] for example, discovered that obedience took priority over the act of sacrifice. Ps 40:6; 51:16–17; and Prov 21:3 make the same point, and the prophets continually rebuked Israel for their lack of obedience in the midst of sacrifice.[97] The attitude of the one offering the sacrifice is all-important. Thus, Paul may intend to present Christ's faithfulness as an exemplar of proper sacrifice.[98] But if Paul were to identify Christ as the one who offers the sacrifice, then a subjective understanding of the genitive may be implied. Paul, however, makes no such connection. Rather, he makes it clear in verse 25 that it is God who presents (προέθετο) the sacrifice. If anyone is faithful in presenting the sacrifice, it is God. Indeed, God's faithfulness is not a new concept introduced here; Paul picks up the theme from Rom 3:3.

Overall, the subjective genitive does not provide the best reading of the text. The example of Abraham's trust in God argues for the objective genitive reading, as does the lack of Pauline emphasis on Christ's faithful-

94. Fitzmyer, *Romans*, 121.

95. 1 Sam 2:29–30.

96. 1 Sam 15:22.

97. E.g., Isa 1:12–20; Jer 7:22–23; Hos 6:6; Mic 6:6–8.

98. Given that many of these texts refer to *doing* what is right, does this mean that a faithful sacrifice must be accompanied by works in order to be efficacious? Paul himself could be accused of such a requirement—the call to live a holy life is never far from his thought, as Rom 12–15 suggests. Paul argues, however, that the attitude of trust in God is temporally prior to the works that naturally flow from such trust (Rom 4:11). The point of the rebuke in the OT verses cited above is that the sacrifice was offered without the necessary spirit of faith/trust in God (as evidenced by the lack of mercy and righteousness elsewhere in the person's life).

ness elsewhere. The apparently redundant language in 3:22 is used to emphasize the inclusion of all people based on faith in Christ, not to indicate a different understanding of faith. The sacrificial language demonstrates what Christ has accomplished for believers, i.e., that in which believers are to trust: their sins have been wiped away by Christ's ultimate sacrifice of atonement. Finally, the objective genitive reading fits well with Paul's emphases elsewhere in Romans, most notably 10:12, which has strong parallels with 3:30 (see the section, "Other Passages in Romans," below).

Before offering an interpretation of 3:21–26, we need to consider what Paul means in verse 26 when he refers to God's forbearance, and why he feels it important to include this statement in his debate about faith and works. Paul asserts in verse 25a that the sacrifice of Jesus was for the purpose of demonstrating God's righteousness, and 25b–26 further states that this demonstration was necessary on account of the "passing over" of the sins previously committed. Verse 26 has nearly parallel language to 25b in describing the "demonstration of the righteousness of God" and further clarifies 25b by stating that this demonstration was for the "present time." Paul's language thus emphasizes the temporality of the events. What God did previously was for the purpose of demonstrating God's righteousness *now*. This "now," for Paul, is the time inaugurated by the Christ-event.[99]

But what was it that God did previously? Paul says that God, in his forbearance, "passed over" the sins previously committed. What does "passed over" mean? Whose sins are they? In response to the first question, the term πάρεσιν could refer to either "passing over"[100] or "forgiving."[101] The former definition interprets Paul as saying that God temporarily suspended judgment of past sins, but now judgment has been rendered (and God's righteousness preserved) through Christ, and those who have faith in him shall live. The latter definition interprets Paul as saying that God has now pardoned past sins as a result of Christ's death. Yet this latter

99. Dunn states, "The death of Christ is envisaged as forming a pivotal point in history with God's righteousness demonstrated there having effect for both the past and the future" (*Romans*, 174).

100. Stowers (*Rereading*, 105) notes that "passing over" should not be confused with forgiveness; see also Barrett, *Romans*, 79; Johnson, *Romans*, 54; Witherington, *Romans*, 109.

101. Fitzmyer, *Romans*, 124; Käsemann, *Romans*, 98; both note that the term meant "pardon" or "remission of penalty" and had legal overtones.

understanding does not make sense of the normal causal meaning of the accusative διά ("on account of," i.e., God demonstrated his righteousness on account of the forgiveness of past sins). How does the forgiveness of sins *cause* the demonstration of God's righteousness? Forgiveness does not necessarily entail righteousness; God's punishment of sins could equally demonstrate God's righteousness. The passage makes more sense if Paul meant "passing over" of sins. God's righteousness certainly would be called into question if God had "passed over" previous sins. God would be forced, "on account of" those past sins, to do something to demonstrate that he was still just. In Christ, sin has been addressed and defeated. Thus, God is vindicated.

Whose sins, then, has God passed over? Paul could be referring to the sins of Israel, or to the sins of the Gentiles, or to the sins of all humankind. That Paul is addressing Jews could be supported by recognizing the repetition of the term ἀνοχῇ from 2:4.[102] Such an interpretation, however, would only encourage the Gentiles in their wrong belief that God had turned his back on Israel. If Israel's previous sins were at last being dealt with through Christ's death, *which most of Israel had rejected*, then surely God had turned with favor to the Gentiles! Yet it is precisely this thinking that Paul reacts against in chapters 9–11. Thus, he would not encourage such thinking in 3:26.

Is Paul then addressing only Gentile sins in 3:26?[103] From the standpoint of Jewish apocalyptic, the fact that the Gentiles remain in power over Israel seems to indicate that God has indeed passed over Gentile sins. Nonetheless, nothing within the context of 3:21–26 singles out the

102. Dunn opts for this interpretation: "His failure to punish Israel's sins, that is, by completely rejecting Israel as his people, did not mean that he was unfairly generous (one of the questions raised by the aborted discussion in 3:1–8" (*Romans*, 181). Not all scholars, however, are convinced that Paul is addressing Jews in 2:4. See, e.g., Stowers, *Rereading of Romans*, 37; and Witherington, *Romans*, 76. Yet Paul's emphasis on the sinfulness of both Jew and Gentile, and thus their equal standing before God, suggests that he does address both groups—the Gentiles in 1:18–32 and the Jews in 2:12—3:8. Dunn (*Romans*, 78–79) argues persuasively that 2:1–11 serves as a general overlapping section to bind the two indictments together.

103. Stowers has suggested that the passage should be interpreted to mean that "God has failed to punish gentiles fully for their sin in the past so that their liability for punishment has accumulated" (*Rereading of Romans*, 105). Israel is fortunate to receive God's punishment immediately, but the gentiles, because of the heaping up of sin over time, will face "a horrible day of reckoning." Nonetheless, God's holding back of his wrath provides an opportunity for the gentiles to repent (106). See also Johnson, *Romans*, 54.

Gentiles as the sole recipients of God's forbearance. Rather, it is more likely that Paul is referring here to the sin of *all*. Paul emphasizes in 3:23 that all have sinned; he does nothing in the present verse to indicate a change of subject to an indictment of either Jew or Gentile alone. In addition, the argument of Rom 2:3–4 can influence our understanding of God's ἀνοχῇ in 3:26 (as Dunn suggests), although we must not transfer the subject of 2:3–4 into 3:26: God passed over previous sins, both Jew and Gentile, in order to provide opportunity for both Jew and Gentile to come to repentance at the present time. Had he not held back his just judgment against sinners, who would be left to witness God's righteousness and grace in Christ? This passage suggests that God's plan from the beginning was to demonstrate his righteousness by justifying all who believe through their faith in Christ. God did not pass over sins previously without a plan for how to address those sins.[104] The implication of 3:25–26 is that God, because he is just, passed over the previous sins (withholding his judgment) with a view toward dealing with those sins later by means of the sacrificial death of Christ. Thus, Paul affirms a strong continuity between what God had done previously and what he has now accomplished in Christ.[105]

In addition, the language in Rom 3:24 regarding humans falling short of the "glory" of God is significant in this respect. Robert W. Yarbrough argues that Paul's references to the glory of God provide a tie to salvation history: "Paul continually affirmed God's glory in part because he knew himself to be caught up in a salvation-historical drama begun at creation, sustained through Old Testament epochs, fulfilled in Jesus's cross and resurrection, and consummated at some yet-to-be-determined juncture."[106] This suggests that when Paul uses the language of glory, he is underscoring the plan of God that stretches from the beginning of history; those who sin are no longer included in this divine plan, except when they cling to the redemption provided by Christ's sacrifice.[107] Paul's argument in Rom 3:21–26 therefore emphasizes that God has not abandoned his previous plans, and this point will be significant for Paul when he addresses the question of God's righteousness in chapters 9–11.

104. As Dunn (*Romans*, 175) states, if God has simply passed over previous sins, then God would not be just.

105. See also Gal 3:15–26.

106. Yarbrough, "Paul and Salvation History," 324.

107. For a good summary of the meaning of the term "redemption," see Fitzmyer, *Romans*, 122–23.

It is now possible to offer an interpretive paraphrase of 3:21–26 as a preparation for understanding Paul's argument in 3:27–31. Up to this point in his letter, Paul has argued that both Jew and Gentile face the righteous condemnation of God because both are sinful. In 3:21–26, Paul provides the first part of the explanation of how God has remedied this dire situation:

> But now (in the new age inaugurated by the Christ-event) a righteousness of God (i.e., God's faithfulness to his promises and his just judgment) has been revealed, and the Law and the prophets are witnesses. This righteousness of God is through faith in Christ to *all* of those who believe. The reason that all are included is that there is no distinction (between Jew and Gentile), since all have sinned and fallen short of the glory of God. Those who have faith are now justified by his graceful gift through the redemption of Jesus Christ. God displayed him as a sacrifice of atonement by his blood, through faith, in order to demonstrate his righteousness—because in God's forbearance, he had passed over previous sins. He did this in order to demonstrate his righteousness in the present time, showing that he is just (in that he deals with those previous sins) and that he justifies those who have faith in Christ.

Thus, in these few short verses, Paul proclaims that God is just and trustworthy because of what he has accomplished in the Christ-event. The overwhelming sin that Paul had presented in 1:18—3:20 has been addressed by Christ's sacrifice, and the justifying effects of this redemptive offering are accessible to all who have faith in him.

This sets the stage for the resumption of the diatribal question-and-answer format in verses 27–31. Having established the unity of the means of justification, Paul returns in verse 27 to the question of distinctiveness regarding Jews and Gentiles. Given what Paul has just said about all being justified before God on the same basis, the logical question for Paul (through the voice of the interlocutor) is, "Where then is boasting?" This clearly calls to mind the preceding discussion; boasting was first mentioned in 2:17 and 23, where Paul addressed his Jewish interlocutor's pride in his possession of the Law.

Given the previous discussion regarding the New Perspective, it is important to consider what Paul meant by "boasting" here. New Perspective proponents argue that Paul reacted against Jews who boasted in their special privilege as the elect people of God, separated from the

Gentiles.[108] Traditional approaches, however, take the view that boasting involves an individual's reliance on one's own ability to please God.[109] Yet this is one area where the differences have been overplayed; there is a sense in which both views are correct. Paul's focus is on the Christ-event: no one can be justified apart from faith in Christ. Thus, any boasting is excluded—whether boasting in a person's own law-keeping abilities or boasting in a sense of national pride. Neither will make a person righteous, since, as Paul has already pointed out in 3:23, all have sinned and fallen short of the glory of God.[110]

In the second half of verse 27, Paul explains that boasting is not excluded based on the law/principle of works, but on the law/principle of faith. The phrase τῶν ἔργων could refer here to the Torah,[111] or it could retain the general sense of "principle."[112] The Roman audience, however, would most likely understand Paul's reference in verse 27 as a reference to the Torah. First, the question regarding the law is in answer to the charge that boasting is excluded; in 2:17 and 23, it is the Jewish interlocutor who has boasted in having the Law, i.e., the Torah. Second, as noted previously, the whole context of the letter deals with the question of the Jew-Gentile relationship. Finally, the context of 3:21–31 contains several references to law, all of which refer to the Torah (vv. 21, 28, 31). It would be difficult indeed to imagine that the Torah is not in view in verse 27. Thus, the "law of faith" in verse 27 is "the Law as read through the eyes of faith . . . In other words, the Law *read as Paul has already claimed it should be read* is the

108. Dunn, *Romans*, 185. Similarly, N. T. Wright argues that boasting is based on covenant election: "Paul is not here talking about every individual Jew, as is regularly supposed, but about the *national* boast which declares that ethnic Israel as a whole remains inviolate" (*Paul*, 117).

109. See, e.g., Barrett, *Romans*, 82; Fitzmyer, *Romans*, 359.

110. One of the benefits of this more all-inclusive interpretation of Paul's polemic is that it addresses the different emphases in the various ideologies of Jewish groups from the Second Temple period. Regardless of whether a Jew focuses on personal purity or national righteousness, Paul has the same answer: apart from Christ, all is for naught.

111. E.g., Dunn, Cranfield, Hübner.

112. E.g., Bultmann, Sanders, Räisänen, Fitzmyer, Byrne. Ito ("ΝΟΜΟΣ [ΤΩΝ] ἘΡΓΩΝ and ΝΟΜΟΣ ΠΙΣΤΕΩΣ," 247–49) takes both positions, arguing that on a superficial hearing of the letter, the Romans would have taken the term to mean general principles. Upon deeper reflection on the letter, however, they would come to understand Paul's language as a reference to the Torah, especially since vv. 29, 30 and 31 all implicitly address the Torah. Ito further concludes that the "law of faith" here refers to that part of the law which describes Abraham's faith (257).

νόμος πίστεως."[113] Such an interpretation is also consistent with Paul's claim in verse 21 that the Law (i.e., Torah) is a witness to this righteousness through faith. Paul is claiming that the Law, properly understood, testifies regarding human sinfulness and the need for redemption; God's promise is thus fulfilled through Christ's sacrifice.[114] This is further emphasized in verse 28, where Paul reiterates his claims of 3:21–26 that a person—any person, whether Jew or Gentile—is justified by faith apart from works of the Law.

Verses 29–30 form yet another, related approach for Paul to the question of the inclusion of the Gentiles. He uses the basic conviction of Judaism, the Shema, in order to convince the Jewish interlocutor that Yahweh is God of the Gentiles as well as of the Jews. Most commentators, however, make two mistakes—one grammatical and one theological—in interpreting this passage. First, they locate the conclusion of this passage in the wrong place, arguing (at least implicitly) that 30a provides the protasis of Paul's argument, and both 29 and 30b provide the apodosis.[115] Second, they understand the reference to the Shema as *primarily* a reference to a creational universalism. The combined effect of these assumptions is that the universal creational aspect of God provides the ground for the idea that God justifies both Jew and Greek on the same basis. In this view, there is almost a chiastic arrangement here, in which verse 29 provides the conclusion (universalism), verse 30a provides the premise (God is one), and verse 30b provides a restatement of the conclusion (God universally justifies on the basis of faith).

113. Hays, "Three Dramatic Roles," 153–54.

114. As Das states, "Boasting is excluded only when the Jew views the law from the perspective of faith. Then they see that the law itself never offered a valid boast, since it never saved (3:21–26) . . . God never justified on the basis of the law but rather on the basis of faith" (*Paul, the Law*, 202).

115. Stuhlmacher, for example, argues that Paul "grounds the universality of justification for Jews and Gentiles by referring to Deut 6:4" (*Romans*, 66). Clearly, Stuhlmacher is taking 30a as the protasis, but considers 30b to be part of the apodosis. Similarly, Fitzmyer argues that "no Jew would have denied that Yahweh was the God of all human beings," and Paul uses this understanding to insinuate the equal standing of Jew and Gentile (*Romans*, 364–65; similarly, see Dodd, *Romans*, 63). Here it seems that Fitzmyer takes 29 and 30a as the protasis and 30b as the apodosis. Hays ("'Have we Found Abraham?'" 84) takes a different approach when he suggests that 30a and the first half of 30b are the protasis ("If indeed God, who will justify the circumcised on the basis of faith, is one"), whereas the second half of 30b provides an elliptical apodosis ("he will also justify the uncircumcised through faith").

But in looking at the passage more closely, it becomes apparent that 30a and 30b are *both* part of the protasis of this first-class conditional statement.[116] The εἴπερ ("if indeed") controls the entire verse, not just 30a. This is indicated by the fact that 30b is introduced by means of the relative pronoun ὅς. The idea that both Jew and Gentile are justified by faith serves to clarify who the one God of 30a is,[117] and cannot begin the apodosis. An apodosis is grammatically independent,[118] and 30b is not.[119] Thus, in describing the one God, Paul is simply restating in 30b what he has already argued in 3:21–26, that all are justified by faith, and he uses this reiteration to support the assertion of verse 29 that the God of the Jews is also the God of the Gentiles.[120] In addition, the structure of the argument in verses 29–30 is very similar to the structure of verses 27–28, as Jan Lambrecht notes: "This statement [verse 28] is not a new idea. Rather it is the basic insight that was reached by the lengthy exposition of Rom 1:16—3:26 and more particularly 3:21–26 . . . The convictional statement

116. In the first class condition, the protasis is assumed true for the sake of argument. Wallace notes that "not infrequently" in the NT, the author bases his argument "on what both speaker and audience already embrace as true." He cites Rom 3:29–30 as an example and further notes that in such instances "it is not the protasis that is in doubt, but the apodosis" (*Greek Grammar*, 694). Thus, even though it is a conditional sentence, the oneness of God is not what is in question here.

117. A relative clause typically "describes, clarifies, or restricts the meaning of the noun" with which it is connected (Wallace, *Greek Grammar*, 336).

118. Ibid., 684.

119. Hays's conclusion is more plausible than the traditional argument, since he identifies an apodosis that could be grammatically independent. Nonetheless, his argument is not convincing for two reasons. First, it forces the reader of the letter to supply missing information (another verb) in order to achieve the intended meaning, whereas the text as constructed makes sense without resorting to any grammatical acrobatics. For someone hearing the letter for the first time, there are no clues within the text itself that suggest a reading other than the obvious one is preferable. Second, it makes the argument of v. 30 independent of v. 29. Yet the Jew/Gentile distinction in v. 29 is parallel to the circumcised/uncircumcised language in v. 30, indicating that these verses are closely tied together. Under Hays's interpretation, the reader could leave out v. 29 altogether and still achieve Paul's meaning. Under my proposal, v. 29 is an integral part of Paul's argument and could not be so easily eliminated. Thus, vv. 29–30 should be interpreted as follows: "Because God is the One God who impartially justifies both Jew and Gentile through faith, this means that God is not only the God of the Jew, but also the God of the Gentile."

120. Thompson comments, "To think that the oneness of God in v. 30a in any way causes or grounds the justifying activity of God in v. 30b is to impute more to the relative clause here than is acceptable and to misunderstand the logic of the verse" ("Inclusion of the Gentiles," 543). He argues that the relative clause is purely descriptive of God.

of v. 28 grounds v. 27. In vv. 29–30 a very similar conviction is used to make clear that God is also the God of the Gentiles."[121] In Paul's mind then, the oneness of God is tied to his character as one who impartially judges Jew and Gentile alike. It is this understanding of God that allows Paul to conclude that Yahweh is also the God of the Gentiles. It seems, then, that in this context Paul is more concerned with the uniqueness, the character, of the one God than with his numerical oneness. Because of who this one God is (i.e., he maintains a single standard for all people), he necessarily is God of both Jew and Gentile.

Furthermore, Paul's word choice here is intentional. In describing God's justifying activity in 30b, Paul does not use the term "Jew" or "Gentile," but instead uses the terms "circumcision" and "uncircumcision." Thus Paul emphasizes that God justifies the law-obedient Jew but also the lawless Gentile; Paul makes it clear that circumcision is not necessary for justification. Thus, God is the God of Jews *as Jews*, and he is also the God of Gentiles *as Gentiles*. Paul is making a radical statement, a positively oxymoronic claim in the face of Jewish election: The one God, Yahweh of the Jews, is none other than Yahweh of the Gentiles. While this may not seem astonishing to those scholars who argue, as Stuhlmacher, that no Jew would deny that God is God of the Gentiles, too, it is critical to make a distinction between a simple theoretical assent to God's sovereignty (to which all Jews would readily agree) and Paul's weightier statement here. Paul is asserting that the one God who offers special care, protection, and guidance for the Jew is also the one God who offers special care, protection, and guidance for the Gentile. He is not simply stating God is *over* the Gentiles (as a distant sovereign), but he is God *of* the Gentiles. The distinction is important. Paul sees that in the Christ-event the Gentiles are not quietly slipped into heaven through the back door of faith, but rather they are given full and equal access to the blessings of the one God, and this without Torah.

In order to more fully understand the impact of Paul's statement, it is time to recall the earlier discussion of Jewish attitudes toward Gentiles. The attitude found in some of the texts was very negative toward Gentiles (e.g., *2 Baruch* and *4 Ezra*). In other texts, "righteous" Gentiles would be accepted by God. In practice in the first century, this meant that Jews were willing to accept proselytes; one did not have to be born a Jew in order to

121. Lambrecht, "Paul's Logic in Romans 3:29–30," 527.

be included in the people of God. Although God-fearing Gentiles were accepted, they were accepted on *Jewish* terms. Gentiles could receive God's blessings by becoming Jews; God's promise to bless the nations was perceived as a blessing that came *through* Judaism.

Thus we should ask how a first-century Jew might respond to the idea that the Gentiles will now equally share in God's blessings without first becoming Jews. If, as Paul suggests, Yahweh is the God of the Gentiles *qua* Gentiles, then they are receiving blessings that a Jew might well perceive ought to belong to Israel alone.[122] Election meant that God was the Jewish God and preserved special honor for Israel, over and against whatever other blessings God had in store for the nations. As Moo states, "To be sure, Jews also believed that God was God of the whole world. But the limitations they placed upon this concept illustrate the radicality of Paul's argument. For, in Judaism, God was God of Gentiles only by virtue of his creative work, while only the Jews enjoy any meaningful relationship with God . . ."[123] Thus, in Paul's statement of 3:30, it would be easy for Jews to perceive Paul as wiping out Jewish distinctiveness. It is this fear that leads to the question of 3:31, "Do we then nullify the law by this faith?"

But lest we get ahead of ourselves, we will further consider the second mistake frequently made by interpreters of Rom 3:30. The theological underpinning for Paul's argument does not lie *primarily* in the understanding that God created all things and therefore must be a universal God; rather, it lies in the understanding that God is impartial. His character, i.e., the righteousness of God, is at issue here, as in other places in Romans, most notably chapters 9–11. This is not to deny that creational aspects are present as well—Rom 1:19–20 clearly demonstrates this emphasis. But in 3:30 Paul defends the inclusion of the Gentiles on the grounds of the character of the Jewish God as an impartial God.

It is important to note that Paul's argument contains an unspoken assumption. For him, the one God is the God who is revealed in the Jewish Scriptures, and that God is not arbitrary or capricious. Hypothetically, a single God with sovereignty over all nations could arbitrarily judge dif-

122. This is not to deny that the OT has, in places, a decidedly universal outlook. Cf., Gen 12:3; Pss 67:3–6; 82:8; 97:6; 105:1; 117:1; Isa 42:6; 49:6; 56:6–7; Jer 46:46; 48:47; 49:6, 39. But it is notable that even in these verses, the blessings come to the nations *through* Israel (e.g., Isa 49:6): the nations are dependent on Israel as the mediator of the blessings.

123. Moo, *Romans*, 251.

ferent peoples according to different standards. There is nothing in the *numerical* oneness of God that requires God to be impartial. But for Paul, any arbitrariness is unthinkable. The God he knows judges equitably and is not arbitrary.[124] This premise, which Paul has already included in his discussion in 2:9–11, has led to Paul's conclusion in 3:21–26 that justification is by faith for *all* who believe, Jew and Gentile alike. God is just and thus cannot judge people on the basis of different standards, especially since all people ultimately have the same status before God, i.e., they are all sinners. Jews must not make the mistake of thinking that special privilege in one area (i.e., designation as God's people) translates into special privilege in all areas (i.e., a "get-out-of-jail-free card" where sin is concerned). Although God chose Israel to be his people, to receive the Law, the land, etc., such status does not change God's justice; sin is sin regardless of the identity of the one who commits it. This is the picture presented in Rom 1–2. As Bassler states, "Divine judgment has been radicalized to the point that all physical distinctions have been eliminated before God, who inquires only about deeds."[125] But this seemingly pessimistic view of God's impartiality also translates into the optimistic view of God's impartial grace.[126] Because God is not arbitrary and God's justice remains the same, so does God's standard for grace—a standard that is met through faith. The unstated conviction underlying Paul's argument is this: Because the one God is of unimpeachable character, and because it would be unfair to judge equal people (i.e., sinners, both Jews and Gentiles) with an unequal standard, then God must have a single standard for all people. As a result of this conviction, Paul is able to argue that Yahweh must therefore be the God of the Gentiles.

Thus the monotheistic statement does not emphasize a quantitative solution as much as a qualitative solution: the one God who is over all is equitable and not arbitrary. God accepts the Gentiles on the same basis as the Jews. For Paul, unlike for non-Christian Jews, the Law does *not*

124. See, e.g., Deut 10:17; 2 Chr 19:7; and Mal 2:9. Note that this latter passage directly precedes a verse describing the oneness of God.

125. Bassler, *Divine Impartiality*, 152.

126. Bassler uses the term "impartial grace" to describe Paul's argument in 3:21–31 (see "Centering the Argument," 165). Bassler's work emphasizes the importance of God's impartiality for understanding Paul's rhetoric. "Whether justifying on the basis of faith or judging on the basis of performance God makes no distinction between Jew or Greek. In either case he shows no partiality" (*Divine Impartiality*, 166).

provide the basis of a person being identified as a member of the people of God. Rather, God's single standard of faith in Christ offers the basis of this identity. Hence, the one God of the Jews necessarily must also be the one God of the Gentiles.[127]

The conclusion of Paul's argument, then, is that God's impartiality, which requires God to judge sinful Jew and sinful Gentile alike and this through faith, means that God is the God of both the Jew and the Gentile equally. Yet the wording of the statement requires closer scrutiny. Paul uses two different prepositions to describe justification of Jews and Gentiles by faith: ἐκ in the former and διά in the latter. Despite the speculation by some scholars that Paul intends to connote a continuing distinction between Jew and Gentile,[128] both Paul's all-inclusive language through-

127. Despite the focus on people groups here, Paul's argument does not focus on the need to create a single family. As noted in chapter 3, N. T. Wright argues that the particularism of the Jewish law prevented God from having the one family that he intended; the Law created multiple families—those who followed it and those who did not. As I pointed out, however, a Jew could have simply argued that the one family of God comes through the Law. Everyone had access to God provided they accept the Law; ultimately, this was little different than Christianity's claim that everyone had access to God provided they have faith in Christ. *Thus, if the one-family argument is the heart of Paul's polemic against many of his Jewish contemporaries, then Paul's gospel has not solved the problem of multiple families.* Johnson astutely recognizes this difficulty: "Certainly it would be inconsistent with Paul's whole argument to claim that one had to be Christian in order to have access to God—for then God could neither be truly one nor truly fair. Then the particularity of the Christian religion would simply replace the particularity of Judaism, providing an expanded but in principle equally restricted range of accessibility to God" (*Romans*, 64). Although Johnson is correct in identifying the particularism of Christianity (resulting in an "in" group and an "out" group, just as with Judaism), he incorrectly argues that particularism prevents God from being truly one or truly fair. Rather, I would argue that Paul's impartial God is both one and fair if he indeed upholds a single principle of justice for all people. It is only when this God maintains multiple standards that his oneness, as Paul understands it, becomes compromised—which would be the case if he maintained a different standard for Jews and for Gentiles. The New Perspective's focus on the Jew-Gentile debate, boundary markers, and national righteousness has led proponents to over-emphasize these dimensions of Paul's thought; thus, the "one family" of God has been interpreted as the focus of Paul's polemic. Certainly one of Paul's major concerns is the inclusion of the Gentiles. But this is not the whole story. Paul's concern with the Law does not concern one family; rather, it concerns the Law's inability to offer life—a problem which has now been corrected through the life-giving Spirit.

128. See, e.g., Schlatter, *Romans*, 105; Gager, *Origins of Anti-Semitism*, 217; Gaston, *Paul and the Torah*, 123. Stowers ("ΕΚ ΠΙΣΤΕΩΣ and ΔΙΑ ΤΗΣ ΠΙΣΤΕΩΣ," 669), e.g., argues that Paul uses διά when Gentiles are in view and ἐκ when either Jews or both are in view. He suggests that Paul expresses Jesus's atoning life and death on behalf of the

out 3:21–31 and his emphasis on the impartiality of God suggest that, as far as justification is concerned, both Jews and Gentiles meet the same standard. The exchange of prepositions is the result of stylistic variation and does not indicate any substantive change in Paul's thought.[129] Dunn makes a convincing point: "Paul would not want to imply a continuing distinction, since it is precisely the common ground and medium of faith which has rendered insignificant the distinction circumcision/uncircumcision so far as the relationship with the God who is one is concerned . . ."[130] Indeed, it simply does not make sense, given Paul's larger argument of equal standing before God, for Paul to insert a distinction here. Certainly if Paul were intending to nuance his argument further, he would need to explain the distinctions rather than simply change prepositions without further comment.

As Paul comes to the conclusion of his argument, he states the logical question that the Jewish interlocutor would ask, given Paul's leveling of the playing field between Jew and Gentile: "Do we nullify the law through this faith?"[131] Paul's response, "May it never be!" reaffirms his commitment to Judaism. He further explains that his gospel upholds the Law. This transitional statement not only closes this ten-verse section, but also leads Paul into chapter 4, where he uses the example of Abraham to illus-

---

Gentiles by using διά. Paul is writing to Gentile churches about Gentile concerns, and therefore never fully explains how Christ's death relates to the Jews, although it may be that ἐκ πίστεως denotes a more basic relationship. "It is clear, however, that he does not assimilate the two into a generic Christianity. Both Jews and Gentiles share in blessings ἐκ πίστεως of Abraham and Jesus, although not in identical ways" (ibid., 674). Stowers's argument, however, is tentative at best. He notes himself that there is "obvious circularity" in his argument because it depends on accepting a certain reading. Stowers's claim that Paul addresses only Gentiles in Romans, however, does not hold up under scrutiny. For example, he claims that in 3:22 Paul is addressing only Gentiles, and thus διά is the term used for Gentiles. As demonstrated above, however, Paul is clearly addressing *all* people, both Jew and Gentile, as the language of 3:22–23 clearly indicates. Thus, Stowers's claims of distinctive language for Jew and Gentile fails to convince.

129. See, e.g., Schlier, *Römerbrief*, 118; Witherington, *Romans*, 112 n. 56; Käsemann, *Romans*, 104; Barrett, *Romans*, 84; Cranfield, *Romans*, 2:222; Mounce, *Romans*, 119 n. 29.

130. Dunn, *Romans*, 189.

131. For the interpretation of καταργοῦμεν, see Mounce, *Romans*, 120, n. 30. He argues that despite the wide range of meaning for the verb, the contrast with ἱστάνομεν ("to establish, confirm") indicates that καταργοῦμεν should be taken to mean "nullify."

trate how, from the beginning and prior to the Law, God reckoned people righteous on the basis of faith.[132]

This investigation into 3:21–31 has clarified Paul's overall argument and the purpose served by his one-God language in 3:30. Paul has detailed, in ten short verses, a complicated theology in defense and explication of God's righteousness. Through the Christ-event, God has finally addressed the problem of human sin, a problem which both Jew and Gentile alike face. Because all fall short of what God requires, no one is in any better position to receive favor from God. Yet everyone is equally able to receive God's favor if they believe in Christ, whom God offered up as a sacrifice of atonement to deal with humanity's sin. As a result, no one is able to boast before God, since no works of the Law (whether moral obedience or nationality markers) can take care of this sin—only faith can, a faith which is attested by the Law itself. God's impartiality (an aspect of his righteousness) is preserved through this one standard of faith. Thus the one God of the Jews, who blesses and protects his people, is also the one God of the Gentiles, and promises blessings and protection for the Gentiles as well. Yet this apparent leveling of the playing field does not cancel the Torah; rather it fulfills the Torah, which was always intended not as an end itself, but as a means of pointing the way to the end (fulfillment), i.e., Christ.

Paul's allusion to the Shema in verse 30 thus serves several purposes. First, it primarily highlights God's impartiality. Numerical oneness is not the issue as much as the character of the one God as revealed in Scripture. Second, God's oneness entails a universal emphasis. Although creation is part of this universality and is certainly in Paul's mind, uppermost in Paul's thought is the idea that the one God must treat Jew and Gentile alike. Since both are able to approach God by means of faith, this entails a radical expansion of the understanding of the identity of the people of God. Third, God's impartiality and justification on the basis of faith means that the Law must necessarily take a subsidiary position to that of faith; the Law is not an end in and of itself. Rather, it convicts a person of sin and points toward faith as the means of attaining a right relationship with God. Fourth, although Paul's rendition of the Shema here does not include Christ (as it did in 1 Cor 8:6), 3:21–31 clearly argues that God's righteousness is demonstrated, defined, and confirmed by means of the

132. See Käsemann, *Romans*, 105.

Christ-event.[133] Without the Christ-event, God's righteousness would be open to question. Thus, even when Paul does not explicitly include Christ in the Shema, he nonetheless implies that the one God is the one God because of his actions in and through Christ.

Overall, then, Paul's use of one-God language in 3:30 is neither cursory nor coincidental. Paul uses his fundamental understanding of God to make sense of what God has accomplished in the Christ-event. Without the insights provided by his theology, Paul would not have determined that a single standard of justification applies to both Jew and Gentile, nor would he have reached the conclusion that God is the protector and provider of both Jew and Gentile. Ultimately, without the vision developed out of his one-God theology, Paul would not have been able to promote the unity of Jew and Gentile within the Roman church.

OTHER PASSAGES IN ROMANS

In order to fully understand how Paul's one-God language functions in Romans, we need to consider how Paul describes the relationship between the one God and Christ elsewhere in the letter. Does Paul's strong monotheistic language cause him to limit or subordinate the role of Christ? Or does he nonetheless describe Jesus in terms functionally similar to God? The answers to these questions will help inform the dynamics of Paul's one-God language.

The first of these passages is 1:1–9. Several significant features arise in these verses. First, as is Paul's custom, he greets his audience in 1:7 by offering grace and peace from both God the Father and the Lord Jesus Christ. As I argued in chapter 2, this may denote Paul's understanding of the similar functions of Yahweh and Jesus.[134] This is especially important here because Paul has not previously had the opportunity to discuss his Christology with this church, yet he is able to use this language without further explanation. He is able to describe a recently executed criminal as

133. Christoph Demke states: "Sein Einzig-Sein ist also von vornherein ein Sein in relatione zu Jesus Christus und durch ihn für jedermann" ("'Ein Gott und viele Herren,'" 476).

134. Johnson comments, "We notice . . . the powerful understanding of the resurrection of Jesus that Paul can assume without any explanation among his readers. He can wish for them grace and peace not only from the living God but also from 'Jesus Messiah.' Jesus is therefore not simply an executed criminal from the past. He is a present and powerful 'Lord'" (*Romans*, 20).

the "Lord" who is now able to dispense grace and peace, and he trusts that such a claim will be embraced!

Second, Paul uses the terms "gospel of God" (1:1) and "gospel of his Son" interchangeably (1:9).[135] There is nothing in these verses to indicate any difference in content; Paul is not preaching two gospels.[136] The phrase "gospel of God" also occurs in Rom 15:16; 1 Thess 2:2, 8, 9; and 2 Cor 11:7. In 1 Thessalonians Paul also refers to the "gospel of Christ" at 3:2. In 2 Corinthians, Paul uses "gospel of Christ" (2:12; 9:13) as well as the "gospel of the glory of Christ" (4:4). Thus, the interchange that occurs in Romans is not unique to Paul's thinking nor is it a late development in his thought.

Is this variation in the description of the gospel message unconscious, or does Paul have a specific reason for altering his language? I have argued throughout this study that Paul was concerned to preserve the continuity of salvation history, and this emphasis is evident in Paul's language here. By varying his description of the gospel message, Paul is claiming that the new message of Christ is really not such a new proclamation. Rather, it is the fulfillment of God's promise and was planned from the beginning.[137] The gospel of Christ is not independent of the Jewish God, nor is God's plan separate from what has occurred in the Christ-event. The interchangeable language serves to highlight this fact.

The first phrase, "gospel of God," is likely a genitive of origin denoting the good news originating from God.[138] The second reference should be taken as an objective genitive, the "gospel concerning his Son."[139] Nonetheless, this does not result in a hard distinction between these two descriptions, since God's activity is defined through the activity of Christ. The good news of God does not exist apart from what has occurred through Christ. Thus, while the phrases do not necessarily imply functional equivalence between Christ and God, they do imply that God's

135. Ibid., 22.

136. See Gal 1:8 for Paul's assertion that he preaches only one message.

137. Dunn argues: "the issue at stake was the continuity between the revelation embodied in the Jewish Scriptures and Paul's concern for a universal outreach. Paul's assertion is emphatic. The gospel to which he was set apart is in complete continuity with God's earlier revelation to Israel" (*Romans*, 22).

138. In agreement with Fitzmyer, *Romans*, 232.

139. Dunn, *Romans*, 29.

identity and Christ's identity are inextricably bound up with one another and mutually redefine one another.[140]

Finally, it is important to investigate Paul's use of the term "Son of God" for Jesus. As noted in chapter 1, the phrase has a number of different meanings. Thus, we need to narrow down precisely what Paul meant by the term in this instance. Two clarifications regarding the structure of the text are in order first. It is possible that in 1:3–4 Paul is quoting a pre-Pauline tradition.[141] It is difficult to reconstruct with precision the extent of any material Paul might have incorporated into his text, and ultimately, Paul makes it clear that he affirms the statement regarding Christ's origins.[142] As a result, we should focus on the final form presented by Paul here.

The second structural question concerns the precise description involved. A clarification is necessary regarding whether "with power" modifies "established"[143] or "Son of God."[144] The former interpretation emphasizes the power in the establishment of Christ as the Son of God, whereas the latter emphasizes Jesus's own power as the Son of God. Given the connection with Christ's resurrection and Paul's understanding that

140. Barrett notes this interconnectedness: "Paul's theology is theocentric in that God is the source of salvation and thus of the Gospel, and of the theology that rests upon the Gospel; christocentric in that the historical manifestation of the truth of God lies in the deeds of Jesus Christ" (*Romans*, 18). See also the work of Richardson, who argues that Paul's language about God throughout his letters is interconnected to Christ. He suggests that Paul's Christ-language is grammatically subordinate to his God-language, which emphasizes God's role as originator and goal. "Yet a kind of equality between God and Christ is implied in the form of the opening salutations, in the exercise by the exalted κύριος of divine functions and prerogatives, and in the occasional application to Christ of a LXX text referring to God. Certain divine attributes, notably grace, power, love and glory, are attributed also to Christ, indicating God as the source, Christ the means" *(Paul's Language about God*, 309). All of these uses indicate that "Paul's thought and writings are *both* theocentric *and* Christocentric; Paul's language about God and his language about Christ are so intertwined that neither can properly be understood without the other" (312).

141. See the discussion in Moo, *Romans*, 45–46, n. 31.

142. Hurtado argues that it is Paul's final product that must be investigated: "If a writer incorporates into his/her text without refutation or criticism elements of a tradition, this is surely because the author accepts these elements and indeed regards them as expressive of his/her own thoughts. . . . All that Paul says about Jesus without criticism is directly indicative of Paul's Christological beliefs, whether particular statements are original with him or echo the statements and formulas of others also" ("Jesus's Divine Sonship," 220).

143. E.g., Godet, *Romans*, 79; Hodge, *Romans*, 19–20.

144. E.g., Moo, *Romans*, 48; Dunn, *Romans*, 14; Käsemann, *Romans*, 12.

Christ currently sits at God's right hand (i.e., designating power), the latter interpretation is preferable.

The term "Son of God" can convey a wide variety of meanings. Nonetheless, Paul's use is specific. Consistently Paul uses the definite article with divine sonship language, suggesting that Paul employs not a general concept, but specifically claims for Jesus "a unique favor, approval, and authority" relating directly to Christ's standing with God.[145] Furthermore, as will be discussed in the section "Other Passages in Romans," below, God's love for humanity is shown in the actions of his Son; it is not enough that "a righteous man" has died as an atoning sacrifice. Rather, God demonstrates his *own* love through sending his Son (5:8, 10). This suggests that "son of God" describes a very close relationship to God indeed.

Yet this raises the question of whether "the Son of God" implies the preexistence of Christ. The phrase *in general* does not necessarily mean that Jesus came from heaven,[146] but as crafted by Paul, the phrase may well imply preexistence.[147] The specific language of 1:3 is instructive in this regard. Here Paul uses the verb γενομένου ("came into being"), which is not the verb usually used of birth; Paul may well make this odd word choice in order to imply preexistence.[148] Such usage is consistent with Paul's descriptions elsewhere.[149]

Another issue arising from Paul's use of "Son of God" terminology concerns when this uniqueness occurred. Does "τοῦ ὁρισθέντος υἱοῦ θεοῦ ἐν δυνάμει" imply an adoptionist Christology (i.e., that Christ only became Son at the resurrection), or that the sonship Christ already had was somehow amplified at the resurrection? The term ὁρισθέντος most often means "appointed," which would seem to imply that Christ only

145. Hurtado, "Jesus's Divine Sonship," 225.

146. As observed by Dunn, *Romans*, 12. The concepts that might correlate Jesus with preexistence are either not distinctive enough or are late, he argues. As I asserted in chapter 2, however, Dunn's view does not adequately explain Paul's arguments elsewhere, where preexistence is clearly implied in Paul's language.

147. If Paul is indeed using an earlier creed or hymn in his formulation, then this could suggest that the early church, and not just Paul, understood the distinctively Christian use of the phrase in this way.

148. Osborne, *Romans*, 30. See also Moo, *Romans*, 46; and Witherington, *Romans*, 32.

149. E.g., Rom 8:3 and 10:6 (see the section, "Other Passages in Romans," below); 1 Cor 8:6; 10:4; Phil 2:5–11. See also Col 1:17.

became the Son at the resurrection and exaltation.[150] The difficulty with the adoptionist argument is that it runs counter to Paul's understanding of Christ's preexistence; Christ's sonship was not something that came only at the resurrection.[151] Moo notes Paul's phrasing here: it is the Son who is appointed Son. This tautologous language suggests not a change in essence, but a change in status or function.[152] Thus, even though the language of appointment may denote something new, this does not necessarily mean that sonship itself was new.

Furthermore, part of Paul's logic elsewhere (Gal 4:3–7) depends on the idea that the adoption of believers as sons occurs through the actions of the natural son, Christ.[153] Humans have gone from slave to son in status; although Christ is elsewhere also described as a slave/servant (Phil 2:7), this was not his original status (2:6). In addition, the idea of Jesus being "appointed" to his position has parallels elsewhere in the New Testament[154] and is likely the result of allusions to 2 Sam 7:14 and Ps 2:7 in Rom 1:3–4.[155] Paul thus uses the term "appointed" in order to call to mind these texts, which are messianic. He wishes to emphasize that Jesus is the promised Messiah. The term "appointed" is merely a tool to reach a messianic conclusion; it is not the conclusion itself.[156]

The next question arising from the uniqueness of Christ's sonship involves the meaning of the contrast between flesh and spirit. Several

150. Dunn argues that the term denotes an act of God which gave Jesus a new status: "According to the creedal formula, then, Jesus became something he was not before, or took on a role which was not previously his before . . ." (*Romans*, 13–14).

151. See Michel, *Brief an die Römer*, 40; Barrett, *Romans*, 20; and Fitzmyer: "Before the resurrection Jesus Christ was the Son of God in the weakness of his human existence; as of the resurrection he is the Son of God established in power and has become such for the vivifying of all human beings." (*Romans*, 234–35).

152. Moo, *Romans*, 48.

153. This, of course, assumes that Paul is not being inconsistent in his argument throughout his letters (*contra* Räisänen). Indeed, this study has observed that Paul is quite consistent in his treatment of the relationship between God and Christ.

154. E.g., Acts 10:42, 17:31.

155. Allen ("Old Testament Background") argues that ὁρίζω and προορίζω in the NT refer to Ps 2:7. See also Scott (*Adoption as Sons of God*, 227–44), who connects Rom 1:3–4 with 2 Sam 7:14 in his work.

156. Whitsett ("Son of God") argues that the messianic texts serve to underline Paul's argument about the righteousness of God being fulfilled in Christ. Not only is Jesus the promised Messiah, but the nations are blessed in him (through the inclusion of the Gentiles) as God had promised to Abraham.

different interpretations are possible, including the contrast of Jesus's humanity and divinity,[157] a contrast between Jesus's physical lineage as Messiah and his inner, spiritual qualification for that role,[158] or a contrast between the earthly and spiritual eons.[159] None of these solutions are without difficulties. The first interpretation takes the verb to mean "demonstrate" rather than "appoint," even though the latter is more true to NT usage elsewhere.[160] Thus, it is difficult to see how an ontological aspect is "appointed" to Christ.

The second interpretation understands "spirit" to refer to Jesus's own spirit, rather than the Holy Spirit. Yet this explanation is not without difficulties, either. Although "Spirit of holiness" is an unusual way of referring to the Holy Spirit, Holy Spirit language is fluid; in several places, Jesus's spirit is very closely connected with the Spirit of God.[161] Furthermore, nowhere in the Pauline corpus does Paul use πνεῦμα to refer to Jesus's personal inner spirit over against the Holy Spirit. When Jesus's spirit is mentioned, it is always connected, in some way, to the Spirit/Spirit of God. Thus, the kind of external/internal dimension necessary for this interpretation is not consistent with Paul's terminology elsewhere.

The third interpretation emphasizes the eschatological dimension found elsewhere in Paul's thought, but it too suffers from difficulties. This interpretation requires that σάρξ here has a negative connotation. Yet Paul is able to use the term neutrally elsewhere (9:3, 5) as a means of describing a person's physical lineage. Thus, it is not necessary here to interpret "flesh" as representing the former, evil age. In addition, while it is true that Paul envisions a past eon and a new eon ushered in by Christ, we must ask at what point is the new eon ushered in—at Jesus's birth, his baptism, his death on the cross, his resurrection, or his ascension? Rom 1:4 indicates that Christ's resurrection is the defining moment for his appointment as Son. Yet, as we just observed in 3:21–31, the "now" time is ushered in by Christ's death. One could argue that Christ's death would be meaningless were it not for his obedient life, which is what qualified him to be the sacrifice of atonement; one could also argue that unless Christ had been

157. E.g., Hodge, *Romans*, 18–20; R. Mounce, *Romans*, 61.

158. E.g., Fitzmyer, *Romans*, 236.

159. E.g., Moo, *Romans*, 49–50; Ridderbos, *Paul*, 64–68.

160. Moo, *Romans*, 49.

161. Rom 8:9; 2 Cor 3:17–18; Gal 4:6; Phil 1:19; see also Eph 3:16–17.

sent by God in the first place, all the other arguments would be moot. The point is that all of these events encompass the ushering in of the new era; we should not put too fine a point on the moment of time when the new eschaton occurred. Yet what we find in 1:4 is indeed a fine point in time: Christ's resurrection. Thus, it appears that Paul has something else in mind in this verse.

Of the three options above, the first is preferable. Paul clearly refers in verse 3 to Jesus's human, physical nature and emphasizes the messianic implications via his reference to the seed of David. The antithesis in verse 4 thus highlights something other than Christ's physical characteristics. If the verb γενομένου in verse 3 is indeed hinting at the unusual circumstances of Christ's birth, then Paul himself may be indicating that we should understand verse 4 in regard to Christ's supernatural origination. As noted in 1 Corinthians and Galatians, Paul understood Jesus to take on certain divine functions, and Paul uses divine language of Jesus. It is thus not inconceivable that he would do so here. As argued above, the unexpected verb ὁρισθέντος likely occurs here because it alludes to messianic passages in the Jewish Scriptures. Indeed, verse 2 refers to the Scriptures, thus preparing the reader to think about that witness (i.e., the promise of the coming messiah) in verse 3. The appointment language specifically makes this connection: the one who is Son of God was appointed to be the Messiah. That he has been appointed with power may serve to highlight the restoration of Jesus's exalted status that the divine Christ left behind when he took human form (Phil 2:6–7). In addition, in the only other place in Romans in which Paul refers to Christ κατὰ σάρκα (9:5), similar questions arise regarding Christ's identity.[162] Although κατὰ πνεῦμα does not appear there, if Paul is indeed referring to Christ as God (see below), then it is possible that Paul is foreshadowing in 1:3–4 what he wishes to say in 9:5 and the ensuing argument.

Overall, the verses examined from the opening chapter of Romans suggest that Paul compacts a great deal of theology and Christology in these first few verses. The greeting suggests Christ shares similar functions with God. The intermingling of "gospel of God" and "gospel of his Son" does not identify Christ and God as the same, but nonetheless suggests that Christ and God define one another; their identities are reflected

162. The only other place in the entire Pauline corpus where Christ and κατὰ σάρκα are connected is in 2 Cor 5:16, but in this passage the phrase has an entirely different meaning ("from a human point of view").

and established in each another. Finally, Jesus as the Son has a unique relationship with God; Paul hints at Christ's preexistence, affirms his messianic status, and emphasizes the restoration of Christ's exalted status at the resurrection.

In the next passage for consideration, 5:8–11, Paul says that God demonstrates his love through the act of Christ dying on the cross. Paul explains in verse 9 that Christ's death justifies believers through his blood and they are thus saved from God's wrath. Reconciliation is the result (v. 10). The concepts of blood, wrath and reconciliation are reminiscent of 3:21–26. The intriguing question arises as to how *God's* love is demonstrated through the actions of *Christ*. We might instead expect the passage to state that Christ's love is demonstrated through Christ's actions, or that God's love is demonstrated through God's actions. Instead, a crossover between the two appears. Furthermore, the Greek here emphasizes God's *own* (ἑαυτοῦ) love.[163]

The implication from these verses is that the relationship between God and Christ is so close that the actions of the one define the character of the other.[164] In addition, the sonship language makes the relationship

163. Some commentators fail to notice the oddity of this description, while others take more notice. Stowers, for example, makes no mention of this language. The nearest he comes to acknowledging the closeness of the relationship is to state that "God and Christ in concert had accepted the gentile readers into a relation of help and friendship when they were ungodly . . ." (*Rereading of Romans*, 323). Fitzmyer, on the other hand, observes the connection and states, "Because *ho theos* is the Father, whose love is poured out 'through the Spirit' (5:5) and now manifested in Christ's death, this triadic text becomes a Pauline starting point for later Trinitarian dogma" (*Romans*, 400). Hurtado also emphasizes the Son of God language in 5:1–11. He sees this language as intentionally bringing out the emotions of Paul's audience, emphasizing the "divine investment" of the Christ-event: "We are reconciled to God through the death of *God's Son*" ("Jesus's Divine Sonship," 228–29). Fitzmyer and Hurtado are right to highlight the uniqueness of this language. How can God's love be shown when he sends someone else to do his work? N. T. Wright makes a similar observation: "The death of God's son can only reveal God's love (as in, e.g., Rom 5:6–10) if the son is the personal expression of God himself. If will hardly do to say 'I love you so much that I'm going to send someone else'" ("Jesus and the Identity of God," 48). As these interpreters suggest, God's love would be a truly exemplary deed only if God makes some act of self-sacrifice; the sonship language is thus *necessary* for Paul's argument. God's love for his people is shown in his willingness to send his own son to make reconciliation. In Christ's sacrifice, God sacrifices, and the people receive atonement.

164. Bauckham notes that "the terms 'Father' and 'Son' entail each other. The Father is called Father only because Jesus is his Son, and Jesus is called Son only because he is the Son of his divine Father. Each is essential to the identity of the other" ("Biblical Theology," 228).

even more intimate. It is not as if a prophet or priest has performed some action as a representative of God; rather, because the relationship is one of unique sonship, the association is closer.[165] The fact that it is God's Son who dies emphasizes the status of Jesus, for if Jesus were not closely connected to God, it would be impossible for God to show his love through an act of Christ. Paul then uses this familial relationship to emphasize the value of the unredeemed in God's eyes. That God wanted his enemies to live (v. 10), even if it meant his Son would die, suggests the value God places on those who are his enemies. Paul heightens his argument even further by stating that if this is how God felt about humans while they were still enemies, then imagine how much more motivation God has to save those who have now been reconciled to him. Paul's use of the close familial bond between Father and Son thus serves to accentuate God's love for the redeemed.[166]

The next passage for consideration is 8:3. In this verse God sends his Son in the likeness of sinful flesh to be a sin offering. The fact that this is God's *own* Son is emphasized in the Greek with the use of the term ἑαυτοῦ. Thus, once again, Paul emphasizes the uniqueness of Christ's sonship and the close relationship of Jesus with God. In addition, the idea of God *sending* his Son may imply Christ's preexistence. As noted in chapter 3, "sending" does not *necessarily* contain this connotation. God sends his prophets, for example, and they clearly were not considered to be divine. Nevertheless, the coupling of "sending" with the idea of sonship may hint in this direction.[167] "Sending" involves leaving one place to go to another; in the specific case of a son, this would imply leaving his home to go to another place. In the case of the Son of God, this would imply leaving

165. This is reminiscent of my argument in chapter 3, where Christ is the superior mediator over against Moses.

166. It is worth noting that in this section (5:1–11) N. T. Wright regards the Shema being fulfilled. He interprets v. 5 to refer to the believer's love for God: "The *Shema* is at last fulfilled: in Christ and by the Spirit, the creator/covenant God has created a people that, in return for redemption, will love him from the heart. The people defined as God's covenant people by faith are the true covenant people, inheriting all the covenant blessings" ("Romans and the Theology of Paul," 45). The Shema is not cited in 5:1–11, but Wright sees the spirit of the Shema being made complete. Other commentators have not made this connection.

167. Byrne states, "The sending statement conveys a sense of divine 'invasion from outside' into the human realm, while also stressing the depth of divine identification with the human condition" (*Romans*, 236).

heaven—an idea that Paul touches upon in 10:6 (see the section, "Other Passages in Romans," below).

Furthermore, Paul also hints at Christ's divinity by stating that Jesus came in the likeness (ὁμοιώματι) of sinful flesh. Paul is not introducing here a docetic idea that Christ only appeared to be human;[168] rather, he implies that because Jesus came as a human, he is able to fulfill the requirements for the sin offering on humanity's behalf.[169] Nonetheless, the term ὁμοιώματι is significant because it implies something other than complete equivalence, i.e., that in some way Jesus was different from the rest of humanity. Although a number of possibilities emerge,[170] it is most likely that Paul intends to describe Jesus as fully human but yet without sin, i.e., not sharing in sinful flesh. This interpretation is suggested by the reference to a sin offering. The Jewish Scriptures state that any such offering was required to be without blemish (e.g., Lev 9:2–3). Thus, for Paul's sacrificial motif to work in his argument, he needed to take care to avoid ascribing any blemish to Christ. The use of ὁμοιώματι serves this purpose. In addition, the argument that follows bases the ability of believers to resist the flesh on having the Spirit of Christ. If Paul implies that Christ entirely identified with *sinful* flesh, then he would be contradicting himself to argue that the Spirit of Christ helps one avoid sin. Thus, the logic of Paul's argument (because of the implications of the cultic sacrifice and the connection with the life-giving Spirit) demands that Christ be distanced from complete identification with sinful flesh.

This brief reference, then, is laden with weighty theological implications. Despite strong one-God language in 3:30, Paul does not lower his estimation of Christ. Rather, his language appears to include Christ within the divine identity. The oneness of God does not preclude the inclusion of the Son.

168. Schlatter argues: "*Homoiōma* is to be understood concretely; concerning the body of Jesus it denotes that it was made just like ours. There are no docetic notions to be introduced; Paul's formulation rules them out deliberately" (*Romans*, 174).

169. Moo notes that of the 54 occurrences of περὶ ἁμαρτίας in the LXX, 44 refer to sacrifice, and thus the same meaning is likely intended in this passage (*Romans*, 480 n. 48). His conclusion is also supported by my findings in 3:25, where Paul's language refers to a sacrifice of atonement. Once again we see the richness of the Old Testament background in Paul's argumentation.

170. For the various possibilities, see Cranfield, *Romans*, 379–82. See also Branick, "Sinful Flesh," and the response by Gillman, "Another Look at Romans 8:3."

The next passage for consideration is 8:9–11:

> But you are not in the flesh; you are in the Spirit, since the Spirit of God dwells in you. Anyone who does not have the Spirit of Christ does not belong to him. But if Christ is in you, though the body is dead because of sin, the Spirit is life because of righteousness. If the Spirit of him who raised Jesus from the dead dwells in you, he who raised Christ from the dead will give life to your mortal bodies also through his Spirit that dwells in you.

In these verses, Paul's language about the Spirit continually shifts between the Spirit of God to the Spirit of Christ and back again. In verse 9a, believers are in the Spirit, "since the Spirit of God dwells in you." But in 9b, Paul says that anyone who does not have "the Spirit of Christ" does not belong to him. In verse 10, it is still Christ's spirit that is in the believer, but in verse 11 the language shifts again. Here it is the spirit of "him who raised Jesus from the dead," i.e., God, who will also give life to the believer through "his Spirit."

The major question for our purposes concerns the level of distinction, if any, Paul finds between the Spirit, the Spirit of God, and the Spirit of Christ in this passage. Are these concepts unified in Paul's thinking?[171] Or does he make significant distinctions?[172] Do these verses provide the foundations for later Trinitarian theology?[173] What impact does this have on his monotheistic beliefs in general?

On the surface, at least, it may appear that Paul does not make a distinction between the various descriptions of the Spirit. In these verses,

171. Byrne argues that any distinction is tenuous: "To be 'in Christ Jesus's (as in vv 1–2) or 'in the Lord' or 'in the Spirit' or, conversely, to have Christ (v 10) or the Spirit '(dwelling) within you' amounts very much to the same conception of Christian life lived within the influence of the risen Lord who, as 'Last Adam,' has become 'life-giving Spirit'" (*Romans*, 240). Dunn goes even further in arguing that Christ and the Spirit are perceived as one (*Romans*, 430). See also Dunn's article, "II Corinthians 3.17." The numerous phrases regarding the Spirit (whether of God or of Christ) in the passage are equivalent, he argues. The result of Dunn's view is that Paul maintains a Spirit Christology rather than a pneumatology distinct from Christ.

172. Moo, for example, states: "What this means is not that Christ and the Spirit are equated or interchangeable, but that Christ and the Spirit are so closely related in communicating to believers the benefits of salvation that Paul can move from one to the other almost unconsciously" (*Romans*, 491). He argues that both the Spirit and Christ dwell in the believer.

173. Such a conclusion is reached by, e.g., Dunn, *Romans*, 433; Johnson, *Romans*, 130–31; Fitzmyer, *Romans*, 481; Moo, *Romans*, 491.

Paul tells believers that the Spirit is in you, God is in you, and Christ is in you. Yet all of these references ultimately mean that the believer is able to overcome the sinful nature and will live (vv. 10, 11, 13).

We should ask, however, *why* Paul varies his descriptions of the Spirit. It appears that he does, in fact, have a rhetorical reason for doing so. The structure of the argument suggests that Paul is making an argument about God in verse 9a, then he makes a sort of parenthetical statement about Christ in verses 9b–10, and then he returns to his main argument about God in verse 11. The revisiting of the main argument is signaled by the repetition of "πνεῦμα . . . οἰκεῖ ἐν ὑμῖν" from verse 9 in verse 11. Paul simply makes a stylistic variation when he changes "God" in verse 9 to "the one who raised Jesus from the dead" in verse 11. The reason for the parenthetical statement about Christ in verse 10 is that Paul wants to focus on the righteousness effected by Christ and thus make further connections with what he has already said in 6:1–14, which he summarized in 8:2.[174] That God is the main subject is supported by the language of 8:3, where God initiates the solution to sin by sending his Son. Paul makes the general statement in verse 4 that the Law is fulfilled by those who walk in the spirit, not in the flesh. In verses 9–11 he connects this idea with the Roman believers by clarifying that they are in the spirit and not in the flesh. The reason he can say this is because believers have the Spirit of God in them (v. 9a), and as a result they will receive life through that Spirit (v. 11). Parenthetically, he further explains his understanding of the current state of the believer by tying the work of Christ into the discussion once again. As Paul maintained in 6:1–14 (and summarizes in 8:2), it is through Christ that sin and death have been broken. Believers are now dead to sin but alive to God because of Christ's justification. The argument comes full circle when Paul reassures the believers that God will make them not only spiritually but also physically alive through his Spirit.[175]

174. Fee argues, "Paul did *not* in fact perceive the Risen Christ to be one and the same as the Spirit, or that he thought of both as indwelling 'side by side,' as it were. The expression 'Christ in you' is to be understood as shorthand for 'having the Spirit of Christ' from the preceding clause" ("Christology and Pneumatology," 326).

175. Fee argues that Paul's return to spirit of God language in v. 11 provides "clear evidence that Paul saw the Spirit and his role as distinct from that of Christ and his role, even though in terms of 'indwelling,' Paul seems also clearly to understand that since the Spirit is both 'of God' and 'of Christ,' this is how God and Christ both indwell the believer in the present aeon—by the Spirit" ("Christology and Pneumatology," 326).

The structure of the argument, then, suggests that Paul is not completely identifying the Spirit of God with the Spirit of Christ, although the ideas are closely related. Paul's language later in chapter 8 also confirms that a distinction exists. In 8:26–27, the Spirit intercedes for believers presently *on earth*, whereas in 8:34 Christ intercedes for believers *in heaven*.[176]

In most cases Paul clearly distinguishes Christ and the Spirit; in the few texts where a commingling appears linguistically, it is possible to discern Paul's rhetorical purposes for such apparent equivalence.[177] Ultimately, when Paul makes such a close association between Christ and the Spirit, he is maintaining the inseparable link between knowing Christ and receiving the Spirit. As Barrett remarks, "What Paul means is that 'Spirit in you' is impossible apart from 'Christ in you.' Union with Christ is the only way into the life of the Age to Come, of which the distinguishing mark is the Spirit."[178] Indeed, this close connection is inescapable. It is only because Christ has dealt with sin that believers now have access to the Spirit, and it is only through the Spirit that God gives life.

The primary significance for this study lies in observing (as Fee puts it) the ease with which Paul shifts between "Spirit of God" and "Spirit of Christ." This shift "is the strongest kind of evidence for Paul's high Christology, that a person steeped in the OT understanding of the Spirit of God as Paul was, should so easily, on the basis of his Christian experience, designate him as the Spirit of Christ as well."[179] The fact that it is difficult to untangle the distinctions in meaning between the Spirit of God and the Spirit of Christ in this passage gives evidence for the closeness of God, Christ, and the Spirit. Despite strong one-God language elsewhere in the letter, Paul does not back away from making significant connections between the Spirit of God and the Spirit of Christ.

Another pair of passages that require further investigation are 8:31–39 and 14:1–12, because Paul does a poor job of identifying who

176. Ibid., 331. Fee also finds distinctions between Christ and the Spirit in Rom 9:1 and 15:30.

177. Fee argues, for example, that in 2 Cor 3:17 Paul uses a form of midrash pesher to explain that in the previous typology "the Lord" stands for the Spirit in the OT passage he just cited, and thus "The Lord is the Spirit" does not actually denote equivalence (ibid., 319).

178. Barrett, *Romans*, 159.

179. Fee, *God's Empowering Presence*, 548. Fee further argues that the two phrases "refer to the one divine being; this interchange suggests the closest possible links—ontological links, if you will—between the Father and the Son."

he is referring to when he uses the term "Lord." Both God and Jesus have been mentioned in the surrounding context, and this makes it even more difficult to discern Paul's subject.

The first section, 8:31–39, discusses the love of God and Christ for the believer. In verse 35, Paul asks who can separate the believer from the love of Christ (τῆς ἀγάπης τοῦ Χριστοῦ);[180] in 8:39, Paul states that nothing in all creation will be able to separate the believer from the love of God (τῆς ἀγάπης τοῦ θεοῦ), although he adds that it is the love of God "in Christ Jesus our Lord." This leaves us with the question, however, of the identity in verse 37 of the one "who loved us" (τοῦ ἀγαπήσαντος ἡμᾶς). It appears that verse 37 may refer to the love of Christ, since verse 35 speaks of Christ's love, and many interpreters have taken it this way.[181] Others, such as Dunn, see the aorist participle as referring to "God's love expressed in the gift of his Son."[182] Either way, what we find is that Paul's thought here is very similar to that in 5:8. God's love is ultimately expressed through Christ's actions and entails Christ's love for the believer.

Two other characteristics of this section are worthy of note. The unity between God and Christ is also seen in verse 32, where Paul refers again to Christ's sonship. As with previous passages, Paul emphasizes that it is God's *own* son (τοῦ ἰδίου υἱοῦ). This highlights Jesus as the son in a direct, not adoptive, sense.[183] Although believers are adopted children of God (8:23), the Son Jesus is a natural child. This point strengthens Paul's argument regarding the depth of God's love for believers: God was willing to send his natural Son in order to adopt many sons.

The close connection between God and Christ is also seen in verse 34, where Paul alludes to Ps 110:1, identifying Christ as the heavenly intercessor for believers. If we keep in mind that this exaltation is applied to someone recently executed as a criminal, this statement is astonishing.

180. A number of textual variants exist in v. 35, suggesting that the interchange of ideas here was not any clearer to the earliest readers than it is to us. Some manuscripts have "love of God," whereas others have "love of God in Christ Jesus," although most have "love of Christ."

181. E.g., Fitzmyer, *Romans*, 534; Johnson, *Romans*, 147.

182. Dunn, *Romans*, 506. He finds the interchange of terms "striking," and argues that Paul is thinking in Jewish terms—Jesus as Messiah expresses the covenant love of God for his people.

183. Fitzmyer, *Romans*, 531. He comments, "In not sparing his own son, God the judge has thus already pronounced sentence in favor of Christians, his adopted children; hence there is no reason to expect anything different from him hereafter."

None of the other "messiahs" in Second Temple Judaism had ever come to be spoken of in this way.[184] In addition, the Psalm suggests that Christ has been exalted to a position higher than that of any angelic being, and it is this position that brings comfort to the believer in Rom 8:31–39: "The success of his advocacy over that of any challenge is assured, since his resurrection and exaltation to God's right hand was God's own doing, the mark of God's own authorization and approval of those he represents."[185] Paul brings his description of the gospel to a climax in chapter 8 with his statement that nothing can separate the believer from the love of God that is found in Christ Jesus. God's promise to his people has come to fulfillment in Christ; the sin that once separated believers from God has been dealt with in the work of Christ, and believers now have life through the Spirit and communion with God.

This section of Paul's letter, then, emphasizes the closeness of Christ and God in several ways: through Christ's exaltation, through his unique Sonship, and through the interchange of language about the love of God and Christ.

In addition to 8:31–39, 14:1–12 also finds Paul using the term "Lord" without clarifying whether he means an earthly master, Jesus, or God. The context involves Paul's exhortation to the weak and the strong in the Roman church as they disagree about "disputable matters" such as diet and holy days.[186] In verse 4, Paul asks, "Who are you to judge someone else's servant?" He then states that to his own "lord" each person stands or falls. "And he will stand, for the Lord is able to make him stand." In verse 6, the person who regards one day as special does so to "the Lord," he eats meat to "the Lord," with the reason being that he gives thanks to "God." Whoever abstains does so to the "Lord" and gives thanks to "God." Paul argues that if a person lives, he lives to "the Lord" or dies to "the Lord." He concludes, "So, whether we live or die, we belong to the Lord." Then in verse 9 Paul continues by saying, "For this very reason, Christ died and

184. Dunn, *Romans*, 504.

185. Ibid., 511.

186. Although the identification of the "strong" and "weak" are not directly relevant to the discussion here, it is important to distinguish between this discussion and the one in 1 Corinthians. While on the surface this section appears congruous with 1 Cor 8–10, it is in fact a different question that Paul addresses. The Corinthian conflict dealt specifically with the question of idol meats, whereas nowhere in the Romans context does Paul address idolatry. Thus, the two letters communicate similar concerns regarding how Christians who disagree ought to treat one another, but the specific issues are distinct.

returned to life so that he might be the Lord of both the dead and the living." In verse 10, Paul claims that all will stand before "God's" judgment seat—although a number of manuscripts state that it is "Christ's" judgment seat.[187] Then in verse 11, Paul quotes Isa 45:23, in which every tongue will confess to "God." Paul sums up in verse 12 that everyone will give an account to "God."[188]

Most often when Paul uses the term "Lord," he refers to Jesus. Of course, the context can easily change this designation. Thus, in verse 4, most commentators consider the first use of κύριος to refer to an earthly master.[189] This makes good sense of the context; Paul answers the question regarding another person's servant, and thus that servant's master would be the natural subject of his response. The second use of κύριος in verse 4, however, appears to refer to either Christ or God as the ultimate master to whom a believer is responsible. On the one hand, Paul focuses in Romans on God as the ultimate source of all things. Thus, "God" may well be in view here.[190] On the other hand, Paul frequently refers to the Lordship of Christ; hence such a reading would not be out of place.[191]

187. Fitzmyer (*Romans*, 692) notes that the best manuscripts have "God"; he regards the alternate reading as a copyist's attempt to harmonize the text with the language found in 2 Cor 5:10.

188. Some manuscripts (e.g., B, F, G, 6, 424c) delete the reference to God, although most earlier manuscripts retain the reference (e.g. a, A, C, D).

189. E.g., Käsemann, *Romans*, 365; Fitzmyer, *Romans*, 689; Witherington, *Romans*, 329; Johnson, *Romans*, 214; Dunn, *Romans*, 796.

190. Dunn, for example, argues: "Throughout this chapter God is consistently presented as the one with whom ultimate authority and judgment lie, and Christ is a more subordinate figure . . ." (*Romans*, 803). Fitzmyer also finds God to be the subject of most of the passage, including the references to "Lord" in verse 6: "Ever since v 4 Paul has been speaking of *Kyrios*, and one may wonder whether he means God or Christ. In view of the parallelism in this verse, it seems best to understand *Kyrios* in the OT sense of God. This reading is suggested too by v 11, where Paul uses Isa 49:18" (*Romans*, 691). Fitzmyer notes that Paul extends the lordship to Christ in v. 9 and v. 14.

191. Käsemann (*Romans*, 370–71), for example, points to 1 Cor 3:21–23 as a parallel, denoting that all things are lawful so long as the believer is under Christ's lordship. As noted in chapter 2, however, 1 Cor 3:23 places God at the head of the list; in Käsemann's defense, 4:1 does refer to the believer as a "servant of Christ," which appears roughly parallel to our language here. Moo (*Romans*, 841) also sees the second half of verse 4 as a reference to Christ, although he admits that this conclusion is not certain. He acknowledges that the interchange of "Lord" with "God" in v. 6 could indicate that God is intended as "Lord." Nevertheless, he argues that the parallels of v. 6 with v. 8 suggest that Christ is the referent, since v. 9 clearly indicates Christ is the "Lord" and is closely connected to v. 8. Moo further argues that the lack of an article does not pose a problem for

It is worth noting that Paul refers to "the Lord Jesus Christ" in 13:14 as he exhorts the Romans against quarrelling and the desires of the flesh. This verse transitions into the discussion of 14:1, which begins with a warning to avoid quarrelling. Thus, although Paul refers to God in verse 3, there is nothing in this verse to indicate that Paul has shifted his use of "Lord" from Christ to God. Furthermore, if Paul meant "God" when he used "Lord," then we must ask why Paul did not simply say, "Those who eat, eat in honor of the Lord, since they give thanks to him." Rather, it seems Paul intends to distinguish between the two. Yet even in distinguishing, he establishes an incredibly close link. The way to honor Christ is to give thanks to God. Again the interdependence of God and Christ is evident.

This section identifies God as the ultimate judge (v. 11). This is consistent with Paul's language elsewhere in Romans, e.g., 2:16 and 3:6. Note that in 3:16, however, God judges *through* Jesus Christ. Certainly elsewhere Paul identifies Christ himself as judge (2 Cor 5:10).[192] There need not be an inconsistency between these phrases. The frequent reference to Ps 110:1, where Christ sits at God's right hand and in essence shares God's throne, suggests that Christ and God share the function of judgment.

Thus, once again Paul's language appears to be interchangeable between God and Christ, and Paul makes no great effort to distinguish the two. Perhaps he is not conscious of the difficulty and assumes his readers will understand his references. But it seems more likely that Paul intentionally uses language that ties Christ and God together and suggests their interconnectedness.

The next passage, 9:5, poses a major challenge for interpretation in that it is difficult to know where to place the appropriate punctuation.[193] For our discussion, it is important to quote the Greek: ὧν οἱ πατέρες καὶ ἐξ ὧν ὁ Χριστὸς τὸ κατὰ σάρκα ὁ ὢν ἐπὶ πάντων θεὸς εὐλογητὸς εἰς τοὺς αἰῶνας ἀμήν. Although a number of interpretive possibilities

---

this interpretation. Although Paul more frequently uses the article with "Lord" when he denotes Jesus, it is still common for Paul to use anarthous references to Christ as "Lord" (ibid., 843 n. 78).

192. Moo argues that this indicates not that Paul conceives of two different judgments, but rather that "he views God and Christ as so closely related that he can shift almost unconsciously from one to the other . . ." (*Romans*, 847 n. 105).

193. For a list of scholars promoting various solutions, consult Harris, *Jesus as God*, 152 n. 18–19, 154 n. 22.

exist, the basic issue involves whether Paul states that the Messiah *is* God over all, or whether Paul ends his list of the prerogatives of Israel with Messiah, full stop, and then begins a new sentence offering a doxology to God. If Paul does call Christ "God" here, then it is the only place in the undisputed Pauline letters where he makes this claim outright.

That 9:5 may well be a reference to Christ as God is strongly supported by the sentence structure itself. Independent doxologies usually start with the word "blessed" rather than with the subject of the doxology.[194] It is possible that 9:5 is a descriptive doxology to Christ; although the use of ἀμήν after a descriptive doxology (rather than after a volitive doxology) is unusual, Paul himself offers a precedent in 1:25.[195] In addition, a description of Christ's divine status provides a natural contrast with the κατὰ σάρκα of 9:5a, similar to what appears in 1:3–4.[196]

On the other hand, several factors potentially suggest that 9:5 may not be a reference to Christ as God. The specific context here, as well as Paul's theocentric focus in the letter, could argue for an independent doxology to God. Paul is offering a list of advantages given to the Jew by God; thematically, it would be appropriate to end the list with a praise offered to God for these blessings.[197] Indeed, Wilckens argues that in this context, Paul's focus is not to magnify Christ, but "Paulus ziehlt auf die Superiorität des erwählenden Gottes."[198] Thus, a doxology to God better serves Paul's larger argument. In addition, chapters 9–11 have very little reference to Christ, and thus such a strong christological statement at the beginning of the section might seem out of place, especially when the doxology that concludes the section (11:36) appears strictly theological.[199] Perhaps one of the strongest arguments for this viewpoint is the lack of God language for Christ elsewhere in the Pauline epistles.[200] Not only this, but as Kuss

194. Fitzmyer states: "In Paul's writings such a doxology is never joined asyndetically with what precedes or with the subject expressed first; it usually continues from what precedes as an integral part of the sentence . . ." (*Romans*, 549).

195. Harris, *Jesus as God*, 163–64.

196. Kammler also notes this parallel ("Die Prädikation Jesu Christi," 167).

197. Dunn argues, "A devout Jew would naturally end a recollection of God's goodness to Israel with such a benediction to Israel's God, and a Jewish Christian would naturally think of 'the Christ/Messiah' as one of the most important examples of that goodness" (*Romans*, 522).

198. Wilckens, *Brief an die Römer*, 2:189.

199. Harris, *Jesus as God*, 153.

200. Johnson argues that θεός is "jealously reserved for 'God the father'" in the NT

argues, the other six uses of εὐλογητός in the New Testament all apply to God, not to Christ.[201] Thus, Kuss translates Paul's words in 9:5: "Der über allem ist, nämlich Gott, (sei) gepriesen in die Aionen."[202]

Nonetheless, a number of compelling reasons exist for supporting the interpretation that Paul is calling Christ "God" in 9:5. The grammatical considerations provide a weighty argument in favor of this interpretation—as noted above, independent doxologies begin with the word "blessed," not with the subject. Even so, Ps 67:19–20 (LXX) provides the lone exception to this rule.[203] Although one could argue that this exception provides a precedent for an independent doxology in Rom 9:5, the unusual wording of the psalm does have another explanation. The LXX contains the word "blessed" twice when there is, in fact, no corresponding word in Hebrew to the first use of the term. It is thus likely "an erroneous double translation."[204] Bruce Metzger notes that it would be odd indeed for Paul, who would have been so used to hearing "blessed be God," to change the standard formula in this single instance.[205] To this observation I would add that it would be odd for Paul's audience as well, especially since Paul gives no indication that he is changing the standard doxological formula. Thus, the Romans would be more likely to hear Paul's words as a description of Christ.[206]

Furthermore, *if* Paul had strictly separated the identities of Christ and God in his letters, and *if* Paul's one-God language suggested that he jealously guarded the numerical oneness of Yahweh, then it would be more likely that the language here also protects the numerical uniqueness of God. But this is not what this study has found in Paul's letters. Rather, the letters that contain the strongest monotheistic language paradoxically

---

(*Romans*, 157). Similarly, Schmithals points out that Jesus cannot be called God here "weil Paulus Jesus nie 'Gott,' geschweige den 'Gott über alle(s)' nennt . . ." (*Römerbrief*, 333).

201. Kuss, "Zur Römer 9:5," 298. See also Wilckens, *Brief an die Römer*, 189.

202. Kuss, *Römerbrief übersetzt und erklärt*, 678.

203. The relevant portion of the text reads: γάρ ἀπειθοῦντες τοῦ κατασκηνῶσαι κύριος ὁ θεὸς εὐλογητός εὐλογητός κύριος . . .

204. Metzger, "Punctuation of Rom. 9:5," 107, n. 24.

205. Ibid., 107.

206. Many of the patristic writers (e.g., Tertullian, Irenaeus, and Hippolytus) understood Paul's language in this way, although it is possible that their concerns to defend against Arianism colored their interpretation.

also describe Christ in terms that are normally reserved for God. The Lord Yahweh is now the Lord Jesus Christ. God demonstrates his love by sending his Son. The Spirit of God is found only in those who have the Spirit of Christ. All things come from the Father and through the Son. Paul's language consistently intertwines the work of Christ and God so that, at times, it is hard to distinguish who the referent is. It is only a small step from this implied equivalence of Christ and God to a direct statement of this equivalence.

Furthermore, and despite Kuss's argument that "blessed" is not used of Christ, prayers to Christ—although infrequent—nonetheless appear within the Pauline epistles. The most obvious example is the maranatha prayer ("Our Lord, come!") in 1 Cor 16:22. In 2 Cor 12:8–9, Paul states that he called upon the Lord three times to remove the thorn in his flesh. In 1 Thess 3:11–13, Paul makes a "prayer-wish" to God and the Lord Jesus to direct his way to the Thessalonians; he then asks "the Lord" to help the Thessalonians increase their love for one another and to strengthen their hearts.[207] This study has already noted the "grace and peace" formula in the beginning of Paul's letters, and the close connection between Christ and God found there. These passages illustrate that a doxology to Christ is not beyond Paul's conceptual capacity.

In addition, contextually Paul's use of "God" for Christ is not at all out of place. In this section Paul is answering the question of the righteousness of God. If God has not fulfilled his promises to the Jews, then how can the Gentiles possibly trust that God will keep his promises to them? Beker takes this logic another step: "Moreover, such a rejection of Israel by God would simply cut the connection of the gospel to its foundation in the Hebrew Scriptures and degrade the God of Jesus Christ into the God of Marcion—a 'new God' who has no relation either to creation or to Israel's salvation history."[208] Thus, Paul's emphasis at the beginning of the section on Israel's continuing prerogatives serves to tie together what God has done in the past with what God has done in Jesus Christ. (Paul's warning against Gentile boasting in chapter 11 serves the same purpose.) There would be no better way for Paul to affirm this unity than to conclude his rendition of Jewish privilege with the proclamation that

207. Hurtado uses the term "prayer-wish" for passages, like this one, that read like a prayer. These prayer-wishes "most likely reflect actual prayer practices . . ." (*Lord Jesus Christ*, 139).

208. Beker, "Faithfulness of God," 14.

the *Jewish* Messiah is one and the same as the *God* of the Gentiles. Lest the Romans take 3:29–30 too far, Paul affirms here that God is not only the God of the Gentiles, he is *still* the God of the Jews.[209]

If this interpretation is correct, then the letter to the Romans provides an extraordinary combination of theological and christological thinking. The strongest statement of Jewish monotheistic theology stands together with the strongest statement of christological identity; they are not in tension, but rather complement each other in their purposes. The first affirms to the Jews that God is *also* the God of the Gentiles; the second affirms to the Gentiles that their God is *still* the God of the Jews. It is only in these complementary statements that God through Jesus Christ can be Lord over all things.[210] This description of complex oneness, in which diversity nonetheless expresses unity, serves as a model for diverse peoples to express their unity as the new people of God. Paul's intertwined theology and Christology work together to affirm the righteousness of God, now demonstrated to all people.

The next passage for consideration is 10:5–13. Here Paul's allusion to Deut 30:11–14 radically transforms the message that originally urged the observance of the Torah into a statement promoting the righteousness that comes through faith. In Deuteronomy, Moses claims that no one need go into heaven or descend into the abyss in order to discover the Law; rather, it is in their mouths and hearts so that they may obey. Paul dramatically alters this statement so that it applies to Christ's life and death. In doing so, he implies Christ's preexistence and incarnation.[211]

209. Ultimately, for the purposes of this letter, Paul is playing an excellent game of church politics. His letter is primarily addressed to the Roman church (the majority of whom are Gentiles), but Paul expects that this influential church will spread word of his viewpoint to Jerusalem. Thus, Paul understands his secondary audience to be very concerned with Jewish-Christian identity. As Paul affirms Jewish priority (repeatedly, "for the Jew first, then the Gentile"), he hopes not only to bring unity to the Roman church, but also to defend his own ministry and promote the acceptance of the gift he plans to bring to Jerusalem.

210. Bassler's arguments concerning the impartiality of God affirm this observation. The theme flows throughout chapters 9–11. Although only a remnant of the Jews exists now, Paul argues that the Jews will ultimately be included, and the plans of God for *all* people will be fulfilled (11:32). "Thus the situation is now the reverse of that which prevailed earlier, when the Jews were the heirs of salvation and all but a few Gentile proselytes firmly excluded. But if God in his impartiality could not permit the first situation to prevail (Chapters 1–3), no more can he endure the second" (*Divine Impartiality*, 162).

211. Fitzmyer states that v. 6 is "an indirect allusion to the incarnation of Christ; this

This conclusion is supported by the logic of Paul's argument, in which he pits the witness of Deuteronomy against the law-keeping witness of Lev 18:5 (which he quoted in 10:5).[212] Those who wish to please God by means of an attitude of works act as if they are on a quest to seek Christ in heaven or in the underworld and thus attain righteousness themselves.[213] Yet they cannot achieve this, because it has already been accomplished for them. They only need profess their faith in Christ to receive life. Paul's ascent-descent language serves to describe the full extent of Christ's activity—from preexistence in heaven to his resurrection from the realm of the dead—in order to demonstrate the completeness of Christ's work. Nothing further can be done to secure salvation. There is nowhere else to go to seek it: Christ has been active and successful in all realms. Thus, human striving simply cannot achieve what has already been wholly accomplished by Christ.

Paul's focus is this passage is soteriological. That is, his intention is not primarily to describe Christ's participation in the deity of God. Rather, he starts with the presupposition that Christ preexisted with God and uses the concept to further his argument regarding Jews and Gentiles. The fact that Paul does not believe it necessary to explain to the Roman church, which he has never before visited, the intricacies of this aspect of his Christology suggests that Paul assumes their agreement on this point.[214] Of course, he has already declared in 9:5 that Christ is God, so

---

is the closest one comes in the Pauline letters to such an idea . . . " (*Romans*, 590). For a contrasting opinion, see Dunn (*Romans*, 605–6), who argues that the language refers not to the incarnation but to Christ's exaltation and resurrection. In Dunn's view, Paul argues against those who think it would be easier to believe the Gospel if Christ came again from heaven (where he now reigns) or if he descended into the realm of the dead and returned. Yet Dunn's rationale does not fit with the order of the text. If this were Paul's argument, we would expect him to list descending first and ascending second (as noted by, e.g., F. Watson, *Paul and Hermeneutics*, 340 n. 48).

212. F. Watson's description of Paul's antithetical hermeneutic is once again helpful in discovering Paul's meaning.

213. F. Watson, *Paul and Hermeneutics*, 340–41. Watson argues, "The continuing practice of the law as the way to righteousness and life presupposes that God has *not* acted in Christ, in his descent from heaven to take human form and in his resurrection from the dead (cf. Rom 10:6–9). But in fact, God *has* so acted, and his action intends its own acknowledgment in human mouths and hearts" (335).

214. Paul may be aware of the basic theological underpinnings of the Roman church as a result of his conversations with Priscilla and Aquila and others.

the preexistence language here will not be any more shocking than what the Romans have already heard.

This astonishing language about Christ continues in verses 9–13. This section has the greatest affinity with Rom 3:29–30, for it is in 10:12 that Paul states, "For there is no distinction between Jew and Greek; the same Lord is Lord of all and is generous to all who call on him." This verse touches on the theme of God's impartiality, which Paul has presented in several places throughout Romans. In 2:11, Paul says that God judges Jew and Gentile alike based on whether they do evil or good (2:9–10), but the wording is slightly different. Paul says there is no προσωπολημψία, "favoritism," with God. In 3:22, however, the same wording appears as in 10:12: there is no distinction (οὐ γάρ ἐστιν διαστολὴ). But in 3:22 there is no distinction because all have sinned.

Although Paul does not again quote the Shema, he nevertheless presents a similar argument to 3:30 in 10:12 by arguing that the same Lord is over all (γὰρ αὐτὸς κύριος πάντων). Yet in 10:12 God's impartiality is defined in a different way—not as judgment/justification, but as grace. Paul says that God is generous to *all* who call on him (πλουτῶν εἰς πάντας τοὺς ἐπικαλουμένους αὐτόν), and that is why there is no distinction between Jew and Gentile. With this language he intentionally calls to mind the argument in 3:21–31.[215] Nonetheless, Paul switches from a theological emphasis in 3:30 to a christological emphasis in 10:12.[216] A number of observations support this contention. Here "Lord" is a reference to Christ,[217] as denoted by verse 9. Paul makes no indication that he has shifted referents. In addition, Paul uses an Old Testament text that originally referred to God (Joel 2:32) and applies it now to Christ. The Old Testament concept of calling on Yahweh is monotheistic in nature,[218] but Paul now applies it to Christ! Furthermore, in verse 12 Paul declares that

215. Dunn states, "In calling Christ 'Lord of all' he echoes, no doubt deliberately, the argument used in 3:29–30: if Jews believe God is one, then he must be God of Gentiles as well as Jews; so if Christ is 'Lord of all' he is Lord for both Jew and Greek" (*Romans*, 617).

216. As noted by Bassler (*Divine Impartiality*, 161), *contra* Dunn (Dunn, *Romans*, 617), who argues that Paul's point is one of salvation history, not Christology.

217. Fitzmyer, *Romans*, 592.

218. Schmidt notes that the Old Testament texts place "a particular stress on the fact that believers like the patriarchs and Elijah call on the one, true and eternal God and on His name . . . this God and not the Canaanite Baal is the true God . . . " ("ἐπικαλέω," 3:499).

this Lord is "Lord of all," a decree reminiscent of his proclamation of God elsewhere (11:36). Thus, once again we have passages in which God and Christ appear functionally equivalent. Even more astounding is that the impartiality of the one God, which grounded Paul's argument in 3:29–30, is now attributed to Christ. The character of the one God is likewise the character of Jesus Christ.

Part of Paul's rationale for the specific emphasis in these verses may be to provide a needed corrective, lest the Gentiles take their Christology too far. It would have been easy in the Hellenistic world to assimilate Jesus into the many gods of Greek culture.[219] But the language of verse 9 prevents this conclusion by once again inextricably linking the work of God and Christ.[220] Verse 9 may serve another function as well. Dunn calls it the "equivalent of the Shema."[221] In reciting the Shema, Jews proclaimed themselves members of Israel; in acknowledging Jesus as Lord, believers proclaim themselves members of the new Christian community.

In this section, then, Paul reviews his earlier arguments from chapter 3, reaffirming that the impartiality of God (3:29–30) and Christ (10:12) means that both Jew and Gentile have access to God on the same basis—that of faith in Christ Jesus, whom God raised from the dead. The interconnectedness of God and Christ is therefore integral to Paul's soteriology.

The next passage, 11:36, is important to investigate precisely because of what it does *not* say. Paul concludes chapters 9–11 with a doxology to God, with the final verse being very reminiscent of 1 Cor 8:6—except that Paul offers this doxology solely to God, and Christ is not included: "For from him and through him and to him are all things. To him be the glory for ever. Amen."

219. Barrett argues that by insisting on the claim that God raised Jesus from the dead, Paul emphasizes subordination. "Christ is not an independent demigod, but one who was what he was only in virtue of his ordination by and unbroken union with the Father . . . The Christian faith therefore is not one cult among many, nor is Christ one 'lord' among many; he is, and the Church accordingly rests upon, the one unique act and self-revelation of God" (*Romans*, 201). For the question of subordinationist Christology, see the discussion in chapter 2, "Passages that Imply a Hierarchy Between Jesus and God."

220. Rowe observes, "God, Jesus Christ, and the gospel are so bound up with each other that to speak of one is to speak of the others . . . To reject and disobey the gospel is to reject and disobey God and Jesus Christ/God in Jesus Christ/what God has done through Jesus Christ, etc." ("Romans 10:13" 138–39 n. 10).

221. Dunn, *Romans*, 607.

Since I have already discussed this passage in chapter 2, I will not go into detail here, other than to suggest why Paul leaves Christ out of the equation. Romans is a later letter, and so we might expect to see the same formulation here. But the context is clearly different; in 1 Corinthians, Paul was dealing with the Jewish-Christian God over against paganism, whereas here Paul is addressing God's faithfulness to the Jews.[222] Paul ends by highlighting the unexpected nature of God's plan for salvation history. To do so, he cites Old Testament texts that emphasize God's otherness. To include Jesus, and inherently his tangible humanity, at this point would draw the Romans's attention from the point Paul wished to make: God, who is the source and sustainer of all things, is beyond human comprehension.

The next passage for consideration is 15:6: ". . . so that together you may with one voice glorify the God and Father of our Lord Jesus Christ." Dunn has forcefully argued that this passage, which has parallels elsewhere,[223] indicates that Paul used the title κύριος as a means of distinguishing Christ from God. It is not only that Paul sees Yahweh as the God of Jesus, but he is the God of the *Lord* Jesus Christ. Thus, at least here, "the roles of the one God and of the exalted Christ are kept distinct."[224]

It is important to remember, however, that Paul uses κύριος in association with God's fatherhood of Christ, which I have already argued denotes Christ's unique identity. There is almost a sense of containment here which, given the Hellenistic audience, makes sense. As noted above, Paul wanted to guard against the Gentiles turning Christ into just another god in the pantheon. By uniting Christ with God through fatherhood language, Paul emphasizes the uniqueness and superiority of the Christian God. By calling Yahweh the God of Christ, Paul limits the scope of Christ's power and authority. He is not a rival God who has defeated the Old Testament Yahweh; rather, Christ fulfills the plan of the Old Testament God. He is united with, but does not extend beyond, the one who was and always is God.

222 Witherington (*Romans*, 278) hypothesizes that in Rom 11:36 Paul is speaking for the Jews who are yet to be saved, and they would embrace a theological, not Christological, doxology. It seems quite unlikely, however, that Paul would end his entire argument by accommodating unbelievers.

223. 2 Cor 1:3; 11:31; Col 1:3; Eph 1:3.

224. Dunn, *Romans*, 841.

The final passage from Romans for consideration is 16:25–27. In the concluding verses of Paul's letter we find this final doxology. It is possible that this doxology was added to the text of the original letter;[225] the manuscripts disagree on its placement in the letter, and the language is rather unusual for Paul. Although it is difficult to determine with any certainty, the doxology is likely authentic.[226] The themes contained within 25–27 reflect the themes present throughout the letter: "my gospel" (2:16), the mystery long hidden (11:33–36), now revealed through the prophetic writings (1:2; 3:21), so that all nations might believe (3:22–23, 29–30; 10:12–13). Nonetheless, the evidence taken from these verses must be weighed cautiously.

The question facing us here is whether the praise in the doxology (v. 27) is offered to God or to Christ, since grammatically either could be the case (μόνῳ σοφῷ θεῷ διὰ Ἰησοῦ Χριστοῦ ᾧ ἡ δόξα εἰς τοὺς αἰῶνας, ἀμήν). "To whom be the glory forever" could modify Christ, since it is the closest antecedent, or it could modify "the only wise God," since the dative ᾧ is parallel to these datives.[227]

Given what this study has already discovered regarding the close connection between God and Christ, it seems probable that Paul is offering glory to both God and Christ, for even if the reference is to God, Paul makes it clear that the glory is "through Jesus Christ." Once again, Jesus's actions define who God is; God's ultimate glory is a result of the gospel of grace that comes only through Christ Jesus.

CONCLUSIONS

Paul's monotheistic language occurs most explicitly in 3:30, but is also reflected in 10:12 and the theme of impartiality that runs throughout the letter. Paul is not primarily concerned here with numerical oneness, but

225. E.g., Cranfield, *Romans*, 808; Dunn, *Romans*, 916; Fitzmyer, *Romans*, 753.

226. Scholars who believe it is an original Pauline composition include, e.g., Moo, *Romans*, 937; Witherington, *Romans*, 400; Osborne, *Romans*, 418–19.

227. Barrett prefers the former option: "The defective construction may serve to remind the reader that glory should be ascribed at once to God the Father, the Creator (i. 20), in whose unfathomable wisdom and mercy (xi. 33–6) the work of salvation was planned, and to Jesus Christ his Son, through whom and in whom redemption was effected (iii. 26; v. 8)" (*Romans*, 287). Dunn argues, on the other hand, that "to him be the glory" should be attributed to God and is appropriate if it is intended as a liturgical response: "All begins and ends with God" (*Romans*, 916–17).

rather with the unique character of the God who is one. For Paul, the one God is faithful to his promises, and this righteousness is revealed in the sacrificial death and resurrection of Christ. The one God whom Paul proclaims is not an arbitrary God, capriciously choosing one people over another. Rather, God does not show partiality. This means that God justifies all peoples on the same basis—that of faith. This is especially true since no one people group has a claim to greater status than another—all have sinned and therefore have equal standing before God. As a result, the one God is necessarily the God of both Jews and Gentiles. On one level, Jews would easily affirm such a statement; their understanding of the one God meant that God was the universal creator and sustainer of the world. As such, God is clearly sovereign over all the nations. But most Jews believed that any blessings the Gentiles would receive from Yahweh would come through Israel. Gentiles could receive the blessings of God *if* they embraced Judaism; God blessed the righteous, and the righteous were the ones who followed God's covenant. Given this attitude of first-century Jews toward the Gentiles, Paul's proclamation in 3:29–30 is a radical statement indeed, for Paul proclaims that God will bless the Gentiles *qua* Gentiles, and they will receive the same inheritance as the Jews. Both Gentiles and Jews receive this blessing through faith in Jesus Christ.[228]

The result of this understanding of God's impartial character is that, even though the explicit language of oneness occurs infrequently, it nevertheless establishes the rest of Paul's arguments. God's impartiality provides the foundation on which the justification of *all* people rests. This unity between Jew and Gentile is a primary focus of the letter, as the structural analysis has suggested.

If Paul's monotheistic understanding thus forms an integral part of his argument, we might expect to see a more theological focus, and possibly greater evidence of Christ's subordination in the text. What appears instead is a focus in which theology *and* Christology shape one another. Certainly Paul's letter to the Romans has a great focus on theology, as evidenced by the prevalence of θεός-centered language. But Christ does not fade into the background; rather, Paul continually interconnects God and Christ in such a way that makes it clear that they are defined by one another. The oneness of God is not simple or merely numerical, but it is

228. In one sense, the Jews are right: the blessing of the Gentiles does come through Judaism, but only because Jesus's physical descent is through the line of David, as Paul points out in 9:5.

expressed in this complexity of the divine identity. God is the God who is righteous because he offered Jesus as a sacrifice of atonement and raised him from the dead; Jesus is the Christ because he is God's Son who was raised from the dead and now sits at God's right hand. He is Lord of the living and the dead, and God will judge all people through him. Hence, even though Paul does not use his Christianized Shema in Rom 3:30 as he does in 1 Cor 8:6, Christ is not absent from Paul's thinking. As 3:21–26 describes, the righteousness of God is demonstrated precisely in the atoning work of Christ. When Paul says in 3:30 that the one God justifies both the circumcised and uncircumcised through faith, this is shorthand for saying the one God does so through *faith in Christ*.

Not only do God and Christ define each other, but their functions at times overlap. It is the Spirit who indwells and empowers the believer, but Paul in some cases describes the Spirit as the Spirit of God and in some cases as the Spirit of Christ. Both God and Christ show their love for the believer through the death of God'sSon.[229] Furthermore, in places Paul describes both Christ's humanity and deity. He uses both aspects to maintain the unity between Jew and Gentile. Because Yahweh is God over all and is impartial to all, he is also the God of the Gentiles. But because the Christ who the Gentiles worship is not only the Jewish Messiah but also the Jewish God, this means that the God of the Gentiles is *still* the God of the Jews; the connection has not been severed in any way. Thus, we also see texts that may appear on the surface to subordinate Christ to God (e.g., 15:6). Paul's purpose in these texts, however, is to prevent the Gentiles from rejecting the God of the Jewish Scriptures in favor of a new God. As much as Paul needed to maintain the unity of the Jewish and Gentile Christians, he also needed to maintain the unity of the one God, the God who from the beginning planned to bring salvation to all people through faith in Jesus Christ.

229. Yet they show their love in different ways: God sends his Son, while Jesus is obedient even to the point of death. Thus, God and Christ should not be strictly equated. Rather, some things Christ does are not part of the functions performed by God (e.g., his sacrificial death on the cross or his intercessions at God's right hand), and some actions of God are not part of the functions performed by Christ (e.g., Paul always refers to God raising Jesus from the dead; Jesus does not raise himself).

5

Conclusions: Dynamic Oneness in Paul's Thought

THIS STUDY BEGAN WITH the observation that scholars frequently discuss the importance of God only in passing. Donaldson, for example, states that "A discussion of Paul's *theo*logical defense of his gospel for Gentiles . . . will not take us very far. Nevertheless, it provides us an opportunity for an initial survey of the field, a convenient way of raising the questions to be explored more fully in subsequent chapters."[1] On the contrary, this study has shown that Paul's *theo*logical convictions provide more than a convenient starting point. Rather, his foundational convictions about the one God provide the framework for the rest of his arguments. Paul's ethics flow from the conviction that loving the one God necessarily involves loving humanity. His understanding of the relationship between the promise and the Law derives from his fundamental belief that one God has planned, promised, and delivered; the one God is not arbitrary and thus has not changed his mind in the middle of history. Furthermore, one of the reasons the promise is greater than the Law is that the mediator of the promise shares in God's divinity, and thus provides superior mediation to that of Moses. Paul's concept of the one impartial God also leads him to the conclusion that the one God is God of the Gentiles, too. All of Paul's arguments about justification, grace, the will of God, and ethics derive fundamentally from his convictions regarding the oneness of God. Therefore, even though his one-God language may appear infrequently, scholars should not underestimate the importance of it in shaping the rest of Paul's arguments. To do so would only truncate Paul's rationale and seriously misunderstand his overall paradigm.

1. Donaldson, *Paul and the Gentiles*, 81.

Before answering the questions raised in the introduction of this thesis, I will make a few general observations regarding Paul's one-God language. One striking aspect is that Paul does not use monotheistic premises to confront directly and correct the theology of the churches to whom he writes. Nowhere does he set out to explain systematically his understanding of the relationship between God and Christ. Given the fact that he is writing to *churches*, i.e., to those who already have a fundamental understanding of who Christ is in relation to God and God's purposes, it is understandable that Paul does not detail his theology at length. Rather, he assumes a shared understanding about the identity of God and Christ—an understanding based in the monotheistic faith of the Jews—and he uses this foundation to support his larger argument. This observation in itself is significant. The lack of disagreement over the identity of Christ in relation to God suggests one of two possibilities. Either the church is so young that the individual members have not yet fully considered the ramifications of issues such as the divinity and humanity of Christ, or these concepts were so foundational that a common understanding of Christ's identity is precisely what bound the first believers together into these communities.

Certainly it is true that the theological understandings of the incarnation and the Trinity are developed into a *formal* creed only at a later date; the confessional language that Christians still use today did not gain its structure until the fourth century at Nicea. Nevertheless, this does *not* mean that corresponding ruminations were absent from Paul's writings, or that the churches to which he wrote completely lacked any consideration of such possibilities. As this investigation has observed, Paul continually uses similar language for Christ and God, and he assigns similar functions to both. In some cases, he may be making use of earlier hymns or creeds. This suggests that Paul and his followers had already reached a basic understanding about Christ's identity in relation to God. Paul feels free to use this shared tradition to underscore his main arguments, arguments that involve the practical outworking of Paul's conceptualization of the relationship between the one God and Christ.

This study has found that as these practical applications change, so do Paul's purposes in inserting language about the one God. In 1 Cor 8–10, the larger argument involves a question of ethics: how should believers treat one another when they disagree over the meaning and ramifications of their behavior? In essence, Paul chastises the Corinthian "strong" for divorcing their theological knowledge from their ethics. Paul argues instead that the two cannot be separated, and that a proper understanding of and love for the one God necessarily involves an attitude of self-sacrificing love toward one's brothers and sisters in Christ.

In Galatians, Paul's use of monotheistic language does not involve ethics, but rather a question of the relative value of the old and new covenants. The question of the continuity of salvation history comes into sharp focus. Paul addresses the issue by contrasting the mediators Moses and Christ and emphasizing Christ's superiority. Christ's participation in the divine identity and his dispensation of the Spirit, who empowers believers in a way that the Law could not, are greater than any benefits offered by Moses.

Although Paul's utilization of one-God language in Romans is closer to that of Galatians than that of 1 Corinthians, he presents this theology in yet another context. In Rom 3:30, Paul emphasizes the character of God as the defining factor for the inclusion of the Gentiles. The God who is one is one precisely because this God is the universal creator, sustainer, and ruler of all things; the one God is not arbitrary, and because this is so, this God judges both Jew and Gentile by the same standard. Since both Jew and Gentile have sinned and fallen short of the glory of God, the Jew has no reason to boast in any special status before God; rather, God offers grace to all who have faith in Christ. If that is the case, then surely the God of the Jews must likewise be the God of the Gentiles.

When we compare the variations in the use of Paul's one-God language, some interesting questions arise. For example, both Galatians and Romans are concerned with the role of the Law and, ultimately, the continuity of salvation history. Yet Paul employs a different tactic in each letter. Whereas in Galatians he focuses on Christ's superiority by virtue of his participation in the identity of the one God, in Romans he stresses the impartial character of God. What accounts for this different strategy? The answer may involve the specific issues arising in each individual church. In Galatia Paul must answer Gentiles who ask whether they can be justified on their own without observance of the Jewish Law. To answer this question, Paul compares the mediators of the two covenants. In Rome, Paul is addressing Gentiles and Jews who ask whether God is faithful or whether he has abandoned Israel; why should the Gentiles trust a God who has a record of not keeping his promises? Paul thus must defend God's character, and he does so by appealing to God's impartiality.

Another question arises when we compare 1 Corinthians and Romans. The latter has a stronger emphasis on God and thus we might expect more descriptions of God's superiority to Christ. But instead this study has observed that 1 Corinthians has more language that appears to subordinate Christ to God. What explains this? This study has argued that Paul's terminology includes a boundary-setting function that prevents Christ from being viewed as separate from or more exalted than the God of the Jews. This task is pressing for Paul in Corinth, where he is dealing with a community that takes pride in their knowledge and their spiritual gifts. Yet at the same time, they do not understand the ethical ramifications of their commitment to the one God. As intellectualism and a self-centered focus threaten to spiral out of control, Paul may well be envisioning the potential harm to come. The church knows Christ but does not appear to understand accurately the implications of the Jewish Scriptures. Thus, Paul employs boundary-setting language in order to firmly establish that the new work of Christ is inextricably tied to God. Jesus is Lord, but that is to the glory of the one God. Jesus is not an independent deity. This argument takes a different form in Rome, where the major concern involves the relationship between various ethnic groups. Thus, in Romans, Paul must affirm that the God of the Gentiles *still* lays claim to being the God of the Jews. Thus, in Corinth Paul argues that Jesus is not a new God; in Rome, Paul argues that the one God has not abandoned Israel for a new people.

Paul's very different contexts in 1 Corinthians, Galatians, and Romans are all supported by one-God language. This is what is meant by "dynamic oneness." Paul's concept of the one God is not static or rigid. It does not simply indicate numerical oneness over against the Greek pantheon. Rather, Paul brings out different nuances of his understanding of the uniqueness of the one God in support of a great variety of arguments. In one place Paul emphasizes the love of God, in another, God's impartiality. Elsewhere he emphasizes the continuity of God's plans. Occasionally the one-God motif is alluded to rather than stated directly, such as in Rom 10:12. It is thus more prevalent than is sometimes granted. Paul can mine the rich depth of his understanding of the one God in a variety of situations for a variety of purposes. Paul's theology of the one God therefore provides a vital and compelling underpinning for his entire discussion.

One question that arose in chapter 1 was whether Jews understood the oneness of God quantitatively or qualitatively. In this study I have argued that, for Paul, the oneness of God primarily involves not his numerical oneness, but rather his uniqueness: God is creator, ruler, designer, and ultimate judge of the universe. All things have their source in God and ultimately work together for God's purposes. God's unique *activity* is what makes God the one God over all else. But ultimately, for Paul, God's defining moment is found in the identity and activity of *Christ*. God sent his preexistent Son to fulfill all that the Law required, and through Christ's death and resurrection God has been proved to be both just and loving. Thus, God and Christ mutually define one another through their actions; the oneness of God is complex.

Paul's conviction that the oneness of God primarily involves uniqueness, rather than quantitative measure, came about as the result of both his experience of the risen Christ and his reinterpretation of the Jewish Scriptures. His identification of innate tensions within the Scriptures helped him to make sense of his experience, and his experience helped him to interpret the difficulties he found within the Scriptures. God's oneness is not threatened by the theoretical possibility of multiple participants in the divine identity (e.g., Glory or Sophia) precisely because experience and Scripture inform and further define one another. Spiritual experiences are interpreted and constrained by the limits of Scripture; in turn, Scripture is explained and nuanced by experience. Thus, when Paul experiences the risen Jesus, he is able to turn to Ps 110:1 to begin to understand Christ's exaltation. When Paul reads Gen 12:3, his experience that the Spirit had already come upon the Gentiles helps him to understand that the blessing of the nations occurs by faith.

This correlation between experience and hermeneutics helps us to decide between the three options presented in chapter 1 for describing the first Christians' view of the relationship between Jesus and God: 1) either Jesus was not exalted to the level of divinity, 2) he was considered divine as the result of an intentional departure from Judaism, or 3) he was proclaimed to be divine within newly understood parameters of Jewish monotheistic beliefs. Paul's experience, combined with his antithetical hermeneutic, suggest that he was able to affirm simultaneously both the inclusion of Jesus within the divine identity and his Jewish monotheistic roots. Paul believed he was conforming to the witness of Scripture when he applied language to Christ that was functionally equivalent to the language he used of God, when he used Old Testament Yahweh texts to refer to Christ, and when he described Jesus as God.

Furthermore, this study also began by asking about the specific way in which Paul made sense of the relationship between God and Christ. Despite the exaltation of Christ, the hierarchical language cannot be ignored. In exploring these passages, however, I argued that the apparently hierarchical language serves an unexpected function. Rather than defining a subordinate relationship between God and Jesus, it serves a boundary-setting function that responds to the potential for disconnecting the relationship between Christ and God. That is, Paul's language demonstrates that the exalted Christ has not superseded the one God; Jesus is not a new God, nor is Yahweh an outmoded deity. Rather, the oneness of God shows the unified will and purpose of the Father and Son; the plans of the one God have not changed. Instead, they come to their fulfillment in Christ.

Paul uses this close relationship between Christ and God, this complex oneness, to emphasize the one plan for salvation history. God had always intended to save his people through faith in Christ. God is not arbitrary; God has not changed his mind. Thus, the promises to Israel will still be fulfilled. Those promises, however, include the blessing of the nations, and this has indeed occurred in the actions of Christ on behalf of all people. This understanding of the continuity of salvation history flows directly from Paul's belief in the uniqueness of the one God and Christ's participation in God's divinity. Thus the entrance requirement for the people of God has been radically redefined, based on faith in what God has done through Jesus Christ. But Paul cannot stress enough that God had always intended for this to be the case. The Jewish Scriptures serve as a witness to this plan of faith, starting with Abraham. Because the nature of the one God includes God's impartiality, Jews and Gentiles alike are redeemed on the basis of faith. Ultimately, this means that God is God over the Gentiles, too, and not merely the Jews alone. It is difficult to overstate the importance of the continuity of salvation history for Paul's Gospel paradigm.

Another question for which this study sought clarification involved the titles used of Jesus. Early on I argued that Paul named Jesus as the Jewish Messiah ("Christ") and intentionally used the term "Lord" to connote deity. The phrase "Son of God" was more ambiguous; however, it became clearer, especially in chapter 4, as a designator for the unique divine Father-Son relationship between God and Christ. The sending language that often accompanies this phrase implies Christ's preexistence, and the familial language itself argues for a very close relationship between God and Christ. God cannot show his love for his people through Christ apart from a close connection between Father and Son. Even the logic of Paul's metaphor regarding the adoption of believers as children of God hinges on the fact of Christ's natural sonship.

These observations help us to understand why, when Paul's one-God language does appear, Paul does not simultaneously diminish his language regarding the exalted Christ. Although we might naturally expect language of subordination and hierarchy in the same places where Paul emphasizes the supremacy of God, this is not in fact the case. Instead, 1 Corinthians, Galatians, and Romans contain the strongest one-God language in Paul's writings, yet these letters do not diminish the view of Christ presented therein. It is precisely in these same letters where Paul describes Jesus as sharing in the functions of the one God and even being called God. Because Jesus and God mutually define one another, exalted language cannot be stripped away from the one without diminishing the accomplishments of the other. God is all in all, but this is only through Christ.

The final issue considered in chapter 1 concerned ethics within the new people of God. This study has emphasized, especially in chapter 2, that the vertical dimension of loving God *necessarily* involves the horizontal dimension of loving one's neighbor. Thus it is no accident that Paul begins his section on idol meats in 1 Corinthians with a reference to the oneness of God. True worship of the one God does not involve mere assent to theological principles, but it also involves a demonstration of love of neighbor *as* a demonstration of love of God. Conversely, to sin against one's neighbor is to sin against Christ (1 Cor 8:12). For Paul, then, the daily moral life of the community reflects the oneness of God in that proper ethical behavior between believers bears witness to the power of the one God to bring unity to his creation.

From these conclusions further questions arise that are beyond the scope of this study. If we investigated Paul's other letters, where the language about the one God is not as explicit, would we reach similar conclusions? Does Paul craft his overall argument differently, or does an undercurrent of monotheistic belief still influence the larger argument? Significant texts to explore include 1 Thess 1:9–10, which refers to the "living God," and Phil 2:5–11, which arguably contains the strongest statements about the exalted Christ. Is the christological language stronger in this latter text because of the lack of explicit one-God language? Or is Paul's monotheistic theology evident here as well?

In addition, it would be informative to explore the disputed letters in order to see if the trajectories established here hold true or are modified in any way. Key texts include Eph 4:4–6, which promotes unity through a list that includes both "one Lord" and "one God and Father of all, who is above all and through all and in all," and 1 Tim 2:5, where the author proclaims the oneness of God in the same breath as the oneness of the Lord Jesus, who is the mediator between God and humanity. What function do these statements play within the larger argument? Are they foundational to the author's thinking, as I have argued here? Is the concept of oneness in these passages dynamic or static?

From study alone, however, I would suggest a number of improvements for approaching Pauline theology. First, any discussion of Paul's thought should begin with an in-depth discussion of his *theo*logy, with particular attention paid to his understanding of the oneness of God, especially as it involves God's unique activity. Also, Paul's Jewish background and his continued commitment to the one God should be underscored. Paul envisions continuity between Judaism and believers in Christ; the one plan of the one God has been brought to fulfillment in Christ. The character of the one God is integral to this discussion as well. The one God is not arbitrary and does not change his mind or abandon his plans. This certainly affects how Paul views the gospel and the role of faith in the lives of Jews and Christians.

Second, when considering Christology, the close relationship between Jesus and God must be acknowledged. Because this complex oneness involves unique activity more so than numerical oneness, the divinity of Christ should not be ruled out on an *a priori* basis. Instead, the unique actions of God and Christ can be seen to define not only themselves, but also each other. When Paul describes Christ as having similar functions as God when he applies Old Testament Yahweh texts to Christ, he is making a significant statement about Christ's identity. Yet Paul is still careful to maintain a Jewish understanding of the supremacy of Yahweh. Christ is not a god who supersedes Yahweh, but the two work in concert together within the oneness of their divinity.

Third, any discussion of the people of God, especially the relationship between Jews and Gentiles, should also reflect an understanding of the oneness of God. This goes back to the character of God. Because of who Yahweh is, because God is just and not arbitrary, the righteousness of God is found in his single standard for all peoples. Thus God is God over both Jew and Gentile. Paul's gospel message flows from this understanding. His Christology and soteriology stem from his belief in the oneness of God, and this emphasis should not be overlooked.

Finally, any discussion of ethics should note not only Paul's theological foundations, but also the specific aspect of God's oneness. The relationship of Paul's ethics to the Jewish Shema should be fully examined. Loving the one God necessarily involves actions that demonstrate love for others. Thus, when Paul willingly sets aside his own rights—in imitation of Christ—for the benefits of other Christians, this is a result of his theological convictions regarding how to properly display loyalty to the one God.

In conclusion, the oneness of God in Paul's thought provides a significant foundation for his gospel message. The infrequency of Paul's explicit mention of the one God belies the importance of this aspect of his theology. Paul has made major decisions regarding the faithfulness of God, the identity of Christ, and the practical outworking of the gospel message based on this dynamic understanding of the one God. Furthermore, Paul's use of this theology is flexible; he is able to apply this concept to a variety of issues and situations within the early church. This flexibility reveals the comprehensive effects of the oneness of God on Paul's thinking.

Bibliography

Abrahams, I. *Studies in Pharisaism and the Gospels*. Cambridge: Cambridge University Press, 1917.

Allen, Leslie. "The Old Testament Background of (προ-) ὁρίζειν in the New Testament." *NTS* 17 (1971) 104–8.

Allison, Dale. "Mark 12.28–31 and the Decalogue." In *The Gospel and the Scriptures of Israel*, edited by Craig A. Evans and W. Richard Stegner, 270–78. Sheffield: Sheffield Academic, 1994.

Arnold, Clinton. "The 'Exorcism' of Ephesians 6:12 in Recent Research: A Critique of Wesley Carr's View of the Role of Evil Powers in First-Century AD Belief." *JSNT* 30 (1987) 71–87.

———. "Returning to the Domain of the Powers: *Stoicheia* as Evil Spirits in Gal. 4:3, 9." *NovT* 38 (1996) 55–76.

Aune, D. E. "Apocalypticism." In *DPL*, 25–35.

Badenas, Robert. *Christ the End of the Law: Romans 10.4 in Pauline Perspective*. JSOTSup 10. Sheffield: JSOT Press, 1985.

Balz, Horst, and Gerhard Schneider, editors. *EDNT*. 3 vols. Grand Rapids: Eerdmans, 1990–93.

Bandstra, Andrew J. "The Law and Angels: *Antiquities* 15.136 and Galatians 3:19." *CTJ* 24 (1989) 223–40.

Barclay, John. *Obeying the Truth: A Study of Paul's Ethics in Galatians*. Studies of the New Testament and Its World. Edinburgh: T. & T. Clark, 1988.

Barker, Margaret. *The Great Angel: A Study of Israel's Second God*. Louisville: Westminster John Knox, 1992.

———. "The High Priest and the Worship of Jesus." In *The Jewish Roots of Christological Monotheism: Papers from the St. Andrews Conference on the Historical Origins of the Worship of Jesus*, edited by Carey C. Newman et al., 93–111. Supplements to the Journal for the Study of Judaism 63. Leiden: Brill, 1999.

Barrett, C. K. *A Commentary on the Epistle to the Romans*. New York: Harper, 1957.

———. *The First Epistle to the Corinthians*. 2nd ed. BNTC. London: Black, 1971.

———. *Freedom and Obligation: A Study on the Epistle to the Galatians*. London: SPCK, 1985.

———. *Paul: An Introduction to His Thought*. Louisville: Westminster John Knox, 1994.

Barton, Stephen C. "Christian Community in the Light of the Gospel of John." In *Christology, Controversy and Community. New Testament Essays in Honour of David R. Catchpole*, edited by D. G. Horrell et al., 279–301. NovTSup 99. Leiden: Brill, 2000.

———. "The Unity of Humankind as a Theme in Biblical Theology." In *Out of Egypt: Biblical Theology and Biblical Interpretation*, edited by Craig Bartholomew et al., 233–58. Scripture and Hermeneutics 5. Grand Rapids: Zondervan, 2004.

Bassler, Jouette M. "Centering the Argument: A Response to Andrew T. Lincoln." In *Romans*, Vol. 3 of *Pauline Theology*, edited by David M. Hay et al., 160–68. Minneapolis: Fortress, 1995.

———. *Divine Impartiality: Paul and a Theological Axiom*. SBLDS 59. Chico, CA: Scholars, 1982.

Bauckham, Richard. "Biblical Theology and the Problems of Monotheism." In *Out of Egypt: Biblical Theology and Biblical Interpretation*, edited by Craig Bartholomew et al., 187–232. Scripture and Hermeneutics 5. Grand Rapids: Zondervan, 2004.

———. *God Crucified: Monotheism and Christology in the New Testament*. Carlisle: Paternoster, 1998.

———. "The Throne of God and the Worship of Jesus." In *The Jewish Roots of Christological Monotheism: Papers from the St. Andrews Conference on the Historical Origins of the Worship of Jesus*, edited by Carey C. Newman et al., 43–69. Supplements to the Journal for the Study of Judaism 63. Leiden: Brill, 1999.

Becker, Jürgen. *Paul: The Apostle to the Gentiles*. Translated by O. C. Dean Jr. Louisville: Westminster John Knox, 1993.

Becker, O. "μεσίτης." In *NIDNTT*, 1:372–76.

Beker, J. Christiaan. "The Faithfulness of God and the Priority of Israel in Paul's Letter to the Romans." *HTR* 79 (1986) 10–16.

———. *Paul the Apostle: The Triumph of God in Life and Thought*. Philadelphia: Fortress, 1980.

———. *The Triumph of God: The Essence of Paul's Thought*. Minneapolis: Fortress, 1990.

Betz, Hans Dieter. *Galatians: A Commentary on Paul's Letter to the Churches in Galatia*. Hermeneia. Philadelphia: Fortress, 1979.

Bietenhard, H. "Name." In *NIDNTT*, 2:648–56.

———. "ὄνομα." In *TDNT*, 5:242–83.

Bilezikian, Gilbert. "Appendix: A Critical Examination of Wayne Grudem's Treatment of *Kephalē* in Ancient Greek Texts." In *Beyond Sex Roles: What the Bible Says about a Woman's Place in Church and Family*, 215–52. 2nd ed. Grand Rapids: Baker, 1985.

———. "Hermeneutical Bungee-Jumping: Subordination in the Godhead." *JETS* 40 (1997) 57–68.

Bockmuehl, Markus. *Jewish Law in Gentile Churches: Halakhah and the Beginning of Christian Public Ethics*. Edinburgh: T. & T. Clark, 2000.

Borgen, Peter. "'Yes,' 'No,' 'How Far?': The Participation of Jews and Christians in Pagan Cults." In *Early Christianity and Hellenistic Judaism*, 15–43. Edinburgh: T. & T. Clark, 1996.

Bornkamm, Günther. "The Letter to the Romans as Paul's Last Will and Testament." In *The Romans Debate*, edited by Karl P. Donfried, 16–28. Peabody, MA: Hendrickson, 1991.

Bousset, Wilhelm. *Die Religion des Judentums im späthellenistischen Zeitalter*. Edited by Hugo Gressman. 3rd ed. HNT 21. Tübingen: Mohr/Siebeck, 1966.

Branick, Vincent P. "The Sinful Flesh of the Son of God (Rom 8:3): A Key Image of Pauline Theology." *CBQ* 47 (1985) 246–62.

Braude, William G., trans. *The Midrash on Psalms*. 2 vols. Yale Judaica Series 13. New Haven: Yale University Press, 1959.

Brown, Colin, editor. *NIDNTT*. 3 vols. Exeter: Paternoster, 1976.

Bruce, F. F. *1 and 2 Corinthians*. NCB. London: Oliphants, 1971.

———. *Commentary on Galatians*. NIGTC. Exeter: Paternoster, 1982.

———. *New Testament History*. London: Nelson, 1969.

Büchsel, Friedrich. "εἰδωλόθυτον." In *TDNT*, 2:378–79.

Bultmann, Rudolf. *Theology of the New Testament*. 2 vols. New York: Scribner's, 1951.

———. "καυχάομαι." In *TDNT*, 3:645–53.

Burton, Ernest de Witt. *The Epistle to the Galatians*. ICC. Edinburgh: T. & T. Clark, 1921.

Byrne, Brendan. "Interpreting Romans: The New Perspective and Beyond." *Int* 58 (2004) 241–52.

———. "Interpreting Romans Theologically in a Post-'New Perspective' Perspective." *HTR* 94 (2001) 227–41.

———. *Romans*. SP 6. Collegeville: Liturgical, 1996.

Caird, G. B. *Principalities and Powers*. Oxford: Clarendon, 1956.

Callan, Terrance. "Pauline Midrash: The Exegetical Background of Gal 3:19b." *JBL* 99 (1980) 549–67.

Calvert-Koyzis, Nancy. *Paul, Monotheism and the People of God: The Significance of Abraham Traditions for Early Judaism and Christianity*. JSNTSup 273. London: T. & T. Clark, 2004.

Calvin, John. *The Epistles of Paul the Apostle to the Galatians, Ephesians, Philippians and Colossians*. Edited by David W. Torrance and Thomas F. Torrance, translated by T. H. L. Parker. Calvin's Commentaries. Edinburgh: Oliver and Boyd, 1965.

Campbell, Douglas A. "Romans 1:17—A *Crux Interpretum* for the ΠΙΣΤΙΣ ΧΡΙΣΤΟΥ Debate." *JBL* 113 (1994) 265–85.

———. "Towards a New, Rhetorically Assisted Reading of Romans 3:27—4:25." In *Rhetorical Criticism and the Bible*, edited by Stanley E. Porter et al., 355–402. JSNTSup 195. London: Sheffield Academic, 2002.

Capes, David. *Old Testament Yahweh Texts in Paul's Christology*. Tübingen: Mohr/Siebeck, 1992.

Carr, Wesley. *Angels and Principalities: The Background, Meaning, and Development of the Pauline Phrase* hai archai kai hai exousiai. Cambridge: Cambridge University Press, 1981.

Casey, P. M. *From Jewish Prophet to Gentile God: The Origins and Development of New Testament Christology*. Louisville: Westminster John Knox, 1991.

———. "Lord Jesus Christ: A Response to Professor Hurtado." *JSNT* 27 (2004) 83–96.

———. "Monotheism, Worship and Christological Developments in the Pauline Churches." In *The Jewish Roots of Christological Monotheism: Papers from the St. Andrews Conference on the Historical Origins of the Worship of Jesus*, edited by Carey C. Newman et al., 214–33. Supplements to the Journal for the Study of Judaism 63. Leiden: Brill, 1999.

Cervin, R. E. "Does κεφαλή Mean 'Source' or 'Authority Over' in Greek Literature? A Rebuttal." *TJ* 10 (1989) 85–112.

Charlesworth, James H., editor. *The Old Testament Pseudepigrapha*. 2 vols. New York: Doubleday, 1985.

Chester, Andrew. "Jewish Messianic Expectations and Mediatorial Figures and Pauline Christology." In *Paulus und das antike Judentum*, 17–89. WUNT 58. Tübingen: Mohr/Siebeck, 1991.

Cheung, Alex T. *Idol Food in Corinth: Jewish Background and Pauline Legacy*. JSNTSup 176. Sheffield: Sheffield Academic, 1999.

Childs, Brevard. *Old Testament Theology in a Canonical Context*. Philadelphia: Fortress, 1985.

Cohon, Samuel S. "The Unity of God." *HUCA* 26 (1955) 425–79.

Collins, John J. *Apocalypticism in the Dead Sea Scrolls*. New York: Routledge, 1997.

———. *The Apocalyptic Imagination: An Introduction to the Jewish Matrix of Christianity*. New York: Crossroad, 1984.

Collins, Raymond F. *First Corinthians*. SP 7. Collegeville: Liturgical, 1999.

Conzelmann, Hans. *1 Corinthians: A Commentary on the First Epistle to the Corinthians*. Translated by James W. Leitch. Hermeneia. Philadelphia: Fortress, 1975.

Cosgrove, Charles H. *The Cross and the Spirit: A Study in the Argument and Theology of Galatians*. Macon, GA: Mercer University Press, 1988.

Cranfield, C. E. B. *A Critical and Exegetical Commentary on the Epistle to the Romans*. 2 vols. ICC. Edinburgh: T. & T. Clark, 1975–1979.

———. "'The Works of the Law' in the Epistle to the Romans." *JSNT* 43 (1991) 89–101.

Cullmann, Oscar. *Christ and Time: The Primitive Christian Conception of Time and History*. Translated by Floyd V. Filson. London: SCM, 1951.

———. *The Christology of the New Testament*. London: SCM, 1959.

Dahl, Nils Alstrup. *Jesus the Christ: The Historical Origins of Christological Doctrine*. Edited by Donald H. Juel. Minneapolis: Fortress, 1991.

Dahms, John V. "The Subordination of the Son." *JETS* 37 (1994) 351–64.

Danker, F. W., W. Bauer, W. F. Arndt, and F. W. Gingrich. *Greek-English Lexicon of the New Testament and Other Early Christian Literature*. 3rd ed. Chicago: University of Chicago Press, 2000.

Das, A. Andrew. *Paul and the Jews*. Library of Pauline Studies. Peabody, MA: Hendrickson, 2003.

———. *Paul, the Law, and the Covenant*. Peabody, MA: Hendrickson, 2001.

Davies, W. D. "A Note on Josephus, *Antiquities* 15:136." *HTR* 47 (1954) 135–40.

Davis, P. G. "Divine Agents, Mediators, and New Testament Christology." *JTS* 45 (1994) 479–503.

Dawes, Gregory W. "The Danger of Idolatry: First Corinthians 8:7–13." *CBQ* 58 (1996) 82–98.

De Lacey, D. R. "Jesus as Mediator." *JSNT* 29 (1987) 101–21.

———. "'One Lord' in Pauline Christology." In *Christ the Lord: Studies in Christology Presented to Donald Guthrie*, edited by Harold H. Rowdon, 191–203. Leicester: InterVarsity, 1982.

Delling, Gerhard. "διατάσσω." In *TDNT*, 8:34–39.

Demke, Christoph. "'Ein Gott und viele Herren': Die Verkündigung des einen Gottes in den Briefen des Paulus." *EvT* 36 (1976) 473–84.

Dodd, Brian. "Romans 1:17—A *Crux Interpretum* for the ΠΙΣΤΙΣ ΧΡΙΣΤΟΥ Debate?" *JBL* 114 (1995) 470–73.

Dodd, C. H. "ἔννομος Χριστοῦ." In *More New Testament Studies*, 134–48. Manchester: Manchester University Press, 1968.

———. *The Bible and the Greeks*. London: Hodder and Stoughton, 1935.

———. *The Epistle of Paul to the Romans*. MNTC. London: Hodder and Stoughton, 1932.

Donaldson, Terence L. *Paul and the Gentiles: Remapping the Apostle's Convictional World*. Minneapolis: Fortress, 1997.

Donfried, Karl P., editor. *The Romans Debate*. Rev. ed. Peabody, MA: Hendrickson, 1991.

Duncan, George S. *The Epistle of Paul to the Galatians*. London: Hodder and Stoughton, 1934.

Dunn, James D. G. "II Corinthians 3.17—'The Lord is the Spirit.'" *JTS* 21 (1970) 309–20.

———. "Christology as an Aspect of Theology." In *The Future of Christology: Essays in Honor of Leander E. Keck*, edited by Abraham J. Malherbe et al., 202–12. Minneapolis: Fortress, 1993.

———. *Christology in the Making: A New Testament Inquiry into the Origins of the Doctrine of the Incarnation*. 2nd ed. Grand Rapids: Eerdmans, 1996.

———. *The Epistle to the Galatians*. BNTC. London: Black, 1993.

———. "Once More, ΠΙΣΤΙΣ ΧΡΙΣΤΟΥ." In *The Faith of Jesus Christ: The Narrative Substructure of Galatians 3:1—4:11*, by Richard B. Hays, 249–71. 2nd ed. Grand Rapids: Eerdmans, 2002.

———. *The Partings of the Ways: Between Christianity and Judaism and their Significance for the Character of Christianity*. London: SCM, 1991.

———. *Romans*. 2 vols. WBC 38A–B. Dallas: Word, 1988.

———. *The Theology of Paul the Apostle*. Grand Rapids: Eerdmans, 1998.

———. *The Theology of Paul's Letter to the Galatians*. New Testament Theology. Cambridge: Cambridge University Press, 1993.

———. *Unity and Diversity in the New Testament: An Inquiry into the Character of Earliest Christianity*. Philadelphia: Westminster, 1977.

———. "Was Christianity a Monotheistic Faith from the Beginning?" *SJT* 35 (1982) 303–36.

Ellis, E. Earle. "Preformed Traditions and Their Implications for Pauline Christology." In *Christology, Controversy and Community: New Testament Essays in Honour of David R. Catchpole*, edited by David G. Horrell et al., 303–20. NovTSup 99. Leiden: Brill, 2000.

———. "'Wisdom' and 'Knowledge' in 1 Corinthians." *TynBul* 25 (1974) 82–98.

Elwell, Walter. "The Deity of Christ in the Writings of Paul." In *Current Issues in Biblical and Patristic Interpretation: Studies in Honor of Merrill C. Tenney*, edited by Gerald F. Hawthorne, 297–308. Grand Rapids: Eerdmans, 1975.

Encyclopaedia Judaica. 16 vols. Jerusalem: Keter, 1972.

Engberg-Pedersen, Troels. *Paul and the Stoics*. Louisville: Westminster John Knox, 2000.

———. "Response to Martyn." *JSNT* 86 (2002) 103–14.

Epp, Eldon Jay. "Jewish-Gentile Continuity in Paul: Torah and/ or Faith? (Romans 9:1–5)." *HTR* 79 (1986) 80–90.

Esler, Philip F. "Ancient Oleiculture and Ethnic Differentiation: The Meaning of the Olive-Tree Image in Romans 11." *JSNT* 26 (2003) 103–24.

———. "Paul and Stoicism: Romans 12 as a Test Case." *NTS* 50 (2004) 106–24.

Exler, F. J. *The Form of the Ancient Greek Letter of the Epistolary Papyri (3rd c. B.C.–3rd c. A.D.): A Study in Greek Epistology*. Chicago: Ares, 1923.

Fee, Gordon D. "Christology and Pneumatology in Romans 8:9–11—and Elsewhere: Some Reflections on Paul as a Trinitarian." In *Jesus of Nazareth, Lord and Christ: Essays on the Historical Jesus and New Testament Christology*, edited by Joel B. Green et al., 312–31. Grand Rapids: Eerdmans, 1994.

———. *The First Epistle to the Corinthians*. Grand Rapids: Eerdmans, 1987.

———. *God's Empowering Presence: The Holy Spirit in the Letters of Paul*. Peabody, MA: Hendrickson, 1994.

———. "Paul and the Trinity: The Experience of Christ and the Spirit for Paul's Understanding of God." In *The Trinity: An Interdisciplinary Symposium on the Trinity*, edited by Stephen T. Davis et al., 49–72. New York: Oxford University Press, 1999.

Feldman, Louis. *Jew and Gentile in the Ancient World: Attitudes and Interactions from Alexander to Justinian*. Princeton: Princeton University Press, 1993.

Ferguson, Everett. *Backgrounds of Early Christianity*. 3rd ed. Grand Rapids: Eerdmans, 2003.

Finkelstein, Louis. "The Oldest Midrash: Pre-Rabbinic Ideals and Teachings in the Passover Haggadah." *HTR* 31 (1938) 291–317.

Fitzmyer, Joseph A. "Aramaic Epistolography." *Semeia* 22 (1981) 25–57.

———. "The Christology of the Epistle to the Romans." In *The Future of Christology: Essays in Honor of Leander E. Keck*, edited by Abraham J. Malherbe et al., 81–90. Minneapolis: Fortress, 1993.

———. "A Feature of Qumran Angelology and 1 Cor. 11:10." In *Essays on the Semitic Background of the New Testament*, 187–204. London: G. Chapman, 1971.

———. "*Kephale* in 1 Corinthians 11:3." *Int* 47 (1993) 52–59.

———. *Romans: A New Translation with Introduction and Commentary*. AB 33. New York: Doubleday, 1993.

———. *To Advance the Gospel: New Testament Studies*. New York: Crossroad, 1981.

Fletcher-Louis, Crispin. "The Worship of Divine Humanity as God's Image and the Worship of Jesus." In *The Jewish Roots of Christological Monotheism: Papers from the St. Andrews Conference on the Historical Origins of the Worship of Jesus*, edited by Carey C. Newman et al., 112–28. Supplements to the Journal for the Study of Judaism 63. Leiden: Brill, 1999.

Foerster, Werner. "κύριος." In *TDNT*, 3:1039–95

Forbes, Chris. "Pauline Demonology and/or Cosmology? Principalities, Powers and the Elements of the World in Their Hellenistic Context." *JSNT* 85 (2002) 51–73.

———. "Paul's Principalities and Powers: Demythologizing Apocalyptic?" *JSNT* 82 (2001) 61–88.

Fossum, Jarl E. *The Name of God and the Angel of the Lord: Samaritan and Jewish Concepts of Intermediation and the Origin of Gnosticism*. Tübingen: Mohr/Siebeck, 1985.

Fotopoulos, John. "Arguments Concerning Food Offered to Idols: Corinthian Quotations and Pauline Refutations in a Rhetorical *Partitio*." *CBQ* 67 (2005) 611–31.

France, R. T. "The Worship of Jesus: A Neglected Factor in Theological Debate?" In *Christ the Lord: Studies in Christology Presented to Donald Guthrie*, 17–36. Leicester: InterVarsity, 1982.

Freedman, David Noel, ed. *ABD*. 6 vols. New York: Doubleday, 1992.

Freedman, H., and Maurice Simon, editors. *Midrash Rabbah*. 10 vols. 2nd ed. London: Soncino, 1951.

Fung, Ronald Y. K. *The Epistle to the Galatians*. NICNT. Grand Rapids: Eerdmans, 1953.

Furnish, Victor Paul. *Theology and Ethics in Paul*. Nashville: Abingdon, 1968.

———. *The Theology of the First Letter to the Corinthians*. Cambridge: Cambridge University Press, 1999.

Gager, J. G. *The Origins of Anti-Semitism*. Oxford: Oxford University Press, 1985.

Garland, David E. "The Dispute over Food Sacrificed to Idols." *PRSt* 30 (2003) 173–97.

Gaston, Lloyd. "Angels and Gentiles in Early Judaism and in Paul." *SR* 11 (1982) 65–75.

———. *Paul and the Torah*. Vancouver: University of British Columbia Press, 1987.

Gathercole, Simon J. "Justified by Faith, Justified by his Blood: The Evidence of Romans 3:21—4:25." In *The Paradoxes of Paul*, vol. 2 of *Justification and Variegated Nomism*, edited by D. A. Carson et al., 147–84. Grand Rapids: Baker Academic, 2004.

———. *Where Is Boasting? Early Jewish Soteriology and Paul's Response in Romans 1–5*. Grand Rapids: Eerdmans, 2002.

Giblin, Charles. "Three Monotheistic Texts in Paul." *CBQ* 37 (1975) 527–47.

Gieschen, Charles. *Angelomorphic Christology: Antecedents and Early Evidence*. Leiden: Brill, 1998.

Gillman, Florence Morgan. "Another Look at Romans 8:3: 'In the Likeness of Sinful Flesh.'" *CBQ* 49 (1987) 597–604.

Godet, Frederic Louis. *Commentary on Romans*. Rev. ed. Classic Commentary Library. Grand Rapids: Zondervan, 1956. Reprinted, Grand Rapids: Kregel, 1977.

Goldin, Judah. "Not by Means of an Angel and Not by Means of a Messenger." In *Religions in Antiquity: Essays in Memory of Erwin Ramsdell Goodenough*, edited by Jacob Neusner, 414–24. SHR14. Leiden: Brill, 1968.

Gooch, Peter D. *Dangerous Food: 1 Corinthians 8–10 in Its Context*. Studies in Christianity and Judaism 5. Waterloo, ON: Wilfrid Laurier University Press, 1993.

Goodman, Martin. *Mission and Conversion: Proselytizing in the Religious History of the Roman Empire*. Oxford: Clarendon, 1994.

Goppelt, Leonhard. *Typos: The Typological Interpretation of the Old Testament in the New*. Translated by Donald H. Madvig. Grand Rapids: Eerdmans, 1982.

———. "τύπος." In *TDNT*, 8:246–59.

Gottwald, Norman K. *A Light to the Nations: An Introduction to the Old Testament*. New York: Harper & Row, 1959.

Gray, William. "Wisdom Christology in the New Testament: Its Scope and Relevance." *Theology* 89 (1986) 448–59.

Grudem, Wayne. "Does κεφαλή ('Head') Mean 'Source' or 'Authority' in Greek Literature? A Survey of 2,336 Examples." *TJ* 6 (1985) 38–59.

———. "The Meaning of kephalē ('Head'): A Response to Recent Studies." *TJ* 11 (1990) 3–72.

Guerra, Anthony J. *Romans and the Apologetic Tradition: The Purpose, Genre and Audience of Paul's Letter*. SNTSMS 81. Cambridge: Cambridge University Press, 1995.

Gunton, Colin E. "Trinity, Ontology and Anthropology: Towards a Renewal of the Doctrine of the Imago Dei." In *Persons, Divine and Human: King's College Essays in Theological Anthropology*, edited by Christoph Schwöbel et al., 47–61. Edinburgh: T. & T. Clark, 1991.

Guthrie, Donald. *Galatians*. NCB. London: Marshall, Morgan, and Scott, 1973.

Hagner, Donald A. "Paul's Christology and Jewish Monotheism." In *Perspectives on Christology: Essays in Honor of Paul K. Jewett*, edited by Margaret Shuster et al., 19–38. Grand Rapids: Zondervan, 1991.

Hahn, Ferdinand. "The Confession of the One God in the New Testament." *HBT* 2 (1980) 69–84.

Hannah, Darrell D. *Michael and Christ: Michael Traditions and Angel Christology in Early Christianity*. Tübingen: Mohr/Siebeck, 1999.

Hansen, G. Walter. *Galatians*. Edited by Grant R. Osborne. InterVarsity Press New Testament Commentary 9. Downers Grove: InterVarsity, 1994.

Hanson, Anthony T. *Jesus Christ in the Old Testament*. London: SPCK, 1965.

———. *Studies in Paul's Technique and Theology*. Grand Rapids: Eerdmans, 1974.

Harris, Murray J. *Jesus as God: The New Testament Use of* Theos *in Reference to Jesus*. Grand Rapids: Baker, 1992.

Hartman, Lars. "Into the Name of Jesus." *NTS* 20 (1974) 432–40.

Harvey, A. E. "Son of God: The Constraint of Monotheism." In *Jesus and the Constraints of History*, 154–73. London: Duckworth, 1980.

Hawthorne, Gerald F., Ralph P. Martin, and Daniel G. Reid, editors. *Dictionary of Paul and His Letters*. Downers Grove: InterVarsity, 1993.

Hayman, Peter. "Monotheism—A Misused Word in Jewish Studies?" *JJS* 42 (1991) 1–15.

Hays, Richard B. *Echoes of Scripture in the Letters of Paul*. New Haven: Yale University Press, 1993.

———. *The Faith of Jesus Christ: The Narrative Substructure of Galatians 3:1—4:11*. 2nd ed. Grand Rapids: Eerdmans, 2002.

———. *First Corinthians*. IBC. Louisville: John Knox, 1997.

———. "'Have We Found Abraham To Be Our Forefather According to the Flesh?' A Reconsideration of Rom 4:1." *NovT* 27 (1985) 76–98.

———. "Psalm 143 and the Logic of Romans 3." *JBL* 99 (1980) 107–15.

———. *The Moral Vision of the New Testament: A Contemporary Introduction to New Testament Ethics*. New York: Harper Collins, 1996.

———. "Three Dramatic Roles: The Law in Romans 3–4." In *Paul and the Mosaic Law*, edited by James D. G. Dunn, 151–64. The Third Durham-Tübingen Research Symposium on Earliest Christianity and Judaism: Durham, 1994. WUNT 89. Tübingen: Mohr/Siebeck, 1996.

Heckl, Raik. "Ein Bezugstext für Gal 3:21B." *NovT* 45 (2003) 260–64.

Hengel, Martin. *The Son of God: The Origin of Christology and the History of Jewish-Hellenistic Religion*. London: SCM, 1976.

———. *Studies in Early Christology*. T. & T. Clark: Edinburgh, 1995.

Hiers, Richard H. "Day of the Lord." In *ABD*, 2:82–83.

Hocken, Peter. "The Oneness of God and the Unity of All Creation." *OiC* 20 (1984) 186–90.

Hodge, Charles. *Commentary on the Epistle to the Romans*. Rev. ed. Grand Rapids: Eerdmans, 1953.

Holtz, Traugott. "Theo-logie und Christologie bei Paulus." In *Glaube und Eschatologie: Festschrift für Werner Georg Kümmel zum 80. Geburtstag*, edited by Erich Grässer et al., 105–21. Tübingen: Mohr/Siebeck, 1985.

Horowitz, Herman L. "The Sh'ma Reconsidered." *Judaism* (1975) 476–81.

Horrell, David. *The Social Ethos of the Corinthian Correspondence: Interests and Ideology from 1 Corinthians to 1 Clement*. Edinburgh: T. & T. Clark, 1996.

———. "Theological Principle or Christological Praxis?" *JSNT* 67 (1997) 83–114.

Howard, George. "Romans 3:21–31 and the Inclusion of the Gentiles." *HTR* 63 (1970) 223–33.

Hurtado, Larry. "Jesus' Divine Sonship in Paul's Epistle to the Romans." In *Romans and the People of God: Essays in Honor of Gordon D. Fee on the Occasion of his 65th Birthday*, edited by Sven K. Soderlund et al., 217–33. Grand Rapids: Eerdmans, 1999.

———. *Lord Jesus Christ: Devotion to Jesus in Earliest Christianity*. Grand Rapids: Eerdmans, 2003.

———. *One God, One Lord: Early Christian Devotion and Ancient Jewish Monotheism*. London: SCM, 1988.

———. "Paul's Christology." In *The Cambridge Companion to St. Paul*, edited by James D. G. Dunn, 185–98. Cambridge: Cambridge University Press, 2003.

———. "What Do We Mean by 'First-Century Jewish Monotheism'?" In *SBLSP* 32, 348–68. Atlanta: Scholars, 1993.

Ito, Akio. "ΝΟΜΟΣ (ΤΩΝ) 'ΕΡΓΩΝ and ΝΟΜΟΣ ΠΙΣΤΕΩΣ: The Pauline Rhetoric and Theology of ΝΟΜΟΣ." *NovT* 45 (2003) 237–59.

Jacobs, Louis. "Shema, Reading of." In *EncJud*, 14:1370–74.

Jacobson, Howard. *The Exagoge of Ezekiel.* Cambridge: Cambridge University Press, 1983.

Janzen, J. Gerald. "On the Most Important Word in the Shema (Deuteronomy VI 4–5)." *VT* 27 (1987) 280–300.

Jervell, Jacob. "The Letter to Jerusalem." In *The Romans Debate*, edited by Karl P. Donfried, 53–64. Peabody, MA: Hendrickson, 1991.

Jervis, L. Ann. *Galatians.* NIBCNT. Peabody, MA: Hendrickson, 1999.

Johnson, Aubrey R. *The One and the Many in the Israelite Conception of God.* Cardiff: University of Wales Press, 1961.

Johnson, Luke Timothy. *Reading Romans: A Literary and Theological Commentary.* Macon, GA: Smyth & Helwys, 2001.

———. "Rom 3:21–26 and the Faith of Jesus." *CBQ* 44 (1982) 77–90.

Jonge, Marinus de. "Monotheism and Christology." In *Early Christian Thought in Its Jewish Context*, edited by John Barclay et al., 225–37. Cambridge: Cambridge University Press, 1996.

Kahle, Paul E. *The Cairo Geniza.* 2nd ed. Oxford: Blackwell, 1959.

Kammler, Hans-Christian. "Die Prädikation Jesu Christi als 'Gott' und die paulinische Christologie." *ZNW* 94 (2003) 164–80.

Käsemann, Ernst. *Commentary on Romans.* Translated and edited by Geoffrey W. Bromiley. Grand Rapids: Eerdmans, 1980.

Kittel, Gerhard, and Gerhard Friedrich, editors. *Theological Dictionary of the New Testament.* Translated by Geoffrey W. Bromiley. 10 vols. Grand Rapids: Eerdmans, 1964–1976.

Klausner, Joseph. *From Jesus to Paul.* Translated by William F. Stinespring. London: Allen & Unwin, 1946.

Koester, Craig R. *Hebrews: A New Translation with Introduction and Commentary.* AB 36. New York: Doubleday, 2001.

Kreitzer, L. Joseph. *Jesus and God in Paul's Eschatology.* JSNTSup 19. Sheffield: JSOT Press, 1987.

Kugler, Robert A. *The Testaments of the Twelve Patriarchs.* Edited by Michael A. Knibb. Guides to Apocrypha and Pseudepigrapha. Sheffield: Sheffield Academic, 2001.

Kuss, Otto. *Der Römerbrief übersetzt und erklärt.* Regensburg: Pustet, 1978.

———. "Zur Römer 9:5." In *Rechtfertigung: Festschrift für Ernst Käsemann zum 70. Geburtstag*, edited by J. Friedrich et al., 291–303. Tübingen: Mohr, 1976.

Lake, K. "Shorter Form of Paul's Epistle to the Romans." *Expositor* 7 (1910) 504–25.

Lambrecht, Jan. "Paul's Logic in Romans 3:29–30." *JBL* 119 (2000) 526–28.

Lampe, Peter. *From Paul to Valentinus: Christians at Rome in the First Two Centuries.* Edited by Marshall D. Johnson, translated by Michael Steinhauser. Minneapolis: Fortress, 2003.

Lang, Bernhard. "Der monarchische Monotheismus und die Konstellation zweier Götter im Frühjudentum: Ein neuer Versuch über Menschensohn, Sophia und Christologie." In *Ein Gott Allein? JHWH-Verehrung und biblischer Monotheismus im Kontext der israelitischen und altorientalische Religionsgeschichte*, edited by Walter Dietrich et al., 559–64. Göttingen: Vandenhoeck & Ruprecht, 1994.

———. *Wisdom and the Book of Proverbs: A Hebrew Goddess Redefined.* New York: Pilgrim, 1986.

Lee, Jung Young. "Interpreting the Demonic Powers in Pauline Thought." *NovT* 12 (1970): 54–69.

Lietaert Peerbolte, L. J. "Man, Woman, and the Angels in 1 Cor 11:2–16." In *The Creation of Man and Woman: Interpretations of the Biblical Narratives in Jewish and Christian Traditions*, edited by Gerard P. Luttikhuizen, 76–92. Themes in Biblical Narrative 3. Leiden: Brill, 2000.

Lietzmann, D. Hans. *An die Korinther 1–2.* HNT 9. Tübingen: Mohr/Siebeck, 1949.

Lightfoot, J. B. *St. Paul's Epistle to the Galatians.* 3rd ed. Cambridge: MacMillan, 1869.

Longenecker, Richard N. *Galatians.* WBC 41. Dallas: Word, 1990.

Lull, David John. "'The Law Was Our Pedagogue': A Study in Galatians 3:19–25." *JBL* 105 (1986) 481–98.

———. *The Spirit in Galatia: Paul's Interpretation of* Pneuma *as Divine Power.* SBLDS 49. Chico, CA: Scholars, 1980.

Luther, Martin. *Lectures on Galatians [1535], Chapters 1–4.* Edited by Jaroslav Pelikan. Luther's Works 26. St. Louis: Concordia College, 1963.

MacDonald, Nathan. "The Origin of 'Monotheism.'" In *Early Jewish and Christian Monotheism*, edited by Loren T. Stuckenbruck et al., 204–15. JSNTSup 263. London: T. & T. Clark, 2004.

MacGregor, G. H. C. "Principalities and Powers: The Cosmic Background of Paul's Thought." *NTS* 1 (1954) 17–28.

Mach, Michael. "Concepts of Jewish Monotheism During the Hellenistic Period." In *The Jewish Roots of Christological Monotheism: Papers from the St. Andrews Conference on the Historical Origins of the Worship of Jesus*, edited by Carey C. Newman et al., 21–42. Leiden: Brill, 1999.

Malina Bruce J., and Jerome H. Neyrey. "Honor and Shame in Luke-Acts: Pivotal Values of the Mediterranean World." In *The Social World of Luke-Acts: Models for Interpretation*, 25–65. Peabody, MA: Hendrickson, 1991.

Manson, T. W. "St. Paul's Letter to the Romans—and Others." In *Studies in the Gospels and Epistles*, 225–41. Manchester: Manchester University Press, 1962.

Martens, Elmer A. *God's Design: A Focus on Old Testament Theology.* 3rd ed. North Richland Hills, TX: BIBAL Press, 1998.

Martin, Dale B. *The Corinthian Body.* New Haven: Yale University Press, 1995.

Martyn, J. Louis. "De-apocalypticizing Paul: An Essay Focused on *Paul and the Stoics* by Troels Engberg-Pedersen." *JSNT* 86 (2002) 61–102.

———. *Galatians: A New Translation with Introduction and Commentary.* AB 33A. New York: Doubleday, 1997.

———. *Theological Issues in the Letters of Paul.* Nashville: Abingdon, 1997.

Matera, Frank J. *Galatians.* SP 9. Collegeville: Liturgical, 1992.

Matlock, R. Barry. "Detheologizing the ΠΙΣΤΙΣ ΧΡΙΣΤΟΥ Debate: Cautionary Remarks from a Lexical Semantic Perspective." *NovT* 42 (2000): 1–23.

Mauser, Ulrich. "Galater III.20: die Universalität des Heils." *NTS* 13 (1967) 258–70.

———. “One God Alone: A Pillar of Biblical Theology.” *PSB* 12 (1991) 255–65.

McBride, S. Dean. “The Yoke of the Kingdom: An Exposition of Deuteronomy 6:4–5.” *Int* 27 (1973) 273–306.

McGiffert, Arthur Cushman. *The God of the Early Christians*. New York: Scribner's, 1924.

McKnight, Scot. *A Light among the Gentiles: Jewish Missionary Activity in the Second Temple Period*. Minneapolis: Fortress, 1991.

Meeks, Wayne. “Moses as God and King.” In *Religions in Antiquity: Essays in Memory of Erwin Ramsdell Goodenough*, edited by Jacob Neusner, 354–71. Leiden: Brill, 1968.

Metzger, Bruce M. “The Punctuation of Rom. 9:5.” In *Christ and the Spirit in the New Testament*, edited by Barnard Lindars et al., 95–112. Cambridge: Cambridge University Press, 1973.

Michel, Otto. *Der Brief an die Römer*. KEK 4. Rev. ed. Göttingen: Vandenhoeck & Ruprecht, 1966.

Mickelson, B. and A. “What Does *Kephale* Mean in the New Testament?” In *Women, Authority, and the Bible*, edited by B. Mickelson et al., 97–110. Downers Grove: InterVarsity, 1986.

Mitchell, Margaret. “Concerning ΠΕΡΙ ΔΕ in 1 Corinthians.” *NovT* 31 (1989) 229–56.

———. *Paul and the Rhetoric of Reconciliation: An Exegetical Investigation of the Language and Composition of 1 Corinthians*. Tübingen: Mohr/Siebeck, 1991.

Moberly, Walter. “How Appropriate Is ‘Monotheism’ as a Category for Biblical Intepretation?” In *Early Jewish and Christian Monotheism*, edited by Loren T. Stuckenbruck et al., 216–34. JSNTSup 263. London: T. & T. Clark, 2004.

———. “Toward an Interpretation of the Shema.” In *Theological Exegesis: Essays in Honor of Brevard S. Childs*, edited by Christopher Seitz et al., 124–44. Grand Rapids: Eerdmans, 1999.

———. “‘Yahweh Is One’: The Translation of the Shema.” In *Studies in the Pentateuch*, edited by J. A. Emerton, 209–15. VTSup 41. Leiden: Brill, 1990.

Moo, Douglas. *The Epistle to the Romans*. NICNT. Grand Rapids: Eerdmans, 1996.

Moore, George Foot. *Judaism in the First Centuries of the Christian Era: The Age of the Tannaim*. 3 vols. Cambridge: Harvard University Press, 1962.

Morris, Leon. *The Epistle to the Romans*. Grand Rapids: Eerdmans, 1988.

———. *Galatians: Paul's Charter of Christian Freedom*. Downers Grove: InterVarsity, 1996.

Mounce, Robert H. *Romans*. NAC 27. Nashville: Broadman & Holman, 1995.

Mounce, William D. *Pastoral Epistles*. WBC 46. Nashville: T. Nelson, 2000.

Murphy-O'Connor, Jerome. “I Cor., VIII, 6: Cosmology or Soteriology?” *RB* 85 (1978) 253–67.

———. “Food and Spiritual Gifts in 1 Cor 8:8.” *CBQ* 41 (1979) 292–98.

———. “Freedom or the Ghetto (1 Cor., VIII, 1–13; X, 23–XI, 1).” *RB* 85 (1978) 543–74.

Mussner, Franz. *Der Galaterbrief*. HTKNT 9. Rev. ed. Freiburg: Herder, 1988.

Najman, Hindy. “Angels at Sinai: Exegesis, Theology and Interpretive Authority.” *DSD* 7 (2000) 313–33.

Neudecker, Reinhard. “‘And You Shall Love Your Neighbor as Yourself—I Am the Lord’ (Lev 19,18) in Jewish Interpretation.” *Bib* 73 (1992) 496–517.

Neusner, Jacob. *Sifre to Deuteronomy: An Analytical Translation*. 2 vols. Atlanta: Scholars, 1987.

———. *The Fathers According to Rabbi Nathan: An Analytical Translation and Explanation*. BJS 114. Atlanta: Scholars, 1986.

———, translator. *Mekhilta According to Rabbi Ishmael: An Analytical Translation*. 2 vols. BJS 154. Atlanta: Scholars, 1988.

Newton, Derek. *Deity and Diet: The Dilemma of Sacrificial Food at Corinth*. JSNTSup 169. Sheffield: Sheffield Academic, 1998.

Neyrey, Jerome H. *Paul, in Other Words: A Cultural Reading of His Letters*. Louisville: Westminster John Knox, 1990.

Nickelsburg, George W. E. *Ancient Judaism and Christian Origins: Diversity, Continuity, and Transformation*. Minneapolis: Fortress, 2003.

Nicole, Roger. "C. H. Dodd and the Doctrine of Propitiation." *WTJ* 17 (1955) 117–57.

Nilsson, Martin P. "The High God and the Mediator." *HTR* 56 (1963) 101–20.

O'Brien, P. T. "Principalities and Powers: Opponents of the Church." In *Biblical Interpretation and the Church: The Problem of Contextualization*, edited by D. A. Carson, 110–50. Nashville: Thomas Nelson, 1984.

O'Day, Gail R. "Jeremiah 9:22–23 and 1 Corinthians 1:26–31: A Study in Intertextuality." *JBL* 109 (1990) 269–67.

Oepke, A. "μεσίτης." In *TDNT*, 4:598–624.

O'Neill, John. "The Trinity and the Incarnation as Jewish Doctrines." In *Who Did Jesus Think He Was?* 94–114. Biblical Interpretation Series 11. Leiden: Brill, 1996.

Oropeza, B. J. "Laying to Rest the Midrash: Paul's Message on Meat Sacrificed to Idols in Light of the Deuteronomic Tradition." *Bib* 79 (1998) 57–68.

———. *Paul and Apostasy: Eschatology, Perseverance, and Falling Away in the Corinthian Congregation*. Tübingen: Mohr/Siebeck, 2000.

Orr, William F., and Arthur Walther. *1 Corinthians*. AB 32. Garden City, NY: Doubleday, 1976.

Osborne, Grant R. *Romans*. InterVarsity Press New Testament Commentary. Downers Grove: InterVarsity, 2004.

Paige, Terence. "Stoicism, ΕΛΕΥΘΕΡΙΑ and Community at Corinth." In *Worship, Theology and Ministry in the Early Church: Essays in Honor of Ralph P. Martin*, edited by Michael J. Wilkins and Terence Paige, 180–93. JSNTSup 87. Sheffield: Sheffield Academic, 1992.

Pearson, Birger A. "Hellenistic-Jewish Wisdom Speculation and Paul." In *Aspects of Wisdom in Judaism and Early Christianity*, edited by Robert L. Wilken, 43–66. Notre Dame: University of Notre Dame Press, 1975.

Penchansky, David. *Twilight of the Gods: Polytheism in the Hebrew Bible*. Lousiville: Westminster John Knox, 2005.

Perriman, A. C. "The Head of Woman: The Meaning of κεφαλή in 1 Cor 11:3." *JTS* 45 (1994) 602–22.

Philo. Translated by F. H. Colson and G. H. Whitaker. 10 vols. LCL. Cambridge: Harvard University Press, 1952–1968.

Porter, J. R. "The Legal Aspects of the Concept of 'Corporate Personality' in the Old Testament." *VT* 15 (1965) 361–80.

Rad, Gerhard von. *Old Testament Theology*. Translated by D. M. G. Stalker. 2 vols. Edinburgh: Oliver & Boyd, 1962–1965.

Rainbow, Paul. "Jewish Monotheism as the Matrix for New Testament Christology: A Review Article." *NovT* 33 (1991) 78–91.

Räisänen, Heikki. *Paul and the Law*. 2nd ed. Tübingen: Mohr/Siebeck, 1987.

Reid, D. G. "Elements/Elemental Spirits." In *DPL*, 229–33.

———. "Principalities and Powers." In *DPL*, 746–752.

Rengstorf, Karl Heinrich. "ἀποστέλλω." In *TDNT*, 1:398–406.

Reumann, John. "The Gospel of the Righteousness of God: Pauline Reinterpretation in Romans 3:21–31." *Int* 20 (1966) 432–52.

Richardson, Neil. *Paul's Language about God*. JSNTSup 99. Sheffield: Sheffield Academic, 1994.

Ridderbos, Herman. *The Epistle of Paul to the Churches of Galatia*. Grand Rapids: Eerdmans, 1953.

———. *Paul: An Outline of His Theology*. Translated by John Richard de Witt. Grand Rapids: Eerdmans, 1975.

Ringgren, Helmer. *Word and Wisdom: Studies in the Hypostatization of Divine Qualities and Functions in the Ancient Near East*. Lund, Sweden: H. Ohlssons, 1947.

Robinson, H. Wheeler. *Corporate Personality in Ancient Israel*. Rev. ed. Edinburgh: T. & T. Clark, 1981.

Roetzel, Calvin J. *Paul: The Man and the Myth*. Minneapolis: Fortress, 1999.

Rogerson, John William. "Hebrew Conception of Corporate Personality: A Re-Examination." *JTS* 21 (1970) 1–16.

Rosner, Brian. *Paul, Scripture and Ethics: A Study of 1 Corinthians 5–7*. Grand Rapids: Baker, 1994.

Ross, Allen P. *Creation and Blessing: A Guide to the Study and Exposition of Genesis*. Grand Rapids: Baker, 1988.

Rowe, C. Kavin. "Romans 10:13: What Is the Name of the Lord?" *HBT* 22 (2000) 135–73.

Rowland, Christopher. *The Open Heaven: A Study of Apocalyptic in Judaism and Early Christianity*. London: SPCK, 1982.

Rowley, H. H. "Living Issues in Biblical Scholarship: The Antiquity of Israelite Monotheism." *ExpTim* 61 (1949) 333–38.

Russell, D. S. *The Method and Message of Jewish Apocalyptic*. OTL. London: SCM, 1964.

Saldarini, Anthony J, trans. and comm. *The Fathers According to Rabbi Nathan, Version B*. Edited by Jacob Neusner. SJLA 11. Leiden: Brill, 1975.

Sandelin, Karl-Gustav. "Christ as the Nourishing Rock: 1 Cor. 10:1–13." In *Wisdom as Nourisher*, 161–72. Abo: Abo Akademia, 1986.

Sanders, E. P. *Paul and Palestinian Judaism*. Philadelphia: Fortress, 1977.

Sawyer, John F. "Biblical Alternatives to Monotheism." *Theology* 87 (1984) 172–80.

Schlatter, Adolf. *Romans: The Righteousness of God*. Translated by Siegfried S. Schatzmann. Peabody, MA: Hendrickson, 1995.

Schlier, Heinrich. *Der Römerbrief*. HTKNT 6. Freiburg: Herder, 1977.

Schmidt, K. L. "ἐπικαλέω." In *TDNT*, 3:496–500.

Schmithals, Walter. *Gnosticism in Corinth: An Investigation of the Letters to the Corinthians*. Translated by John E. Steely. Nashville: Abingdon, 1971.

———. *Der Römerbrief: Ein Kommentar*. Gütersloh: Gütersloher, 1988.

Schneemelcher, Wilhelm. "υἱός." In *TDNT*, 8:334–97.

Schnelle, Udo. *Paulus: Leben und Denken*. Berlin: de Gruyter, 2003.

Schoeps, H. J. *Paul: The Theology of the Apostle in the Light of Jewish Religious History*. Translated by Harold Knight. Philadelphia: Westminster, 1961.

Schreiner, Thomas. *The Law and Its Fulfillment: A Pauline Theology of Law*. Grand Rapids: Baker, 1993.

Schultz, Joseph P. "Angelic Opposition to the Ascension of Moses and the Revelation of the Law." *JQR* 61 (1971) 282–307.

Schweitzer, Albert. *The Mysticism of Paul the Apostle*. Translated by William Montgomery. London: Black, 1931.

Scott, James M. *Adoption as Sons of God: An Exegetical Investigation into the Background of* ΥΙΟΘΕΣΙΑ *in the Pauline Corpus*. WUNT, 2nd ser., 48. Tübingen: Mohr/Siebeck, 1992.

Seesemann, Heinrich. "πεῖρα." In *TDNT*, 6:21–36.

Segal, Alan F. "Paul's Jewish Presuppositions." In *The Cambridge Companion to St Paul*, edited by James D. G. Dunn, 159–72. Cambridge: Cambridge University Press, 2003.

———. "'Two Powers in Heaven' and Early Christian Trinitarian Thinking." In *The Trinity*, edited by Stephen T. Davis et al., 73–95. Oxford: Oxord University Press, 1999.

———. *Two Powers in Heaven: Early Rabbinic Reports about Christianity and Gnosticism*. SJLA 25. Leiden: Brill, 1977.

Skehan, Patrick W., and Alexander A. Di Lella. *The Wisdom of Ben Sira*. AB 39. New York: Doubleday, 1987.

Smit, Joop F. M. *About the Idol Offerings: Rhetoric, Social Context and Theology of Paul's Discourse in First Corinthians 8:1—11:1*. Contributions to Biblical Exegesis and Theology 27. Leuven: Peeters, 2000.

Soards, Marion L. *1 Corinthians*. NIBCNT. Peabody, MA: Hendrickson, 1999.

Stauufer, Ethelbert. "θεός." In *TDNT*, 3:65–119.

Stein, Robert H. *Playing By the Rules: A Basic Guide to Interpreting the Bible*. Grand Rapids: Baker, 1994.

Stendahl, Krister. *Final Account: Paul's Letter to the Romans*. Minneapolis: Fortress, 1995.

Stewart, James S. "On a Neglected Emphasis in New Testament Theology." *SJT* 4 (1951) 292–301.

Still, E. Coye. "Paul's Aims Regarding ΕΙΔΩΛΟΘΥΤΑ: A New Proposal for Interpreting 1 Corinthians 8:1—11:1." *NovT* 44 (2002) 333–43.

Stowers, Stanley K. *A Rereading of Romans: Justice, Jews and Gentiles*. New Haven: Yale University Press, 1994.

———. "ΕΚ ΠΙΣΤΕΩΣ and ΔΙΑ ΤΗΣ ΠΙΣΤΕΩΣ in Romans 3:30." *JBL* 108 (1989) 665–74.

Stuckenbruck, Loren. *Angel Veneration and Christology: A Study in Early Judaism and in the Christology of the Apocalypse of John*. WUNT, 2nd ser., 70. Tübingen: Mohr/Siebeck, 1995.

———. "Angels of the Nations." In *Dictionary of New Testament Background*, edited by Craig A. Evans and Stanley E. Porter, 29–31. Downers Grove: InterVarsity, 2000.

———. "Why Should Women Cover Their Heads Because of the Angels? (1Corinthians 11:10)." *Stone-Campbell Journal* 4 (2001) 205–34.

Stuhlmacher, Peter. *Paul's Letter to the Romans: A Commentary*. Translated by Scott J. Hafemann. Louisville: Westminster John Knox, 1994.

———. "The Purpose of Romans." In *The Romans Debate*, edited by Karl P. Donfried, 231–42. Peabody, MA: Hendrickson, 1991.

———. "Recent Exegesis on Romans 3:24–26." In *Reconciliation, Law and Righteousness: Essays in Biblical Theology*, 94–109. Philadelphia: Fortress, 1986.

Tertullian. *Adversus Marcionem*. Books 1–3. Edited and translated by Ernest Evans. Oxford: Oxford University Press, 1972.

Theissen, Gerd. *Social Reality and the Early Christians: Theology, Ethics, and the World of the New Testament*. Translated by Margaret Kohl. Minneapolis: Fortress, 1992.

Thielman, Frank. "The Coherence of Paul's View of the Law: The Evidence of 1 Corinthians." *NTS* 38 (1992): 235–53.

Thompson, Richard W. "The Inclusion of the Gentiles in Romans 3:27–30." *Bib* 69 (1988) 543–46.

Tobin, Thomas H. *Paul's Rhetoric in its Contexts: The Argument of Romans*. Peabody, MA: Hendrickson, 2004.

Turner, M. M. B. "The Spirit of Christ and Christology." In *Christ the Lord: Studies in Christology Presented to Donald Guthrie*, edited by H. H. Rowdon, 168–90. Leicester: InterVarsity, 1982.

Van Winkle, D. W. "The Relationship of the Nations to Yahweh and to Israel in Isaiah XL–LV." *VT* 35 (1985) 446–58.

Vanhoye, A. "Un mediateur des anges en Ga 3, 19–20." *Bib* 59 (1978) 403–11.

Wallace, Daniel B. "Galatians 3:19–20: A *Crux Interpretum* for Paul's View of the Law." *WTJ* 52 (1990) 225–45.

———. *Greek Grammar beyond the Basics: An Exegetical Syntax of the New Testament*. Grand Rapids: Zondervan, 1996.

Walters, James C. *Ethnic Issues in Paul's Letter to the Romans: Changing Self-Definitions in Earliest Roman Christianity*. Valley Forge: Trinity, 1993.

Walton, Francis R. "The Messenger of God in Hecataeus of Abdera." *HTR* 48 (1955) 255–57.

Watson, Duane F. "1 Corinthians 10:23—11:1 in Light of Greco-Roman Rhetoric: The Role of Rhetorical Questions." *JBL* 108 (1989) 301–18.

Watson, Francis. "The Authority of the Voice: A Theological Reading of 1 Cor 11.2–16." *NTS* 46 (2000) 520–36.

———. *Paul and the Hermeneutics of Faith*. London: T. & T. Clark, 2004.

———. "The Triune Divine Identity: Reflections on Pauline God-Language, in Disagreement with J. D. G. Dunn." *JSNT* 80 (2000) 99–124.

———. "The Two Roman Congregations: 14:1—15:13." In *The Romans Debate*, edited by Karl P. Donfried, 203–15. Peabody, MA: Hendrickson, 1991.

Watson, Gerard. *Greek Philosophy and the Christian Notion of God*. Maynooth Bicentenary Series. Blackrock, Co. Dublin: Columba, 1994.

Weiss, Johannes. *Der erste Korintherbrief*. Göttingen: Vandenhoeck & Ruprecht, 1910.

Westerholm, Stephen. *Perspectives Old and New on Paul: The 'Lutheran' Paul and His Critics*. Grand Rapids: Eerdmans, 2004.

———. "The Righteousness of the Law and the Righteousness of Faith in Romans." *Int* 58 (2004) 253–64.

White, John L. "The Ancient Epistolography Group in Retrospect." *Semeia* 22 (1981) 1–14.

———. *Light from Ancient Letters*. Philadelphia: Fortress, 1986.

———. "Saint Paul and the Apostolic Letter Tradition." *CBQ* 45 (1983) 433–44.

Whitsett, Christopher J. "Son of God, Seed of David: Paul's Messianic Exegesis in Romans 2[*sic*]:3–4." *JBL* 119 (2000) 661–81.

Wilckens, Ulrich. *Der Brief an die Römer*. 3 vols. EKKNT 6. Zürich: Benziger, 1980.

Williams, Sam K. *Galatians*. ANTC. Nashville: Abingdon, 1997.

———. "The 'Righteousness of God' in Romans." *JBL* 99 (1980) 241–90.

Willis, Wendell Lee. *Idol Meat in Corinth: The Pauline Argument in 1 Corinthians 8 and 10*. SBLDS 68. Chico, CA: Scholars, 1985.

Wilson, Robert R. *Prophecy and Society in Israel*. Philadelphia: Fortress, 1980.

———. "The Prophetic Books." In *The Cambridge Companion to Biblical Interpretation*, edited by John Barton, 212–25. Cambridge: Cambridge University Press, 1998.

Winger, Michael. "The Law of Christ." *NTS* 46 (2000) 537–46.

Wink, Walter. *Naming the Powers: The Language of Power in the New Testament*. Philadelphia: Fortress, 1984.

Winter, Bruce W. *Roman Wives, Roman Widows: The Appearance of New Women and the Pauline Communities*. Grand Rapids: Eerdmans, 2003.

Witherington, Ben. *The Acts of the Apostles: A Socio-Rhetorical Commentary*. Grand Rapids: Eerdmans, 1998.

———. *Conflict and Community in Corinth: A Socio-Rhetorical Commentary on 1 and 2 Corinthians*. Grand Rapids: Eerdmans, 1995.

———. *Paul's Letter to the Romans: A Socio-Rhetorical Commentary*. Grand Rapids: Eerdmans, 2004.

Wright, Christopher J. H. *Deuteronomy*. NIBCOT 4. Peabody, MA: Hendrickson, 1996.

Wright, N. T. *The Climax of the Covenant: Christ and the Law in Pauline Theology*. Edinburgh: T. & T. Clark, 1991.

———. "Jesus and the Identity of God." *ExAud* 14 (1998) 42–56.

———. "New Perspectives on Paul." Paper presented at the 10th Edinburgh Dogmatics Conference, August 25–28, 2003. Online: http://www.ntwrightpage.com/Wright_New_Perspectives.htm.

———. *The New Testament and the People of God*. Christian Origins and the Question of God 1. Minneapolis: Fortress, 1992.

———. "One God, One Lord, One People." *ExAud* 7 (1991) 45–58.

———. *Paul: Fresh Perspectives*. London: SPCK, 2005.

———. *The Resurrection of the Son of God*. Christian Origins and the Question of God 3. Minneapolis: Fortress, 2003.

———. "Romans and the Theology of Paul." In *Romans*, vol. 3 of *Pauline Theology*, edited by David M. Hay et al., 30–67. Minneapolis: Fortress, 1995.

Yarbrough, Robert W. "Paul and Salvation History." In *The Paradoxes of Paul*, vol. 2 of *Justification and Variegated Nomism*, edited by D. A. Carson et al., 297–342. Grand Rapids: Baker Academic, 2004.

Yeo, Khiok-Khng. *Rhetorical Interaction in 1 Corinthians 8 and 10: A Formal Analysis with Preliminary Suggestions for a Chinese, Cross-Cultural Hermeneutic*. Edited by R. Alan Culpepper and Rolf Rendtorff. Biblical Interpretation Series 9. Leiden: Brill, 1995.

Index of Subjects

Index of Modern Authors

Index of Scripture and Other Ancient Sources

OLD TESTAMENT

Genesis

Exodus

Leviticus

Romans

1 Corinthians

1 Timothy

2 Timothy

Titus

Philemon

Hebrews

APOCRYPHA

1 Maccabees

2 Maccabees

4 Maccabees

Sirach

Tobit

Wisdom of Solomon

PSEUDEPIGRAPHA

Apocalypse of Abraham

Apocalypse of Zephaniah

GREEK AND LATIN SOURCES

www.ingramcontent.com/pod-product-compliance
Lightning Source LLC
LaVergne TN
LVHW020535100826
845148LV00010B/1477

* 9 7 8 1 6 0 6 0 8 3 2 6 0 *